An Introduction
To Soviet Foreign Policy

RICHARD F. ROSSER
Professor of Political Science
United States Air Force Academy

PRENTICE-HALL, INC., Englewood Cliffs, N.J.

To Donna and the Boys

DK
266
.R66

Current printing (last digit)

10 9 8 7 6 5 4 3 2 1

P-13-497487-5

C-13-497495-6

Library of Congress Catalog Card Number: 75-78803

Printed in the United States of America

PRENTICE-HALL INTERNATIONAL, INC., *London*
PRENTICE-HALL OF AUSTRALIA, PTY. LTD., *Sydney*
PRENTICE-HALL OF CANADA, LTD., *Toronto*
PRENTICE-HALL OF INDIA PRIVATE LTD., *New Delhi*
PRENTICE-HALL OF JAPAN, INC., *Tokyo*

PREFACE

This book attempts to introduce Soviet foreign policy to the student and layman. As such, it builds on the work of hundreds of scholars as well as on primary sources. Yet any errors, of course, are mine. I have tried to use the most convincing material available to construct the story, but all students of the field know that analysts of Soviet foreign policy face a slippery task. No one has the final or complete answer. I recall A. J. P. Taylor's comment about one of the best works in the field, "On Soviet foreign policy generally during the interwar period there is only M. Beloff, *The Foreign Policy of Soviet Russia, 1929-1941.*" Taylor added, "Inevitably it is for the most part conjecture."

I owe particular thanks to my colleagues in the Department of Political Science at the United States Air Force Academy for encouragement and advice. Specifically, Captain Edward Warner gave invaluable criticism on every section of the manuscript; Lieutenant Colonel Byron Tatum, now missing in action in Vietnam, thoroughly evaluated the first several chapters. Lieutenant Colonel Allen Chew and Lieutenant Colonel George Collins of the Academy's Department of History aided me on the historical section. Professor Frederick C. Barghoorn of Yale Univer-

39401

sity gave helpful comments on the first few chapters, as did Professor Alvin Z. Rubinstein of the University of Pennsylvania. Professor Adam Ulam of Harvard University commented on the entire manuscript. I owe a special debt to Professor W. W. Kulski of Duke University who introduced me to Soviet studies and who continues to inspire students with his dedicated scholarship. Finally, I would like to thank James J. Murray, III, and Mrs. Helen S. Harris and the staff of Prentice-Hall, Inc., for their invaluable assistance in preparing the manuscript.

The analysis in this book reflects my personal view of Soviet foreign policy and should not be construed as representing the official policy or opinion of the United States Air Force or the United States Government.

RICHARD F. ROSSER

CONTENTS

v

MAPS

INTRODUCTION

What are the Soviets doing now? Are they searching for a détente or becoming more militant? Diplomats, intelligence officers, presidents, and prime ministers must find the answer; citizens should at least be curious. The question cannot be ignored, for the USSR is a dynamic and powerful nation. Its foreign policy sends shock waves around the world.

The analytical task can seem hopeless. Soviet foreign policy, Winston Churchill once said, is "a riddle wrapped in a mystery inside an enigma." [1] Many still share the Prime Minister's frustration.

But Churchill exaggerated. We are not wholly ignorant about Soviet foreign policy—defined as the total effort of the Soviet Union to influence the world. We can examine what Soviet leaders have done in the past, thereby revealing recurring themes and continuing motivations. These make some sense out of past, present, and future Soviet policy. In short, we can demonstrate that Soviet foreign policy is neither a riddle, a mys-

---

[1] In the next breath Churchill offered a rarely quoted solution: "But perhaps there is a key . . . Russia's national interest." From a radio broadcast on October 1, 1939, quoted in Winston Churchill, *The Gathering Storm* (Boston: Houghton Mifflin Company, 1948), p. 449. (See the section on "national interest" in Chap. 1 below.)

1

tery, nor an enigma—only somewhat confusing. The purpose of this book is to attempt such an analysis.

Before launching the analysis, I want to examine two elementary yet essential considerations for the study of Soviet foreign policy. The first deals with methodology: the sources available for an analysis of Soviet foreign policy, and the difficulties in using these sources. The second consideration is quite different, but still basic. Soviet capability to achieve foreign policy objectives is always relative to that of other states. The Soviet Union does not exist in a vacuum, but in an international system made up of other nation states and supranational organizations. I therefore spend a few pages sketching the limitations placed on Soviet foreign policy by the international system, as well as the limitations placed on that policy by such factors as Russia's natural resources, the state of Soviet technology, and military power.

THE DIFFICULTIES
IN ANALYZING
SOVIET FOREIGN POLICY

Several factors inhibit the complete understanding of any nation's foreign policy. First, foreign policy is a human product. It shares the fate of all human thoughts and actions, never presenting a complete and wholly logical pattern. Soviet foreign policy, for example, is made by men tempered by Lenin's pragmatism, yet capable of passion; men guided by the "science" of history yet working with a curious, antique view of Western society. In addition, Soviet foreign policy is often a *reaction* to the imperfectly planned policies of other nations, formulated by other, fallible humans.

There is a second factor militating against full understanding of any foreign policy. We can never know enough about the motivations, emotions, and actions of the decision makers in international politics. No matter how hard we try, we cannot think like the leaders of another nation (or even of our own nation). Therefore, analysis of any foreign policy is less than perfect. It is based on incomplete information about never consistently predictable actions.

Unfortunately, we face additional difficulties with Soviet foreign policy. Attempts to unravel even the day-to-day policies of the USSR, let alone the basic motivations behind these policies, are often frustrating and inconclusive. The unusual difficulty in studying Soviet foreign policy is rooted in the peculiar nature of the Soviet society. Two basic factors obscure the analysis. First, the leaders of the USSR have practically total control of the sources of information in their country. What was the agenda, for example, of the last meeting of the Soviet Communist Party

Politburo, or more basically, when was the meeting? Second, the USSR is ruled by a single, monolithic political party with a highly developed ideology, the professed goals of which transcend mere national concerns. For years the Communist Party of the Soviet Union was the nucleus and the only fount of leadership and support for a movement committed to communizing the world. This revolutionary impulse gave—and continues to give in some degree—Soviet foreign policy a unique, dual aspect. The same small group of men is concerned not only with the traditional problems of a territorial state, but also with the cause of world revolution. (As will be shown, the needs of the first generally prevail over the second.)

Since the study of the foreign policy of any country must concentrate on the decision makers of the state, the sources of information in the Soviet Union are: (1) the spoken and written word of the Soviet leadership; (2) observation of their conduct; (3) personal contact with Soviet leaders.[2]

The Spoken and Written Word   The Soviets are famous for producing reams of ideological statements defending and explaining their every public move. The marathon speeches of Premier Khrushchev were especially well-known. In theory, the reasons for particular Soviet foreign policies should be adequately publicized.

Nevertheless, the first difficulty is present in the ideological tone of the spoken and written word. Every formal policy is explained in Marxist-Leninist terms, and because the ideology claims to be the "scientific" key to the secrets of history, everything is pictured as if the Soviets had expected it all along. If we rely solely on what is written, the Soviets appear to have a corner on rationality, and to be gifted with the ability to anticipate events in the most remote country. No ideology can possibly account for every happening in the world; the Soviets often are simply reacting to the moves of other nations.

A second difficulty arises from the Marxian terminology itself. Any careful examination of Soviet communications requires a knowledge of Marxist-Leninist ideology. This is particularly the case when studying polemics between communists. Note, for example, the remarks in the 1961 Program of the Soviet Communist Party regarding the deviations of certain fraternal communist parties:

> Revisionism, Right opportunism . . . is the chief danger within the Communist movement today. The revisionists . . . in effect play the role of pedlars of bourgeois-reformist ideology within the Communist movement.

[2] Other less tangible factors, of course, are often used to explain Soviet behavior: i.e. national character, geography, pervasive themes in Russian history, and so forth. These are examined in Chap. 1, as are the pitfalls in their use as analytical tools.

. . . Another danger is dogmatism and sectarianism, . . . which lead to the dissociation and isolation of Communists from the broad masses, doom them to passive expectation or incite them to Leftist, adventurist actions in the revolutionary struggle, and hinder correct appraisal of the changing situation and the use of new opportunities for the benefit of the working class and all democratic forces.[3]

In the 1961 Program, the Soviets labeled the Yugoslavians as the chief revisionists. But it took a knowledge of the ideological terminology (and Soviet foreign policy) to know that the charges of dogmatism and sectarianism referred to the Chinese.[4] However, even common, everyday terms such as "democracy" and "freedom" have entirely different connotations to a communist than the meanings we give them. And the communist meaning can only be fully understood after an examination of the whole ideological system.

But an understanding of the ideological terminology only gets one over the first hurdle. "Kremlinologists" such as Myron Rush claim that communists have purposely developed a system of esoteric communication to pass on limited indications of top-level decisions to party members and bureaucratic subordinates. This system functions especially in the struggle for political power, which naturally affects Soviet foreign policy, and results in subtle allusions concerning the trend in the struggle. Thus the Central Committee of the Soviet Communist Party, says Rush, hinted at Stalin's downgrading by Khrushchev at the Party's Twentieth Congress (1956) just a few days before the Congress convened. In their birthday greetings to Voroshilov, then the formal head of state, the Committee altered the standard formula. Voroshilov became an "associate of Lenin," not an "associate of Lenin and Stalin." Rush suggests the ability to interpret such esoteric language comes from participating actively in the Soviet system, an opportunity obviously closed to Western analysts. To some degree, outside observers can compensate for this lack by rigorous examination of numerous Soviet documents.[5]

In addition to these difficulties with the written or spoken word, there is a third general problem for the analyst. Soviet formal pronouncements often have a high propaganda content when reporting current events.

---

[3] Jan F. Triska, ed., *Soviet Communism: Programs and Rules* (San Francisco: Chandler Publishing Co., 1962), p. 53.

[4] The Chinese communists are even more prone to use the jargon of Marxism-Leninism. Note an excerpt from the Chinese communist theoretical journal, *Red Flag*, November 16, 1962, which answers the above Soviet charges: "All Communists must work hard to raise their ability to distinguish Marxism-Leninism from revisionism, to distinguish the way of opposing dogmatism with Marxism-Leninism from that of opposing Marxism-Leninism with revisionism under the cover of opposing dogmatism, and to distinguish the way of opposing sectarianism with proletarian internationalism from that of opposing proletarian internationalism with great-nation chauvinism and narrow nationalism under the cover of opposing sectarianism."

[5] See Myron Rush, *The Rise of Khrushchev* (Washington: Public Affairs Press, 1958), Appendix 2.

This information is intended for the Soviet citizenry and foreign governments; the real "line" is reserved for the inner few. A striking illustration of such conscious deception occurred during Soviet efforts to prepare a communiqué justifying Russian intervention in Poland during the fall of 1939. (The division of Poland had been arranged by the secret protocol to the Nazi-Soviet Non-Aggression Pact of August 1939.) Foreign Minister Molotov told the Germans that the USSR wanted to make Soviet intervention plausible. At the same time, the Russians hoped to avoid having the USSR appear to be an aggressor. Molotov's suggestion, naturally repugnant to the Germans, was to insert a clause in the Soviet communiqué stating that the USSR felt "obligated to intervene to protect its Ukrainian and White Russian brothers" from a "third power" (Germany). The Soviet government, according to the foreign minister, saw no other possible argument for public consumption. The USSR until that point had not concerned itself with the plight of Soviet minorities in Poland. After German objections, Stalin personally wrote an even more cynical communiqué: Germany and Russia had joined together "to restore peace and order in Poland, which has been destroyed by the disintegration of the Polish state. . . ."

A fourth problem is a lack of vital information. Often even the most basic facts are unknown. For instance, many of the fundamental details concerning the Sino-Soviet dispute were lacking until the Chinese and Soviet leaders decided to publicize their positions.

Analysts of Soviet foreign policy also are denied sources of information common in Western countries. The controlled Soviet press prohibits any meaningful public debate of foreign policy. There are no Soviet equivalents of a Walter Lippmann or a James Reston. The lack of real democracy means the leaders do not have to defend their policies before a critical parliament. There are some closely controlled debates on domestic issues in the Supreme Soviet, but no discussion of foreign policy alternatives. Intraparty disputes on foreign policy occasionally surface after the fact. However, such information must be handled with care because of its use in the power struggle. In the late 1950's, for example, Khrushchev implied that the "anti-Party" group (Malenkov, Molotov, and other losers) had opposed most of his foreign policy initiatives. At best, this was tenuous evidence of the anti-Party group's true position. Soviet leaders also write few memoirs to aid the unraveling of their foreign policy.[6] Trotsky, the one man who did write, was assassinated at his Mexican hideaway in 1940.

[6] Beginning in the early 1960's, a few Soviet diplomats began to publish apparently authentic commentaries on their experiences. See Ivan Maisky, *Who Helped Hitler* (London: Hutchinson & Co. [Publishers] Limited, 1964). Mr. Maisky was Soviet ambassador to Britain from 1932-1943. A famous earlier work, Maxim Litvinov's *Notes for a Journal* (New York: William Morrow & Co., Inc., 1955) is a rambling account of the foreign minister's career, and a partial, if not complete, forgery.

These four basic difficulties with the spoken and written word can easily lead to the conclusion that it is a waste of time to read any Soviet sources about international affairs. The language in which Soviet statements are couched seems too abstruse, and if one understands the terminology, there are hidden meanings. Yet, even a rudimentary knowledge of the ideology can remove some pitfalls in interpreting Soviet communications. The reader can understand, for example, the meaning of "peaceful coexistence." Moreover, there may be an esoteric method of communication, but this does not prevail when the basic aims and strategy of the communist movement are discussed. And certainly these aims and strategy are as clearly stated as those of any other political movement. There also is no clear evidence that cynical manipulation of the central assumptions of the ideology takes place. The present leaders still seem to believe, for example, in the final triumph of communism.

Our analysis is aided by another factor. There is a limit to the distortion or falsification which can be introduced for propaganda purposes. The news must be partly credible in a totalitarian society because the communications media are necessary to control and guide the citizenry, especially lower ranking party members and sympathizers. (Soviet leaders also may believe what seems propaganda to us—the Soviet claim until recently, for example, of the danger of Western intervention in the Soviet Union.)

In summary, the Soviets may conceal the particular reasoning for their current tactics, the possible alternatives considered, and who was for what policy. But Soviet open communications do seem to reveal the basic approach of the leaders to foreign affairs, their patterns of reasoning, and the fundamental assumptions on which they act.

Observation of Soviet Conduct   When there is a conflict between what the Soviets say and what they do, their actions would seem to be a better guide to true motivation. But there are pitfalls in accepting these actions at face value. We often lack full details, and sometimes basic facts, about their conduct. And if we analyze their conduct alone, we may be led to believe the Soviets are hard-headed cynics attempting to maximize national power (or capability). Naturally they seek power— but for what end? It makes a difference whether their central concern is national security or the militant promotion of world communism.

Another factor complicating a study of Soviet actions is the rapid fluctuation and seeming incongruity in tactics often characteristic of Soviet foreign policy. Confusion reigned when the Soviets installed missiles in Cuba during the fall of 1962. This hardly was in keeping with the professed Soviet belief in peaceful coexistence. Many Western analysts were at a loss to explain the sudden switch to tactics reminiscent of the Cold War. Such twists in Soviet foreign policy, however, begin to make sense when viewed against the basic factors motivating or conditioning the acts of the Soviet leadership, in particular, the Marxist-Leninist ideology.

Personal Contact with Soviet Leaders An understanding of the character of the leaders is extremely important when analyzing the foreign policy of the Soviet state. This policy is not made by a few highly placed robots working from some pre-ordained master plan for world conquest found in Marx or Lenin. Soviet foreign policy is made by individuals, each with his own particular personality trait and psychological makeup. Lenin, Stalin, and Khrushchev, to name only the most prominent of the oligarchy, differed remarkably in their manners of playing politics and methods of leadership. And these differences inevitably affected their "styles" in foreign policy.

On the other hand, all Soviet leaders have been conditioned by the ideology in regard to goals, world outlook, and basic patterns of action. Personal observations of the Soviet leaders should be tempered by this probability, but often they are not. Intelligent laymen have concluded after one audience with a high Soviet leader that he is remarkably like the chairman of the board of directors of a large corporation in trouble with his stockholders. Overemphasis on the personalities of the Soviet leaders also tends to inflate the irrational element in the making of foreign policy and to neglect the stabilizing influence of the Marxist-Leninist ideology and continuing Russian national interests. Khrushchev's secret anti-Stalin speech in 1956, for example, contained little criticism of the former dictator's foreign policy. Stalin was branded a neurotic tyrant in domestic politics, yet he had acted "rationally" and in conformity with the tenets of Marxism-Leninism in world politics.

The three primary sources of information therefore must be used with care. Neither the spoken and written word of the Soviet leaders, observation of their conduct, nor personal contact with them can provide the definitive clue to Soviet motivations and actions. At any given moment one source may seem to reveal the truth; that very source may later prove wrong. Only a balanced, judicious—and skeptical—attitude toward all three sources is safe.

SOVIET CAPABILITY

Soviet capability is defined as the ability of the Soviets to achieve their foreign policy objectives.[7] The leadership, if it hopes

[7] "National power" is often used in place of "capability." "Power" is not used in this analysis because it tends to connote primarily *military* power, or at least some type of coercion or threat of coercion. "Capability," however, is a more neutral term. It can include gaining one's objectives through force *or* consent. My analysis of capability basically follows that used by Harold and Margaret Sprout in *Foundations of International Politics* (Princeton, N.J.: D. Van Nostrand Co., Inc., 1962).

to continue ruling, must consider capability when formulating Soviet objectives. The constant pursuit of overambitious aims can lead to disaster. Capability thus limits and, some would argue, even determines Soviet objectives.

The factors determining Soviet capability are the "givens" Soviet leaders must (or should) consider when making foreign policy. Two basic categories are involved: (1) external factors—those determinants which come from the world outside the Soviet Union; namely, the nature of the international system at any particular time; (2) internal factors—those determinants of Soviet capability peculiar to the Soviet Union, such as its geographic setting, military strength, economic base, and population.

External Factors   The first external factor determining Soviet capability is rooted in the competitive nature of the international system, of which the organized national communities called *states* are the basic units. The Soviet Union, although a very large state, is only one of more than a hundred. The system is further complicated by the increasing number of supranational organizations. The United Nations and the European Economic Community, for example, are beginning to acquire personalities separate and distinct from the states which are their member organizations.

Whether the USSR has the *capability* to achieve its foreign policy objectives depends to a great degree on the capabilities and objectives of other states. When other states oppose the objectives of the USSR, it may be successful if its capability is relatively greater, and vice versa.

The Soviets, of course, need not be isolated. They can acquire external aid for the Soviet cause by gaining allies. Such an addition increases Soviet capability and decreases that of Russia's opponents. Thus the alignment of states at any one time is a significant factor and must be considered by the Soviet leaders in formulating their foreign policy. After the Revolution of 1917, for instance, they had little choice but to assume the defensive in view of the hostility between the critically weak and isolated Soviet Union and the surrounding capitalist world. In the 1960's the USSR, aided by a number of other communist states, has considerably greater flexibility in choosing its policies.

Another external factor limiting Soviet capability is the constant state of flux characteristic of the international system. International politics is a very complex process of action and reaction. When the Soviet Union acts in relation to the smallest, most insignificant state in Africa, a reaction probably will be triggered in the United States. American action toward the same state may trigger a Soviet reaction. Furthermore, action by either superpower, the United States or the USSR, will cause responses in many other states and possibly in supranational organizations.

Action by one state does not *automatically* trigger a response in another for several reasons. States are not always in competition with one another. Much cooperation and agreement is necessary merely to exist on this planet. For example, all have a common interest in stifling deadly, communicable diseases, or in arranging for the efficient movement of the mails. Moreover, responses to the actions of one state may be slow in coming simply because these actions are not viewed as an immediate threat; thus Hitler was belatedly recognized as a menace to all of Western civilization.

The sheer complexity of this maze of events makes Sir Harold Nicolson question whether policy makers of any state can really *plan* a coherent foreign policy. Anyone who has watched so-called policies being applied to daily problems, remarks Nicolson, knows how seldom the course of events is really determined by conscious, calculated action. Often what we later think was planned has been directed by that most potent of all factors—"the chain of circumstance." [8]

The remaining external determinant comes from the dynamic forces at work in the international system. There seem to be certain basic trends in each era, beyond the control of any one state, which are altering the pattern of international relationships in a given direction. The "revolution of rising expectations," nationalism, and the collapse of Western colonial empires are some of the major dynamic forces in our century.

No one state can initiate such basic trends, although it may hurry them along. The Soviets constantly attempt to accelerate the collapse of Western colonialism; however they are not responsible for initiating the downfall of the colonial system. The Soviets, drawing on their Marxist-Leninist ideology for guidance, actually have a fairly realistic view of their limited ability to influence such great uncontrollable movements. Marxian economic determinism places relatively little importance on the role of individual men or states in determining the general course of history.

Technology is another type of dynamic force changing the state system. The impact of the airplane on traditionally impenetrable national interiors is well known. This impact has been greatly increased with the development of nuclear weapons, and now we have ballistic missiles. The nation-state is obsolete as a defensive unit if other nation-states use such weapons against it. Who is responsible for these developments? The advance of technology, like the collapse of colonialism, is beyond the control of one man or one nation, but the results of developing technology and dying colonialism affect *all* states—and thus their capabilities to achieve national goals.

Internal Factors   Most of the external factors just listed are beyond the direct control of the Soviet policy makers. However, the Soviets have more latitude in manipulating the *internal* factors affecting

[8] Sir Harold Nicolson, *The Congress of Vienna* (London: Constable & Co. Ltd., 1946), p. 17.

their national capability. (These are sometimes called "elements" of national power.) Internal factors consist of *tangible* elements, such as the state's geographic setting, population size and characteristics, natural resources, industrial and agricultural systems, and armed forces. "Tangible" means elements which generally can be measured by objective criteria. The Soviet gross national product, for instance, can be calculated and the number of men under arms determined.

Intangible elements are those which exist yet cannot be quantified. These also constitute a vital part of Soviet capability. Intangible factors include national morale or public opinion, the degree to which the Marxist-Leninist ideology creates loyalty to the regime, the effectiveness of the political structure in controlling the society, national prestige, the general caliber of the leadership, and even the impact on the leaders of their Marxist-Leninist view of the world.

Although the Soviets have more freedom in manipulating internal rather than external factors, the degree to which they can control the various internal elements differs greatly. The internal elements least susceptible to manipulation are the geographic setting and the supply of natural resources; these often can be decisive in determining capability because of their impact on a nation's military and economic strength. A certain minimum size and quantity of resources are necessary today to develop a significant national capability.

But if resources exist, men have to use them effectively. The continuing Soviet agricultural "Achilles' heel" is only partly due to poor geographic conditions—the short growing season and extremes of heat and cold in the northern half of Russia, as well as the little rain and poor soil in much of the south (with the notable exception of the Ukraine). Many authorities believe production problems also are caused by the forced collectivization of the peasants and the low prices paid for their produce by the state. These factors in turn have curbed the peasants' incentive. Both decisions, of course, are conscious, planned acts by the Soviet leaders.

The Soviets also cannot change the fact that certain of their country's geographic features are mixed blessings. If the USSR is weak, her frontier, which is the longest and most exposed border in the world, gives enemies easy access to the vast central Russian plain. If the USSR is powerful, the same border offers countless opportunities for the Soviets to exert pressure on their neighbors.

Other tangible elements of national capability are easier to manipulate. The forced industrialization of the USSR was the result of a calculated decision by Stalin; the USSR could have remained a predominantly agricultural country. The size and composition of the Soviet armed forces could be radically altered in a few years. Population characteristics—

particularly growth rate, health standards, and educational levels—could be altered over extended time periods.

Intangible factors such as national morale or the attractiveness of the ideology also can be manipulated, but results are never certain. The story is told of a movie on New York slums shown to Moscow audiences during World War II. Soviet propagandists counted on their public's being appalled at the living conditions of the "average" American citizen. Moscow filmgoers instead were amazed at the number of clothes stretched out to dry between the tenement buildings, more clothes than the average Russian could ever hope to have.

Soviet leaders thus face many limitations on their national capability and consequently on their policy choices. These limitations can be ignored; however, Marxism-Leninism requires that leaders carefully calculate the relative capabilities of the USSR and its opponents before any movement is made. Particular policies backfire because Soviet leaders miscalculate, not because they fail to calculate. They overestimate their own capability and underestimate that of their opponents. Soviet leaders naturally are not alone in making such mistakes, given the difficulties in determining national capability noted above.[9]

Utilizing Soviet Capability   Once Soviet leaders have decided on a certain foreign policy objective, they have to pick the *techniques* needed to apply their capability.[10] The economic system of the USSR, listed as one of the internal factors making up Soviet capability, does not automatically enable the Soviets to gain control of an underdeveloped country in sub-Saharan Africa. Planners must decide how to use the economic *capability* of the Soviet system to fashion the economic *techniques* of foreign aid, technical assistance, directed foreign trade, and so forth. The other three classic techniques are diplomacy, propaganda, and the use of force in its various forms. Soviet use of these techniques will be illustrated throughout the second part of this book.

We may now examine briefly the approach of the remaining text. Part One deals with the most fundamental question of analysis—what the Soviets are after, or *why* they act as they do in international politics. Chapter 1 investigates nine suggested roots of Soviet action, discarding six as affecting but not determining Soviet behavior. Chapters 2 and 3 analyze in depth the nature of the ideological root, since this is the most complex of the three that do determine Soviet behavior.

---

[9] The ideology of Marxism-Leninism, of course, has a peculiar impact on the ability of Soviet leaders to accurately analyze capability. This impact is brought out during the discussion of the advantages and disadvantages of the ideology in the formulation of Soviet foreign policy (see Chap. 3).

[10] "Techniques" sometimes are called "instruments of national power." They are designated "tactics" in Marxist-Leninist terminology.

Part Two demonstrates the interaction of these three roots through an examination of the major periods in Soviet foreign policy. This part forms a brief history of Soviet foreign relations since 1917, with emphasis on Soviet tactics in each period. The Conclusion of the book discusses the evidence for the continuing existence of the Marxist-Leninist ideology as a primary motivating factor in Soviet foreign policy.

FURTHER READING

Short bibliographies of books and articles for further reading have been placed at the end of each chapter. These lists necessarily are highly selective since the literature on Soviet foreign policy is now enormous. The lists do not include sources in the Russian language because this book only introduces the subject of Soviet foreign policy. The lists should be used together with books and articles referenced in the footnotes. Where referenced books are especially useful, they are repeated in the bibliographies.

Armstrong, John A., *Ideology, Politics, and Government in the Soviet Union.* New York: Frederick A. Praeger, Inc., 1962. See the Preface for problems in methodology.

Campbell, Robert W., *Soviet Economic Power.* Boston: Houghton Mifflin Company, 1966. 2nd ed. Introductory survey.

Cressey, George, *Soviet Potentials, A Geographic Appraisal.* Syracuse, N.Y.: Syracuse University Press, 1962. Discussion of "tangible" elements of capability.

Institute for Strategic Studies, *The Military Balance, 1968-1969.* London: The Institute for Strategic Studies, 1968. Published annually. Best summary of Soviet military strength.

Lydolph, Paul E., *Geography of the U.S.S.R.* New York: John Wiley and Sons, Inc., 1964. Widely used textbook.

Mellor, R. E. H., *Geography of the U.S.S.R.* London: Macmillan & Co., Ltd., 1964. Good survey of Soviet resources.

Morgenthau, Hans, *Politics Among Nations,* 4th ed. New York: Alfred A. Knopf, Inc., 1966. A classic in international relations. Good discussion of concept of "power" and elements of power.

Reshetar, John S., Jr., *Problems of Analyzing and Predicting Soviet Behavior.* Garden City, N.Y.: Doubleday & Company, Inc., 1955. A pioneering work on this problem.

Zagoria, Donald S., *The Sino-Soviet Conflict, 1956-1961.* Princeton, N.J.: Princeton University Press, 1962. See "A Note on Methodology."

one

THE BASES
OF
SOVIET FOREIGN POLICY

1

THE ROOTS
OF
SOVIET FOREIGN POLICY

The motivations behind the foreign policy of the Soviet Union are complex. There is no simple explanation of Soviet behavior: Soviet foreign policy is not merely a geographically-determined search for warm water ports or the desire to conquer the world for communism. Yet we can't avoid the question because there is no "school solution." Soviet motivations must be carefully analyzed because our foreign policies toward the Soviet Union and often other countries are based on assumptions, stated or unstated, about why the Soviets act as they do. And the success of our foreign policies may hinge on the accuracy of these assumptions.

The motivations we must examine are those of the Soviet political leadership. Those persons acting for the state in foreign affairs are of central importance in the examination of the foreign policy of any country; but in a political system such as the Soviet Union where decision making is concentrated at the top, the ruling political leaders have a unique, supreme role in foreign affairs.

The relatively free hand of the Soviet rulers, however, is limited by the many factors discussed previously which account for Soviet national capability. Unlimited goals recklessly pursued—such as the establishment of a totally communist world—undoubtedly will fail because such goals are presently beyond Soviet capability. (The Soviets can't even control other communist states.) Particular foreign policies derived from Soviet motivations must have some possibility of success if the Soviets are to continue operating. Of course some people question whether the Soviets really have any opportunity to consciously plan foreign policy, but even if this extreme view is accepted, it is still true that the Soviets can react in various ways. (There naturally are exceptions. In June 1941, the USSR had very little choice when Nazi Germany attacked—surrender or fight.)

We are looking for the reasons why the Soviets act or react as they do in foreign affairs. We also are assuming they are not complete prisoners of their environment, but have some control over their destiny. The initial set of theories considered does not share this assumption. These theories tend to be deterministic, and indicate a single dominant motive behind Soviet foreign policy. The set includes (1) the Soviet explanation of the basis of Soviet foreign policy; (2) the geopolitical explanation; (3) the search for security, or reacting to the "balance of power"; (4) the Russian heritage; (5) the national (and Bolshevik) character theories; and (6) totalitarianism.

The second set of theories implies that the Soviets have some control over their destiny, and offers a more convincing explanation for Soviet behavior in foreign affairs. This set includes (7) the maintenance of power by the elite; (8) the preservation of the national interest; and (9) the impact of the Marxist-Leninist ideology, or "communism."

THE FIRST SET

The Soviet Explanation   It is only fair to give the Soviet explanation of the motivations behind Soviet foreign policy. Karl Radek, one of Stalin's chief spokesmen during the 1930's on international affairs (later sentenced to 10 years' imprisonment during the great purge), wrote in the American journal *Foreign Affairs* (January 1934):

> Foreign policy is a function of domestic policy. It solves problems which result from the development of a given society, a given state, under definite historical conditions. . . . Its aims are seen to be shaped by the economic and political structure of changing forms of society. Therefore they are not permanent but on the contrary variable. The attempt to represent the foreign policy of the Soviet Union as a continuation of Tsarist policy is ridiculous. . . . It used to be an axiom of Tsarist policy that it should strive by every available means to gain possession of the Dardanelles and of an ice-free port on the Pacific. Not only have the Soviets not attempted to seize the Dardanelles, but from the very beginning they have tried to establish

the most friendly relations with Turkey; nor has Soviet policy ever had as one of its aims the conquest of Port Arthur or Dairen.

The Soviets, during and after World War II, attempted to gain these very objectives. But in 1934 Radek was giving a Marxist-Leninist explanation. He went on to put the geographical influence in its place:

> It is silly to say that geography plays the part of fate, that it determines the foreign policy of a state. Tsarist policy originated not in geographical conditions, but in the privileges of the Russian nobility and the demands of young Russian capitalism.

Radek then described the guiding motivation behind Soviet foreign policy—peace. Radek's formula is still held to be accurate. The standard Soviet explanation is that peace is the only possible policy for the USSR because it is a "socialist society." The desire for war cannot be found in such a society because there is no exploiting capitalist class, and the "working people" are in control. War is due to the evil of imperialism, foisted on the world by the monopoly capitalists in the industrialized countries.[1]

The Geopolitical Explanation   There have been serious attempts to show that Soviet foreign policy is primarily guided by geopolitical considerations. Geopolitics deals with the *opportunities* and *limitations* on the capabilities of states derived from two broad categories of hypotheses: (1) the layout and configuration of the lands and seas, climate, or resources; and (2) the distribution of people, or some set of social institutions or other behavior patterns. Too often, however, geopolitical hypotheses applied to Russia have been presented as compulsive drives forcing the Tsarist Russian—and now Soviet—leaders to expand in a particular direction or to work for some vitally necessary geographic objective. Robert J. Kerner, for instance, in *The Urge to the Sea* (1943) argued that a constant urge to secure routes to the open seas along all Russia's borders has dominated both Russian and now Soviet foreign policy. If Russia does not control such outlets, she is not independent. Foreign states commanding them can restrict Russian trade and invade

---

[1] While the above explanation of the basis of Soviet foreign policy is generally adhered to by Soviet writers, it has been qualified on occasion by some of the more realistic commentators. For example, a Soviet authority on diplomacy wrote in 1950: "Marxism teaches that economic factors determine the foreign policy and diplomacy of a state only in the long run, and that politics and diplomacy are, in a certain sense, conditioned by the concrete historical period and by many other elements (not excluding even, for instance, the geographical situation of a given country)." [F. I. Kozhevnikov, "Engels on 19th Century Russian Diplomacy," *Sovetskoye Gosudarstvo i Pravo*, December 1950, quoted in "Soviet Foreign Policy," by Vernon Aspaturian, in *Foreign Policy in World Politics*, ed. Roy C. Macridis, 2nd ed. (Englewood Cliffs, N.J.: Prentice-Hall, Inc., 1962), p. 135.]

at will. Tsarist Russia consequently was always in conflict with bordering countries over control of seaports and of inland water routes leading to them. Soviet foreign policy, according to Kerner, is basically a continuation of this historic pattern. Soviet moves in the Far East, Middle East, and Germany, for example, are fundamentally attempts to control the sea routes to and from the Soviet Union.

The noted American geographer, George Cressey, also believed Russia's drive to secure seaports, particularly warm water ports, to be the primary determinant of both Tsarist and Soviet foreign policy. In *The Basis of Soviet Strength* Cressey wrote: "The history of Russia may be written in terms of its search for ocean ports. The Russian Bear will not be content until it finds warm water, and this is equally true regardless of whether the government be a czarist autarchy or Soviet socialism." [2] Cressey later modified this view, acknowledging that the motivations behind at least *Soviet* foreign policy were based on ideological, economic, and strategic considerations. Nevertheless, he considered the last factor most important because it dealt with the Soviet Union's security needs, dictated in turn by her geographical setting. The relative vulnerability of this setting, Cressey argued, has required the creation of a ring of buffer states surrounding the USSR, with the notable exceptions of Turkey and Iran, from Finland to Korea. Cressey felt that "intrigue in Afghanistan and Manchuria are also part of the Russian Bear's desire to reach warm-water ports." [3]

Another geopolitical hypothesis elevated to the status of a basic drive is the so-called "Eurasian" tendency in all of Russian history. This school of thought is best personified in the writings of the Russian émigré historian, George Vernadsky.[4] The history and policies of Tsarist and now Soviet Russia, argued Vernadsky, are due to the country's geographical structure. Russia is a huge self-contained mass—a "Eurasia"—a world apart politically and culturally. Within this sprawling geographical unit, the natural direction of Tsarist Russian expansion was *east* because of the absence of geographical barriers in that direction. Soviet foreign policy merely carries on this drive, emphasizing expansion eastward with the goal of controlling all of Asia.

Robert Strausz-Hupé has offered a direct refutation of the "eastward" compulsion in Soviet foreign policy.[5] Russian foreign policy, both Tsarist

[2] George B. Cressey, *The Basis of Soviet Strength* (New York: McGraw-Hill Book Company, Inc., 1945), p. 242.

[3] George B. Cressey, *How Strong is Russia?* (Syracuse, N.Y.: Syracuse University Press, 1954), p. 127.

[4] George Vernadsky, *Political and Diplomatic History of Russia* (Boston: Little, Brown and Company, 1936).

[5] Robert Strausz-Hupé, "The Western Frontiers of Russia," in *New Compass of the World*, ed. Hans W. Weigert *et al.* (New York: The Macmillan Company, 1949), pp. 150-61.

and Soviet, is characterized by "matchless simplicity of conception and persistence of effort." The central aim is to defend the country, with primary attention given to the geographically vulnerable Western frontier. Russia has turned to Asia or the Middle East, asserted Strausz-Hupé, only when blocked in her efforts to secure the Western border. The surface complexity of Russian foreign policy comes from the difficulty of establishing "natural" frontiers in Eastern Europe due to the shape of the lands and the intermingling of nationalities, and, in the case of *Soviet* foreign policy, the "ideological language which the Soviet regime affects."

Evidence can be marshalled to support all such geopolitical hypotheses. Both Russian and Soviet leaders have wanted warm water ports and have expanded Eastward and Westward. Security considerations, as Cressey suggested, have undoubtedly been behind the creation of communist regimes in Eastern Europe. But all these policies have been conscious choices of the leadership, pursued when Russian or Soviet capability has permitted; they are not the result of compulsive drives. Soviet interest in Eastern Europe, for instance, at least partly seems to be motivated by the desire to expand communism. Moreover, Tsarist and Soviet governments may have expanded in the same direction. But this does not necessarily mean that the *motivation* for expansion is the same, only that the Soviets live in the same country with the same neighbors as the Tsars. Lastly, continuing technological advances already have affected what traditionally have been considered necessities for Russian security. Buffer states, for example, give relatively little protection in the age of the intercontinental missile. Geography presents opportunities and limitations which can change. It is not a fixed determinant of Soviet foreign policy.

The Search for Security, or Reacting to the "Balance of Power"   A third explanation of the motivating force behind Soviet foreign policy asserts the Soviets simply have been reacting to the realities of international politics. Any dreams of promoting world communism were quickly shoved aside in the search for national security necessitated by an anarchic international political system.

Frederick L. Schuman presented one version of this approach in *Government in the Soviet Union* (1961). Like all rulers, the Soviet leaders see the necessity of achieving security against the "hostile designs, actual or potential" of other great powers. And these powers, suggested Schuman, are seeking security by maximizing the USSR's *insecurity*.[6] The Soviet leaders thus are basically reacting to circumstances beyond their control. The Marxist-Leninist ideology, Schuman believed, is important only in amplifying Soviet mistrust and hatred of the West, which feed

[6] This pattern of action and reaction in the international system was described in the Introduction to this book as one of the external factors affecting Soviet capability.

upon and are caused by Western mistrust and hatred of the Soviets. Neither West nor East is really to blame. Both sides are caught in a vicious whirlpool, fed by the potentially violent current of international politics.

A more convincing version of the Soviet search for security necessitated by the international system is found in Barrington Moore's *Soviet Politics—The Dilemma of Power* (1956). The main outlines and twists and turns of Soviet foreign policy, Moore suggested, represent typical reactions to changes in the distribution of political power in the world. There is no *basic* difference between the foreign policy of the USSR and that of any other state. All nations, Moore argued, must engage in "balance of power" politics or face national disaster. The essence of the balance of power game is that when any state attempts to expand (as did Nazi Germany), other states will ally to meet the threat. This hopefully reestablishes the previous equilibrium of the international system (as did the Allied coalition against Germany).

Moore hastened to point out, however, that the specific way and the exact timing of Soviet reactions to changes in the power distribution are affected by the Marxist-Leninist ideology, just as democratic beliefs affect the way Western powers react. The Soviets, for example, continued to see the German Social-Democrats (traditional rivals of the communists for the support of the working class) as their main enemies until after Hitler came to power.

It is certainly true that the search for national security necessitated by the international political system has played an important role in determining Soviet foreign policy, particularly before World War II. It is not so certain that this has been the case since World War II, or will be the case in the future. Hans Morgenthau, probably the foremost advocate of the balance of power theory, suggests that the appearance of the two superpowers, the United States and the USSR, has drastically affected the workings of the international system. If one of the superpowers feels threatened it cannot redress the balance by allying with other powers because these nations cannot add significant strength to the side of the threatened state. Similarly, the threatening state does not gain its major strength from its allies. The "balance" can only be maintained by an old fashioned arms race between the two superpowers.[7]

The crucial question is what motivating factor in which state is responsible for this arms race? And the Marxist-Leninist ideology of the Soviet leaders postulating inevitable world communism and describing almost every act by Western "imperialist" powers as evilly motivated must take the lion's share of the blame. Only advocates of this ideology

[7] *Politics Among Nations*, 3rd ed. (New York: Alfred A. Knopf, Inc., 1961), esp. Chap. 21.

could interpret the rapid American disarmament after World War II or the Marshall Plan as schemes seriously threatening Soviet security.

The Soviets now have achieved a nuclear deterrent capability. They should no longer be afraid of surprise attack by another state or combination of states. But the Soviet leaders still seem conditioned by the Marxist-Leninist view of international politics. Communists apparently will only feel really secure if they control the whole world. In the meantime, Soviet feeling of *relative* security may have been increased by their possession of nuclear weapons and the growth of the communist bloc.

The Russian Heritage   No rulers, regardless how revolutionary, can escape the impact of history on their country. One group of interpreters of the Soviet system therefore argues that the historical patterns and traditions formed deep in the Russian past basically determine the general social and political structure—and foreign policy—of contemporary Soviet Russia. Any changes wrought by the Soviet leaders are superficial; underneath life in Russia goes on as always.

The general continuity between Tsarist and Soviet Russia has been argued most forcefully by British historians Bernard Pares and John Maynard, and Nicholas Berdyaev, the brilliant émigré Russian philosopher. Berdyaev in *The Origin of Russian Communism* (1937) saw "Bolshevism" as the third appearance of Russian autocratic imperialism, first seen in the Muscovite Tsardom and then in the empire of Peter the Great. Bolshevism stood for a strong centralized and militarized state, but so had old Russia. Bolshevism instituted a dictatorship, similar to the ruling pattern of the Tsars, and not "unfamiliar democracy." Bolshevism made use of the characteristics of the Russian mind—its religious instinct and dogmatism, its search for social justice, its messianism and faith in Russia's own path of development. Bolshevism was successful because it was more faithful to certain Russian "primordial" traditions than other prescriptions for reform. Communism, believed Berdyaev, was the inevitable fate of Russia.

Edward Crankshaw, a veteran correspondent for the London *Observer*, saw the Russian past as determining Soviet *foreign* policy in particular.[8] Crankshaw emphasized that the Soviets inherited an empire, not a country. This empire merely expressed a fact of international politics: the domination of the weak by the strong in the self-interest of the strong.[9] Russian imperialism under all regimes, Crankshaw suggested, is essentially the same as Roman, British, or American "imperialism."

[8] "Russia's Imperial Design," *The Atlantic Monthly*, November 1957. Also see his *Cracks in the Kremlin Wall* (New York: The Viking Press, Inc., 1951).

[9] Crankshaw, it can be argued, implies that the international system, not history, determines Soviet foreign policy. Nevertheless, he is commonly discussed in relation to the historical school.

According to Crankshaw, Tsarist Russian imperialism manifested itself at different times in basically three ways, all designed to increase the power and influence of the homeland: there was the *strategic* drive to increase national security, the *economic* drive to increase national wealth, and the *missionary* drive to impose the better way of life in the homeland on "inferior" cultures.

Soviet foreign policy, Crankshaw believed, represents a continuation of this traditional Russian imperialist dynamic, complicated and reinforced by a "distorted Marxism." The Soviets are not attempting to communize the world. On the contrary, Soviet moves to control Eastern Europe parallel the strategic and economic drives behind the formation of the Russian empire. The messianic features of communism, where they influence Soviet foreign policy, are a continuation of Tsarist Russia's "Third Rome" Complex—carrying the torch of civilization for the world after the fall of Constantinople—and later, her promotion of Pan-Slavism.

Other writers emphasize specific features of the Russian heritage as determining Soviet foreign policy. Arnold Toynbee, who attempted to put all civilizations in historical perspective in *A Study of History,* saw Russia, first Tsarist and now Soviet, as the main offshoot of the Byzantine civilization (the "second Rome").[10] The Soviets do not share the Western cultural heritage. On the contrary, they are continuing the historic conflict between the Byzantine civilization and the surrounding alien civilizations. Fundamental characteristics of Byzantium are revealed in both Tsarist and Soviet Russia: a historical destiny to bring salvation to the world; a fear and hatred of a corrupt and heretical Western civilization; a sense of infallibility; and a totalitarian political system. Russia has borrowed two things from the West, admitted Toynbee: technology, to build the industrial and military base to compete with the West; and Marxism, an "ideological heresy" to battle "liberal Western ideological orthodoxy." (He reasoned the world has become so westernized that the Russians can only win with a Western "heresy"; Orthodox Christianity does not have a chance of converting the infidels.)

Obviously the Soviet leaders cannot ignore history as they might wish, and obviously there are great similarities between Tsarist and Soviet Russia. But we must not push similarities so far as to fall into the trap of historical determinism. Questions remain about historical data "proving" continuity, and about the interpretation of this data. For instance, from the 1917 Revolution until Stalin reconquered most of the former outposts of the Tsarist Empire after World War II, the Soviet Union's pattern of expansion looked much like that of Tsarist Russia. This did *not*

---

[10] Toynbee's argument can be found in "Russia and the West," a selection from his *The World and the West,* reprinted in *Readings in Russian Foreign Policy,* ed. Robert A. Goldwin (New York: Oxford University Press, Inc., 1959), pp. 680-88.

mean the motives behind this expansion were necessarily Tsarist motives, but only that the Soviets had to expand in the same geographical directions as their Tsarist predecessors because they both started from the same place. Furthermore, Tsarist Russian messianism, represented by the "Third Rome" and Pan-Slav movements, is basically different from communism. These two pre-revolutionary concepts were not officially supported by the Tsarist regimes.[11] The Tsarist governments, it can be argued, were essentially similar to other European governments in their desire for empire and relatively limited territorial objectives. The Tsars held no global aspirations or commitments as do the Soviets.

The revival of Russian nationalist symbols in the 1930's and the russification of the USSR's non-Great Russian populations often are given as evidence of resurgent Russian nationalism.[12] However, it is highly questionable whether nationalism in these instances is the motive or the instrument. Much evidence indicates the Soviets, particularly during World War II, merely used Russian nationalism (the Russian nationality is the largest in the USSR) to prop up an unstable regime. Moreover, russification seems primarily an instrument of the regime to suppress non-Russian nationalities, not necessarily to make them "Russians." (The required teaching of Russian to all non-Great Russians, for example, reflects the necessity of any large, centralized state to have a common language, and Russian is spoken by more people in the USSR than any other tongue.) Existing Soviet nationalism is a complex amalgam (in Marxist-Leninist terminology) of Soviet patriotism, proletarian internationalism, and the "progressive" national traditions (primarily Great Russian) of the peoples of the USSR.[13]

The National (and Bolshevik) Character Theories   In the last few decades, cultural anthropologists and psychologists have made some of the most interesting attempts to explain the basic roots of Soviet behavior. The central concept used by these analysts is "national character": the belief that members of a given culture share certain common ways of managing their emotional drives and meeting the tensions or frustrations generated by their society. These general behavior patterns are culturally determined and differ, often greatly, from culture to culture. In the case of the USSR, almost all such analyses have been of the Great Russian character.

Geoffrey Gorer, a British anthropologist (aided by John Rickman, a

[11] The Tsarist government's aims for Eastern Europe nevertheless hinted of Pan-Slavism, while the same concept had ignited Russia's war against Turkey in 1877.

[12] See Nicholas Timasheff, *The Great Retreat* (New York: E. P. Dutton & Co., Inc., 1946).

[13] See Frederick Barghoorn, *Soviet Russian Nationalism* (New York: Oxford University Press, Inc., 1956).

British psychiatrist), gave one intriguing explanation of Soviet behavior using the national character concept in *The People of Great Russia* (1949). From material gathered in several hundred interviews, Gorer argued that the practice of tightly swaddling the Russian infant (still apparently done in many parts of Russia) produces a privation-gratification cycle. When swaddled, Russian babies are lonely and filled with rage at being constricted. When finally freed, they are bathed, fed and given unlimited attention. This alternation of complete restraint without gratification, and complete gratification without restraint, builds into a Great Russian the tendency to swing wildly from submissiveness to violence, from apathy to anxiety. From this hypothesis, which he repeatedly pointed out was only one source of influence on the Russian character, Gorer suggested several "political maxims" for Russian behavior. The following are of particular interest regarding Soviet foreign policy: suspicion by both the elite and the masses of the outside world springs from unconscious and thus irrational sources, and cannot be eliminated through rational actions by outsiders; both the elite and the masses feel the need to continually expand their national boundaries until met by superior force; when superior force is met, strategic retreat is a highly acceptable maneuver and not humiliating because as Russians they have pushed outward to their utmost ability; attempts to persuade the Russians to admit error in their ideology are futile because admitting one error destroys the whole system of truth, and consequently Russian self-esteem is destroyed.

Henry V. Dicks offered a second explanation of Russian behavior based on intensive psychiatric interviews, lasting between 15 to 18 hours. The subjects were 29 defectors from the USSR (mostly Great Russians).[14] Dicks, like Gorer, stressed the ambivalence of Russian character, but he made an important distinction between the traditional national character found in the masses, particularly the peasantry, and that of the elite. Both character types, Dicks believed, make up the Russian character. Their interaction is particularly important. The masses, for instance, alternate between the tendency to rush enthusiastically into every experience, and the tendency toward melancholia, suspicion, and grudging acquiescence in the need for a strong authority to restrict the excesses of their Russian nature. To counter this capriciousness in the masses and provide the firm arbitrary authority required, the elite must be puritanical and strong enough to renounce the gratifications sought by the average Russian.

Dicks said relatively little about the relevance of his findings to Soviet foreign policy. However, he did offer a suggestive theory: the elite, facing

[14] H. V. Dicks, "Observations on Contemporary Russian Behavior," *Human Relations*, V (May 1952), 111-75.

intense inner conflict in the society because of the pressing need to produce a new managerial and technological class, have projected any fail-
ures onto "foreign out-groups" (defined as foreign "spies" sabotaging industrialization) which "encircle" the USSR.

A third attempt to analyze Russian character concentrates entirely on
the "Bolshevik" elite (the left wing of the Russian communist party led
by Lenin before 1917, later the Communist Party of the Soviet Union).
Nathan Leites pioneered this approach in *A Study of Bolshevism* (1954).
After a detailed study of the writings of Lenin and Stalin using the techniques of psychoanalysis, Leites concluded that Bolshevik behavior—
rigid, suspicious, unyielding, constantly aggressive—stems primarily from
Lenin's unconscious reaction to powerful tendencies in the nineteenth-
century Russian intelligentsia. These Russians were introspective, always
searching for metaphysical truths; Bolsheviks therefore must have a certainty of purpose and a commitment to specific action. They need the
constant goals of work and service to the party to counter the Russian
intelligentsia's traditional fear of a life with no purpose, of an existence
filled with compulsive gratifications arousing guilt, and ending in a
flirtation with death. From all this emerges the Bolshevik "operational
code" for political action, which Leites summarized in the Russian couplet
kto-kovo, literally, "who-whom," but really who *gets* whom. The rules
of the operational political code derived from this formula consist of such
maxims as pushing to one's limit, acting when ready, refusing to be
provoked. Indefinite peaceful coexistence becomes impossible, although
temporary agreements with the enemy can be considered. The party
members never forget the basic conflict and push on again at the strategic
moment.

The theories of Gorer, Dicks and Leites seem fanciful. They appear to
rob the Soviets of any pretense of rationality, and imply all their acts are
generated by subconscious impulses. But Lenin, for instance, apparently
knew exactly what he was doing in warning his comrades not to fall into
the habits of the Russian intelligentsia. Furthermore, these hypotheses are
based on very few samples, and, in the case of Leites, exclusively on the
writings of Lenin and Stalin.[15]

Leites, and to some extent Gorer and Dicks, do go beyond traditional
concepts of national character by dealing with the elite. But they tend to
consider all members of the elite group identical in character. Zbigniew
Brzezinski suggests, however, that the "Bolsheviks" today include gen-

[15] A more recent study by Leites, "Kremlin Moods" (Santa Monica, Calif.: The
RAND Corp., 1964), analyzes Khrushchev's speeches and writings. Also see Alexander
George, "The 'Operational Code': A Neglected Approach to the Study of Political
Leaders and Decision-Making" (Santa Monica, Calif.: The RAND Corp., 1967).
George attempts to refine Leites' analysis into "a general belief system about the
nature of history and politics."

eralists, providing the leadership, technical experts, specializing in particular fields of party action, and ideologues, concentrating on ideological problems.[16] The generalizations of Gorer concerning Soviet adult behavior in particular seem based on flimsy reasoning. (Skeptics have labeled Gorer's hypothesis "diaperology.") There is some question whether we yet know enough to draw conclusions about the impact of child-training on the psychological characteristics of the adult.

But these generalizations cannot be completely ignored. Gorer's swaddling hypothesis is considered, by many of his fellow anthropologists, the only coherent explanation of early childhood behavior in Russia.[17] The psychological explanations of Dicks and Leites also are highly suggestive. We should have learned by now not to laugh at the connection between the conscious and subconscious. The chief problem, however, for our analysis is the tenuous, questionable, and often vague relationship between the hypotheses of the "national character" school and the motivations behind Soviet foreign policy.

Totalitarianism   After the appearance of Nazism and the stabilization of Stalin's rule in the Soviet Union, a number of writers began to write about a radically new social form—totalitarianism. Unlike dictatorships or authoritarian regimes, totalitarianism seeks to control *all* phases of life.

The analysts of this new social phenomenon basically agree about the effect of such a system on a state's foreign policy. The state, because of the totalitarian dynamic, is inherently expansionist and aggressive. But these analysts are not exactly sure how this aggressiveness fits into the totalitarian system. Carl Friedrich and Zbigniew Brzezinski in *Totalitarian Dictatorship and Autocracy* (1956) refer to "the struggle for world conquest which is the totalitarian's natural bent. . . . ," and write about "the will to conquer the world which is intimately linked with their ideological preoccupations. It is the outward thrust of that 'passion for unanimity' which brooks no disagreement with what the movement has proclaimed 'as the truth.' "[18] The authors of this work nevertheless ignore external expansion when describing the "syndrome" of the totalitarian dictatorship, the cluster of interrelated traits forming the system: namely, an ideology, a single party, terroristic police, communications and weapons monopolies, and a centrally directed economy.

Hannah Arendt gave a more fully developed and positive explanation

---

[16] Zbigniew Brzezinski, "The Nature of the Soviet System," *Slavic Review*, XX, No. 3 (1961), 351-68.

[17] Clyde Kluckhohn, "Studies of Russian National Character," *Human Development Bulletin* (University of Chicago), February 5, 1955, pp. 39-60.

[18] *Totalitarian Dictatorship and Autocracy* (Cambridge, Mass.: Harvard University Press, 1956), p. 63.

of totalitarian "aggression" in *The Origins of Totalitarianism* (1958). The totalitarian leader, she argued, is attempting to gain total control over the individual. To do this, he can never permit a normal society to develop with stable laws and institutions. He must create a "fictitious world," based on the myths of the totalitarian movement. But it is difficult to maintain this fiction because of factual information leaking through the "iron curtain." And here is the rub: such leaks can only be eliminated if the totalitarian leader controls the whole world. Otherwise the leader may lose whatever power he now has. "Even a single individual," Hannah Arendt asserted, "can be absolutely and reliably dominated only under global totalitarian conditions." The struggle to dominate the whole world therefore is an inherent part of every totalitarian system.[19]

Even if we accept the concept of totalitarianism as the key to Soviet society, it is doubtful whether external aggressiveness comes primarily from totalitarianism: specifically, the compulsion of the leaders to gain total control of the world. The Soviet leaders probably would be happier if they could completely shut out the Voice of America. But is this irritant or the existence of other sources threatening to penetrate the Soviet Union reason enough to compel the Soviets to seek control of the world? Unrelenting Soviet aggressiveness, it might be argued, would place a worse strain on party control of society than now exists. For such pressure on the West would probably result in war. And we know that World War II tested party control of Soviet society. Stalin, for example, had to use nationalism, not ideology, as the main prop for his regime.

The Soviet leaders, of course, do create a "fictitious world" in one respect: the myth of an eternally hostile "imperialist camp." This fiction helps justify the maintenance of strong internal controls and powerful armed forces. But the belief in a hostile world opposing the "socialist camp" stems basically from the Marxist-Leninist ideology, not the totalitarian system.

But perhaps the most serious criticism of the totalitarian explanation of Soviet foreign policy is that the concept seems increasingly irrelevant. Although many analysts still refer to the Soviet system as "totalitarian," there is growing recognition that the control of the leader (or leaders) is far from total. The Soviet leaders seem involved in a constant struggle for power, which will be described later, and they must pay attention to emerging "interest groups" such as the military, the managerial elite, the intelligentsia, and so forth.[20] Soviet foreign policy is only one element in the resulting political process; this policy is hardly the single-minded pursuit of one dictator for total world control.

[19] *The Origins of Totalitarianism*, 2nd ed. (New York: The World Publishing Company, 1958), pp. 391-92.

[20] See H. Gordon Skilling, "Interest Groups and Communist Politics," *World Politics*, XVIII, No. 3 (1966), 435-51.

THE SECOND SET

The remaining three theories seem to offer more convincing explanations of Soviet behavior in foreign affairs. And this motivational trilogy—the maintenance of power by the elite, the preservation of the "national interest," and the habits of thought and action derived from the Marxist-Leninist ideology—seems to form an interlocking and mutually reinforcing influence conditioning Soviet behavior. The Soviet leaders do not and probably cannot always separate out these various reasons for their actions. Any conflict among the three is also, at least officially, glossed over. We actually rupture the fabric by examining each influence separately. But this must be done because there seems to be a degree of difference in the influence of each motivation on Soviet foreign policy, depending on the situation. Furthermore, the three must be examined individually since some authorities argue for the *continual* primacy of one or more of the motivations.

The Maintenance of Power by the Elite   Many writers have suggested that the ruling elite in the Soviet Union desire to maintain and increase their power above all else. The elite supposedly determine their policy decisions, both foreign and domestic, by the formula: "Will such an action increase our political power?" There are several variations on this theme, some emphasizing the drive for power as the only motivating factor, and others, considerably more sophisticated, admitting the impact of such factors as the ideology.

One of the more sophisticated treatments is W. W. Rostow's *The Dynamics of Soviet Society* (1952). Rostow suggested the one, consistent thread in the story of Soviet communism has been the priority given by the party leaders to the maintenance and expansion of their power, including their willingness to use any method necessary to control the masses. This priority of the elite is partly due to their love for personal power, but also to one aspect of the Marxist-Leninist ideology: the conviction, especially evident in Lenin's writings, that the communist party is the chosen instrument for the achievement of progress. The party believes it must maintain power because it has the duty—and *moral* right —to determine the correct path and to force the majority to follow. Other aspects of the ideology, such as the original goal of giving political authority directly to the trade unions and soviets (the workers' and soldiers' councils organized before the November communist revolution), have been dropped when in conflict with this pursuit of power.

The expansion of Soviet power beyond the USSR, Rostow believed, holds second priority to the maintenance of internal control. This expansion was primarily for defensive purposes before 1945, but now it is offensive in nature. The roots of expansionism, argued Rostow, are: (1) the Marxist-Leninist goal of world communism, which after a fashion has become a habit of thought; (2) more important, the internal stability of the regime supposedly is dependent upon the USSR's maintaining the view of a hostile *external* world, in turn justifying Soviet hostility; (3) the habits of handling power within the USSR now condition the regime's external behavior; the regime cannot operate comfortably unless it monopolizes power internally; and this habit makes it difficult for the elite to operate internationally in situations where power is shared or diffused.

George F. Kennan gave a similar explanation of the motivations behind Soviet foreign policy in his now famous article, "The Sources of Soviet Conduct" (*Foreign Affairs*, July 1947). Kennan, then head of the State Department Policy Planning Staff, argued that the circumstances immediately after the November communist revolution made it absolutely necessary for the party members to establish dictatorial power; they were an insignificant minority attempting to fight civil war and foreign intervention. The elite nevertheless did not seek power for its own sake. The party leaders, Kennan believed, were convinced they alone knew what was good for society, and were prepared to accomplish that good once their power was consolidated against both internal and external enemies.

By 1947 (the time of Kennan's article) the consolidation of power still was not complete. Little justification, however, could now be found for arguing the continuing existence of *internal* threats to the regime. Emphasis therefore was shifted to the menace of foreign imperialism. The ideology indicated the world was hostile and Russian history tended to substantiate this belief, even if the external threat was not always founded on reality. The party, nevertheless, had to insist on the threat's existence to justify the dictatorship.

The main aim of the regime in foreign affairs, because of its concern for security, was to make sure it filled "every nook and cranny available to it in the basin of world power." But Kennan believed there was no time-table or compulsion for this expansion. Following the teachings of Lenin and remembering the lessons of Russian history—the caution, circumspection, flexibility and deception learned from "centuries of obscure battles between nomadic forces over the stretches of a vast unfortified plain"—the Soviet leaders would accept retreats philosophically until they could apply pressure toward the desired goal. (Kennan suggested United States policy toward the Soviet Union thus should be "a long-term, patient but firm and vigilant containment of Russian expansive tendencies.")

The Kremlinologists have a third variation on the power theme. These analysts, whose technique was noted in the Introduction, are concerned with what they believe to be a permanent struggle for power *among* the members of the elite group. This is the "who-whom" couplet internalized; or, which Bolshevik is "doing in" which former comrade. Kremlinology first was practiced by Franz Borkenau and Boris Nicolaevsky, now by Myron Rush, Robert Conquest, Donald Zagoria and others—and necessarily by every intelligence organization and foreign ministry.

Exactly what causes the power struggle is not always defined. Robert Conquest in *Power and Policy in the U.S.S.R.* (1961, Chap. 2), suggests that it stems primarily from the force of the ideology on the minds of thousands of senior party officials and their inevitable differences in interpreting this ideology. Where foreign policy is concerned, there are two distinct lines: a "forward" policy, and one of more gentle pressure. These seem very broadly to match concurrent domestic trends. An overall Left policy favors the creation of the communist society at home and throughout the world by a crash program, while a Right policy is more concerned with solving immediate problems more slowly. (Soviet Left and Right foreign policies are analyzed in Chap. 3 of this book.)

Conquest argued that a particular party leader frequently adopts a Right or Left policy because it aids him in the political struggle, not because of the merits of the policy. Khrushchev was virtually forced into a Left position during his struggle with Malenkov after Stalin's death because Malenkov held what could be most easily attacked as a Right position. Most of the other top leaders, in short, combine "flexible tacticism with an inflexible drive to power." [21] (The top positions, noted Conquest, go to the politically ambitious, where rulers are selected through a political process and not by royal lineage or other fixed methods.)

The link between the ideology, the compulsion of the elite to maintain power, and the internal struggle among the elite should now begin to appear. The ideology justifies and even compels the maintenance of power, and, fed by the natural love of power found in most politicians, is the source of the internal struggle.

The preservation of power by the elite is intimately connected with the preservation and promotion of the "national interest," to be discussed next. Anything advancing the interests of the Soviet state advances the interests of the elite (or at least those members of the elite in control). In this respect, Kremlinology requires a word of caution. If Conquest's thesis is accepted, the national interest may not be served by the elite. A contender for power may adopt an aggressive Left policy, totally un-

[21] Contemporary "Kremlinologists" prefer to call their art the "conflict school" of analysis. The original Kremlinologists were concerned primarily with the power struggle. The conflict school is concerned with power but also with policy questions involved in the struggle. See Carl A. Linden, *Khrushchev and the Soviet Leadership, 1957-1964* (Baltimore, Md.: The Johns Hopkins Press, 1966), esp. the Introduction.

suited for the particular international situation, if the policy promises to advance his political position. Undoubtedly, the internal struggle has dictated certain turns and twists in Soviet international strategy and tactics. But all Soviet leaders necessarily need to pay attention to the realities of international politics, to the external and internal factors determining Soviet capability. Otherwise, they cannot continue to rule. This need in turn places a limit on the kinds of policies that a member of the elite can adopt at any one time, regardless of the demands of the power struggle.

The Preservation of the National Interest   Every state has a national interest, even though it may be difficult to define. And every state's national interest must be served, even in Russia where Soviet rulers are formally committed to an ideology transcending national concerns. George Kennan has written:

> Anyone who has looked reasonably closely at political history will have had many occasions to observe that the very experience of holding and exercising supreme power in a country saddles any ruler, whatever his own ideological motives, with most of the traditional concerns of government in that country, subjects him to the customary compulsions of statesmanship within that framework, makes him the protagonist of the traditional interests and the guardian against the traditional dangers. . . . However despotic he may be, and however far his original ideas may have departed from the interests of the people over whom he rules, his position of power gives him, as Gibbon once pointed out, a certain identity of interest with those who are ruled.[22]

The Soviet leaders are no different. From the first they could not avoid concern for "Russia." Bolsheviks personally might despise the masses, but they couldn't ignore them—along with the traditional interests of the country. In Leninist terms, Russia was the base for all future revolutions. The desires and needs of the people and the country had to be served to preserve this base.

Early in their regime, the Soviet leaders began to rationalize any apparent conflict between the goals of world communism and the national interest. This, of course, had not always been the case. At the very beginning of the new Soviet state, Lenin, basically an "internationalist," claimed:

> We defend not a Great-power status; there is nothing left of Russia except for Great-Russia; we do not defend national interests. We declare that the

[22] *Russia and the West Under Lenin and Stalin* (Boston: Atlantic-Little, Brown and Company, 1961), p. 392.

interests of socialism, the interests of world socialism, are superior to national interests and to the interests of states.[23]

Yet even Lenin showed traces of an emotional attachment to the
motherland. Apparently it was difficult for the most hardened revolutionary to be unsentimental about Russia. Lenin wrote in 1915: "Is the
feeling of national pride foreign to us, the Great-Russian, class-conscious
proletarians? Of course not! We love our language and our country." [24]
Stalin was just as patriotic. He stated at the end of World War II: "I
drink first of all to the health of the Russian people because it is the
leading nation of all the nations belonging to the Soviet Union . . . .
but also because it has a clear mind, a firm character and patience." [25]

Lenin, Stalin, Khrushchev, and the present Soviet leaders have never
forgotten Russia. But this attachment has been more than simple Russian
nationalism. The devotion of the Soviet leaders to "Russian" interests is
bound up with commitments to the Marxist-Leninist ideology, the third
part of the motivational trilogy. And the protection of the national interest
naturally is necessary for the preservation of their personal power, the
first primary motivation discussed.

The Soviets *publicly* have seen no basic conflict between Soviet national
and communist interests.[26] In their view, anything advancing the interests
of the USSR advances the interests of world communism. Many non-
Soviet communists appeared to believe this—at least through the 1930's.
It was logical to give first priority, for example, to the defense of the
Soviet Union. This base was indispensable for future revolutions. Moreover, the USSR controlled the international communist movement, making
it wise policy to accept the Soviet line.

But even in this period some non-Russian communists began to see a

[23] Quoted in W. W. Kulski, *Peaceful Coexistence* (Chicago: Henry Regnery Co.,
1959), p. 38.

[24] *Ibid.*, p. 39.

[25] Barghoorn, *Soviet Russian Nationalism*, p. 27.

[26] This supposed identity of interests may not last. In a speech to the Supreme
Soviet on December 12, 1962, Khrushchev appeared to differentiate between national
interests of communist states and the interests of the socialist camp, and indicated
national interests on occasion might have to come first. Replying to Communist
Chinese attacks on the USSR for having "appeased" the United States by withdrawing missiles from Cuba, Khrushchev said no one should accuse China for permitting "remnants of colonialism"—Hong Kong and Macao—on her territory. The
Chinese obviously had "good reasons" for permitting the existence of these colonies,
and would take care of the problem in their own time. Khrushchev told the Chinese:
"Settle this matter in accordance with the interest of your own country and of the
whole socialist camp." *New York Times,* December 13, 1962. This differentiation also
is creeping into Soviet defense statements. In the speeches of Soviet admirals on Navy
Day, July 30, 1967, the mission of the Soviet Navy was said to be the defense of
Soviet "state interests" anywhere in the world as well as the defense of the "members
of the commonwealth" (meaning other socialist countries). *Christian Science Monitor,*
August 9, 1967.

divergence between what they considered best for world communism, and what the Soviets claimed to be best. The dramatic signing of the Nazi-Soviet Non-Aggression Pact in 1939, and the subsequent orders for all communists to embrace the Germans and hate the Western capitalists, made certain party members outside the USSR believe the whole communist movement was being sacrificed (as it was) for the security of the USSR.

The differences today between the Soviet national interest and the interests of world communism are vividly illuminated by the split within the communist bloc and the attendant charges of "great power chauvinism" and "narrow nationalism." The conflict within the bloc in turn seems largely based on the Soviet *national* interest, versus the Chinese *national* interest, versus the Rumanian *national* interest, and so on. However, this begs the question. We still must define the Soviet national interest—a rather complex task. Since the Soviets imply that no difference exists between their national interest and that of world communism, perhaps we can look for certain "interests" which would be pursued by *any* government controlling what is now the USSR. There may be certain immutable goals which any "Russian" regime must strive for.

The basic national goal of any leader of Russia, it can be argued, must be national survival. This is the *minimum* objective—a certain degree of security.[27] Another question then arises. What do you need to provide Russian security? One clue comes from Russian history. Cyril Black, for example, has suggested that Russian leaders traditionally have pursued security through four general categories of objectives: (1) the stabilization of frontiers to protect the motherland by defeating neighboring powers, extending Russian control over relatively uninhabited territories, or relying on existing natural barriers; (2) the attempt to establish favorable conditions for economic growth, long recognized by Russian statesmen as important for national security and one of the motivations behind the desire for ice-free ports; (3) the unification of territories considered Russian by virtue of dynastic, religious, or national claims if they could add to Russian strength and provide defense in depth; (4) participation in alliances, both short- and long-term, and in international organizations designed to promote international security.[28]

From the peace settlement of 1921 to that of 1947, Black believes,

---

[27] The national interest could, of course, be directed primarily toward the promotion of a higher standard of living for the populace, toward world peace, etc. But today the term generally refers to the promotion of national security, and it will be used in this manner. However, the possible existence of other *higher* Soviet national interests are noted at the end of this section. The possible existence of these other interests differentiates this motivation from (3) "the search for security."

[28] "The Pattern of Soviet Objectives," in *Russian Foreign Policy* (New Haven, Conn.: Yale University Press, 1962), ed. Ivo J. Lederer, pp. 3-38.

the immediate objectives of Soviet foreign policy were determined primarily by security needs. This was evident in Soviet pursuit of the same four general categories of objectives. However, only the furthering of economic interests through the provision of ice-free ports had been relatively unaffected by the peace settlement. Soviet achievement of the other three categories of objectives had been drastically restricted. The Soviet Union's western frontier was, by traditional standards, very unstable. Many Ukrainians and White Russians now were under foreign rule. Finally, Soviet ability to form alliances or participate in international organizations to protect Russian security had been hampered by the Russian Revolution.

The problem with such an analysis is that a Western scholar, not the Soviet leaders, is defining the Soviet national interest. And the Soviets, as noted previously, formally deny any difference between this interest and that of world communism. The primary concern of a Russian leader serving the national interest must be to achieve a certain degree of national security. But security for a Soviet leader steeped in Marxism-Leninism is quite different from security for a Tsarist official. Marxism-Leninism predicts the Soviets will be in perpetual conflict with hostile imperialist states until the world is communized. This extends the requirements for the *complete* satisfaction of their national interest far beyond those Professor Black lists.

Yet there surely are *degrees* of security for the Soviets. Certainly domination of Eastern Europe makes them feel much more secure than the possession of some island chain in the Indian Ocean. There also probably exist certain *minimum* requirements the Soviet leaders consider absolutely necessary for national security—requirements for which they would fight. We cannot list these requirements. Even the Soviets probably would hesitate to do this, assuming they could. Too much depends on the circumstances, Soviet motivations, and Soviet capability. In 1918 the new Soviet government, largely because of Lenin's forceful leadership, agreed to a drastic butchering of European Russia with the Treaty of Brest-Litovsk. It is doubtful whether the USSR today, with its present capability, would agree to a similar ultimatum. The contemporary Soviet "Brest-Litovsk"—an area which the Soviets want, but do not consider necessary for survival—probably lies geographically far to the west of the heart of Russia. (The more a nation has, the more it tends to consider vital.) In 1962, Cuba apparently was a contemporary "Brest-Litovsk." In the next decade, Berlin may qualify.

These *minimum* Soviet security requirements probably correspond roughly to the national interest which would be pursued by any "Russian" government. (The national interest of any "Russian" government probably would cause trouble for the West.) Furthermore, these requirements, until satisfied, must take precedence over all other state goals—in particular, over the furthering of world communism. The history of Soviet foreign policy presented in the second part of this book will show that this has been the case since 1917. When Soviet *minimum* security is in jeopardy, the Soviets present world communism in muted form. When the Soviets seem to feel relatively secure, the pursuit of world communism is more energetic. World communism is the publicly stated, long-range *maximum* goal, always second in priority to the *minimum* goal of national security. Other communist states, and certain non-communist states, may consider the maximum Soviet goal as not merely furthering communism, but also a *higher* Soviet national interest. But the Soviets probably can equate this higher national interest—be it prestige, dominance of the communist bloc or some other goal—with the interests of world communism.

The Impact of the Marxist-Leninist Ideology   By now there should be some awareness of the impact of Marxist-Leninist ideology on Soviet foreign policy. But the extent of this impact remains to be discussed. The ideology has a profound influence on Soviet behavior in foreign affairs: (1) it establishes certain long range goals for Soviet foreign policy; (2) it provides the Soviet leaders with a system of knowledge on which to build their view of the world; (3) it gives them a method for analyzing foreign policy problems; (4) it furnishes strategy and tactics to achieve the ultimate ends; (5) it justifies the party's continuance in power, and thus the moral right of the party leaders even to make foreign policy; (6) it provides a unique method of control which, at least until the development of several independent communist states, has served to unify and coordinate the activities of communists all over the world; and (7) it serves as an important "technique" for the expansion of Soviet influence.

Some of these aspects of the ideology have been touched upon, particularly in relation to the national interest and the maintenance of power by the elite. But the complex nature of the ideological impact on Soviet foreign policy and the extreme importance of understanding this impact require a more detailed treatment. Chapter 2 thus contains a summary of those theoretical aspects of the ideology relevant to an understanding of Soviet behavior in world affairs. Chapter 3 describes the specific impact of the ideology on Soviet foreign policy: among other things, the evidence indicating the ideology does affect Soviet decisions in foreign affairs, the qualities it imparts to this decision making, and the advantages and disadvantages of the ideology for reaching sound decisions.

FURTHER READING

Aspaturian, Vernon V., "Internal Politics and Foreign Policy in the Soviet System," found in *Approaches to Comparative and International Politics,* ed. by R. Barry Farrell. Evanston, Ill.: Northwestern University Press, 1966. Essay on interplay of domestic interests and foreign policy in the political process.

Aspaturian, Vernon V., "Soviet Foreign Policy," found in *Foreign Policy in World Politics,* ed. by Roy C. Macridis, 2nd ed., Englewood Cliffs, N.J.: Prentice-Hall, Inc., 1962. Lengthy essay with analysis of Soviet motivations.

Aspaturian, Vernon V., *The Soviet Union in the World Communist System.* Stanford, Calif.: The Hoover Institution on War, Revolution, and Peace, Stanford University, 1966. Part of series on various communist states and their place in "communist system."

Bauer, Raymond A., *Nine Soviet Portraits.* New York: John Wiley & Sons, Inc., and M.I.T. Press, 1955. Fascinating composite characterizations based on refugee interviews.

Bell, Daniel, "Ten Theories in Search of Soviet Reality," found in *Soviet Society, A Book of Readings,* ed. by Alex Inkeles and Kent Geiger. Boston: Houghton Mifflin Company, 1961. Interpretative essay on Soviet system in general.

Beloff, Max, *The Foreign Policy of Soviet Russia, 1929-1941,* Vol. II. London: Oxford University Press, 1949. Chap. 15 contains essay on "The Principles of Soviet Foreign Policy."

Berdyaev, Nikolai, *The Origin of Russian Communism.* London: G. Bles, 1948.

Broderson, Arvid, "National Character: An Old Problem Re-examined," found in *International Politics and Foreign Policy,* ed. by James M. Rosenau. New York: The Free Press of Glencoe, Inc., 1961. Summarizes state of research on "national character."

Clarkson, Jesse D., "Toynbee on Slavic and Russian History," *Russian Review,* XV, No. 3 (1956). A critique of Toynbee's theory.

Dallin, Alexander, ed., *Soviet Conduct in World Affairs.* New York: Columbia University Press, 1960. Good collection of essays on Soviet behavior.

Garthoff, Raymond L., "The Concept of the Balance of Power in Soviet Policy-Making," *World Politics,* IV (1951). Scholarly analysis.

Glaser, William A., "Theories of Soviet Foreign Policy: A Classification of the Literature," *World Affairs Quarterly,* XXVII, No. 2 (1956). Somewhat dated but still useful.

Goldwin, Robert A. *et al.,* eds., *Readings in Russian Foreign Policy.* New York: Oxford University Press, 1959. Contains several essays on motivations behind Soviet foreign policy.

Gorer, Geoffrey and John Rickman, *The People of Great Russia.* London: Cresset Press, 1950.

Gurian, Waldemar, ed., *Soviet Imperialism: Its Origins and Tactics*. Notre Dame, Ind.: Notre Dame University Press, 1953. Essays on relationship between Marxian ideology and Russian nationalism as motivating forces in Soviet foreign policy.

Hermens, F. A., "Totalitarian Power Structure and Russian Foreign Policy," *Journal of Politics*, XXI, No. 3 (1959).

Kerner, Robert J., *The Urge to the Sea*. Berkeley and Los Angeles, Calif.: University of California Press, 1942.

Khvostov, V. M. and L. N. Kutakov, "The Foreign Policy of the Union of Soviet Socialist Republics," found in *Foreign Policies in a World of Change*, ed. by Joseph E. Black and Kenneth W. Thompson. New York: Harper & Row, Publishers, 1963. A Marxist-Leninist interpretation by two Soviet specialists.

Kohn, Hans, *Pan-Slavism; Its History and Ideology*. Notre Dame, Ind.: University of Notre Dame Press, 1953. Sees Soviet expansion after World War II as Slavic messianism Russian style.

Kulski, W. W., *Peaceful Co-Existence*. Chicago: Henry Regnery Co., 1959. Emphasizes motivations of ideology and national interest.

Lederer, Ivo J., ed., *Russian Foreign Policy*. New Haven, Conn. and London: Yale University Press, 1966. Excellent collection of essays contrasting Soviet and Tsarist behavior in "Russian" foreign policy.

Leites, Nathan C., *A Study of Bolshevism*. New York: Free Press of Glencoe, Inc., 1953.

Mackinder, Sir Halford J., *Democratic Ideals and Reality*. New York: Henry Holt and Company, 1942. Originally printed in 1919. Contains Mackinder's "heartland concept."

Moore, Barrington, *Soviet Politics—the Dilemma of Power*. Cambridge, Mass.: Harvard University Press, 1950. Study by sociologist of interaction between ideology and Soviet political system in foreign and domestic policy.

Morrison, John, "Russia and the Warm Waters," found in *U. S. Naval Institute Proceedings*, 1952, pp. 1169-79. Criticism of "urge to the sea" thesis.

Pentony, DeVere E., ed., *Soviet Behavior in World Affairs*. San Francisco, Calif.: Chandler Publishing Co., 1962. Good collection of articles on the motivations behind Soviet foreign policy and on current tactics.

Robinson, Thomas W., "A National Interest Analysis of Sino-Soviet Relations," *International Studies Quarterly*, XI, No. 2 (1967).

Rostow, W. W., *The Dynamics of Soviet Society*. New York: W. W. Norton & Company, Inc., 1967. New edition updated by Edward J. Rozek.

Schuman, Frederick L., *Government in the Soviet Union*. New York: Thomas Y. Crowell Company, 1961.

Triska, Jan F. and David D. Finley, *Soviet Foreign Policy*. New York: The Macmillan Company, 1968. A major effort toward applying the latest methodological approaches of political science to the *how* and *why* of Soviet foreign policy.

Tucker, Robert C., *The Soviet Political Mind*. New York: Frederick A. Praeger, Inc., 1963. Contains particularly interesting analysis of Stalin's approach to foreign affairs.

Wolfe, Bertram D., *Communist Totalitarianism*. Boston: Beacon Press, 1961, Rev. ed. Forceful argument for existence of totalitarian system in USSR.

2

THE MARXIST-LENINIST
IDEOLOGY

Marxism-Leninism, as communists label their ideology, is one of the three basic motivational roots of Soviet foreign policy. A knowledge of Marxism-Leninism also is necessary to understand the other two roots: the Soviets describe the national interest and justify their maintenance of power in ideological terms.

This chapter examines the basic assumptions of the ideology, paying special attention to those aspects which form the *theoretical* foundation for Soviet action in international politics. Communist strategy and tactics therefore receive major attention. In Chap. 3 we examine the *actual* impact of the ideology on Soviet foreign policy—how the ideology affects the Soviet leaders in their daily dealings with the real world.

MARXISM-LENINISM:
IDEOLOGY, NOT SCIENCE

The science of Marxism-Leninism, the Soviets assert, reveals the true workings of history. Statesmen armed with this science possess an immeasurable advantage in international politics; they have the key to the future. Provided the principles of the science are carefully adhered to, communist leaders can be certain of success.

Communists, of course, are not as lucky as they would have us believe. They have not discovered an infallible key to the historical process. Marxism-Leninism, which is based on communist theory, is not a science: it fails three basic tests. First, a theory to be scientific should be grounded on experience. Although lip service is paid to history, communism is founded on a series of unproven assumptions. Second, the theory should be formulated in a logical and coherent manner. There is superficial logic in communism, but the theory underneath is often disorganized and contradictory. Third, a scientific theory should be readily revised if experience dictates that it is obsolete. Communists reject free criticism of their doctrine. They are reluctant to face unpleasant facts which contravene basic assumptions.

If anything was inevitable about communism, it was the transformation of the *theory* into an *ideology*—roughly, a system of abstract ideas which claims to explain the general nature of society, asserts what the goals of this society should be, and specifies an action program for their achievement. The Marxist-Leninist *ideology* uses communist *theory*, developed primarily by Marx and Lenin, to explain reality, establish long-range goals, and provide a guide to action in specific situations.[1]

Changes in communist theory also were inevitable if the ideology was to have continuing significance. No theory dealing with human behavior can possibly predict all future events and specify the correct action necessary to move closer to the ultimate goal. In unforeseen instances the "high priests" must practice "creative Marxism." This is a most delicate task because there is only one "correct" interpretation of the theory, and an onerous one because changes have been necessary from the very first.

Soviet practitioners of creative Marxism naturally do not work in a vacuum. There is and can be no slavish, mechanistic interpretation of the gospel according to Marx and Lenin. Soviet leaders, for example, cannot construct a proper communist foreign policy just by reading the "sacred writings." (It would be equally absurd to assert that American foreign policy can be formulated from a close analysis of the works of John Locke or Thomas Jefferson.) Soviet theoreticians when ruminating are affected by the current international situation, the state of the USSR's domestic economy, geographical limitations on national capability, the Russian historical heritage, subconscious compulsions, the development of nuclear weapons—the list could be endless.

In short, the leaders of the Communist Party of the Soviet Union reach pragmatic solutions to their daily problems within the general framework of the Marxist-Leninist ideology. As a result, the ideology re-

---

[1] Communists today ignore the obvious contradiction between the terms "science" and "ideology." They refer to the "scientific, communist ideology," explaining that this is a true ideology because it reflects the science of historical materialism.

flects both the stated assumptions of the doctrine and the total historical and social experience of the Soviet leadership. Indeed, the original doctrine would long ago have lost its usefulness without the leavening influence of experience.

THE IDEOLOGY: MARXISM

The "science" upon which the ideology depends for its theoretical support was not originally a Russian product. The founders of the doctrine, Karl Marx and his collaborator Friedrich Engels, were both German. The impact of the Russian heritage and experience on the doctrine began with Lenin, who, although he claimed to be an internationalist, could not avoid the influence of his Russian environment.

The writings of Marx, Engels, and Lenin are the classics of Marxism-Leninism, or "communism," as it is often called. We shall be particularly interested, however, in the works of Lenin. His modifications of the original doctrine of Marxism made the ideology live by giving it relevance to the real world. Lenin's followers, especially Stalin and Khrushchev, introduced further modifications. However, the changes made in Marxism by the Soviet leaders, which they insist are not changes, must not be overemphasized. These leaders still seem basically committed to the final goal of world communism and operate with the world view of Marx and Engels. The contributions of the founders therefore must be briefly considered.

Dialectical Materialism   The science of Marxism-Leninism, according to its believers, reveals to man, for the first time, the fundamental laws of history. Through the use of reason and the scientific method, man can finally explain why and how society has developed and where it is going.[2]

The key concept which Marx discovered and which explains all of man's history, is dialectical materialism. Materialism means that the critical factor determining man's situation is the material base of his particular society, specifically its mode of production—the way in which men produce and distribute the society's wealth. Since the mode of production is so fundamental, it also determines the basic character of the whole social and cultural superstructure. In each society, for example, men are organized into two basic classes, depending on whether they own the means of production or whether they work for the owners, or, as a communist would put it, whether they are the exploiters or the

---

[2] Terms such as "capitalism," "socialism," "imperialism," "bourgeoisie," "united front," and so forth, unless otherwise noted, should be given their communist connotation. Initially, these terms may be set off by quotation marks. Where the quotation marks are omitted, the communist meaning still applies.

exploited.[3] The mode of production even determines such abstract ideas of a society as justice and morality, such organizational concepts as its form of government and its laws, even its music and art. Mankind as a whole supposedly has passed through four general types of societies—primitive-communal, slave, feudal, and capitalist—and is now living in the epoch of the transition to the next, higher type, communism, the first phase of which is called socialism.

Marx borrowed the dialectic from Hegel, the German philosopher, to explain how society progresses by means of a change in the mode of production.[4] The term "dialectic" comes from a Greek word which originally meant the art of arriving at the truth through exposing the contradictions found in the arguments of the parties to the dispute. There are three basic steps in the dialectical process. In the first step—the thesis—a proposition is stated. In the second step—the antithesis—a counter proposal is made. The third step—the synthesis—combines what is true in both the thesis and the antithesis and discards what is false, arriving at a new and higher truth. Soon the synthesis is found to have flaws and the process starts over again.

The transition from one step to another, however, is not a smooth or simple process. The dialectic operates in history, communists assert, through insignificant and imperceptible *quantitative* changes. At a given point these accumulated *quantitative* changes rapidly and abruptly explode, producing a major *qualitative* change. Genuine progress thus involves a "leap" from one step to a higher step.

The Class Struggle   The change in the mode of production is the factor which sets the dialectic in operation, but the dialectic operates in society through the medium of the class struggle. An example of the dialectic at work can be seen in the capitalist stage of history. New machines lead to a change in the mode of production, permitting at this juncture large scale mass production. The new system of manufacturing in turn calls into being the proletarian class—the factory workers.

Mass production inevitably creates a surplus of goods. The surplus exists because the "property relations" of the capitalist period are relatively static, and are now in "contradiction" with the more rapidly changing mode of production. "Property relations" refer mainly to the form of

[3] In actual practice, communists recognize considerable complexity in the class structure. They divide, for example, the exploited into the workers and peasants, and redivide the peasants into the exploiting, rich peasants, and the exploited middle and poor peasants. Communists also assert that the classes which exist under communist-style socialism cooperate with each other. No exploiting classes exist in such societies.

[4] The use of dialectical materialism to explain society and its history is called historical materialism.

ownership of the means of production; in the capitalist stage of history it is private ownership by the capitalist class.

The conflict between the mode of production and the property relations is translated into societal conflict between the capitalist (or bourgeois) class and the proletarian class. The exploiting capitalists will neither permit free distribution of the surplus goods nor raise the wages of the workers so that they may buy the surplus. The contradiction can only be resolved when the society as a whole owns the means of production, permitting the economic system to work for all the people and not just for the capitalist class.

The capitalists, of course, are not overjoyed about relinquishing their wealth and power to the proletariat. Neither was the feudal aristocracy eager to yield to the capitalist class—the bourgeoisie—when that class emerged as a result of the changes in the mode of production. An inevitable struggle occurs between the old class, still in control of the society, and the new, rising class. The result is violent revolution: the "leap" to the new, higher stage of society. (Creative Marxism now indicates this fundamental change in certain instances may be peaceful.)

Marx stated in *The Communist Manifesto* that the history of all hitherto existing society was the history of class struggles. Such struggles would continue, he predicted, until the final stage of communism when all people would own the means of production in common. With the society no longer divided into exploiters and exploited, classes would cease to exist and the dialectic would stop.

THE IDEOLOGY:
LENIN'S THEORY OF REVOLUTION

The emphasis in Marx is on explaining the grand sweep of history and the forces behind it. But the emphasis in Lenin is on engineering the necessary revolutions. He modified and amplified the original theory to make it a guide for action. (Lenin in fact emphasized that the theory was of no value unless it *was* a guide to action.) Marx and Engels were certain socialism was inevitable in the near future. Lenin believed socialism was *theoretically* inevitable, but as a realist he could see that careful planning would be necessary to bring about the required revolution. Certain aspects of the theory might even have to be altered to keep it in tune with the real world.

At the beginning of the twentieth century, Marxism was in danger of losing touch with reality. The world was not developing as the communists had predicted; capitalism was not dying. The workers in the most advanced capitalist countries, contrary to Marx, were losing their revolutionary fervor and were yielding to the promise for reforms within the capitalist system. Moreover, the proletariat in these countries was not becoming poorer, but was experiencing better living conditions. Socialist revolution looked far away, particularly in Russia where the capitalist stage of economic development was just beginning.

Imperialism   Lenin found a way out of this discouraging turn of events in his highly important work, *Imperialism* (largely based, as Lenin admits, on the work of John Hobson, an English middle-class social critic, and Rudolf Hilferding, an Austrian Marxist). Lenin explained that the "primary contradiction" between the mode of production and the property relations of the capitalist societies, exemplified in the conflict between the bourgeoisie and the proletariat, had not developed into revolution because the capitalists had found a way out of that contradiction.

Capitalism had progressed to a new level—in Leninist terms, its highest stage. In the most advanced countries, capital was now concentrated in the hands of huge monopolies. These monopolies, which naturally controlled the governments of their countries, had expanded throughout the world in search of cheap raw materials, new markets for their products, uses for excess capital, and, above all, cheap labor. New and higher profits resulted from this search (centering in the area now called "underdeveloped"). The capitalists thus had money to bribe the leaders of the proletariat with economic concessions and could make political concessions to the lower classes in general. In addition, the workers were caught up in the fierce nationalism engendered by the imperialist competition. It hardly was surprising that the revolutionary enthusiasm of the proletariat had waned.

Lenin was merely realistic about the lack of revolutionary possibilities in the more advanced capitalist countries (although for questionable reasons). But he was not ready to give up all hope of revolution. Creative Marxism was required; and Lenin supplied it. According to his theory of imperialism, the primary contradiction between the bourgeoisie and the proletariat in each capitalist country had been temporarily brought under control by the capitalists. But the capitalist predicament could not be solved so easily. The conflict previously concentrated within each industrial nation simply had been transferred to the international level. The world had become one huge capitalist system, producing two new contradictions. First, there was an international counterpart of the class struggle within each country. The relatively few, advanced capitalist countries had become the exploiters of the rest of the world. Second, a contradiction had developed between the rival imperialist powers. Monopolies within each of the capitalist countries had reduced the anarchic domestic competition only to see it reappear in a much more deadly form on the international scene. Now it involved whole nations, and conflicts over colonies and spheres of influence could only be resolved by war (specifically, communists would reason, World Wars I and II).[5]

A further contradiction began to plague the world capitalist system with the founding of the first socialist state, the USSR. There were now "two camps"—the camp of socialism and that of capitalism. The camp of socialism represented the "progressive" forces in the world in conflict with "reactionary" capitalism. Stalin viewed this contradiction as the most fundamental of all.

Revolution in the Age of Imperialism   Because of these new contradictions, revolutionary possibilities were actually greater than before the rise of imperialism. But the type of country ripe for revolution had changed. Instead of having to wait for developments in the relatively few highly industrialized nations, communists could look for revolution in all but the most backward societies.[6] The total world situation was now more significant than the maturity of the particular economic system. The country qualifying as the "weakest link" in the world capitalist system at any given time would be the logical place for revolution. This could be a country going through the very painful, early stages of industrialization. Here the capitalists would be mercilessly exploiting the new, comparatively weak proletariat and the much larger peasant class. In 1917 there was a "weak link" of this type—Russia.

An additional problem had to be faced in the event that a revolution could develop in such a relatively backward country. In the years before World War I, Lenin theorized that Russia still lacked her bourgeois-democratic revolution led by the capitalist class. According to a strict interpretation of Marx's writings, this would have to precede any socialist revolution under the leadership of the proletariat. The working class could only gain the required strength for its own, later revolution during such a capitalist phase of development.

Lenin was not prepared to wait. The Russian bourgeoisie, he argued, would not push their own revolution because it had to be a liberal revolution—and they were not basically liberal. Therefore, the proletariat

[5] Stalin, during his report on the Central Committee to the Fourteenth Party Congress in 1925, broke this contradiction into two parts: (1) the contradictions between the victorious imperialist countries in World War I and the beaten imperialist powers (between the Western Allies and Germany); (2) the contradictions between the victors (between Japan and England and the United States, etc.).

[6] Stalin said in 1924 that there had to be at least "a certain minimum" of industrial development and culture. Otherwise, revolution could have occurred somewhere in central Africa. Today, however, even this qualification is in doubt in view of the obvious communist interest in the Congo and other African countries. Historicus, "Stalin on Revolution," *Foreign Affairs*, XXVII, No. 2 (1949), p. 183.

would have to carry out *both* the bourgeois and socialist revolutions. And since the proletariat would be so weak on the eve of the bourgeois revolution, it would have to get aid from other quarters. Prime candidates would be the peasantry, hungry for land, the dissatisfied national minorities, wanting self-determination, and those liberal members of the bourgeoisie ready for revolution.[7]

The result of the bourgeois revolution would be "a revolutionary-democratic dictatorship of the proletariat and the peasantry." This arrangement, however, would only be temporary. Communists would push on at the earliest moment toward the proletarian-socialist revolution. To do otherwise would give the bourgeoisie time to solidify its position and make the inevitable socialist revolution more difficult.

Lenin would not attempt to predict the time required before the proletarian revolution could take place. (He was too sensible to attempt to forecast the date of any revolution in any country—even Russia.) In practice, communists have taken power during the bourgeois revolution and proceeded as quickly as possible to their own revolution. This strategy has come perilously close to ignoring the Marxian requirement of the logical development of a society through the capitalist to the socialist stage.[8] But regardless of its lack of doctrinal purity, Lenin's theory of revolution emerged as the general pattern for subsequent communist revolutions. (Recent significant deviations are noted later in this chapter.)

Requirements for Revolution Communist leaders may have a "weak link" to exploit; however, they still have the difficult decision as to just when this link is ripe for revolution. Their task is eased somewhat through guidelines laid down by Lenin. Three "objective" factors have to be present, he stressed, for a revolutionary situation to exist in a particular country. (Objective factors are those historical forces which, although they can be *modified* by conscious human action, determine the basic pattern of history regardless of human will.) First, there must be a national crisis. This can result from a disastrous economic

---

[7] For an excellent discussion of the three general strains of Russian Marxist thought (the views of Lenin, Trotsky and the Mensheviks) about the coming revolution in Russia, see Bertram D. Wolfe, *Three Who Made A Revolution* (New York: The Dial Press, Inc., 1948), pp. 289-98.

[8] Soviet theorists now indicate that the bourgeois and socialist revolutions may merge into a single revolutionary process. During the Russian Revolution, the democratic revolution was essentially anti-feudal. In a number of countries today this revolution is directed from the outset against the "extremely reactionary, monopolistic wing" of the bourgeoisie as well as against the survivals of feudalism. In other words, the democratic revolution is directed against essentially the same enemy as is the socialist revolution. The East European "popular-democratic" revolutions after 1945 are cited as examples. *Fundamentals of Marxism-Leninism,* 2nd rev. ed. (Moscow: Foreign Languages Publishing House, 1963), p. 487.

depression or from the strains created internally by imperialist wars, particularly in those less developed countries where exploitation is at its worst. The situation in Russia itself on the eve of the revolution in 1917 is a classic example. A crisis also can arise because of the inability of the government to cope with pressing, national problems. The second objective factor occurs when the ruling class loses faith in its ability to continue governing. The third factor results from the first two: the masses are fed up with the ensuing chaos and are ready for revolution.

A country experiencing such conditions would seem to be heading inevitably toward revolution. But for Lenin, objective factors were not enough to insure the revolution—or at least the "correct" type of revolution. Objective factors are blind forces; they must be given direction. This can only come from the members of a tightly organized, highly disciplined party of professional revolutionaries guided by the scientific doctrine of Marxism-Leninism. Conscious human effort, a "subjective" factor, is required for the proper type of revolution—a revolution moving a country toward communism.

In summary, Lenin did not share Marx's optimism about the immediate possibilities for progressive revolutions. Lenin was too much a realist in his short-range analysis to believe that things were developing exactly as Marx had predicted. But both he and his Soviet followers were and are orthodox Marxists in believing that world capitalism will collapse and that communism will be victorious. Lenin also followed the basic postulates of dialectical materialism in his theory of revolution. A band of communists cannot bring off a revolution anywhere, anytime. Lenin insisted that certain objective conditions produced by the inexorable movement of fundamental historical forces must be present.

Lenin's *conditions* for revolution, on the other hand, differed considerably from those of Marx, who emphasized that meaningful economic and political revolutions were only possible at certain stages of economic development. The proletarian revolution, for example, could occur only in a mature, capitalist society. Such turning points of history for Marx did not basically hinge on national chaos, a revolutionary mood of the masses, and the pending collapse of the ruling class.

THE IDEOLOGY:
STRATEGY AND TACTICS OF REVOLUTION

Lenin's objective conditions only indicate the basic requirements for a revolutionary situation. The communist party in each country must prepare the *subjective* conditions. It must mobilize the proletariat and its allies and lead them into battle at the precise moment promising victory—when objective conditions are ripe.

Lenin's strategy and tactics of revolution are an aid for the proper preparation of subjective conditions. Lenin laid out general principles to be followed. He refused to formulate complete, detailed plans for revolution. Communist leaders therefore cannot refer to some obscure passage in Lenin for specific policies. They must make decisions on the spot as the situation dictates. Lenin provided a *guide* to revolutionary success— no more.

Calculating the Class Forces   The correct strategy and tactics for a particular party, Lenin stressed, are determined by a very careful and accurate calculation of the power of the country's classes and their current relationships, particularly, the relative strength of the bourgeoisie and the proletariat. Once this is done, the basic direction of the attack can be derived. If the enemy is weaker, the communists *must* attack, if stronger, they *must* retreat. (This, of course, needs to be related to the revolutionary situation, described previously, and to whether the revolutionary tide is ebbing or flowing.) If a party leader fails to follow the dictates of this basic Leninist principle, he is not a good communist.

Unfortunately, it is not easy to correctly estimate the balance of forces in a particular situation. There is no definitive listing available of what factors must be considered in determining, for instance, whether the proletariat in a certain country is stronger than the bourgeoisie. Stalin did give a clue in 1921 that such things should be considered in calculating the relative power of the proletariat and its enemies as the greater or lesser degree of their organization and class-consciousness, and the presence of particular traditions and particular forms of their political movement. But a communist might be wrong in calculating only these factors. "Forces" seem to be any factors which may affect class capabilities in the inevitable struggle. Lenin opened the floodgates when he stated in *Left Wing Communism* that "tactics must be based on a sober and strictly objective estimation of *all* the class forces (in neighboring states, and in all states the world over) as well as of the experience of revolutionary movements." [9]

The calculation of the balance of forces is further complicated because certain forces can either hinder or aid the communist cause, depending on the situation. Lenin stated, for example, that a revolutionary party had to be ready to use everybody and everything in pursuit of its goal. Any

---

[9] In 1962 Soviet theoreticians stated: "The course and outcome of the class struggle in any country have never been so dependent on the general correlation of class forces and the state of international relations as in our epoch." See "The Nature and Specific Features of Contemporary International Relations," *International Affairs* (Moscow), No. 10 (1962), pp. 93-98.

group must be considered a potential ally if it hurts the enemy's forces, even if this ally is "temporary, vacillating, unstable, unreliable, and conditional." (The calculator errs, naturally, if the ally later proves too unreliable.)

The communists, of course, do not explicitly recognize these difficulties in their calculations. Supposedly their doctrine is scientific, eliminating guesswork. Any intelligent Marxist-Leninist should be able to arrive at exactly the same appraisal of the balance of forces. But communists are human and their doctrine as we have indicated is not scientific. Consequently, the most serious intra-party debates often arise over just such questions. Lenin, Trotsky and Bukharin, all brilliant dialecticians, disagreed over whether the new Soviet revolutionary government should accept the German terms of the Treaty of Brest-Litovsk in 1918. And the central question was over the relative power of each side. Lenin won the argument. The losing comrades were accused of being "non-Marxist" in their particular estimates. There could be no real disagreement because the doctrine was scientific; therefore, the losers simply had failed to apply the doctrine's principles.

The specific bill of particulars leveled against party leaders in such instances is that they have made one of two basic mistakes: underestimating or overestimating the enemy's forces. Underestimating makes one a Left deviationist, an "adventurist" ready to take very risky action against a superior enemy. Overestimating leads to "opportunism," a deviation to the Right, and the failure to act in spite of having superior force on your side. Communists refuse to admit that neither the power of nation-states nor the intricate power relationships in a particular country can be measured accurately.

Revolutionary Strategy Once the balance of forces has been calculated, the leaders of a particular communist party can determine the correct strategy and tactics for their national revolution. These, of course, are Lenin's strategy and tactics, which, Stalin reminds us, constitute "the science of leadership in the revolutionary struggle of the proletariat." [10] (A recent authoritative updating of the whole ideology, the *Fundamentals of Marxism-Leninism*, emphasizes that more than "science" is involved. Political leadership depends not only on "a correct, scientifically trustworthy analysis of the situation," but also on "great ability, skill and real artistry. . . .") [11]

Strategy and tactics are commonly considered military terms. It is not unusual for communists to use them, however, if we remember that the

---

[10] *Foundations of Leninism* (New York: International Publishers Co., Inc., 1932), p. 86. A collection of lectures given by the emerging Soviet dictator in 1924.

[11] *Fundamentals of Marxism-Leninism*, p. 347.

ideology predicts continual class *war* until communism is achieved. Lenin, who had been greatly influenced by von Clausewitz's classic, *On War*, first used the terms. Like Clausewitz, Lenin saw political life as a continual struggle. But when the terms strategy and tactics were applied to class conflict instead of military conflict, they naturally received a Marxian connotation.

A clear definition of the communist meaning of strategy is found in *Foundations of Leninism*. According to Stalin:

> Strategy is the determination of the direction of the main blow of the proletariat at a given stage of the revolution; the elaboration of a corresponding plan of disposition of the revolutionary forces (the main and secondary reserves); the struggle to carry out this plan during the whole period of the given stage of the revolution.[12]

Strategy refers to the overall plan for communist action in a given stage of a country's revolution, and remains basically unchanged throughout that stage. Each national communist party has a strategy to fit the particular situation in its country because each country is at a certain stage of economic development with unique political conditions.

In theory there has never been one overall strategy for the world communist movement. But from the early days of the Comintern in 1919 until the collapse of close Soviet control over the world communist movement in the 1950's, the strategies of individual communist parties were in fact generally subordinated to the strategy of the Soviet Union.

Today, the Soviets admit that the working class movement should develop on a "national" basis. But they remind all other communist parties that the communist movement is "international" by its very essence—having a common ideology, common aims, and a common enemy. The *Fundamentals of Marxism-Leninism* states: "While remaining politically and organizationally independent, the Communist Parties *voluntarily, by mutual agreement,* proceeding from the unity of their views on the international problems of the working class, unite their actions, jointly elaborate, if necessary, a unified line of conduct, and act as a unified international force safeguarding the interests of the working people of all countries, world peace and security."[13]

Stalin indicated in *Foundations of Leninism* that the Soviet revolution had progressed through two strategic stages and had entered a third. The Soviet Communist Party had constructed separate strategic plans to fit

---

[12] Stalin, *Foundations of Leninism*, p. 87. A recent Soviet definition of strategy states that it is "the general line of the Party directed towards accomplishing the main tasks of a given historical stage, taking the existing correlation of forces between the classes as a starting point." *Fundamentals of Marxism-Leninism*, p. 345.

[13] *Fundamentals of Marxism-Leninism*, p. 356.

each stage. During Stalin's lifetime, every other communist party was ordered to follow a similar pattern.[14]

The task of each communist party was to apply the strategic plan appropriate to the situation in its country. The plan for the first stage was applicable if a country had not yet had a bourgeois-democratic revolution. This corresponded to the period in Russia from 1903 to the March revolution in 1917. The communists disguised their true goals by promoting a "minimum" program: land reform, civil rights, an effective parliament. The party wanted feudalism (or autocracy) overthrown and was perfectly willing to help the bourgeoisie in this task. At the same time, the party hoped to keep control of the masses so that it could push on to the second strategic stage—the promotion of the socialist revolution. (This stage corresponded to the period in Russia from the liberal democratic revolution of March 1917, to the Bolshevik Revolution in November of that year.) During the second stage, the party worked to overthrow the bourgeois government and seize absolute power.

The party began the third strategic stage with a successful proletarian-socialist revolution. (Russia entered this stage with the Bolshevik Revolution.) The "maximum" program was introduced in the third stage, including nationalization of the economy and party control of all phases of the society. The governmental form was the classic "dictatorship of the proletariat." [15]

Stalin's rigid prescription for revolutionary progress in each country began to collapse even before his death. His formula had been applicable mainly to relatively backward, or "underdeveloped," countries. The first deviation came with the formation of the communist regimes in Soviet-dominated Eastern Europe at the end of World War II. The time was not ripe for the creation of carbon copies of the Soviet revolution. The Western powers were still officially interested in seeing truly democratic governments formed in these countries. Local communist parties still had much internal opposition. Obviously the proletarians could not launch

---

[14] W. W. Kulski, *Peaceful Coexistence* (Chicago: Henry Regnery Co., 1959), pp. 76-79.

[15] The 1961 Program of the Soviet Communist Party implies that the USSR has entered a fourth strategic stage. The final victory of socialism is complete (the struggle to build socialism is the first phase of communism), and the society has made the transition to the full-scale construction of communism. The dictatorship of the proletariat, the state form during the third strategic stage, has been replaced by a "socialist state of the whole people." The "dictatorship" is out of date because coercion is no longer needed against classes or social groups, only against individuals. See the *Fundamentals of Marxism-Leninism*, pp. 594-99. Khrushchev's successors made no references to the "socialist state of the whole people" at the Twenty-third Party Congress in 1966. They may have considered the transition to the fourth strategic stage premature.

violent revolutions against the bourgeoisie. Likewise, the dictatorship of the proletariat, the required next stage after the socialist revolution, was theoretically impossible. (This dictatorship has as its main aim the complete destruction of the institutions of the former bourgeois-democratic state and the expropriation of the dominant capitalist ruling class. Lenin had candidly called it unrestricted power, exercised by the proletariat, and resting on force.)

Creative Marxism supplied a new formula to fit the situation. Instead of bourgeois-democratic or socialist revolutions, the Eastern European states had "national-democratic" revolutions. The people rid themselves of Nazi "accomplices" (landlords and monopoly bourgeoisie) and foreign imperialism. Furthermore, these were relatively non-violent revolutions. "The forces of reaction were inhibited and paralyzed in their activity," admitted Polish party leader Gomulka, by the presence of the Red Army.[16]

The state arising from this new type of revolution was a "people's democracy," a hybrid between the old bourgeois-democratic and the new socialist state form in the USSR. Instead of one-party rule, national coalitions existed. Members of the bourgeoisie, the traditional exploiting class, were participants in the coalition. Former state institutions often were retained, where they could be creatively infused with a new "class content." Rumania and Bulgaria even kept their monarchies. In each case, the avowed aim of the local communist parties was for the new people's democracies to press on to socialism—completely avoiding the oppressive dictatorship of the proletariat.

But such diversity—and heresy—could not last. Because of declining Western interest in the area and the apparent Soviet fear of a new war between the Soviet bloc and Western capitalism, Stalin began to tighten Soviet control over Eastern Europe. Tito's defection in 1948 only accentuated the process. The general applicability of Soviet revolutionary experience for *all* communist parties was now reasserted by Moscow. The "democratic" coalitions would remain, but the communist parties in each country would have no constitutional limits on their power. The people's democracies were declared merely a new *form* of the dictatorship of the proletariat, an essentially accurate description in view of the new, completely dominant position of the local communists.

Meanwhile, the Soviets were having doctrinal problems with the new Asian communist states, China and North Korea. Mao Tse-tung's "New Democracy" was hailed by the Chinese as a brilliant contribution to the storehouse of Marxism. The Chinese were willing to accept people's democracy as equivalent to new democracy. But they asserted capitalism was being rooted out in Eastern Europe, as it had been in Russia, by

[16] Z. Brzezinski, *The Soviet Bloc* (New York: Frederick A. Praeger, Inc., 1961), p. 27.

violent means. China, having a relatively weak capitalist class, could eradicate this evil by peaceful methods. Therefore, the Chinese communists refused to consider their new democracy as equivalent to a dictatorship of the proletariat. They proclaimed that the Chinese peasantry, petty bourgeoisie, and national bourgeoisie would march all the way to socialism under the hegemony of the proletariat.

The Chinese heresy was a little more difficult to heal than that of the Eastern European communist parties. The breach was only closed when the Soviets admitted at their Twentieth Party Congress in 1956 that the Chinese path to socialism was a fully legitimate variant of the dictatorship of the proletariat. (The Chinese introduction of communes in 1958 reopened debate on Mao Tse-tung's method of achieving communism.)

The original meaning of the dictatorship appeared to be even more drastically watered down when Khrushchev talked, at the Twentieth Party Congress, of employing the parliamentary method of achieving socialism. This was probably designed to improve the fortunes of the French and Italian Communist Parties. Communists in such advanced capitalist countries had seen the standard formula of a violent proletarian revolution become increasingly less realistic in the face of strongly entrenched capitalist classes. A peaceful transition to socialism was now held theoretically possible since the communists and their allies, by winning parliamentary majorities, might be able to carry through the necessary fundamental social changes.

The possibility of such a peaceful transition, however, was seriously limited in practice. It obviously was not feasible, remarked Khrushchev, in countries where capitalism was still powerful and had huge military and police machinery (effectively ruling out France and Italy). Where then could such a transition take place? Mikoyan, a member of the Party Presidium, stated that Lenin foresaw a possibility in a small bourgeois country with socialist countries for neighbors. Mikoyan offered as examples Czechoslovakia, Bulgaria, Rumania, Hungary and Poland. He neglected to mention the vital factor which made possible such peaceful revolutions—the presence of Soviet troops in or on the borders of these countries.

Such explicit qualifications surrounding this peaceful method of achieving socialism should have placed it in proper prospective. But the "new" method was hailed in some quarters as a basic change in communist strategy. Actually it was merely a restatement of previous declarations by Lenin and Stalin holding out only slim hope for eliminating the necessary, violent transition to socialism.

The extreme flexibility of class alignment and institutional forms now considered possible for the transition to socialism, however, are very important. The contemporary Soviet guide for practical revolutionists, the

Fundamentals of Marxism-Leninism, emphasizes that the future may bring other forms of "working-class dictatorship or of a democracy performing the same functions." For example, there is now a basis for broader social and political alliances in the advanced capitalist countries because the monopoly bourgeoisie in such countries is in opposition to the entire society, including certain sections of the middle bourgeoisie. The use of "coercion" therefore may be "restricted to a narrower field." [17] The resulting political movement is "a democracy of a new type representing the interests of the broad mass of the working people and other progressive sections of the population." [18] The national liberation movements in the underdeveloped areas, predicts the *Fundamentals,* may also give rise to "new forms of working people's political power." Lenin wrote that "the subsequent revolutions in Oriental countries . . . will undoubtedly display even greater peculiarities than the Russian Revolution." [19]

Regardless of which strategic stage a particular communist party believes applicable to its country, there are certain questions which must be answered to formulate the strategic plan of action. In *Foundations of Leninism* Stalin separated strategy into five parts to illustrate the required decisions. For instance, during the second strategic stage of the Russian Revolution (March to November 1917), (1) the *objective* was the overthrow of imperialism in Russia and withdrawal from the imperialist war; (2) the *main force* of the revolution was the proletariat; (3) the *reserves* (aiding the main force) were the peasantry, the proletariat in neighboring countries, and "indirect" reserves such as the obvious crisis of imperialism in World War I; (4) the *direction of the main blow* was against those groups most likely to betray the revolution by surrendering elements of the main force to the enemy; these potential traitors in 1917 were the petty-bourgeois democrats (Mensheviks and Socialist-Revolutionaries); and (5) the *plan for the disposition of forces*—the question of which classes should be allied with the main force—indicated that the proletariat had to ally with the poor peasantry.

---

[17] *Fundamentals of Marxism-Leninism,* p. 536.

[18] *Ibid.,* p. 482.

[19] *Ibid.,* p. 538. Current Soviet doctrine predicts that the transition to socialism may even take place in some developing countries "without the direct leadership of the working class and at least in the initial stage—under the leadership of the progressive forces which gradually go over to the position of scientific socialism." The Chinese incidentally consider this formulation rank heresy—the idea that nonsocialists will bring about socialist revolutions in spite of themselves. See B. N. Ponomarev, ed., *Mezhdunarodnoe Revoliutsionnoe Dvizhenie Rabochego Klassa* (The International Revolutionary Movement of the Working Class) (Moscow, 1964), p. 325. Cited in Herbert S. Dinerstein, "Soviet Policy in Latin America," *American Political Science Review,* LXI (1967), 83. This article contains a good summary of contemporary Soviet thought on the developing countries.

The authors of the *Fundamentals of Marxism-Leninism* suggest the same general decision-making process to formulate the general strategic line. But they criticize Stalin for being led astray by analogies from "military science." In politics, for example, one must deal with social classes and forces, not ready-formed armies and reserves. Political leaders cannot command their forces into battle because economic classes act under the influence of their own interests and not on the order of a commander. In addition, Stalin is criticized for having directed the *main* blow on occasion at the wrong enemy. He should have aimed it at the European bourgeoisie (particularly Hitler's rising party) in 1928. Instead, he portrayed the socialists as the main enemy and facilitated the rise of fascism.[20]

Revolutionary Tactics   Tactics are subordinate to strategy. They are designed to win particular battles, and not the whole war. Tactics may change many times during a given revolutionary stage, while the strategic plan remains fixed.

The inability to distinguish between wildly fluctuating tactical moves and the overall, relatively fixed strategic plan has been the cause of much confusion in the West. Many interpreted the abolition of the Comintern in 1943 as evidence that the Soviets were abandoning their strategic aim of promoting world communism through active cooperation and coordination of all communist parties. It later became apparent this had been a *tactical* move, leaving the basic strategy unaltered.[21]

The problem of analyzing tactical moves is complicated by the willingness of a communist to use *any* tactic if it will serve the cause. Lenin, in fact, demanded such flexibility in *Left-Wing Communism*, subtitled "A Popular Essay in Marxian Strategy and Tactics":

> To carry on a war for the overthrow of the international bourgeoisie, a war which is a hundred times more difficult, prolonged, and complicated than the most stubborn of ordinary wars between states, and to refuse beforehand to maneuver, to utilize the conflict (even though temporary) among one's enemies, to refuse to temporise and compromise with possible (even though transitory, unstable, vacillating and conditional) allies—is not this ridiculous in the extreme? Is it not as though, when making a difficult ascent of an unexplored and hitherto inaccessible mountain, we were to refuse be-

[20] *Fundamentals of Marxism-Leninism,* pp. 345-47.

[21] Confusion over the difference between strategy and tactics occasionally extends to party members. Andrei Zhdanov of the Soviet Party Politburo remarked in 1947 at the launching of the Cominform, the Comintern's successor: "Some comrades understood the dissolution of the Comintern to imply the elimination of all ties, of all contact, between the fraternal Communist parties. But experience has shown that such mutual isolation of the Communist parties is wrong, harmful and, in point of fact, unnatural."

forehand ever to move in zigzags, ever to retrace our steps, ever to abandon the course once selected to try others? [22]

Communists must use every *illegal* method available; every kind of trick, lie, concealment, or bit of cunning which may advance the cause. But they also use *legal* methods, participating in "reactionary" bourgeois parliaments if only to discredit bourgeois democracy. "Revolutionaries who are unable to combine illegal forms of struggle with every form of legal struggle," Lenin emphasized, "are poor revolutionaries indeed." [23]

The Ebb and Flow of the Revolutionary Tide   Communists do give us some aid in analyzing their tactical moves. They insist that tactics must be in tune with the direction of the revolutionary tide in a particular strategic period. Strategy stays the same within a given period. But within this period the revolutionary situation may change drastically. At one moment, revolution is ripe; at another, the non-communist government in power (in the first or second revolutionary stage) gains control of a chaotic situation. There is no constantly rising tide of revolution. On the contrary, there is a rhythm, an "ebbing" and "flowing," to the process. And communists must adjust their tactics to the direction of this tide. Otherwise, they will be swimming against the current of history.

Offensive Tactics   A classic description of tactics for use in a capitalist country during a revolutionary "flood" tide is found in the program adopted by the Comintern at its Sixth World Congress in 1928. When the tide is flowing as it supposedly was in 1928, communists must advance. They employ *offensive* (Left) tactics, and prepare for a direct attack upon the state. Party propaganda is full of "transitional" slogans, emphasizing the need to overthrow the ruling class and transfer power to the proletariat and its allies. Measures to bring about this transfer include the organization of workers' "soviets" (councils) to take over industry, peasant committees to seize the property of big landowners, strikes and demonstrations, including armed demonstrations, and finally, a general strike combined with armed insurrection against the ruling class.

Defensive Tactics   When the revolutionary tide is ebbing, communists introduce *defensive* (Right) tactics because retreat is required. Party propaganda now contains "partial" slogans. Instead of urgent calls for revolution, the party tailors its program to the everyday needs of the working class. Obviously popular issues are emphasized: the

---

[22] *Left-Wing Communism* (New York: International Publishers Co., Inc., 1940), p. 52.
[23] *Ibid.,* p. 77.

1928 Comintern program listed wages, the working day, the right to organize, and, in the case of peasants, taxes and mortgage indebtedness.

During the ebb period, the party also uses the "united front" tactic. The most widely known type of united front is organized "from above" through agreements by communists and leaders of non-communist working class groups on a common program containing items of burning interest for the non-communists. Sometimes, this agreement is based on issues in the communist partial program of 1928. In the 1930's, communists capitalized on the fear of fascism as the cement for a variant of the united front called the "popular front," and more recently, on the desire for peace. Anti-imperialism has been especially useful for common programs in underdeveloped countries. In any case, communists use the united front to try to gain control of the working class (or peasant) movement by proving themselves the real champions of the common man. Hopefully, this posture will give them a mass following for future revolutionary action.

The party faces inherent difficulties, however, in carrying out united front tactics from above. In advanced capitalist countries such as France and Italy, communists are attempting to cooperate with non-revolutionary socialist parties—their traditional rivals for leadership of the proletariat. Communists must call "comrade" the very men they vilify as the worst traitors of the working class movement during Left periods. And many socialist leaders remember Lenin's pointed remark in *Left-Wing Communism* that communists support socialists "as the rope supports the hanged man." Furthermore, even if an agreement between communists and non-communists is reached, communist leaders find difficulty avoiding charges of (1) "opportunism"—losing revolutionary fervor through contact with the socialists, or (2) "sectarianism"—showing too much revolutionary zeal or refusing to collaborate as agreed, thus causing the downfall of the front.

A second form of the united front is organized "from below." This tactic is generally characteristic of Left periods. The united front from below involves attacks on the leadership of other working class groups. Communists attempt to win these groups over to their side by local, grass-roots collaboration with the non-communist rank and file. Such collaboration may have to cease, of course, during the decisive struggle. Communists are compelled to fire even at proletarians when they are on the enemy's side because of "deficient class consciousness."

United front tactics should not be confused with the creation of "front" organizations. Very early in his revolutionary career, Lenin saw the need in *What is to be Done* (1902) to create a variety of mass organizations, either overtly or covertly controlled by the communist party, to spread communist influence as far as possible. With their highly disciplined and carefully selected membership, the Bolsheviks necessarily had shallow roots. But front organizations such as Soviet trade unions and professional organizations enrolled great masses of people who could be manipulated to serve the cause. This tactic later was extended with varying success to the international level, beginning with the "International Workers' Aid" founded in 1921 to collect funds for emergency food shipments to the famine-stricken USSR.[24]

Tactics Neither Left nor Right   The definitive designation of particular tactics or sets of tactics as offensive or defensive, Left or Right, is dangerous and misleading. As the communist movement has grown in age and size, its leaders, particularly the Soviets, have shown great flexibility and ingenuity in choosing tactics. Though the tendency always existed, communists increasingly combine traditionally defensive and offensive tactics in the same period. During a shift to the Right in the early 1950's, communists in Western Europe used the united front from below—a basically Left wing maneuver—instead of the Right wing united front from above.[25] Communists may have sensed a reluctance on the part of European socialist leaders to repeat the "popular front" of the 1930's. Communists also may have wanted to avoid the ideological difficulties of the united front from above. Furthermore, communist policy for the advanced capitalist countries now envisages united fronts from above carrying a nation all the way to socialism. The traditional *defensive* united front thus becomes an *offensive* tactic. A third factor complicating the categorization of particular sets of tactics has existed since the early days of the USSR: the pursuit, for example, of Right tactics by the USSR, and Left tactics by communist parties in other countries.

Opportunists or Idealists   A survey of communist tactics suggests that party leaders are essentially Machiavellian opportunists *par excellence,* interested only in achieving absolute power. Communists appear willing to use *any tactic* if it promises success, and they seem totally indifferent to common standards of Western morality.

But this conclusion is based on a misunderstanding of the relation of strategy to tactics and of the communist view of morality. Lenin reminds his followers that the ability to make all the necessary practical compromises, to maneuver, to make agreements, zigzags, and retreats must be combined with the strictest loyalty to the ideas of communism. The final

---

[24] See Robert H. Bass, "Communist Fronts: Their History and Function," *Problems in Communism,* IX (1960), 8-16.

[25] Marshall D. Shulman, *Stalin's Foreign Policy Reappraised* (Cambridge, Mass.: Harvard University Press, 1963), pp. 120-22.

goals of the movement must not be forgotten even though one may have to make repugnant compromises with the enemy. And such compromises never signify surrender, only the need to circumvent impassable ravines. Communists were told in the 1920's that the defensive united front from above was "nothing other than a method of revolutionary agitation and organization." [26]

Communists also resent being branded immoral by Western standards. They insist that there is no abstract or universal code of morality. Marxism-Leninism proves that moral codes, like all other abstract facets of a culture, are part of the superstructure created by the economic base of the society. Any tactic is good which aids the dialectical movement of the society toward the ultimate end of all societies—communism. Any action is justified which aids the destruction of the old, exploiting society and the creation of the new, higher stage. Anything a communist does is by definition moral; the truly immoral are those who hinder "progress."

FURTHER READING

Anderson, Thornton, ed., *Masters of Russian Marxism*. New York: Appleton-Century-Crofts, 1963. Excerpts from writings of Plekhanov, Lenin, Martov, Trotsky, Kollontai, Bukharin, Stalin, and Khrushchev.

Berlin, Isaiah, *Karl Marx: His Life and Environment*. New York: Oxford University Press, 1959. Much material on the ideology in a classic biography.

Black, Cyril E. and Thomas P. Thornton, eds., *Communism and Revolution*. Princeton, N.J.: Princeton University Press, 1964. Contains three essays on communist revolutionary theory by Black, Thornton, and Andrew C. Janos.

Carew-Hunt, R. N., *The Theory and Practice of Communism*. New York: The Macmillan Company, 1957. 5th ed. One of the best commentaries.

Connor, James E., ed., *Lenin on Politics and Revolution: Selected Writings*. New York: Pegasus (Publishers), 1968. Representative collection of Lenin's writings over a thirty-year period on politics and revolution.

DeGeorge, Richard T., *The New Marxism: Soviet and East European Marxism since 1956*. New York: Pegasus (Publishers), 1968. Changes in Marxism-Leninism since 1956, and the divergencies among East European Marxists.

Deutscher, Isaac, ed., *The Age of Permanent Revolution: A Trotsky Anthology*. New York: Dell Publishing Co., Inc., 1964. Excellent collection by leading authority on Trotsky. Also see his classic 3-volume biography on Trotsky.

Deutscher, Isaac, *Stalin; a Political Biography*. New York: Oxford University

---

[26] Jane Degras, ed., *The Communist International*, II (London: Oxford University Press, 1960), published for the Royal Institute of International Affairs, 193.

Press, 1967, 2nd ed. The classic political biography. One third deals with aspects of Soviet foreign policy.

Drachkovitch, Milorad M., ed., *Marxist Ideology in the Contemporary World: Its Appeals and Paradoxes.* New York: Frederick A. Praeger, Inc., 1966. Seven essays by Western specialists on present impact of Marxian ideology and its future in the West, the Communist states, and the developing nations.

Freedman, Robert, ed., *Marx on Economics.* New York: Harcourt, Brace & World, Inc., 1961. Writings on economics carefully arranged to present a logical statement.

Gregor, A. James, *A Survey of Marxism: Problems in Philosophy and the Theory of History.* New York: Random House, Inc., 1965.

Gruliow, Leo, ed., *Current Soviet Policies,* I-V (IV with Charlotte Saikowski). New York: Frederick A. Praeger, Inc., 1953–. Records of various Congresses of Soviet Communist Party, beginning with the 19th. Valuable for party line at various stages.

Hook, Sidney, *Marx and the Marxists.* Princeton, N.J.: D. Van Nostrand Co., Inc., 1955. Short excerpts from Marx, Engels and Soviet leaders with summary of the ideology.

Khrushchev, Nikita S., *For Victory in Peaceful Competition with Capitalism.* New York: E. P. Dutton & Co., Inc., 1960. Good sample of Khrushchev's thought from his speeches and statements in 1958-1959.

Kulski, W. W., *Peaceful Co-Existence.* Chicago: Henry Regnery Co., 1959. Detailed, well-documented material on the ideology as it relates to foreign policy.

Kuusinen, O. V. *et al., Fundamentals of Marxism-Leninism.* Moscow: Foreign Languages Publishing House, 1963, 2nd. rev. ed. Essential for current Soviet interpretation of the creed.

Lenin, V. I., *Imperialism: The Highest Stage of Capitalism.* New York: International Publishers, 1939.

Lenin, V. I., *What is to be Done?* New York: International Publishers, 1943.

Marcuse, Herbert, *Soviet Marxism—A Critical Analysis.* New York: Columbia University Press, 1958. A provocative interpretation; attempts to analyze Soviet system on its own terms.

Mayo, Henry B., *Introduction to Marxist Theory.* New York: Oxford University Press, 1960. Lucid survey of Marxist theory.

McNeal, Robert H., *The Bolshevik Tradition: Lenin, Stalin, Khrushchev.* Englewood Cliffs, N.J.: Prentice-Hall, Inc., 1963. Essays on three Soviet leaders.

McNeal, Robert H., ed., *Lenin, Stalin, Khrushchev: Voices of Bolshevism.* Englewood Cliffs, N.J.: Prentice-Hall, Inc., 1963. Compact collection of important statements by major Soviet leaders noted in title. Companion volume to McNeal's *The Bolshevik Tradition.*

Meyer, Alfred G., *Leninism.* New York: Frederick A. Praeger, Inc., 1962. Analytical study of Lenin's thought.

Meyer, Alfred G., *Marxism.* Cambridge, Mass.: Harvard University Press, 1954. Marx's thought, with emphasis on Marxism as system of social analysis.

Morgan, George Allen ("Historicus"), "Stalin on Revolution," *Foreign Affairs,* XXVII, No. 2 (1949). Lengthy essay on Stalin's interpretation of Marxism-Leninism.

Schapiro, Leonard, ed., *The U.S.S.R. and the Future.* New York: Frederick A. Praeger, Inc., 1963. Essays on significance of 1961 Party Program, together with 1961 and 1919 Programs.

Selznick, Phillip, *The Organizational Weapon; a Study of Bolshevik Strategy and Tactics.* New York: McGraw-Hill Book Company, 1952. Comprehensive analysis of how a communist party is organized; its strategy and tactics.

Strausz-Hupé, Robert, and others, *Protracted Conflict.* New York: Harper & Row, Publishers, 1959. Argues for a communist plan for world-wide "conflict management."

Triska, Jan F., "A Model for Study of Soviet Foreign Policy," *American Political Science Review,* LII (1958). Attempts to integrate strategy and tactics into an overall model.

Triska, Jan F., ed., *Soviet Communism: Programs and Rules.* San Francisco, Calif.: Chandler Publishing Co., 1962. 1961 Party Program, together with 1919 Program and Party Rules of 1952 and 1961.

Ulam, Adam B., *The Unfinished Revolution.* New York: Random House, Inc., 1960. An argument for the special applicability of Marxism to the transition from pre-industrial to industrial society.

Wetter, Gustav A., *Dialectical Materialism: A Historical and Systematic Survey of Philosophy in the Soviet Union.* New York: Frederick A. Praeger, Inc., 1958. Detailed analysis of Soviet philosophy and its Marxist foundation.

Wetter, Gustav A., *Soviet Ideology Today.* New York: Frederick A. Praeger, Inc., 1966. Commentary by Western specialist on *Fundamentals of Marxist Philosophy* (Moscow, 1958). Main emphasis on Marxian philosophy with some treatment of current strategy and tactics.

3

THE IMPACT
OF
THE IDEOLOGY ON
SOVIET FOREIGN POLICY

As a prelude to the general analysis of the ideological impact, we must discuss the evidence for assuming Marxism-Leninism affects Soviet behavior in foreign affairs. This is one of the most heated topics in the whole field of Soviet foreign policy. Consequently, it is only fair to indicate the case for and against such an assumption.

The general analysis begins in the second section with the specific contributions of Marxism-Leninism to Soviet foreign policy. In particular, the ideology gives the Soviet leaders certain long-range goals for the USSR, a system of knowledge with which to view the world, a method of analysis, and strategy and tactics. The third section describes how the Soviets phase tactics to match the supposed ebb and flow of world revolution.

The ideological contributions produce certain attitudes in the Soviet elite toward international politics, analyzed in the fourth section. Marxism-Leninism imbues them with certainty of success, a sense of righteousness, patience, and expansionist tendencies.

In the last section of this chapter, the advantages and disadvantages of the ideology's impact on the formulation of Soviet foreign policy are assessed. The tendency is to assume Marxism-Leninism only muddies Soviet thinking. This isn't necessarily so. The ideology in some respects adds rationality to Soviet calculations. More important, it requires Soviet leaders to plan ahead—giving Soviet foreign policy a dynamism often lacking in foreign policies of non-communist states.

THE EVIDENCE
FOR THE IMPACT OF THE IDEOLOGY
ON SOVIET BEHAVIOR

We must begin the argument with a warning. It is impossible to give definitive proof of the ideology's impact on the actions of the Soviet leadership. Nevertheless, we will examine five kinds of evidence which stress the impact of the ideology on Soviet behavior in general.

An Analogy A fairly provocative analogy is offered first. Some people claim that the idealistic, abstract goals of communism have little or no influence on Soviet political behavior. The ideology is considered a cynical sham disguising the leadership's crude drive for power. Ironically, this parallels the communist assertion that ideals have a negligible impact on Western statesmen. According to Marxist-Leninist theory, Western foreign policy is basically determined by the Western economic system—"imperialism." The Western democratic ideology merely defends and disguises the economic interests of the ruling capitalist class. We *know* the communists are wrong in their analysis. But, can we prove their error by demonstrating Western statesmen are guided by democratic principles for other than economic reasons? Obviously we can't. Nevertheless, we give our leaders the benefit of the doubt. It might be safer to assume communists also are guided by their professed goals.

The Spoken and Written Word. The second argument, a little more persuasive, offers the spoken or written word of the communist hierarchy as proof of the ideological impact. Western observers marshal statements from top-ranking party leaders, beginning in 1917 or earlier and ending "yesterday," to demonstrate the remarkable consistency of the movement's long-range goals. Analysts imply that such consistency denotes belief on the part of the Soviet high command.[1]

Another, similar technique demonstrates the use of the ideology to explain and justify all actions and policies of the leadership. People point to the Sino-Soviet conflict and the Marxist-Leninist terminology surrounding it. In both above cases, of course, it can be argued that the party

[1] For an extreme example see Anthony T. Bouscaren, *Soviet Foreign Policy, A Pattern of Persistence* (New York: Fordham University Press, 1962).

leaders merely are carrying out a gigantic hoax made necessary by their desire to stay in power.

Political Behavior   Perhaps a more convincing argument is based on what we believe to be true of political behavior in any society. All politicians seem at least partially to be motivated by the desire to wield influence—often termed the "desire for power." But intertwined with the desire for power is a commitment to the proclaimed goals of the society, particularly in societies with highly developed ideologies. This commitment is brought about by pressures in the system, especially the totalitarian system. Even if we could find a communist driven only by a consuming ambition to rule his comrades, such a man must publicly accept the ideology. His continuance in power requires ideological justification. Moreover, the system itself requires him to play "philosopher-king." The practical difference in elite circles between the Marxian idealist and the "power politician" therefore is not very great.[2]

The Indoctrination Process   The fourth piece of evidence is based on the indoctrination process in the Soviet totalitarian system. This process promotes inward acceptance of the ideological goals, as well as mandatory lip-service. Any young "Ivan" aspiring to political leadership or any position of prominence in the Soviet Union cannot escape indoctrination in Marxism-Leninism. He must progress, beginning at a very early age, through the Little Octobrists, Pioneers, and Komsomol (Young Communist League) to Party membership. Ivan's "education" in the ideology naturally increases in intensity as he assumes higher positions. When he achieves Party membership, Ivan is required by the Soviet Communist Party Rules (1961) to "master Marxist-Leninist theory, raise his ideological level, and contribute to the molding and rearing of the man of Communist society." To aid in this task, Ivan proceeds through an elaborate, progressively more difficult series of Party training courses —taking much of his leisure time. In addition he must be ready for remote assignments in the hinterlands if the Party directs. All of these requirements probably make Party membership at this point more of a burden than a privilege. But Ivan must carry out his onerous duties diligently, and preferably, with a smile.

Some would argue that Ivan's inner drive, be it an urge for power or another motivation, remains pure in spite of intensive indoctrination.[3]

---

[2] Robert Conquest ably discusses this aspect of the Soviet political system in *Power and Policy in the U.S.S.R.* (London: Macmillan & Co., Ltd., 1961), p. 20.

[3] Frederick C. Barghoorn in "U.S.S.R. Revisited," *Russian Review* XVIII, No. 2 (1959), stated that a brilliant foreign diplomat told him all Soviet people appeared to be schizophrenics, equipped with "a more or less impervious shell of official stereotypes and slogans, but underneath . . . a human being."

This is questionable. Such an argument implies that Ivan, and his millions of fellow Party members, every day manage a magnificent deception of ideological sincerity with the skill of consummate actors. It seems far more reasonable to assume most communists do believe in the basic principles of their doctrine.

But what about the very top leaders of the Party? Do they still believe in Marxism-Leninism? Probably they do. They were chosen primarily for their diligence in Party activity, efficiency, and loyalty. Moreover, members of the leadership have spent their whole lives in an atmosphere permeated by the ideology. It is doubtful whether they can suddenly divest themselves of its influence. Bertram Wolfe suggests the ideology for Khrushchev was "the source of his emotions, his sense of the meaning of life, his insight into it, his vision of himself, his power and worth." In Khrushchev's mind, only the ideology justified his continuing rule over the Soviet people.[4]

But if Soviet leaders believe in the ideology, they do not always agree on its application to everyday problems. The ideology is vague and permissive on many issues. "Creative Marxism" has been necessary from the beginning. And the process of developing specific policies from broad ideological guidelines has permitted, indeed required, debates among the party leaders.

Behavior Based on Ideology   The last and best evidence illustrating the impact of the ideology on Soviet behavior in international politics comes from the objective fact of certain Soviet actions in foreign affairs. Throughout Soviet history, for example, the Soviet leaders have carried on generally unsuccessful attempts to subvert almost every nation in the free world. The very first act of the Bolshevik Government, the Peace Decree of November 1917, was a scarcely concealed call for world revolution. To list other well known revolutionary activity: the revolts in Europe in 1918 and 1919; the later attempts at revolution in Germany; the fiasco in China in 1927; again, the call for world revolution in 1928; the very serious crises in France and Italy after World War II created by local communists overt and covert activity; attempted communist revolutions in Indonesia, Malaya, Burma, and the Philippines in the late

[4] "Communist Ideology and Soviet Foreign Policy," *Foreign Affairs*, XLI, No. 1 (1962), 168. The Old Bolsheviks were not exposed to such intense, party-controlled indoctrination. However, the ideological sincerity of that generation of Soviet leaders is not difficult to document. These men endured Tsarist prisons and exile for their beliefs. Revolutionary zeal hardly could have been faked. Paul Axelrod, a Menshevik, freely admitted about his opponent, Lenin: there was not "another man who for twenty-four hours of the day is taken up with the revolution, who has no other thoughts but thoughts of revolution, and who, even in his sleep dreams of nothing but revolution." Quoted in Bertram D. Wolfe, *Three Who Made A Revolution* (New York: The Dial Press, Inc., 1948), p. 249.

1940's; support of Guatemalan leftists in 1954; and meddling by the Soviet ambassador in Guinean politics in 1961.[5]

A warning must now be given. The above evidence does not prove that the Soviet commitment to support revolution is unqualified. The historical chapters of this book will show that Soviet leaders allocate second priority to the promotion of foreign revolution. (The only exceptions came during the first several years of the USSR when revolutionary fervor was at its height. But even then Lenin prevailed over the dreamers.) The Soviet commitment to aid other communist parties rarely constitutes a blank check if Russian security may be compromised.

The Soviet commitment also seems to have changed in intensity and kind. The USSR still aids foreign revolutionaries, but Soviet representatives do not seem to indulge in as much blatant subversion. Perhaps more than in earlier periods, the USSR often downplays aid to local revolutionary groups in the developing countries in order to establish closer relations with the bourgeois-nationalist governments of such countries.

In the future, Soviet leaders may rationalize away the commitment to support *any* communist-led revolution abroad. This trend could be already evident. The main Soviet contribution to building international communism, according to Party theoretician Suslov in February, 1964, will be the example of Soviet economic progress. Max Frankel suggests: "The dreams of worldwide revolution . . . for Communism can possess the heart without forcing the hand."[6]

Meanwhile, Soviet promotion of revolution is often harmful if the only concern of the leadership is to promote Russian national security. Where such activity fails, as it did in most of the cases cited above, Soviet influence generally decreases. As a result, the national security of the USSR suffers. (Soviet security would be better served, one could argue, if Soviet leaders improved relations with other states through traditional diplomacy.)

We can now examine the general nature of the ideology's impact on Soviet behavior in international politics. The specific foreign policy style of each Soviet leader naturally varies. Soviet decision makers are individuals, not automatons. One only need look at the contrast between the reticent Stalin and ebullient Khrushchev. The general patterns of thought

[5] It can be argued that the Soviets are involved in the underdeveloped area today because the United States is also, and the Soviets thus fear the impact on their national security if America should succeed in that area. On the other hand, the Soviets did not show a major interest in the underdeveloped countries until after Stalin's death. And Soviet activity in Asia, Africa and Latin America then became an integral part of Khrushchev's offensive use of the peaceful coexistence theme— not just a defensive reaction against Western policy. See Chap. 10 for details.

[6] "Can We End the Cold War?" *New York Times Magazine*, January 29, 1967.

and action which will be described nevertheless seem to be characteristic of all Soviet leaders.

THE NATURE OF
THE IDEOLOGICAL IMPACT

The Soviet commitment to promote world communism may be only one third of the trilogy of primary motivations discussed in Chap. 1. But the other two primary motivations—the preservation of the leading role of the party elite and the furthering of the Soviet national interest—are expressed in revolutionary terms and rationalized by the ideology. Soviet leaders today, of course, try to be good "bourgeois" diplomats when the occasion demands, arguing for "legitimate" Soviet national interests or world peace. But they cannot always escape their revolutionary conditioning. Khrushchev's outburst at a Kremlin reception on November 26, 1956, hardly contributed to the theme of peaceful coexistence: "Whether you like it or not, history is on our side. We will bury you!" [7]

This ideology, in effect, permeates all Soviet activity in international politics. It is an integral part of the mental environment in which Soviet decision makers think and work. To be specific, the ideology gives the Soviet leaders: (1) certain long-range goals for Soviet foreign policy; (2) a system of knowledge with which to view the world; (3) a method of analysis; and (4) strategy and tactics.

The Long Range Goals The vision of the utopian "never-never land" of Marx and Engels still exists. Lenin, Stalin, Khrushchev, and the present regime may have discarded or radically altered the Marxian road to utopia where circumstances have required (often belatedly, and against opposition). But the essence of the Marxian dream remains. Khrushchev boasted in 1957 during an interview with a Japanese news correspondent: "We are convinced that sooner or later capitalism will perish, just as feudalism perished earlier. The socialist nations are advancing towards Communism. All the world will come to Communism. History does not ask whether you want it or not."

The communist belief may appear child-like, naïve and ridiculous. The continuing force of the vision, however, does not depend on its rationality. Certain fundamental elements of any philosophical system, in-

---

[7] Khrushchev clarified his comment to Los Angeles civic authorities during his tour of the United States in 1959: "The words 'We will bury capitalism' should not be taken literally as indicating what is done by ordinary gravediggers who carry a spade and dig graves and bury the dead. What I had in mind was the outlook for the development of human society. Socialism will inevitably succeed capitalism."

cluding the so-called science of Marxism-Leninism, must be taken on faith. And for communists, faith continues to exist. Milovan Djilas, a leading member of the Yugoslavian Communist Party until his imprisonment, knew Stalin and his cohorts well. Djilas writes:

> Every revolution, and even every war, creates illusions and is conducted in the name of unrealizable ideals. During the struggle the ideals seem real enough for the combatants; by the end they often cease to exist. Not so in the case of Communist revolution. Those who carry out the Communist revolution as well as those among the lower echelons persist in their illusions long after the armed struggle. Despite oppression, despotism, unconcealed confiscations, and privileges of the ruling echelons, some of the people—and especially the Communists—retain the illusions contained in their slogans.[8]

Djilas is noting the increasing gap between reality and ideals in the internal development of communist societies. But there also are problems for Marxist-Leninist theory in external developments. How can communists explain the robust health of modern capitalism? Impoverished workers and exploited peasants obviously are not driving the millions of automobiles clogging American highways.

History has disproved much of Marxian theory. But what appears faulty logic in Marxism-Leninism to Western observers does not seem to bother most communists. They find, for instance, "new" contradictions in capitalism—or they simply ignore embarrassing developments.

In any case, the long-range theoretical predictions and the utopian goals of the ideology generally do not distort daily decisions in Soviet foreign policy.[9] Soviet leaders no longer expect an immediate "socialist" millennium. They do not retire every evening hoping for signs of world revolution when they awake. But they believe world communism will be achieved *someday*. And this faith performs three important functions for Soviet leaders: (1) It justifies their continuance in power, both to themselves and theoretically to the populace. (2) It is the foundation on which they rationalize all of their actions. (3) It sets the general *direction* of Soviet policy, both foreign and domestic. These policies, assuming the leadership's avowed faith in communism is sincere, must reflect an attempt to move toward internal and international communism. Foreign observers, and even other communists, may argue that *particular* policies are destructive of these long-range goals. But it is important only that Soviet leaders believe they are advancing the cause. The final goals also may be vague, yet this does not mean they are non-existent. Few Americans, for example, would question the United States' commitment to

---

8 *The New Class* (New York: Frederick A. Praeger, Inc., 1957), p. 30.
9 Jan F. Triska and David D. Finley have used content analysis to demonstrate this proposition in *Soviet Foreign Policy* (New York: The Macmillan Co., 1968), Chap. IV.

promote "freedom" in the world. On the other hand, it is likely that few Americans could agree on exactly what this concept means.

A System of Knowledge   The system of knowledge that the ideology gives Soviet leadership probably has a more important impact on Soviet foreign policy, particularly on day-to-day decisions, than the long-range goals of the ideology. This system determines the leadership's view of the world. It provides the prism through which they view current happenings. The peculiar *tone* or *style* of Soviet foreign policy follows from this world view.

Several aspects of their outlook particularly affect Soviet behavior in world politics. First, the Soviets believe each nation, as well as the international society, is wracked with conflict. The only exceptions are future communist societies in the socialist stage of development, and the USSR, now in the process of building communism. No antagonistic classes exist in such societies; therefore, conflict does not exist—except that caused by individuals with lingering "bourgeois" tendencies. Second, conflict and *change* are the natural order of things. The *status quo* indeed *is* change. In Marxist-Leninist terminology, the material world is constantly being altered through the clash of contradictions. There is no innate tendency toward harmony of classes or interests in either domestic or international societies.[10] Third, national and international conflict finally will be resolved through struggle, not compromise. The communists, since they are on the side of the progressive forces, will win this struggle. On the nation-state level, particularly in the relations between the socialist and capitalist states, armed struggle may be ruled out. The strength of the peaceful socialist states restricts warlike moves by the imperialists, and the existence of nuclear weapons makes total war useless. But such periods of formal international calm do not stop change. The conflict merely is transferred to a different plane. At the present time, conflict develops on the ideological and economic levels, as well as through revolutions and wars of "national liberation."

A Method of Analysis   The ideology provides the Soviet leaders with certain guidelines for analyzing problems in international politics. The science of Marxism-Leninism tells them how to evaluate any situation to get the "big picture," after which the correct strategy and tactics can be selected.

A communist might go through the following analytical process when examining a problem in foreign policy. (He probably would not con-

---

[10] See Arthur Schlesinger, Jr. *A Thousand Days* (Boston: Houghton Mifflin Company, 1965), pp. 358-74, for an excellent summary of Khrushchev's view on the *status quo*.

sciously recognize it as a process, would not necessarily ask the questions in the order given below, and would assume the more basic "facts.") First, the historical era must be defined. In our time, it is "the epoch of transition to the next formation, the communist formation, the first phase of which is called socialism." Imperialism, "parasitic or decaying capitalism," is on the way out. (Certain backward countries still may be in earlier economic stages such as feudalism.) Second, a communist analyzes the productive relations of the particular country or countries he is dealing with—specifically, who owns the means of production. This tells him who really controls policy-making in a given country. In an imperialist nation such as the United States the monopoly capitalists are in charge; thus, American foreign policy inevitably reflects their interests. Carrying through this analysis for all states reveals enemies, friends, and potential allies. The contradictions—the forces making for change through the dialectical process in each country and the world at large—subsequently become apparent. For example, the Soviets believe the conflict is obvious between the monopoly capitalists and the masses in an imperialist nation, and between the imperialist nations as a whole and the underdeveloped countries.

The above "facts" are fundamental generalizations. The crucial, daily questions facing Soviet decision makers center around current alterations in these basic relationships. Are the quantitative changes, evident in the operation of the dialectical process in a capitalist country, on the verge of becoming qualitative? Is *revolution* in the air? Is the tide within a country's strategic period ebbing or flowing? Are the class forces both within the particular country and the world at large in favor of the communists? These, of course, are the really sticky questions to which Marxism-Leninism provides no clear answer. But the important point to remember is that the ideology conditions Soviet decision makers to ask such questions. Debates on foreign policy, in turn, arise from differing answers to them.

Strategy and Tactics   Once the situation is analyzed, Soviet policy makers select the appropriate strategy and tactics. A change in the general strategy for a particular country is not necessary unless a qualitative revolutionary change is imminent; the usual decision thus involves a choice of tactics.

Tactics come from the vast "storehouse of Marxism-Leninism." New variations, of course, are constantly appearing because the world of the present regime is considerably different from the regime in Lenin's time. Such changes on occasion may be attacked as non-Marxist—their initiator, as a deviationist or revisionist. But in each case, the initiator defends his new tactic as being in the basic spirit of the doctrine. The "storehouse" permits the policy maker great latitude. Any ally, for example, can be used if he aids the advance of communism, regardless of whether he is "temporary, vacillating, unstable, unreliable, and conditional."

THE PROPER PHASING
OF SOVIET FOREIGN POLICY

One particular problem surrounds the selection of the proper tactics for Soviet foreign policy. This is the necessity of keeping Soviet foreign policy in tune with the "ebb" and "flow" of the general revolutionary current. Because of the importance of this requirement for the Soviets, we will discuss the question of "phasing" in some detail.

Soviet leaders soberly calculate current historical trends and the world balance of forces to find (1) whether favorable possibilities exist for the extension of communism, or (2) whether the capitalist world temporarily has stabilized the contradictions making for its inevitable downfall and is mounting its own offensive against the progressive forces of communism. (Soviet calculations are modified by pressing domestic problems, and by often unacknowledged factional disputes among party leaders.)

The conscious attempt of the Soviets to phase their foreign policy to fit current conditions has been noted by many observers. In particular, some authorities have described a marked alternation between two modes of behavior. One mode is essentially offensive, involving hard-line militant policies when conditions are held favorable for the promotion of communism. The other mode is essentially defensive, representing temporary retreat in the face of a superior force.[11] During such a period the revolutionary nature of the ideology is de-emphasized.

Offensive tactics generally have been called "Left," and defensive tactics, "Right." But, as suggested in Chap. 2, communists increasingly combine Left and Right tactics in the same period. (The Soviets affirm such a venerable right wing tactic as peaceful coexistence now as offensive in character.) The designation of a particular Soviet mode of behavior as essentially offensive or defensive is therefore more useful than the traditional designations Left or Right.[12]

[11] For a good summary of Soviet phasing, see Marshall D. Shulman, "Some Implications of Changes in Soviet Policy Toward the West," *Slavic Review*, XX, No. 4 (1961), 630-40. Also see his book, *Stalin's Foreign Policy Reappraised* (Cambridge, Mass.: Harvard University Press, 1963), Chap. 1.

[12] Some type of alternation probably would occur in the foreign policy of any "Russian" government. Any national leader—as the Introduction suggests—is to a great degree the prisoner of his environment. A Russian "democratic" government in the 1930's certainly would have become defensive-minded in view of the Nazi menace. However, the leaders of a Russian democratic government would not have shown the same sensitivity to phasing their foreign policy as the Soviet leaders. Furthermore, their style of action would have differed considerably.

Problems in Defining Periods in Soviet Foreign Policy

Soviet leaders generally run into trouble as soon as they attempt to determine the proper moment to switch from the defensive to the offensive, and vice versa. Indeed, some of the most bitter debates among the leadership have turned on this question. One fascinating revelation of the great difficulty of dividing Soviet policy into offensive and defensive periods appeared in the pages of the Moscow journal *International Affairs* during 1958.[13] Sophisticated Soviet political analysts bared their souls in a debate on classifying various turns in their country's foreign policy. We will examine the difficulties they found, and some additional problems Western analysts face in determining the Soviet line during a given period.

One primary difficulty facing the Soviet analysts was the nature of the basic determinant of periodic changes in Soviet foreign policy. V. Khvostov, a special member of the journal's editorial board, in summing up the debate, attempted to resolve the question. As a Marxist-Leninist he had to maintain that the foreign policy of a country "depends largely on the developments and requirements in its economy, the progress of the class struggle and other domestic factors. All major domestic changes—changes in the social system, revolutions, far-reaching economic and social changes and other historic milestones opening new epochs in a people's history—give rise, as a rule, to changes in foreign policy." The October Socialist Revolution, for example, put an end to Tsarist imperialism and produced an entirely new foreign policy. The impact of external, international developments on Soviet foreign policy, Khvostov warned, nevertheless could not be ignored: "There is always the possibility that external events in other countries precipitate radical changes in the international situation and thus lead to far-reaching changes in the foreign policy of a given state which has not, at the time, experienced any significant domestic changes." But such changes are distinct from the sharp turn brought about by the October Revolution, said Khvostov, and alter nothing in the substance of Soviet foreign policy.

The *number* of sharp turns or strategic stages also was debated. Everyone agreed that the October Revolution brought a decisive change in Russian foreign policy. (This began the third strategic stage in Stalin's revolutionary scheme described in Chap. 2.) But there was considerable dissension when a Soviet analyst claimed the foreign policy of the USSR began a new strategic stage in 1945 with the establishment of a world socialist system. One observer argued the basic principles of Soviet foreign policy remain immutable, quoting Khrushchev's assertion at the Twentieth Party Congress in 1956 that the "Leninist principle of peaceful

[13] See *International Affairs* (Moscow), Nos. 2, 5, 7, 8, 1958.

coexistence of states with different social systems has always been and remains the general line of our country's foreign policy." In his summation, Khvostov took a compromise position, arguing that it was absolutely essential to relate strategic stages in foreign policy to fundamental changes in the *internal* social structure—the completion, for example, of the building of a socialist society. But he concluded: ". . . this discussion has not as yet yielded any conclusive and incontestable criteria for such a division into 'basic strategic stages,' nor has it proved that such a division is expedient." (Three years after this debate, the 1961 Program of the Soviet Communist Party indicated that the Soviet Union was entering a fourth strategic stage—the building of communism.)

The problems in periodization discussed above mainly bother Marxist-Leninists, and seem to be largely academic questions even for them. But another problem brought up in the debate also exists for Western analysts. One Soviet expert stated: "It is hazardous on the strength of some group of specific facts and indices, to break off, at a certain year or month the consistent general foreign policy line of the Communist Party and the Soviet Government." The Soviet author may have had in mind the extended intra-party debate (except during Stalin's later years) and policy experimentation which often precede the dramatic, formal pronouncement of a new foreign policy line. Months of veiled hints to the West and cautious overtures to Hitler, for example, preceded the signing of the Nazi-Soviet Non-Aggression Pact in 1939. Bitter debates on the other hand presaged such vital turning points as the signing of the Treaty of Brest-Litovsk in 1918, and, after Stalin's death, the drastically revised relations with the newly independent underdeveloped countries and other communist states and foreign communist parties.

There is a third set of problems, which Soviet experts either vaguely acknowledge or ignore, in dividing Soviet foreign policy into periods. Offensive turns in Soviet foreign policy do not necessarily correspond with similar turns in Soviet *domestic* policy or the policies of other communist states or parties.[14] Soviet foreign policy during 1933–39 essentially was defensive, but a militant hard-line approach was evident internally during the great purges. The difference today between the prevailing mode of Soviet foreign policy and the foreign policies of other communist parties and states is also obvious. The Soviets accuse the Chinese, for example, of being overly militant and adventurous. But even when the Soviets had relatively complete control of the international communist movement, policies of the foreign communist parties and the USSR were not always kept in agreement. The Sixth Congress of the Comintern in

---

[14] Robert Conquest describes Right and Left policies in Soviet domestic politics. *Power and Policy in the U.S.S.R.* (London: Macmillan & Co. Ltd., 1961), pp. 26-27.

1928 adopted an ultra Left line, but the Soviet government continued its basically defensive posture. During this period, of course, the same men were running the USSR and the world communist movement. The Soviets apparently hoped for new revolutions, but realized the USSR was too weak to aid foreign communist parties.

A fourth problem, primarily plaguing Western analysts, is the existence of both offensive and defensive modes of behavior in one period. Sometimes this represents a geographical difference in tactics. After 1953, for instance, and to some extent as early as 1950, the Soviets went on the defensive in Europe, attempting to preserve their post-war gains. The offensive mode prevailed nevertheless in their machinations to further the disintegration of the colonial system of imperialism, particularly after Stalin's death.

A final problem, again primarily for Western analysts, stems from the fundamental distrust and fear the Soviets have of the West. If one looks at a Soviet analysis of the foreign policy of the USSR, the dominant theme in every period until the late 1950's is *defensive*. There is no talk of militant, Left, Soviet foreign policies. The Soviets are struggling either for peace among the peoples, for collective security, for peaceful coexistence, or against the imperialist "negotiations from strength" policy. And they may believe this. Marshall Shulman suggests the "baldly expansionist" tactics pursued by the Soviets during 1946–1949 may have been defensive in the eyes of Stalin and his colleagues. Marxism-Leninism taught them the inevitability of conflict between capitalism and socialism, and the inherent hostility of Western capitalism to the socialist states.

The fundamental, defensive orientation of the Soviets may now have changed with Soviet possession of a powerful nuclear deterrent. This and other factors have resulted in the Soviet claim of a fundamental shift of the world balance of forces in favor of the socialist states, bringing for the first time the possibility of continued coexistence. However, even if we grant the Soviets were basically defensive-minded until recent years, it is still possible to broadly delineate periods when they thought *offensive* action was called for by the international situation.

A Soviet View of the Periods of Soviet Foreign Policy

Having shown the treacherous pitfalls in periodization both Soviet and Western analysts face, it is instructive to examine a Soviet attempt (Fig. 1). This scheme was one of several proposed during the debate in *International Affairs* in 1958, and was used for a course titled "Soviet Foreign Policy and the Current International Situation" at the Party Institute of Advanced Studies in Moscow during 1957. Its author, incidentally, stated that the scheme was not "perfect." (The commentary is taken verbatim;

Figure 1. Program for a course in "Soviet Foreign Policy and the Current International Situation" *

Part One

Soviet foreign policy and international relations in the period of the developing general crisis of capitalism and the victory of Socialism in the U.S.S.R. (after the triumph of the October Socialist Revolution up to the eve of the Second World War).

Nov. 1917-Nov. 1918   a) The international situation in the period of the triumph of the October Revolution in Russia. The struggle of the Soviet State for peace among the peoples.

1918-1920   b) Soviet Russia's foreign policy in the period of the armed intervention and Civil War.

1921-1924   c) The struggle of the Soviet state to establish economic and diplomatic relations with the capitalist countries. The inception of peaceful co-existence between the states of the two systems.

1925-1929   d) The struggle of the U.S.S.R. against the threat of war and new attempts to organize anti-Soviet intervention in the period of the partial stabilization of capitalism.

1929-1934   e) Foreign policy and international relations in the years of the world economic crisis. The emergence of two hotbeds of war. The struggle of the U.S.S.R. for a system of collective security.

Part Two

The foreign policy of the U.S.S.R. and international relations on the eve of and during the Second World War. The victory of the U.S.S.R. and the freedom-loving peoples over the fascist aggressors.

1935-1939   a) The foreign policy of the U.S.S.R. and international relations on the eve of the Second World War. The struggle of the U.S.S.R. for collective resistance to the fascist aggressors.

Sep. 1939-Jun. 1949   b) The beginning of the Second World War and the foreign policy of the U.S.S.R.

1941-1945   c) The foreign policy of the U.S.S.R. and international relations during the Great Patriotic War.

---

* The (Communist) Party Institute of Advanced Studies, Moscow, 1957. From *International Affairs* (Moscow) No. 7 (July), 1958.

Part Three

International relations after the Second World War, in the period of the transformation of Socialism into a world system and the further aggravation of the general crisis of capitalism.

1945-1949	a)	The radical changes in the international situation as a result of the Second World War. The struggle of the U.S.S.R. and the People's Democracies for a democratic organization of the post-war world, against the imperialist "negotiations from strength" policy.
1950-1953	b)	The aggravation of international tensions as a result of the aggressive actions of the imperialist states. The struggle of the U.S.S.R. and other peace-loving peoples against imperialist aggression and for the preservation and strengthening of peace.
1953-1957	c)	The struggle of the Socialist camp, led by the U.S.S.R., and the other peace-loving peoples for a *détente,* peaceful co-existence and the co-operation of states with different systems, for friendship among the peoples.

the dates for each period have been altered in position, and, in some cases, taken from footnotes.)

A Western View of the Periods of Soviet Foreign Policy My suggested scheme (Fig. 2) is also far from "perfect." It should be interpreted with the following qualifications previously analyzed in this section: (1) the dates separating periods are only approximate; (2) the designation "offensive" or "defensive" refers to the general thrust of Soviet foreign policy during the historical period. Formal Soviet foreign policy obviously may not coincide with this estimation; (3) both offensive and defensive tactics may appear in one period, but one mode seems to be emphasized. (The details of the shifts from one period to another and the particular tactics used in each period will be examined in the historical section of this book.)

THE ATTITUDES IMPARTED
BY THE IDEOLOGY

Because of the impact of the ideology on the whole decision-making process in foreign policy, Soviet leaders have certain peculiar attitudes toward international politics. Prominent among them are (1) certainty of success; (2) a sense of righteousness; (3) patience; and (4) expansionist tendencies.

Figure 2. A Western View of the Periods in Soviet Foreign Policy

Part One

A fear of the capitalist West underlies all Soviet moves. A powerful "capitalist" bloc is thought to be planning the destruction of "socialism."

Generally Offensive Generally Defensive

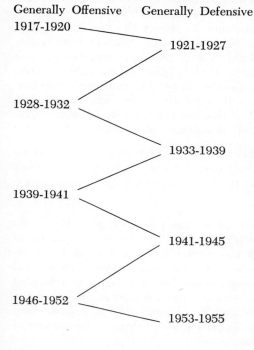

1917-1920	Hopes for world revolution.
1921-1927	Temporary retreat to preserve the Soviet state. "United fronts" for non-Soviet communist parties.
1928-1932	A revolutionary Comintern policy, which the Soviets nevertheless felt too weak to aid.
1933-1939	The beginning of Soviet fear of Germany. Attempts at collective security.
1939-1941	The Nazi-Soviet Non-Aggression Pact. Soviet territorial expansion.
1941-1945	Cooperation with the West to defeat Germany. But Soviet expansion, especially in Eastern Europe, continues.
1946-1952	The "Cold War" begins.
1953-1955	"Defensive" peaceful co-existence. Temporary retreats to correct Stalin's mistakes. (Marshall Shulman in *Stalin's Foreign Policy Reappraised* [1963] cogently argues this defensive swing began in 1950.)

Part Two

The Soviets become more confident of their strength. The balance of forces they begin to imply in 1956 now favor the socialist states. Capitalism nevertheless is still a threat.

1956-1962	"Offensive" peaceful co-existence. Soviets envision all forms of struggle, except nuclear war, between capitalist and socialist states.
1962–	The Soviets appear to have decided a temporary retreat was required in view of the superior American determination revealed during the Cuban missile crisis of 1962.

Certainty of Success   The Soviets feel sure of the eventual success of communism, and thus of their foreign policies. Bertram D. Wolfe vividly describes the origin of the optimism:

> What reason does a man looking with Khrushchev's eyes have for abandoning the view that "capitalist-imperialism" is decadent when it is losing all its colonies, did not show the resolution to protect Hungary's freedom or complete the unification of Korea, failed to make the military moves to prepare its sort of peace during World War II, thereby letting maimed and bleeding Russia pick up all of Eastern Europe, half of Germany, win powerful allies and partners in Asia, expand the "camp of Communism" from one-sixth of the earth to one-fourth, with one-third of the earth's population? We may offer our explanations of all this. None of them would seem to him to refute his simple explanation of "decadence" and "progress." [15]

There is no doubt or uncertainty for the Soviet communist leaders. They are on the side of the fundamental forces making for progress through the operation of the dialectic. Soviet foreign policy consequently must be successful:

> The decisive source of the strength or weakness of a foreign policy, of its historical prospects or lack of prospects, is the correlation of that policy and social progress: its conformity or non-conformity to the laws of social development, to the objective course of the historical process. The victory-bringing strength of Socialist foreign policy lies in it being an *advanced and progressive policy, correctly reflecting the urgent requirements of the development of society's material life, the objective laws of contemporary international development, and in its making use of them in the interests of society, for the good of the working people.*[16]

The "victory-bringing strength" of Soviet foreign policy naturally comes from the Soviet leadership's use of the science of Marxism-Leninism:

> The fact that Soviet foreign policy is based on science is the most important source of its strength and successes. Profound knowledge of the objective laws of international development and the scientific analysis of the world relation of forces enable the Communist Party of the Soviet Union and the Soviet Government to take the right course in the complicated international situation, to foresee the course of events, to discover in time and disrupt the perfidious designs of the warmongers, to determine and carry out whatever steps are necessary in foreign policy to defend with credit the interests of our country and of Socialism and to uphold peace throughout the world.[17]

---

[15] "Communist Ideology and Soviet Foreign Policy," p. 167.

[16] M. Airapetyan and G. Deborin, "Foreign Policy and Social Progress," *International Affairs* (Moscow), No. 2 (1959), p. 22. Italicized portion in Italics in the original.

[17] *Ibid.*, p. 26.

There may, of course, be temporary setbacks. In some cases, the USSR may suffer unforeseen defeat. Naturally the ideology is not at fault. Certain party members simply have failed to apply the precepts of Marxism-Leninism.

A Sense of Righteousness   He who advances communism is acting *morally*. He who opposes communism is acting *immorally*. The science of Marxism-Leninism—and no one can question science—proves beyond doubt that communism will triumph. What is scientifically proven is true. What is *true*, is *good*, and therefore, *moral*.

The certainty of always being right, of marching on the side of inevitable progress, was obvious in Khrushchev's apparent inability to comprehend Western shock at his 1956 outburst: "Whether you like it or not, history is on our side. We will bury you!" For Khrushchev, this was a self-evident truth. It was difficult to understand why anyone should get excited about the inevitable.

Communist self-righteousness also is reflected, Bertram Wolfe argues, in "the unresponsiveness to argument, the stubbornness and repetitiveness of Communist negotiators, the lack of communication in dialogues which are only 'ostensible' dialogues. How can there be genuine dialogue without some consensus? How can there be give-and-take between that which is self-evidently and totally right, and that which is self-evidently wrong, both scientifically and morally?" [18]

Patience   Certainty of success tends to breed patience in a communist. For him the world is marching inexorably toward communism. His own actions can be extremely important in aiding or retarding this progress, but they are not critical. True, the inevitable may seem further and further in the future for some communists. But this is no reason for Soviet leaders to undertake risky international ventures in the name of communism. No specific timetable must be met. Neither Marx, Lenin, Stalin, Khrushchev, nor the present leaders have predicted when the world will be communized. In the meantime, the Soviets are actually poor practitioners of Marxism-Leninism if they consciously jeopardize the existence of that great power base for the extension of communism—the Soviet Union. (Khrushchev's successors obviously thought he was a poor practitioner. They criticized him for "hare-brained scheming," as well as "immature conclusions and hasty decisions and actions divorced from reality, boasting, and empty phrase mongering." One example given was his precipitation of the Cuban Missile Crisis in 1962, the most serious threat to Soviet security since World War II.)

[18] Bertram Wolfe, "Communist Ideology and Soviet Foreign Policy," p. 161.

On the other hand, patience does not mean inaction. If the Soviets must avoid total war, they also must avoid total peace. When the balance of forces is in their favor, they must act. Conflict and change until the millennium are the natural order of things. But *men* actually bring about conflict and change: ". . . historical laws themselves, without people, do not make history. They determine the course of history only through the actions, the struggle and the consciously directed efforts of millions of people." [19]

Expansionist Tendencies   The world's inevitable march toward communism, and the requirement for communists to aid this movement, make Soviet foreign policy inherently "internationalist," or, as it appears to the West, expansionist. Soviet internationalism comes from the continuing assertion that the common interests of similar economic *classes* in different states are much more fundamental and binding than those interests shared by different classes in the same nation-state: "Whoever has mastered the Marxist doctrine and understands the historic mission of the proletariat that Marx discovered is bound to be an internationalist, to strive consciously for the unity and cooperation of the working people of all nations, and to place the common interests of the international working class above partial, local, and narrow national interests." [20] The clarion call of the *Communist Manifesto* of 1848 remains: "Working men of all countries, unite!"

The Soviets have a moral *right* and a *duty* to aid the unification of the world proletariat, for their interests and those of the world's oppressed are one. This obligation inevitably became a vital cornerstone of Soviet foreign policy. Workers of the world, however, found a reciprocal obligation to defend the Soviet Union—even if this meant sacrificing their own hopes of revolution. And while Stalin was alive, this obligation was much more pressing than the Soviet duty to spread communism in other countries.

With the founding of other "socialist" states after World War II, some communists seriously questioned the asserted identity of Soviet foreign policy and the interests of the world proletariat. [21] The Soviets had the duty to support the peoples of the communist bloc. (The "rich" USSR certainly was able to aid the development of fraternal states.) Instead, the Soviets lavished economic aid on India, a capitalist country, and cut off help to Communist China.

Soviet internationalism, as argued earlier, must take second priority to the promotion of the Russian national interest. The Soviet duty to

[19] *Fundamentals of Marxism-Leninism* (2nd ed., 1963), p. 135.
[20] *Ibid.*, p. 305.
[21] See the Yugoslavian charges against the Soviet Union, p. 253.

promote the cause of the world proletariat nevertheless still has sufficient residue to accelerate unrest in many nations.

ADVANTAGES AND DISADVANTAGES OF THE IDEOLOGY IN THE FORMULATION OF SOVIET FOREIGN POLICY

An examination of the impact of Marxism-Leninism on Soviet foreign policy, particularly the impact of its unproven assertions, half-truths, and simple explanations of complex phenomena, easily can lead to the conclusion that the ideology only distorts and harms Soviet foreign policy calculations. This is not necessarily the case. An ideology's impact on foreign policy formulation depends on the nature of the ideology. The ideology can add rationality to the decision-making process as Marxism-Leninism does in some respects, or makes rational action extremely difficult as the Nazi creed did especially in its later stages. Beneficial contributions of Marxism-Leninism to the formulation of Soviet foreign policy will be discussed first, after which the more familiar disadvantages will be listed.

Advantages First, the ideology gives the Soviets a fairly sophisticated appreciation of certain aspects of international affairs. The Soviet leaders look behind the formal structure of the nation-state to examine the internal processes in each society. They naturally place far too much weight on economic factors in their analysis. But they at least realize internal economic problems in each society can cause conflict in international politics. And although they analyze each society according to its economic class relationships, the Soviets are on the right track in visualizing nation-state as the vehicle for the expression of various interests within each society. They do not consider the state an entity separate from or above internal politics, possessing a life of its own, and a single guiding force called the "national interest." The Soviets believe international politics consists of much more than formal, diplomatic contacts between nation-states. This relatively sophisticated view of contemporary international politics was rarely equalled by Western policy makers until recent years.

A second advantage derives from the Soviet view of conflict in international politics as endemic, not artificial or temporary. True, conflict among socialist states is downplayed in their analyses, and cooperation among capitalist states held to be superficial. But the emphasis on conflict as an inevitable part of the nation-state system gave the Soviets for many years a somewhat more realistic conceptualization of the world than was held by some Western statesmen. Under the influence of liberalism, certain Western policy makers viewed world harmony, not "irrational" war, as the natural destiny of man. The Soviet concept of world politics was nearer reality.

Third, the Soviets plan for change because they expect change. Most important, Soviets believe change is the *natural* order of things. Western planners in the field of foreign policy, if planning has been done at all, generally have ignored the contributions theory can make in the planning process. They have placed great pride in their "pragmatic" approach to international politics. Theoretical attempts to explain what is happening in the world often have been frowned upon. This approach may have been sufficient when the Western powers were unchallenged in the driver's seat, and non-Western societies were relatively static and quiet. But with powerful forces now making for change, especially in the underdeveloped countries, those states first recognizing and attempting to direct such phenomena obviously have an advantage.

There is a fourth advantage derived from the ideology. Belief in the inevitability of change and the need to insure change *in the correct direction* require the Soviets to develop and continually experiment with various strategies and tactics. (Lenin insisted political ploys be highly realistic and in tune with the balance of class forces.) In particular, day-to-day variations in the ebb and flow of the revolutionary tide must be observed, and the appropriate tactical device selected. A communist must also remember that each tactic, even if superficially a retreat, must not sacrifice the principles of the movement.

The conscious attempt to perfect political strategies and tactics, preoccupation with phasing these moves to suit the political climate, and the belief that each international incident should be treated in relation to long-range objectives, add rationality to Soviet foreign policy. The long-range goals themselves may be irrational and the world view distorted, but these aspects of the ideology, as argued previously in this chapter, do not seriously affect day-to-day decisions in foreign policy. In brief, the Soviet leadership continues to benefit from the leavening pragmatism of Lenin.

Fifth, the obvious need of the ideology for one authoritative interpreter, and the ideology's justification of totalitarianism, tend to centralize decision-making in one small group, and finally, in one man. This centralization makes possible speed and flexibility in the decision-making process. These desirable qualities in turn are reinforced by the requirement to react immediately to subtle changes in the ebb and flow of the revolutionary tide.

Disadvantages The ideology does not provide answers to all questions, particularly such questions as when and how to apply strategy and tactics. But because Marxism-Leninism is supposed to be a science, Lenin's guidelines for answering these questions should lead all men to the same answer. Obviously the guidelines do not do this. Unless the leader is in complete control, bitter arguments can arise over whether to use this or that tactic. And the burden of proof falls on those trying to change strategies or tactics to meet new conditions. Political gimmicks once found useful are hard to discard. This is true even for non-ideologically oriented politicians. But change is especially difficult where previously successful strategies and tactics have become *dogma*. Tried and proven formulas act as brakes on change. Lenin, for example, continually faced opposition in adjusting the ideology to reality. He made so many changes in his own version of Marxism that eventually he was charged with abandoning "Leninism."

There is a second disadvantage. The ideological necessity to visualize the broad sweep of history has been a major aid in planning. But if Marxian economic determinism has correctly identified certain basic historical trends, the ideology has blinded its adherents to other critical forces at work. Probably the most outrageous error has been the continual underestimation of the force of nationalism, both in the capitalist and in the socialist worlds. Another gross misconception, which has not completely died, is the belief in the revolutionary nature of the world proletariat.

Further disadvantages arise from the tendency of the communist system to elevate one leader, and the need for a single authoritative interpreter for the ideology. These characteristics of the Soviet political system place a great premium on the chosen leader's ideological acumen. The leader's skill in "creative Marxism" determines whether the ideology becomes irrelevant dogma or a helpful analytical guide in international politics. For example, Stalin began to lose touch with reality after World War II, particularly in his understanding of the underdeveloped areas. He asserted that the earlier prediction of Marxism-Leninism about the revolutionary nature of the "national bourgeoisie" was incorrect. Apparently obsessed with fears of a Western onslaught against the Soviet bloc after World War II, Stalin believed Gandhi, Nehru, Sukarno and others were "puppets" of Western imperialism. Because of his position as ideological oracle, Stalin's fears and beliefs became part of the ideology—and harmed Soviet foreign policy.

We have now concluded the first part of *An Introduction to Soviet Foreign Policy*. In Part One theoretical guidelines have been formulated for use in Part Two: a summary of Soviet foreign policy from 1917 to 1968. Attention in the "Short History" will be on specific Soviet tactics during each period of the foreign policy of the USSR. But the operation of the interlocking motivational trilogy—the maintenance of power by the elite, the preservation of the "national interest," and the habits of thought and action derived from Marxism-Leninism—will be described in each period.

FURTHER READING

Airapetyan, M. and G. Deborin, "Foreign Policy and Social Progress," and "The Guiding Force of Socialist Foreign Policy," found in *International Affairs* (Moscow), Nos. 2 and 11 (1959). Soviet view of the impact of Marxism-Leninism on Soviet foreign policy.

Almond, Gabriel, *The Appeals of Communism*. Princeton, N.J.: Princeton University Press, 1954. The psychological appeals, based on interviews with 221 former party members from U. S., Britain, Italy, and France.

Brzezinski, Zbigniew K., "Communist Ideology and International Affairs," found in his *Ideology and Power in Soviet Politics*. New York: Frederick A. Praeger, Inc., 1962. Analyzes unchanging doctrine and flexible ideology.

Chamberlin, William H., "Seven Phases of Soviet Foreign Policy," *The Russian Review*, XV, No. 2 (1956).

Crossman, Richard, ed., *The God That Failed*. New York: Harper & Row, Publishers, 1950. Classic autobiographical accounts of why six communists and "fellow travelers" left the movement.

Daniels, Robert V., *The Nature of Communism*. New York: Random House, Inc., 1962. Survey of all aspects of doctrine and its impact on Russia, the developing countries, etc.

Goodman, Elliot R., *The Soviet Design for a World State*. New York: Columbia University Press, 1960. Argues that Soviet doctrine envisages world state under Russian hegemony.

Katona, Paul, "Right and Left—A Brief Survey," *Problems of Communism*, X, No. 2 (1961). A brief essay on periodization.

Koestler, Arthur, *Darkness at Noon*. New York: New American Library of World Literature, Inc., 1948. Although fictional, one of the best studies of the mentality of the "Old Bolshevik."

Labedz, Leopold, "Ideology: The Fourth Stage," *Problems of Communism*, VIII, No. 6 (1959).

Leonhard, Wolfgang, *Child of the Revolution*. Chicago: Henry Regnery Co., 1958. A foreign communist's training in Russia for Comintern leadership.

Meyer, Frank S., *The Moulding of Communists*. New York: Harcourt, Brace & World, Inc., 1961. The indoctrination process and mental outlook of the typical communist.

Monnerot, Jules, *Sociology and Psychology of Communism*. Boston: Beacon Press, 1953. Communism portrayed as tyrannical secular religion by French sociologist.

Niemeyer, Gerhart and John S. Reshetar, Jr., *An Inquiry into Soviet Mentality*. London: Atlantic Press, 1956. Argue Soviets cannot converse with Western counterparts because their mental worlds completely different.

Ulam, Adam B., "Soviet Ideology and Soviet Foreign Policy," *World Politics*, XI, No. 2 (1959). Argues Soviet need for aggressive foreign policy to justify claims of ideology, and in turn the regime's existence.

Zinner, Paul, "The Ideological Bases of Soviet Foreign Policy," *World Politics*, IV, No. 4 (1952).

two

THE TACTICS OF SOVIET FOREIGN POLICY

4

THE BOLSHEVIKS
ACQUIRE
A COUNTRY
1917-1920

THE SEIZURE OF POWER

At 8:40 on the evening of November 8, 1917, the Bolshevik leadership of the Second All-Russian Congress of Soviets of Workers' and Soldiers' Deputies entered the great meeting-hall of the Smolny Institute, formerly a fashionable finishing school for the daughters of the nobility in a northern suburb of Petrograd (later Leningrad). The Congress had been in session since one o'clock that afternoon; shabby soldiers, grimy workmen, and peasants rubbed shoulders with revolutionary intellectuals, journalists, and students—all awaiting the arrival of Lenin and his comrades. When the time finally came, a thundering wave of cheers greeted the Bolshevik leaders, gray with fatigue yet exultant with their coup d'état. The revolution was hardly assured. It had erupted only two days before with the seizure of key points in Petrograd. But the Bolsheviks were ready to begin the foreign policy of the USSR.[1]

Lenin rose to speak—"great" Lenin to the young American socialist John Reed, recently graduated from Harvard and an eye witness to the

[1] This revolution is often called the "October" Revolution, and the earlier March "liberal-democratic" revolution, the "February" Revolution. The old style "Julian" calendar was still in use, then 13 days behind the Western "Gregorian" calendar.

meeting. Dressed in shabby clothes with trousers too long, his figure short and stocky with "a big head set down in his shoulders, bald and bulging," Lenin gripped the edge of the reading stand, "letting his little winking eyes travel over the crowd as he stood there waiting, apparently oblivious to the long-rolling ovation, which lasted several minutes. When it finished, he said simply, 'We shall now proceed to construct the Socialist order'!! Again that overwhelming human roar." [2]

"The first thing," Lenin proclaimed, "is the adoption of practical measures to realize peace. . . . We shall offer peace to the peoples of all the belligerent countries upon the basis of the Soviet terms—no annexations, no indemnities, and the right of self-determination of peoples." Lenin then read his draft of a Decree of Peace, though the Bolshevik government still had not been formally appointed.

The Decree presaged, in style and content, hundreds of later Soviet pronouncements. It was a strange mixture of propaganda and diplomatic proclamation. Although the Decree was addressed to the "governments of all belligerent nations" as well as to the "peoples" of these nations, it was mainly designed to spur the "peoples" on to revolution against their governments. The final section of the Decree addressed "in particular the conscious workers of the three nations most devoted to humanity and the three most important nations among those taking part in the present war—England, France, and Germany. The workers of these countries have rendered the greatest services to the cause of progress and of Socialism . . . the workers of these countries will understand the duty imposed upon them to liberate humanity from the horrors and consequences of war; and that these workers, by decisive, energetic and continued action, will help us to bring to a successful conclusion the cause of peace—and at the same time, the cause of the liberation of the exploited working masses from all slavery and all exploitation."

Lenin spoke bluntly about the true purpose of the document. He warned the delegates: "This proposal of peace will meet with resistance on the part of the imperialist governments—we don't fool ourselves on that score. But we hope that revolution will soon break out in all the belligerent countries; that is why we address ourselves especially to the workers of France, England and Germany. . . . The revolution of November 6th and 7th has opened the era of the Social revolution. . . . The labor movement, in the name of peace and Socialism, shall win, and fulfill its destiny. . . ."

In spirit with the new era, the Soviet government pledged to abolish "secret diplomacy" and publish all "secret treaties" concluded or confirmed by the previous Provisional Government. (The Tsarist govern-

2 John Reed, Ten Days That Shook the World (New York: Random House, Inc., 1960). See pp. 170-93, for the above session of the Congress.

ment actually was the major culprit, since it was promised, in a series of secret agreements, the Dardanelles in return for Russian support of Allied territorial claims.) Public negotiations for peace, the Soviets suggested, could be carried on by mail, telegraph, formal talks or conferences. An armistice of not less than three months was proposed for the peace talks, in order to permit the participation of "all nationality groups, without exception, who had been involved in the war, or forced to take part." Thus began proletarian diplomacy.

The Congress, faction by faction, gave its approval to the Decree in varying degrees of enthusiasm. (There was still genuine debate in the Soviet government.) Finally, Kamenev, one of the Bolshevik stalwarts, asked for a vote on the document as a whole. One delegate started to raise his hand against, but was submerged by a sea of protest. The vote was unanimous. And as if hit by one overwhelming impulse, the crowd broke into a chorus of the Internationale. A grizzled old soldier sobbed like a child; a young workman, his face shining, chanted "The war is ended! The war is ended!" Peace, most delegates seemed to think, finally had come to war-weary Russia.

Why Peace? The Bolshevik desire for peace had ideo-logical roots. Lenin and his followers held a doctrinally-based hatred of any imperialist war. Lenin poured out his venom in "The War and Russian Social-Democracy (1914)," asserting "neither of the two groups of belligerent countries lags behind the other in robbery, atrocities and the infinite brutalities of war" and referring to "the horrors of the present 'patriotic' barbarism." But given the existence of the imperialistic war cloud, there was a doctrinal silver lining. Capitalism was sowing the seeds of its own destruction through the terrible strains and stresses worked by the war on the nations in the capitalist system. And the Bolsheviks, more internationalist than Russian at this juncture, wanted revolution in all of capitalist Europe. A "socialist" revolt in Russia could—and hopefully would—serve as the spark for the general conflagration. But the Russian experiment could not succeed alone. Leon Trotsky, the newly appointed Commissar of Foreign Affairs, put it baldly to the assembled delegates early on the morning of November 9 (the meeting in which Lenin had proposed the Decree of Peace was still in session): "There are only two alternatives; either the Russian Revolution will create a revolutionary movement in Europe, or the European powers will destroy the Russian Revolution!"

A lone "socialist" government would not have a chance faced by an "imperialist" dominated world—even though the imperialists formally were at war with each other. The Allies, if they could, gladly would give Russia to the Germans in return for the destruction of the Bolsheviks.

The possibility of peace heralded by the Soviets, on the other hand, would bring revolution in the major capitalist countries. Lenin insisted on November 17: "Only a blind man cannot see the ferment that has seized the workers in Germany and in the West." Even though Europe's socialist leaders might be acting like nationalistic patriots, "the rank and file are ready, against the wishes of the leaders, to respond to our summons." The Bolsheviks believed it necessary only to broadcast a plea for peace, and a great ground swell of proletarian opinion everywhere would force warring imperialist governments to stop hostilities. Then would come more socialist revolutions.

The Soviets thus felt compelled to promote peace to further revolution in other capitalist countries, which in turn would protect the new Soviet state from *external* imperialist attacks. But just as crucial a reason for peace was the need to prevent *internal* "counterrevolution." Indeed, it was hard to say which threat presented the greater danger. Trotsky had answered a comrade's query about the expected content of Soviet diplomacy: "I will issue a few revolutionary proclamations to the peoples of the world, and then shut up shop." The overriding governmental task, Trotsky wanted to emphasize, was the *internal* protection and extension of the new regime. (Trotsky also reflected the Bolshevik belief that normal diplomatic relations with other nations would be unnecessary since their bourgeois governments were scheduled to disappear in the coming world revolution.)

On the evening of November 9, the Bolsheviks were not even certain of their control of Petrograd. Kerensky, the deposed leader of the Provisional Government, had fled to the front to organize military intervention against the new Soviet government. (The effort failed.) Non-Russian nationalities wanting independence and rebellious peasants in the Volga Valley, Siberia, central Russia, and, most of all, the Ukraine, were more dangerous. To compound these problems, the Bolsheviks quarreled bitterly among themselves over the right course for the revolution. "Liberal" members of the faction pressed Lenin to widen the base of the government to include representatives from the "mass proletarian organizations." He had excluded most of the non-Bolshevik socialist parties and trade unions from his government. The liberals moreover rebelled at Lenin's use of "political terror."

The Soviets also had no experience in running a government. Experts in the arts of revolution—conspiracy and agitation—the Bolshevik leaders knew nothing of the details of administration. Their lack of experience was not compensated for by a functioning, sympathetic bureaucracy. When Trotsky arrived at his new Commissariat of Foreign Affairs on the morning of November 10, he assembled the entire staff, inherited from the old regime, and went right to the point: "Those for us go to the left, those against us go to the right." All of the some 600 officials went right. Uritsky, a colleague of Trotsky's, was literally thrown out of the Commissariat's Archives Department when he demanded texts of the secret treaties for publication.

But the final and paramount reason for peace, overriding all other internal or external reasons, was the almost compulsive desire of the Russian people to take Russia out of the war. The Provisional "liberal democratic" government born in the earlier March Revolution had fallen primarily because it had not done this. Its leaders, for mixed and sometimes contradictory reasons, had decided to keep Russia in the war. The Allies pressed them at every opportunity to continue the Eastern front. And the liberal leaders of the Provisional Government were bound by feelings of loyalty to the Allied cause, as well as national pride, to continue the conflict. Moreover, what would happen to the liberal revolution in Russia if Germany won the war?

Lenin had no such qualms of conscience. Immediately upon his triumphant arrival in Petrograd in April 1917, Lenin set out to destroy the power of the Provisional Government, particularly the Army.[3] He wanted no armed force at the call of the Government when the time came for the socialist revolution. The collapse of the Russian Army as an effective fighting machine actually was well under way before the Tsarist government fell. The collapse had been aided during the first days of the March Revolution by the infamous "Order No. 1" of the Petrograd Workers' and Soldiers' Soviet, dominated at that time by moderate socialists. (This body, organized on the fall of the Tsarist government, immediately had become a powerful if unofficial rival to the Provisional Government. Other "soviets" later were organized.) The "order" among other things proclaimed military units should be run by committee, except during tactical operations, and abolished the salute off duty. Lenin's tactics went further. He wanted to abolish the army, police and bureaucracy of the Provisional Government. His slogan—"All Power to the Soviets"—was designed for that purpose.

By the November Revolution the Army had been wrecked. It could give no effective support to the Provisional Government, and no effective opposition to the Germans. On the other hand, the Army was not Bolshevik controlled. Lenin admitted the Army voted against the war—and not for the Bolsheviks—with its feet. (Walking away from the front

---

[3] Lenin and other revolutionary leaders had been transported from Switzerland in a sealed train provided by the German General Staff. From this arose the accusation that Lenin was a German agent. The Germans had subsidized the Bolsheviks, but only in a routine manner as part of a larger operation. They hardly expected the Bolsheviks ever to achieve power. Furthermore, Lenin was certainly a poor bet for a servile secret agent. If anything, he was using the Germans.

was an eloquent protest.) In summary, the communist plea for peace was preordained by a war-weary people and an impotent army.

Allied Reaction Foreshadowing future Soviet diplomatic overtures, the Peace Decree was broadcast by wireless and given to the foreign press—not formally communicated to the Allied governments. The Allies were not sure what to make of such a radical procedure. Should they give the Decree serious attention? Were the Bolsheviks really in control, or would the new regime soon collapse? (The Allies still imagined a sizable group of Russians supported the war effort, and thought that this group might gain power.) Even if the Bolsheviks managed to keep power, did this plea for peace *deserve* an answer?

There was the unsavory nature of the Soviet government. United States Ambassador Francis typified Allied reaction to the Bolshevik seizure of power in a letter dated November 8: "It is reported that the Petrograd Council of Workmen and Soldiers has named a Cabinet with Lenin as Premier, Trotsky, as Minister of Foreign Affairs, and Madame or Mlle. Kollontai as Minister of Education. Disgusting." [4] In the Peace Decree, this "disgusting" revolutionary clique had threatened unilateral denunciation of the formal agreement made by Russia and the Allies in 1914 not to make a separate peace. Fighting the war to its bitter end was of primary importance to the Allies, especially France. Clemenceau said he would not release Russia from her obligation to continue the war if "all the celestial powers" asked him to give Russia back her word. The Bolsheviks moreover had addressed the peoples in the Allied nations over the heads of their governments, in effect calling for revolution *against* those governments. The Soviet leaders should not have been surprised when the Allied ambassadors in Petrograd agreed, on November 22, to ignore the Soviet offer for a general armistice and subsequent negotiations for a peace. The Bolsheviks were a "pretended government . . . established by force and not recognized by the Russian people." (On the evening of November 21, Trotsky finally had given the Allied missions formal notice of the Decree—and of the establishment of the Soviet government.)

German Reaction When their wireless operators first picked up the broadcast of the Soviet armistice offer, the Germans were mystified. Although Lenin and the Bolsheviks had been aided at various times by the German High Command, information on the operation was

---

[4] David R. Francis, *Russia from the American Embassy*, April 1916-November 1918 (New York: Charles Scribner's Sons, 1921), p. 186. Madame Kollontai among other things was thought to be an advocate of "free love."

closely held. There also was little knowledge of the details surrounding the November Revolution. Trotsky, whose name was attached to the message, was actually unknown to the Germans. (He had not been one of their "agents" sent from Switzerland.) But any doubt the offer was genuine evaporated when the formal Soviet armistice proposal arrived on November 26.

Surprise now gave way to delight. Major General Max Hoffmann, the brilliant German General Staff Officer in de facto command of the Eastern front, called General Ludendorff, then dominating the German High Command and often, the German government. "Is it possible to negotiate with these people?" Ludendorff asked. "Yes, it is possible," Hoffmann replied, "Your excellency needs troops and this is the easiest way to get them." [5] Hoffmann was referring to the final, desperate offensive on the Western front the Germans then were planning. The fate of Germany and her allies hung on the success of this offensive. For success, reinforcements for the Western front had to be found. An armistice with Russia would provide the vitally needed troops—a gift of almost one million men. Operation "sealed train" had paid off far more generously than the Germans probably ever had hoped.

The Soviets now were moving rapidly toward a separate peace with the Germans—a tactic the Soviets loudly proclaimed was being forced on them by the Allies. In view of the insulting language of the original Decree and Lenin's admission that the Allied governments probably would resist the Soviet offer, some have believed the Soviets wanted a separate peace from the beginning. Wasn't it perfectly permissible—and even mandatory—for a "socialist" government to unilaterally pull out of an "imperialist" war? The Soviets, however, probably were sincere in their clamor for a general cessation of hostilities. They apparently believed general peace, and then revolution in Europe, vital for the security of the new Soviet state. The Allied *governments* might be reluctant to accept Soviet terms, but the *peoples* would be overjoyed at the offer. How could their governments resist? Only with reluctance did the Soviets later accept the bitter truth. The Western masses were neither able nor ready to pressure their governments for peace. Communist analysis of the psychological state of Western society, not for the last time, would prove wrong. The new regime would have to face what Lenin later called "the greatest difficulty" of the Soviet revolution. "A peaceful domestic animal," in Lenin's somewhat biased view, would "lay down with a tiger" and argue peace without annexations and indemnities.

[5] Quoted in John W. Wheeler-Bennett, *Brest-Litovsk, The Forgotten Peace, March, 1918* (London: Macmillan & Co. Ltd., 1956), p. 79. By permission of Macmillan & Co. Ltd, The Macmillan Company of Canada Ltd, and St. Martin's Press, Inc.

BREST-LITOVSK

The Setting   German-Soviet negotiations for the armistice (effective December 17) and then the peace treaty, extended from December 1917 to March 1918.[6] Brest-Litovsk, now a small city on the Western border of the USSR but then the war-ravaged Eastern headquarters of the German Army, was the site. (The Russians had fired the city upon their retreat in 1916.) The cast of characters was uncommon. Wheeler-Bennett wrote: "The whim of history willed that the representatives of the most revolutionary regime ever known should sit at the same diplomatic table with representatives of the most reactionary military caste among all ruling classes."[7]

The Soviet delegation was consciously designed to illustrate the unique character of the new state. Revolutionary window dressing was provided by an old soldier, a handsome sailor, and a happy-go-lucky member of the working class. A good-natured old peasant gave added color. The leaders of the delegation literally shanghaied him when they found on the way to the railroad station in Petrograd that they lacked a representative from the great majority of Russians. Not forgetting equality of the sexes, the Bolsheviks also included little grey-haired Mme. Anastasia Bitsenko, recently freed from a Siberian prison term for assassinating a Tsarist general in 1905. The "negotiators," headed by Adolph Joffe, were typical revolutionary intellectuals. Obviously somewhat better qualified than the working class representatives, they still could not help dropping candid hints over the conference and dinner tables of pending revolution in the countries of the Central Powers.

The Negotiations   There were four phases to the negotiations, the Soviet position becoming more desperate at each stage. The first phase covered the last part of December. The armistice now in effect, the delegations began talks on a treaty of peace.

The Soviets at this juncture still naïvely believed revolutionary propaganda disseminated at the conference table would spark the European revolution. They therefore got the Germans to agree to "open" diplomacy. The talks were fully reported in the press of the world, while every means was tried to get propaganda into Germany. Detailed questions of geography—who got what territory—were of little consequence. The coming European *class* struggle was critical, not whether Lithuania would be given to Germany. The Soviet position outlined by Joffe thus reiterated

---

[6] All the Central Powers—Germany, Austria-Hungary, Bulgaria and Turkey—were represented at the negotiations, but the Germans dominated.

[7] Wheeler-Bennett, *Brest-Litovsk*, pp. 114-15. The story of Brest-Litovsk is taken mainly from this classic on Soviet foreign policy.

the idealistic and propagandistic principles of the Decree of Peace—a *general* peace with no annexations, no indemnities, and self-determination for all peoples. The Germans agreed to negotiate on this basis, providing the Allies also accepted the Soviet terms. That of course was the fly in the ointment. The Germans had little doubt that the Allies would reject a proposal to begin negotiations for a world-wide settlement.

The Soviet delegation was jubilant at the German support of the principle of self-determination. And the Soviets somehow got the impression the Germans were ready, even in the event of a *separate* German-Soviet peace treaty, to withdraw from those areas of the old Tsarist empire then under German control. (This included most of the area of the Baltic states and Poland.)

The Germans moved quickly to clear up the misunderstanding. General Hoffmann bluntly told Joffe that the former Tsarist provinces were exercising self-determination by choosing independence or the status of German protectorates. The Soviets were shocked. Pokrovsky, a member of the delegation, sobbed: "How can you talk of peace without annexation when nearly eighteen provinces are torn from Russia?" [8] Although European revolution was their central objective, the Soviets apparently were not ready to give up all of the former Tsarist empire. On this optimistic note, negotiations were adjourned the following evening (December 28) until January 9, ostensibly to give the Allies a final chance to enter the negotiations.

The Soviets were beginning to get worried. They did not want to give up the occupied areas, but they could not fight to keep them. The Allies moreover gave no sign of joining the peace talks. There was one weapon left—delay. If done properly, this could be the salvation of the new state. The Soviets were convinced the German hard line was possible only because the German workers did not know the true facts of Brest-Litovsk. By stalling for time, internal revolutionary pressure could be brought against the German government. The "delayer" would be Trotsky, now slated to head the Soviet delegation. Trotsky, then 38, was a brilliant, egotistical Marxist polemicist, equally skilled with the tongue and pen, and ideally suited for his new role as procrastinator extraordinary. (Colonel Raymond Robins, one of the unofficial American "representatives" in Petrograd, called Trotsky: "A four-kind son of a bitch, but the greatest Jew since Jesus Christ." [9]) To aid Trotsky's task, the Soviets demanded the negotiations be moved to Stockholm to give their propaganda easier entry into Germany. The Germans refused, realizing Soviet weakness, and the second phase of the talks began January 9 at Brest-Litovsk.

Trotsky harangued the Germans off and on for more than four weeks,

[8] *Ibid.*, p. 125.
[9] *Ibid.*, p. 152.

arguing the forms and principles of self-determination, even discussing the powers of the United States Supreme Court. The Germans, particularly General Hoffmann, progressively got more disgusted with Trotsky's insufferable manner; but, they permitted the debate to continue. The Germans were quarrelling over the correct policy to be used against the Soviets. German attention moreover was riveted on a delegation of young Ukrainian nationalists representing a newly formed Ukrainian government—the "Rada"—which had just arrived at Brest. These delegates stated they were independent of the Soviets (they refused to speak Russian), and that they were ready to talk peace. The Germans decided to encourage this feeling of independence. Most of their vital grain supplies and raw materials were in the Ukraine. By negotiating separately with the Ukrainian delegation, the Germans could let Trotsky talk and still get what they wanted. The separation of the Ukraine would be a terrible loss for the Soviets, who also needed the Ukrainian breadbasket. Pressure on the Soviets to sign a peace logically would increase.

This spectre was brought home to Trotsky on January 18. General Hoffmann spread out a great map showing a blue line from Brest to the Baltic—the future frontier. Below Brest, the Germans would negotiate a border with the Ukrainians.

The adamant German position caused a great crisis for the Soviet leadership. Trotsky immediately left for Petrograd to confer with his government. In the capital, three alternatives were heatedly debated. Bukharin, heading a bare majority, the "left" faction, argued for revolutionary war against European capitalism. The proletarians of Europe deserved the first allegiance of the Soviets; a separate peace to save the skin of the Soviet regime would be a disgusting betrayal of communist ideals. (In 1915 Lenin had proposed such a revolutionary war in the event of socialist success in Russia.)

Lenin, always more coldly realistic than his colleagues, pressed for a second plan. He turned to Bukharin: "My poor friend, go to the front and see if it is possible to fight." Lenin then presented his "21 Theses" on the peace. "The question whether it is possible to undertake at once a revolutionary war must be answered solely from the point of view of actual conditions and the interest of the Socialist Revolution which has already begun. . . . The policy advocated . . . is capable of giving satisfaction to those who crave the romantic and the beautiful but who fail completely to take into consideration the objective correlation of class forces." Lenin vividly summarized the situation: "Germany is only pregnant with revolution. The second month must not be mistaken for the ninth. But here in Russia we have a healthy, lusty child. We may kill it if we start a war." The German terms, Lenin insisted, must be accepted *now*.[10]

[10] *Ibid.*, pp. 188-92.

But Lenin could marshal only 15 out of 63 party leaders for his position. Sensing the mood, Lenin switched his support to Trotsky's proposal, the third alternative. Trotsky wanted neither war nor peace. Before
signing any treaty, Trotsky was determined the Soviets should give the
European proletariat convincing proof of the basic enmity between the
Soviets and the Germans, laying to rest the persistent rumors the Bolsheviks were German agents and hopefully spawning the European revolution. He had written to Lenin: "My plan is this: We announce the
termination of the war and demobilization without signing any peace.
We declare we cannot participate in the brigands' peace . . . after we
declare the war ended . . . it would be very difficult for Germany to
attack us, because of her internal conditions." [11]

Lenin called Trotsky's subtle formula "an international political demonstration" the Soviets could not afford. He was sure Trotsky's alternative
also would fail; Russia could lose even more territory if the Germans
decided to advance. But Lenin was not ready to risk splitting the party.
"We will only risk losing Estonia or Latvia, and for the sake of a good
peace with Trotsky," Lenin chuckled, "Latvia and Estonia are worth
losing." Trotsky had won. The third phase of the negotiations would
begin.

Trotsky returned to Brest-Litovsk at the end of January, free to continue his delaying tactics and authorized to spring "No War—No Peace"
at the convenient moment. It soon came. On February 8, the Germans
signed a separate treaty with the Ukrainian Rada. (That very day, Kiev,
the capital of the Ukraine, fell to Bolshevik forces.) Possibly sensing a
German ultimatum in the air, Trotsky apparently decided the formula had
to be delivered immediately to serve its purpose. On the gray Sunday
afternoon of February 10, the Germans listened to what they thought was
Trotsky's propagandistic prelude to capitulation. Instead, his new tactic
gradually reared its curious head. When Trotsky finished, the delegates
sat speechless. Hoffmann's voice broke the silence: "Unheard of!" The
German legal advisor later exhumed a similar unilateral declaration of
peace after a war between the ancient Greeks and the Scythians.

That night the Soviet delegates left for Petrograd, smugly confident
they had tricked the Germans. In Petrograd the Central Executive Committee of the Soviets unanimously approved Trotsky's action.

The Germans, particularly the German High Command, were not
fooled. On February 16 they announced the war would resume in two
days. Hoffmann wrote in his diary: "No other way out is possible, otherwise these brutes will wipe up the Ukrainians, the Finns, and the Balts,
and then quietly get together a new revolutionary army and turn the

[11] *Ibid.*, p. 185.

whole of Europe into a pig-sty. . . . The whole of Russia is no more than a vast heap of maggots—a squalid, swarming mass." [12] This was to be the publicly announced reason for the pending German attack; in reality, the German High Command felt additional annexations necessary. A few weeks before, Field Marshal Hindenburg had solemnly answered when asked why Germany needed all of the Baltic states: "I need them for the maneuvering of my left wing in the next war." [13] Even more important, however, was the present war. The German High Command agreed the Eastern front had to be consolidated immediately. It also was apparent the Ukraine would have to be taken from the Bolsheviks since the Rada was rapidly sinking.

On hearing the news of the German decision, Lenin turned to Trotsky: "Your test has been tried and it failed. Hoffmann can and will fight. . . . Delay is impossible. We must sign at once. The beast springs quickly." But only after the Germans launched the attack and were making rapid advances did Lenin finally get a bare majority to approve acceptance of the German terms.

The Germans were in no hurry for the Soviet capitulation once their offensive was rolling unhindered. (In one area the Germans moved 150 miles in 124 hours.) On February 21, the Germans therefore dispatched new, much harsher terms. Lenin now put all his prestige on the line, threatening to resign unless the German ultimatum (48 hours) was immediately accepted. On the morning of February 23, Bukharin and the "lefts" still wanted revolutionary war. After hours of debate Lenin only had 7 out of 15 votes of the Bolshevik Central Committee; Bukharin, 4. However, four abstentions (including Trotsky) gave Lenin his demand.

But Lenin still had to face first the Petrograd Soviet, and then the Central Executive Committee of the Congress of Soviets, both meeting that night. As he rose to speak in the assembly hall of the Soviet, Lenin was welcomed with jeers and cries of "traitor." Alexandra Kollontai, a long-time comrade, just had bitterly reprimanded him: "Enough of this opportunism, you are advising us to do the same thing which you have always accused the Mensheviks of doing—compromising with imperialism."

Lenin was unmoved. And he conquered the crowd, with a biting retort for every criticism: "You must sign this shameful peace in order to save the World Revolution, in order to hold fast to its most important, and at present, its only foothold—the Soviet Republic. . . . You think that the path of the Proletarian Revolution is strewn with roses? That we will march from victory to victory with waving flags. . . . The Revolution is not a pleasure trip! The path of revolution leads over thorns and briars. Wade up to the knees in filth, if need be, crawling on our bellies

[12] *Ibid.*, p. 243.
[13] *Ibid.*, p. 109.

through dirt and dung to communism, then in this fight we will win.
. . . We shall see the World Revolution, but meanwhile it is just a very
good fairy-tale, a very pretty fairy-tale. . . ." [14]

The fourth and final phase of the negotiations began when the Soviet
delegation arrived at Brest-Litovsk on February 27. Actually there was
little to negotiate. The Soviets feigned martyrdom, refusing to discuss the
new German terms lest this indicate they had some freedom of choice.
Protesting to the end, they signed on March 3. When the Soviet delegation returned, Lenin forecast the Soviet attitude toward the treaty: "I
don't mean to read it, and I don't mean to fulfill it, except insofar as I'm
forced." Lenin would acknowledge the German occupation. What else
could he do? But he would continue revolutionary propaganda against
the Central Powers though this was forbidden by the treaty.

How disastrous was the treaty? The Germans had taken 26 per cent
of Russia's total population (over 60 million), 27 per cent of her arable
land, 33 per cent of her manufacturing. On the other hand, as George
Kennan remarks, the terms were not inordinately severe when compared
with those the Allies later imposed on Germany. The Bolsheviks never
had controlled the lost territories, and the peoples of these territories had
no desire to be ruled by "Russians" of any type. Russia had fought a war
and lost; a price had to be paid.[15]

ALLIED INTERVENTION AND
THE CIVIL WAR

The negotiations at Brest-Litovsk had been the central
concern of Soviet foreign policy for some three months. But scarcely had
the Soviets signed the treaty than they saw two other dangers: the external threat of Allied intervention in the Soviet Union, and internal
counterrevolution by Russian "exploiting" classes.

Today the Soviets explain intervention and counterrevolution (the civil
war) as a combined operation to crush the new Soviet state, organized
by "international imperialism," specifically "the leading circles" of England, the United States, and France. The capitalists supposedly were
afraid the proletarian state was potential poison for the whole imperialist
edifice. The facts are quite different. The internal opposition, previously
mentioned as one of the compelling reasons for the Soviet Peace Decree,
hardly needed Allied stimulation. Allied aid and armed intervention
merely made more serious an already grave threat to the Bolsheviks.

Internal opposition came from three general groups, uncoordinated

[14] *Ibid.*, p. 260.
[15] George F. Kennan, *Russia and the West* (Boston: Atlantic-Little, Brown and
Company, 1960), p. 41.

and often opposed to each other, united only in hating the Bolsheviks. The first two groups made up the "Whites," committed to destroying the "Reds"; they were (1) former officers of the armed forces under the Tsarist and then Provisional Government, and (2) anti-Bolshevik party politicians and their supporters, ranging from far-right to socialist. The third group had more limited aims. In the borderlands of the former Tsarist empire, non-Russian nationalist movements, often shallowly based, wanted independence from "Russia." There was little interest in the destruction of Soviet power in Petrograd or Moscow. (Because of the fear of further German advances, the Soviets moved their government to Moscow, the old capital of the Muscovite Tsars, in March 1918.) Finland and the Ukraine had attempted separation in 1917 from the Provisional Government. Other nationalist movements existed in Belorussia ("White" Russia); Estonia, Latvia, and Lithuania; the Transcaucasian area —Georgia, Armenia and, Azerbaijan; and among the Moslem inhabitants of Central Asia. Finally, nationalism always had been especially strong in Poland.

What then is the basis for the Soviet charge that the Allies led and supported this motley internal opposition in an all-out attempt to destroy bolshevism? As often happens in Soviet propaganda, there is some fact behind the accusation and this will be shown later. But we can settle the question of motivation now. If there must be one primary reason for Allied intervention, it was the war. Toward the end of November 1917, the Allies recognized Soviet power was relatively secure. The talks of Brest-Litovsk subsequently raised the spectre of a huge German troop movement to the West, and logically, a dreaded German offensive on the Western front the coming spring. How to buttress the Eastern front became a paramount Allied concern. In the search, three different strategies were considered or employed.

First, certain Allied leaders worked for a reformulation of Allied war aims. The Soviet Peace Decree had stolen Western liberal thunder. The Allies thus needed a clear statement of their interest in a humanitarian peace, and especially the principle of self-determination. The reformulation might rekindle enthusiasm in Russia and elsewhere for the Allied cause. Wilson's "fourteen points" address of January 8, 1918, was designed to be such a statement. Speaking to the "Russian people" but also praising the Soviet delegation's efforts at Brest-Litovsk (the second phase of the talks were then beginning), Wilson somehow hoped to bolster Russian resistance to the Germans.

Lenin was pleased—with the propaganda impact Wilson's speech might have on the Germans. Both Lenin and Trotsky refused to believe the bourgeois American President might be sincere in his denunciation of the German terms at Brest-Litovsk and in his protestations of Allied purity. The Soviet leaders apparently thought the United States, France, and England were secretly happy at the pound of flesh Germany was exacting from the new regime. This would make it easier for the Allies later to come to terms with the Germans.

The second strategy to bolster the Eastern front centered on Allied aid to the Soviets. During the gloomy days of the revived German offensive in February 1918, Trotsky and the unofficial Allied intermediaries in Petrograd discussed the possibility of Allied military assistance to the Soviets if the Germans kept coming.[16] The Bolshevik leaders now were ready to consider help from any quarter in a frantic attempt to build a Red Army. One indication of their panic was the manifesto issued on February 21 authorizing the mobilization of the whole able-bodied population for the defense of the "socialist Fatherland." The Soviets also worried about possible Japanese intervention in Siberia, and suggested that the United States might restrain the Japanese as an additional inducement for Russia's acceptance of Allied aid.

Yet the Bolsheviks were uneasy about Allied assistance. Bukharin protested against compromise with any imperialist nation, crying, "We are turning the party into a dung-hill." Lenin, absent from the meeting debating the issue, sent a slip of paper on which he had scrawled, "I request that my vote be added in favor of taking potatoes and arms from the bandits of Anglo-French imperialism." But he indicated the Soviets would accept Allied help only if the German advance continued, threatening the very existence of the new state. However, the German offensive stopped when the Central Powers agreed to the Soviet capitulation, and nothing further came of the negotiations with the Allies. In any case, Paris and London never had been especially enthusiastic about the proposal.

The third Allied strategy was to intervene in Russia, both with Allied troops and financial and military aid for anti-German forces. In the tense winter months during the Soviet peace talks with the Central Powers, Allied military planners saw intervention by an expeditionary force, operating with those Russians still loyal to the Allied cause, as the only logical way to reconstruct the Eastern front.

The British and American political leadership opposed direct Allied military action for the moment. Balfour, the British Foreign Secretary, argued intervention would give the Bolsheviks reason for regarding the Germans as "friends and deliverers." But the British were not against

---

[16] Since the Allies had not recognized the new regime, "unofficial" Allied agents in Petrograd became a main channel of communication with the Bolshevik leaders. For the French, there was Jacques Sadoul, a socialist lawyer attached to the French Military Mission in Petrograd; for the British, Bruce Lockhart, a former British consul in Moscow; for the Americans, "Colonel" Raymond Robins, head of the United States Red Cross Mission in Russia.

giving aid, together with the French, to anti-Bolshevik groups. On December 23, 1917, these two powers signed a secret agreement to divide South Russia for this purpose: the French took the Ukraine; the British, the Caucasus.

The impetus for direct Allied action in Russia was the German offensive in the West, launched in March 1918. The British and French now were eager for any kind of intervention to siphon off German pressure from the Western front. They had few troops to spare, and these were sent to the most critical spots in Russia for the Allied cause: British marines, for example, to guard the huge store of Allied war supplies at the Russian port of Murmansk on the White Sea. It was hoped that the United States and Japan would provide the main contingents. But only the Japanese came through in strength, sending some 72,000 men to Siberia.

The large Japanese force requires an explanation. Japan apparently saw a golden opportunity to wrest Northern Manchuria from prostrate Russia and to gain economic control of Eastern Siberia. Initially the Japanese had hesitated, waiting for American consent to their venture. Japan wanted a free hand in Siberia, but not at the risk of provoking the United States. The Allies subsequently brought great pressure to bear on President Wilson during the first half of 1918 to let the Japanese intervene unilaterally in Siberia, or to send in American forces as part of a joint expedition.

The President finally capitulated to Allied demands for American intervention in July 1918. But American troops were not to be sent for the establishment of an Eastern front or to crush the Bolsheviks. Wilson wanted to avoid direct interference in Soviet *internal* affairs. The decisive factor in Wilson's decision seems to have been his desire to help the Czechoslovak Corps, then scattered through Siberia, from supposed attacks by armed German and Austrian prisoners of war on the loose due to a state of anarchy in the Siberian hinterlands. Actually, the Czechs were fighting Bolshevik forces. (The Provisional Government had organized the Czech Corps, composed of Czech defectors from the Austro-Hungarian army and men from former Tsarist Czech colonies, to fight the Germans. In early 1918, the Allies were trying to get the Corps to the Western front.)

Some 7,000 American troops subsequently landed at Vladivostok, the major Soviet port on the Pacific, in August and September 1918. American troops (approximately 4,500) also joined a small British and French force at the White Sea port of Archangel.[17]

17 Under French leadership, a varied crew of some 45,000 French, Greek, Polish, and Rumanian troops later occupied the Odessa area in Southern Russia, and some 7,500 French and Greek troops occupied the neighboring Crimea. After an unsuccessful attempt over several months to bolster local White forces, both contingents were withdrawn.

The World War ended a few months later, leaving the Allies in a quandary over their Russian adventure. What possible rationale could there now be for keeping Allied forces in Russia—unless the Allies did want to crush the Soviet regime? The lack of common purpose among the Allies, and even within each Allied country, soon became evident. Wilson was completely against the whole concept of "intervention." Lloyd George, the British Prime Minister, argued Bolshevism could not be put down by armed force. At the same time, he considered the new political movement as dangerous for civilization as "German militarism." (Winston Churchill, his Minister of War, wanted to see the Bolsheviks crushed.)

The French were the most anti-Soviet. They held the largest share of the debt of the Tsarist and Provisional Governments, which the Soviets refused to honor as of February 10, 1918. Moreover, the French were especially sensitive to the Soviet "betrayal" of the Allied cause at Brest-Litovsk. Finally, Clemenceau, the French Premier, wanted Bolshevism destroyed or at least "quarantined" because of the fear in 1919 that the Bolshevik "infection" might spread to Europe. Indeed, William Henry Chamberlin calls this fear the decisive reason for continuing the intervention.[18]

Futile attempts to reconcile Allied differences were made at the Paris Peace Conference in January 1919. The Soviets were absent from the conference because of the unofficial war between their government and the Allies. But they were now ready to make important concessions to end the intervention. Certain that the White opposition would collapse without Western support, the Soviets indicated a willingness among other things to compromise on the state debts they had previously refused to pay, and later, to grant a general amnesty to all their opponents. Sudden military successes of the White forces, coupled with the French refusal to have anything to do with the Bolsheviks, quashed negotiations on the Soviet offer.

Shortly after the end of the Peace Conference, the Bolsheviks began to gain the upper hand against their Russian enemies. By now there was no real hope to overthrow the Soviet government, and any reason for continuing the intervention evaporated. The Allied forces therefore, gradually withdrew. European Russia was cleared of Allied troops in 1919. The Americans stayed on in Siberia until early 1920, chiefly to restrain the Japanese. (The Japanese finally left mainland Siberia in 1922 after considerable Allied diplomatic pressure.) The British continued to give substantial economic and military aid to the Whites until 1920, primarily because the British did not want to sacrifice their Russian "allies" of 1918

[18] William Henry Chamberlin, *The Russian Revolution* (New York: The Macmillan Company, 1954), II, p. 152.

to the Bolsheviks. The Allied blockade, extended to Russia at the end of the World War, also continued until January 1920.

Nationalist Movements Separatist movements, previously mentioned as part of the internal opposition, threatened to tear off huge hunks of the new Soviet state all during this period. Some thought the Soviets would approve of such self-determination. As early as 1913, Stalin had proclaimed that right in his first theoretical piece, "Marxism and the National Question." Trotsky had insisted on the principle at Brest-Litovsk. However, it soon became apparent that the Soviets considered separatist movements bourgeois-nationalist and counterrevolutionary if they dismembered a socialist regime. It was perfectly correct for captive nations to rebel against bourgeois governments. But Lenin bluntly stated on January 20, 1918 that the interests of socialism were more important than the right of nations to self-determination. The largest possible base for the future "World Soviet Republic" had to be created, and, in the meantime, a strong bastion was needed for the battle against imperialism.[19]

Most separatist movements eventually were crushed either by the Red Army, local communists, or both. But lip service later was paid to the existence of separate nationalities within the Soviet state. White Russia, the Ukraine, Georgia, Armenia and Azerbaijan became "independent" Soviet republics. Local communist parties, of course, provided the link with the Russian Socialist Federated Soviet Republic (R.S.F.S.R.), proclaimed by the constitution adopted on July 19, 1918.

Some former parts of the Tsarist empire did gain independence. The Soviets permitted Finland to exercise self-determination—in December 1917. Later, the Bolshevik leaders reconsidered their rash move and aided an abortive communist uprising in Finland during the spring of 1918. Other sectors of the old empire—Latvia, Lithuania, and Estonia—gained independence primarily because the Soviets were busy elsewhere. Finally, several Tsarist territories were "liberated" by covetous neighbors. Bessarabia was taken and held by Rumania in 1918. Turkey regained the provinces of Kars and Ardahan, lost to Russia in 1878.

The War with Poland The one national movement seriously threatening Soviet power was Polish. At the Paris Peace Conference an independent Poland had been carved out of Polish territory divided for over a century among Austria, Prussia, and Russia. Since

---

[19] The distinction between "acceptable" and "unacceptable" self-determination appears in Stalin's early work noted above, and even earlier in Lenin's writings. See E. H. Carr, *The Bolshevik Revolution, 1917-1923* (New York: The Macmillan Company, 1951), I, "The Bolshevik Doctrine of Self-Determination," 410-28.

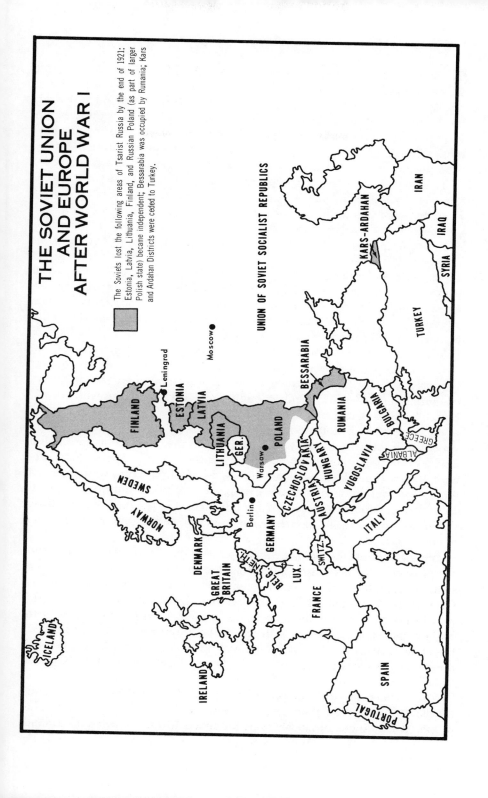

THE SOVIET UNION AND EUROPE AFTER WORLD WAR I

The Soviets lost the following areas of Tsarist Russia by the end of 1921: Estonia, Latvia, Lithuania, Finland, and Russian Poland (as part of larger Polish state) became independent; Bessarabia was occupied by Rumania; Kars and Ardahan Districts were ceded to Turkey.

UNION OF SOVIET SOCIALIST REPUBLICS

Moscow

Leningrad

FINLAND

ESTONIA

LATVIA

LITHUANIA

GER.

POLAND

Warsaw

BESSARABIA

RUMANIA

BULGARIA

GREECE

ALBANIA

KARS-ARDAHAN

IRAN

SYRIA

IRAQ

TURKEY

YUGOSLAVIA

HUNGARY

AUSTRIA

CZECHOSLOVAKIA

SWITZ.

ITALY

GERMANY

Berlin

DENMARK

SWEDEN

NORWAY

NETH.

BELG.

LUX.

FRANCE

GREAT BRITAIN

IRELAND

ICELAND

SPAIN

PORTUGAL

the Soviets were absent from the Conference, the Allies tried to get Poland to accept unilaterally an eastern border based on a rough ethnic division (later called the "Curzon Line.") But Marshall Joseph Pilsudski, the Polish President, had come to power intending to regain the western Ukraine and western White Russia. Although these areas were not ethnically Polish, Pilsudski considered them part of Poland's historic heritage (the Poland of 1772). Russia in turn would be permanently weakened.

The Soviets were eager for peace with Poland because the internal situation in Russia demanded peace. In February 1920, they appeared ready to make significant concessions. But the Poles, in spite of the grave economic crisis in their own country, were suffering from an overdose of nationalism. They opened an offensive against Russia in April 1920 to regain the "lost" territories.

At first the Polish offensive was spectacularly successful. Local Soviet troops were overwhelmed. However, the Bolsheviks moved quickly, organizing in the middle of May a double thrust against the Poles—one offensive in the north through White Russia, the second in the south through the Ukraine. The Poles stubbornly resisted, but by the end of July the Red Army was at the gates of Warsaw, the Polish capital.

The rapid advance was intoxicating for the Soviets. A defensive war to protect the new Soviet state was turning into an offensive war to spread communism. In Moscow, Lenin thought Poland was seething with revolution. The Red Army, now an "international" army serving the interests of an international proletariat and not a "Russian" invading force, would spread communism. It only had to topple the "crust" of the Polish bourgeoisie and a new Polish Soviet Republic would appear. After Poland, Lenin argued, the rest of Europe would fall. Trotsky, in contrast to his cautious optimism about European revolution during the Brest-Litovsk negotiations, opposed further advances. (Later, the Polish workers did prove more nationalist than communist.) But Lenin won and the offensive continued.

Initially, the Allies were tempted to leave the Poles to their fate. But the prospect of a Red Army advancing toward the heart of Europe, then showing symptoms of revolution, required some sort of Allied support for Poland. A French military mission already was on the scene. Additional shipments of munitions were dispatched. Lord Curzon, the British foreign minister, suggested a truce to both parties on July 12, 1920, threatening British and French support for the Poles if the Soviets crossed the border suggested at the Paris Peace Conference (the "Curzon Line").

The Soviets, sensing victory, did not heed the Allied request. Instead, the Soviets submitted their own peace terms to Poland in August. The proposed conditions obviously were designed to turn a defeated Poland into a Soviet satellite. Only a last minute Polish counteroffensive—the "miracle of Warsaw"—saved the new state. The Red Army, partly because of a serious lack of communication between the north and south prongs of the Soviet offensive, rapidly withdrew. Both sides were now exhausted, and the Soviets also wanted to concentrate on subduing the last of the White forces. On October 12 a preliminary peace was signed. Because of the Polish successes in the final weeks of the war, the border was placed considerably to the east of the Curzon Line. Poland thereby gained territory populated predominantly by White Russians and Ukrainians.

PROMOTING
INTERNATIONAL COMMUNISM

This brief outline of the first period in Soviet foreign policy (1917-1920) has dealt mainly with the attempt to defend the new Soviet regime from the Germans, then from the Allies and the internal opposition, and finally from the Poles and other separatist movements. Other Soviet activity, however, was *offensive*. From the first, the Soviets believed proletarian revolutions possible in Europe, and probable in Germany. The horrible strains of the imperialist war had left Europe in ferment. Offensive (Left) tactics were needed only for the spark.

But European revolutions were promoted not just because conditions seemed ripe. The Soviet leaders thought revolution in at least one major European country absolutely necessary if the Soviet state were to survive. Two primary goals of Soviet foreign policy consequently became evident from the beginning of the Soviet state; and, for Lenin and his followers, these goals would always be complementary. The search for national security (the "national interest") went hand in hand with the promotion of world communism. The achievement of more communist revolutions would strengthen Soviet security, while preservation of the "base" (Russia) was necessary for further revolutionary success.

Some of the offensive tactics have been indicated. The first act of the Soviet government in November 1917—the Peace Decree—was a barely disguised call for world revolution, and this Decree set the tone of Soviet propaganda for the first period of Soviet foreign policy. Propaganda was cheap and potentially the most effective weapon available to the Soviets to promote world revolution. Their backs were against the wall militarily, except for temporary victories as in the war with Poland. Little money was available to finance foreign adventures—although the Soviet government publicly announced on December 24, 1917, an appropriation of two million rubles "for aid to the left internationalist wing of the labor movement of all countries."

To expedite propaganda dissemination, Trotsky created a "Press Bureau" and a "Bureau for International Revolutionary Propaganda" in the Commissariat of Foreign Affairs. Ingenious, if sometimes naïve, gimmicks were used to propagate the revolutionary message. Copies of the Peace Decree were dropped behind German lines by Soviet aircraft; a special newspaper in German, *Die Fackel* (The Torch), was printed daily in half a million copies for distribution to the German trenches. Karl Radek, head of the Press Bureau, accompanied Trotsky to Brest-Litovsk in January 1918. As the train pulled into the station, Radek calmly started throwing propaganda pamphlets from the train window to German troops on the platform. "Letters" were sent to workers in other countries: an appeal on August 1, 1918 to the "laboring masses of France, England, America, Italy and Japan" which ended with the ringing exhortation "Down with the gangsters of international imperialism"; a special "open letter" a few weeks later from Lenin to the "American workers," published in Pravda, in which the American millionaires, "those modern slave-owners," were indicted for consenting "to the armed campaign of the Anglo-Japanese beasts for the purpose of crushing the first Soviet republic"; a constant stream of pamphlets in English and French to Allied troops of the interventionist forces, pleading "Be loyal to your class and refuse to do the dirty work of your masters. . . . Go home and establish industrial republics in your own countries, and together we shall form a world-wide cooperative commonwealth." [20]

Letters and pamphlets, however, were not enough. An international organization was needed to plan and lead the revolution in each country when the time came. This was to be the Third International, later called the Communist International—more popularly the Comintern. It would replace the Second International, the prewar worldwide association of socialist parties.

The parties in the Second International had split at the beginning of World War I over whether to support the war efforts of their respective governments. To Lenin's disgust, the moderate socialists prevailed, backing nationalist aims in 1914 rather than international revolution. At the end of the war, the moderate leaders called for a new meeting of the Second International to be held February 1919. Lenin could not permit this "opportunist" organization to again capture the proletariat. The cause of revolution would be delayed indefinitely. Speaking three years later, Zinoviev, the head of the Comintern, clearly revealed Soviet motives: "We were splitters when the Comintern began its work. At that time we could not act otherwise. We had to split the old socialist parties, rescue the best revolutionary elements of the working class, form a rallying

20 Quoted in E. H. Carr, *The Bolshevik Revolution 1917-1923* (New York: The Macmillan Company, 1953), III, 89-90.

point for communist parties in every country. . . . The split was historically necessary; it was a great step forward, a means of winning the masses."[21] Lenin preferred a smaller group under his control, not a larger organization with a will of its own.

The First Congress Unfortunately, Moscow was neither an auspicious place nor was the time favorable in early 1919 for a Soviet-sponsored international conference. The Soviets were cut off from the outside world by the intervention. They knew the conference could not possibly be representative. But some kind of meeting had to be held to offset the scheduled conference of the Second International. Lenin therefore invited "all parties opposed to the Second International" to attend a congress in Moscow to create a Third International. Although the invitation was in the name of the Central Committee of the Soviet Communist Party, Chicherin, the Commissar of Foreign Affairs broadcast the text from Moscow. (The Soviets later denied any formal connection between the Soviet government or its leaders and the Comintern.)

Because the delegates had difficulty in getting to Russia, the conference did not meet until March 1919. George Kennan called it "a rather pathetic affair."[22] There were 35 official representatives, and of these, only five had arrived from abroad specifically for the meeting. Most of the delegates were from the Soviet Communist Party, or had been hand-picked by the Soviets from communist parties in areas bordering Russia, from prisoners of war, or from foreign radicals who happened to be in Moscow. The key foreign delegate at the conference was from Germany, then considered "the classical land of the impending proletarian revolution."[23] The strongest industrial nation in Europe was suffering the terrible pangs of defeat. A revolutionary working class waited to take power. Soviet hopes for European revolution therefore centered on Germany. And Soviet relations with the German communists would form a test case for Soviet policy toward the Comintern.

The German Communist Party, formed only in December 1918, had descended from a radical left group, the Spartacus League. This group had been a very small faction of a large vocal minority, the "Independent Socialists," which had split off from the German Social-Democratic Party. In January 1919, Karl Liebknecht and Rosa Luxemburg, the two brilliant, dedicated revolutionaries heading the new Communist Party, had been arrested and murdered while leading an ill-conceived and premature re-

---

[21] Jane Degras, ed., *The Communist International, 1919-1943* (London: Oxford University Press, 1956), I, 7.

[22] *Russia and the West*, p. 159.

[23] Franz Borkenau, *World Communism* (Ann Arbor: The University of Michigan Press, 1962), p. 34.

volt in Berlin. By the time of the March conference in Moscow, communist leadership in Germany was in a sorry state.

Only a few days before her death, Rosa Luxemburg had instructed the two German delegates designated for the Moscow conference to oppose the formation of a new International. (Only one delegate eventually reached Russia.) The German communists were sure an International founded in Moscow would be a creature of the Bolsheviks, and wanted to forestall the formation of a new organization until greater support was available from other European parties. Above all, Luxemburg disagreed with Lenin's dictatorial methods of dealing with other communists and members of the working class in general. The new German Communist Party, she insisted in December 1918, would "never take power except by the clear and unambiguous will of the great majority of the proletarian masses." [24]

Lenin, of course, was fundamentally opposed to the party *following* the masses in one country or in the world. A tightly knit international revolutionary command had to be created immediately. The only successful proletarian revolution, the Russian, surely was proof enough of the absolute necessity for a disciplined, centrally directed organization.

At the March conference, Hugo Eberlein, the lone German delegate (traveling under the pseudonym "Albert"), courageously stuck to his instructions to oppose the premature formation of a new International. But the pressure on poor Eberlein became so intense that he abstained, rather than mar conference "unanimity," on the critical vote declaring the first "Congress" of the Communist International to be in session.

This act in itself was the most significant accomplishment of the first conference. The world socialist movement had been split. The rest was an oratorical epilogue. In his main speech, Lenin defended the proletarian dictatorship and castigated bourgeois democracy, a direct slap at the "yellow socialist" supporters of the bourgeoisie who had met in February 1919 at a conference of the Second International.

In theory, all communist parties were to be equal "sections" of the Comintern—a worldwide proletarian party. The "interests of the movement in each country," read the invitation to the conference, were to be subordinated to "the common interest of the international revolution." In practice, the Soviets would dominate, and their dominance began at the First Congress. This was partly circumstantial for reasons mentioned— the difficulty of getting to Moscow, and the resulting meager representation from abroad. The Soviets actually seemed sincere in the hope that circumstances soon would be different. They apparently believed Moscow

[24] Quoted by Richard Lowenthal, "The Bolshevisation of the Spartacus League," in *St. Antony's Papers—Number 9, International Communism*, David Footman, ed. (Carbondale, Ill.: Southern Illinois University Press, 1960), p. 27.

would be the *temporary* headquarters of the Comintern. As soon as the revolution triumphed in the West, Trotsky proclaimed, the headquarters would be moved to Berlin, Paris or London.

But as long as the main support of the Comintern necessarily came from the Soviet state, the concerns of the leaders of that state would tend to determine Comintern policy, not the desires of the leaders of weak or embryonic communist parties of other countries. Lenin's concern in 1919 was the preservation of the Soviet state. One of the acts of the first Congress thus was an appeal to the "working masses" of all countries, proclaiming it their duty to use all available means, including revolution, to pressure their governments to stop the intervention, recognize the Soviet government, and establish diplomatic and trade relations with the new regime.

The leadership selected for the Comintern also reflected Soviet control, and indicated that Comintern activity was to be of second importance in the eyes of the Soviets. Two Bolsheviks, Zinoviev and Radek (by birth a Polish Jew), were appointed President and Secretary, respectively, of the Executive Committee of the Comintern (the ECCI). The relatively low priority of Comintern activity was evident, Franz Borkenau suggested, because the Soviets had picked these particular men. Neither had been deemed capable of holding major posts in the Soviet government.[25] (On the other hand, Lenin did consider Radek his number one adviser on German affairs, and Germany was the focal point of Comintern interest.) [26]

The crucial move to secure Soviet control of the Comintern would come at its Second Congress in the summer of 1920. Meanwhile, all of central Europe, hungry and living in chaos, seemed ripe for communism. A Soviet republic emerged in Hungary a few days after the First Congress of the Comintern. The revolution, however, was hardly a communist victory. Bela Kun, the regime's communist leader, was languishing in a Hungarian prison when called to head a coalition government composed of the Hungarian Communist Party and moderate socialists. The former government of this defeated nation had decided to resign rather than capitulate to further territorial demands from the Allies on behalf of Czechoslovakia and Rumania.

In spite of less than complete control, the Hungarian communists managed to initiate many changes based on the Soviet model, including nationalization of the larger industries and the bigger estates. Yet Kun's regime collapsed after four months, the victim of hostile neighbors and internal opposition. Lenin attempted to give military support to the Hun-

---

[25] *World Communism*, p. 165.
[26] Louis Fischer, *The Life of Lenin* (New York: Harper and Row, Publishers, 1964), p. 316.

garian communists when Bela Kun pleaded for help. But the Soviet relief force, which had to cross Rumania, was diverted to meet new threats from the Russian White armies.

A much less successful experiment was the Bavarian Soviet Republic, formed in April 1919. This "Soviet" regime, which lasted less than a month, was hardly a model of communist purity. The two leaders of the revolt had been members of the Social-Revolutionary Party in Russia. Their support came from local anarchists and pacifists.

In other parts of Germany, scattered rebellions occurred in working class areas. But the German Communist Party, still representing a small minority of the German proletariat, was far from controlling or even inspiring revolution in its country. The party leaders in fact lagged behind when rank and file communists joined with other working class groups to put down the "Kapp Putsch" in March 1920, an attempt by reactionary German nationalists to seize the capital.

All revolutionists of leftist tendencies in Germany, Hungary, Austria and elsewhere were inspired by the Russian success. Yet this was the extent of Soviet involvement. In retrospect, Moscow did not seem directly responsible for any of the revolutions outside Russia. But the mere naming of foreign regimes "soviet," and local parties "communist," apparently was sufficient proof for the West of Soviet Russian control. This belief in turn fed Western fears of Soviet "bolshevism."

The Second Congress   The Second Congress of the Comintern opened in Petrograd in July 1920. Although the European revolution had not come about, the Soviet offensive to "liberate" the Polish proletariat opened up entirely new vistas of the millennium. Zinoviev recalled how a great map in the congress hall of the Comintern marked the progress of the Red Army's advance: "The best representatives of the international proletariat" stood before the map every morning and "with breathless interest, with palpitating heart, followed every advance of our armies, and all perfectly realized that, if the military aim set by our army was achieved, it would mean an immense acceleration of the international proletarian revolution." [27] A few weeks later, Zinoviev commented: "I am deeply convinced that the Second World Congress of the CI [Comintern] is the precursor of another world congress, the World Congress of Soviet Republics." [28]

The "best representatives" at the Second Congress were a far different lot than had met a year earlier. Over 200 delegates came from 41 countries. One hundred and thirty-six represented communist parties. These delegates were joined by a motley group of radical labor leaders; British

[27] Quoted by Carr, *The Bolshevik Revolution 1917-1923*, III, 188.
[28] Quoted in *The Communist International, 1919-1943*, ed. by Jane Degras, I, 109.

suffragists turned revolutionists; John Reed, an American eyewitness of the Russian Revolution, pleading for that "oppressed nationality," the American Negro; and, significantly, a scattering of delegates from Asia and the Far East.

Overshadowing all others at the Congress was the monolithic Soviet delegation (other delegations represented diverse strains of thought), and the Soviet controlled group of "foreign" communists living in Moscow. Soviet dominance was accentuated by the enormous prestige the Russians had gained from leading the first successful revolution. An Italian delegate remarked: "What am I compared with comrade Lenin? He is the leader of the Russian Revolution. I represent a tiny communist socialist party." [29]

Two critical issues were debated and resolved. First, the Congress accepted with only two dissenting votes "twenty-one conditions" (19 drafted by Lenin) for admission of a party to the Comintern. The first year of its existence, Zinoviev admitted, the Comintern had been a "propaganda association." It now had to become "a fighting organ of the international proletariat." Fighting demanded centralized organization, iron discipline, and one party line for all "sections" of the Comintern. The obvious model was the Bolshevik party. To a plea by the British delegate for toleration of minor differences in tactics, Lenin retorted there would be no need for an International if such differences were permitted. All parties had to abide by condition 16, which made binding the decisions of the Comintern congresses and the ECCI. Any party member who would not accept the 21 conditions had to be expelled, as well as all "petty-bourgeois elements."

The split of the international working class movement brought about by the First Congress was now permanent. Rigid control from the center was formally instituted. This would be Soviet control. Only new "soviet" states arising from the ashes of Europe could counter the Russian dominance of the Comintern. But such revolutions would fail.

The second critical issue, of greater significance for our times, was the correct communist policy toward the "backward" peoples of the great colonial empires—the area today known as "underdeveloped." The policy finally adopted brought no radical change in doctrine. But new emphasis was placed on the contribution of the colonial peoples to the world revolution. Lenin analyzed the "national and colonial question" for the Congress: (1) The world had been divided into oppressor (imperialist) and oppressed (all other) nations. (2) In the "present world situation" the decisive struggle was between the imperialist states and new Soviet state. Communist parties in both "civilized" and "backward" countries had to

[29] Quoted by Carr, *The Bolshevik Revolution 1917-1923*, III, 199.

start with this fact in formulating their strategy and tactics. For their part, the Soviets were "increasingly representing and really defending" the 70 per cent of the world's population made up of "working" and "exploited" peoples. (3) "World imperialism must fall when the revolutionary onslaught of the exploited and oppressed workers in each country . . . merges with the revolutionary onslaught of hundreds of millions of people [in the colonial empires]. . . ." The Western proletariat and the colonial masses were natural allies. (4) There was, of course, little possibility of true proletarian revolutions in the backward countries (although these countries, with the aid of the proletariat of the advanced countries, could skip the capitalist stage of development). Local communists therefore had to form *temporary* alliances ("national revolutionary movements") with "revolutionary" members of the local bourgeoisie and peasantry. Class origin was unimportant. Was the man anti-British, anti-French? [30]

Why the new interest in the "East"? At this very moment, hopes for revolution in Europe were at their zenith. At the same time, the Soviet regime was harassed by internal and external enemies. Secondly, Europe was still only "pregnant" with revolution. Why not use *all* available forces to bring down imperialism? Bukharin had argued in March 1919, that the Soviets should champion self-determination everywhere in the colonies. Nothing would be lost: "The most outright nationalist movement . . . is only water for our mill, since it contributes to the destruction of English imperialism." [31] The "backward" peoples were to be the auxiliary troops—the reserves of the Western proletariat, and of the Soviet regime. [32]

The supreme optimism of the Second Congress was short-lived. The Red Army's push through Poland collapsed. The German Communist Party again attempted revolution in March 1921, and again the result was disaster. At the Third Congress of the Comintern in July 1921, a chastened

---

[30] M. N. Roy, the Indian delegate, argued for a different emphasis at the Congress: the main thrust of communist activity in the colonial area should be to create "communist" organizations of workers and peasants—not to force the liberation movement "within the narrow frame of bourgeois-democratic nationalism." For a summary of the debate see Carr, *The Bolshevik Revolution, 1917-1923*, III, 251-59. Lenin's view of the proper role of the peasantry in the underdeveloped area is still argued. See the exchange between Karl A. Wittfogel (The Legend of "Maoism") and Benjamin Schwartz (The Legend of the "Legend of 'Maoism'") in *The China Quarterly*, Nos. 1 and 2 (January-March 1960 and April-June 1960), pp. 72-86, and pp. 16-42.

[31] Quoted in Carr, *The Bolshevik Revolution, 1917-1923*, III, 236.

[32] Two special "congresses" later were held for the "auxiliary" forces: the Baku Congress in September 1920—the "first congress of the peoples of the east," with 1,891 delegates mainly from Soviet Central Asia and the Middle East; the Moscow "Congress of the Toilers of the Far East" in January 1922—a much smaller group with foreign representatives mainly from Korea, China, and Japan. At Baku, Zinoviev had cried: "Brothers, we summon you to a holy war, in the first place against English imperialism." Brandishing swords, daggers, and revolvers, Congress members rose from their seats and shouted: "We swear it."

Lenin admitted to the delegates that the international revolution had not "advanced in a straight line as much as we had expected." Instead there was "a certain equilibrium" between the international bourgeoisie and Soviet Russia. This equilibrium signaled the end of the first period of Soviet foreign policy.

SUMMARY

The first period in Soviet foreign policy, from the November Revolution of 1917 to roughly the end of 1920, saw the zenith of Soviet hope for world revolution, and the nadir of Soviet strength. The Soviet grand design for the extension of communism throughout the imperialist world never again would seem so sure of success, nor the Soviet ship of state so close to sinking. In the future, the Soviets would mute the call for world revolution. The pursuit of the national interest or the interests of the elite would often seem paramount.

But even in this first period, all three primary determinants of Soviet policy were evident. World revolution dictated by the ideology was important. But the national interest had to be served and the power of the elite preserved. The peace of Brest-Litovsk was designed to save both the regime and the new socialist fatherland. Some "left" communists wanted revolutionary war, but the healthy, lusty child of Russia needed first attention, not a Germany only pregnant with revolution.

On the other hand, revolution had to be pressed where revolutionary opportunities existed. In spite of extreme national weakness, the Soviets felt obligated to aid the world proletariat if conditions beckoned. But always paramount for a "sensible" Soviet communist would be the preservation of the revolutionary base—the Soviet state. Such a base was necessary if communism were to triumph in other countries. The Comintern would see that "good" communists everywhere shared this view.

FURTHER READING

Since this chapter begins Part Two of the book, the first section of the bibliography below lists general sources for the study of the history of Soviet foreign policy. This section should be consulted for appropriate readings after finishing subsequent chapters in Part Two.

Adams, Arthur E., ed., *Readings in Soviet Foreign Policy*. Boston: D. C. Heath & Company, 1961. Selections from Soviet documents and commentaries by Western experts keyed to periods in Soviet foreign policy from 1917 to 1960.

Bailey, Thomas A., *America Faces Russia: Russian-American Relations from Early Times to Our Day*. Ithaca, N.Y.: Cornell University Press, 1950. Diplomatic relations emphasizing American point of view.

Bishop, Donald G., ed., *Soviet Foreign Relations; Documents and Readings.* Syracuse, N.Y.: Syracuse University Press, 1952. Translations of documents on selected aspects of Soviet foreign policy.

Borkenau, Franz, *World Communism: A History of the Communist International.* Ann Arbor, Mich.: University of Michigan Press, 1962. Vivid, impressionistic account by old Comintern hand of the organization from early days until the mid-1930's. Still the best treatment.

Carr, E. H., *The Bolshevik Revolution, 1917-1923.* 3 vols. New York: The Macmillan Company, 1950-1953. Part of a monumental *History of Russia.* Later series are *The Interregnum 1923-1924,* and *Socialism in One Country, 1924-1926.* Valuable, detailed analyses of early periods in Soviet foreign policy. See particularly Vols. 3, 4, and 7.

Degras, Jane, ed., *The Communist International, 1919-1943: Documents.* 2 vols. London: Oxford University Press, 1956-1960. Published for the Royal Institute of International Affairs. The best collection.

Degras, Jane, ed., *Soviet Documents on Foreign Policy.* 3 vols. covering period 1917-1941. London: Oxford University Press, 1951-1953. Published for the Royal Institute of International Affairs. The most valuable collection for this period.

Drachkovitch, Milorad M. and Branko Lazitch, *Highlights of the Comintern: Essays, Recollections, Documents.* New York: Frederick A. Praeger, Inc., 1966. Excerpts from unpublished memoirs of former Comintern leaders together with eight original essays by Western specialists.

Fischer, Louis, *The Soviets in World Affairs.* 2 vols. Princeton, N.J.: Princeton University Press, 1951. Covers period 1917-1929. Invaluable for his first-hand knowledge of thinking of early Soviet leaders.

Garthoff, Raymond L., *Soviet Military Policy: An Historical Analysis.* New York: Frederick A. Praeger, Inc., 1966. Collection of articles, many dealing with Soviet use of force in foreign policy.

History of the Communist Party of the Soviet Union (Bolsheviks); Short Course. New York: International Publishers, 1939. Official Stalinist history, essential for main lines of Soviet foreign policy through 1937.

Jelavich, Barbara, *A Century of Russian Foreign Policy, 1814-1914.* Philadelphia, Pa. and New York: J. B. Lippincott Co., 1964. Convenient historical survey.

Kennan, George F., *Russia and the West under Lenin and Stalin.* Boston: Atlantic-Little, Brown and Company, 1961. Provocative personal interpretation of the 1917-1945 period with emphasis on the early years.

Kennan, George F., *Soviet Foreign Policy, 1917-1941.* Princeton, N.J.: D. Van Nostrand Co., Inc., 1960. Concise summary of period indicated with excerpts from documents.

Librach, Jan, *The Rise of the Soviet Empire.* New York: Frederick A. Praeger, Inc., 1964. Emphasis on Soviet relations with Eastern Europe.

Meyer, Alfred G., *Communism.* New York: Random House, Inc., 1967. 3rd ed. Short introduction to world communism.

Mosely, Philip E., *The Kremlin and World Politics, Studies in Soviet Policy and Action*. New York: Random House, Inc., 1960. Articles by an American specialist in Soviet affairs covering more than a 20-year period.

Mosely, Philip E., ed., *The Soviet Union, 1922-1962: A Foreign Affairs Reader*. New York: Frederick A. Praeger, Inc., 1963. Thirty selections from *Foreign Affairs* on Soviet foreign policy, internal politics, etc.

Ponomaryov, B. N. *et al.*, *History of the Communist Party of the Soviet Union*. Moscow: Foreign Languages Publishing House, 1960. Official view at time of publishing of Soviet foreign and domestic policy since 1917.

Rubinstein, Alvin Z., *The Foreign Policy of the Soviet Union*. New York: Random House, Inc., 1966. 2nd ed. A collection of readings with introductory essays to each section.

Senn, Alfred Erich, ed., *Readings in Russian Political and Diplomatic History, Vol. II, The Soviet Period*. Homewood, Ill.: Richard D. Irwin, Inc., 1966. Useful collection in paperback with emphasis on pre-World War II period.

Seton-Watson, Hugh, *The Decline of Imperial Russia, 1855-1914*. New York: Frederick A. Praeger, Inc., 1964. Foreign relations and general trends in this period.

Seton-Watson, Hugh, *From Lenin to Khrushchev: The History of World Communism*. New York: Frederick A. Praeger, Inc., 1960. Standard survey of various communist movements.

Slusser, Robert M. and Jan F. Triska, eds., *A Calendar of Soviet Treaties, 1917-1957*. Stanford, Calif.: Stanford University Press, 1959. Chronological listing of Soviet international agreements. Brief summaries of important agreements since 1940.

Ulam, Adam B., *Expansion & Coexistence: The History of Soviet Foreign Policy 1917-1967*. New York: Frederick A. Praeger, Inc., 1968. Historical survey based on primary sources.

Warth, Robert D., *Soviet Russia in World Politics*. New York: Twayne Publishers, Inc., 1963. One-volume diplomatic history from 1917 to 1961.

The second section lists those sources useful for this chapter.

Chamberlin, William H., *The Russian Revolution, 1917-1921*. New York: The Macmillan Company, 1954. Readable, objective coverage of internal and external developments.

Fischer, Louis, *The Life of Lenin*. New York: Harper & Row, Publishers, 1964. A classic, if somewhat disorganized, study of Lenin.

Gruber, Helmut, ed., *International Communism in the Era of Lenin, A Documentary History*. New York: Fawcett World Library: Crest, Gold Medal & Premier Books, 1967. Hard-to-find articles, statements, manifestos, etc. by leaders of various communist movements during this period.

Hulse, James W., *The Forming of the Communist International*. Stanford, Calif.: Stanford University Press, 1964. Study of First and Second Congresses and intervening period.

Kennan, George F., *Russia Leaves the War*, and *The Decision to Intervene*. Princeton, N.J.: Princeton University Press, 1956, 1958. U. S. relations in particular and Allied relations in general with the Soviets from 1917-1920.

Korbel, Josef, *Poland Between East and West: Soviet and German Diplomacy toward Poland, 1919-1933*. Princeton, N.J.: Princeton University Press, 1963.

Morley, James W., *The Japanese Thrust into Siberia, 1918*. New York: Columbia University Press, 1957.

Page, Stanley W., *The Formation of the Baltic States: A Study of the Effects of Great Power Politics upon the Emergence of Lithuania, Latvia, and Estonia*. Cambridge, Mass.: Harvard University Press, 1959.

Pipes, Richard, *The Formation of the Soviet Union: Communism and Nationalism, 1917-1923*. Cambridge, Mass.: Harvard University Press, 1964. 2nd ed. Standard work on the separatist movements.

Sukhanov, N. N., *The Russian Revolution*. New York: Oxford University Press, 1955. Excellent account by eye witness.

Ullman, Richard H., *Anglo-Soviet Relations, 1917-1921*. Princeton, N.J.: Princeton University Press, 1961.

Unterberger, Betty, *America's Siberian Expedition, 1918-1920*. Durham, N.C.: Duke University Press, 1956. Deals mainly with diplomatic aspects of American intervention.

Warth, Robert D., *The Allies and the Russian Revolution: From the Fall of the Monarchy to the Peace of Brest-Litovsk*. Durham, N.C.: Duke University Press, 1954. Best one-volume treatment.

Wheeler-Bennett, John W., *Brest-Litovsk: The Forgotten Peace, March 1918*. London: Macmillan & Co. Ltd., 1963. A classic work on the events leading to Brest-Litovsk and the negotiations.

White, John A., *The Siberian Intervention*. Princeton, N.J.: Princeton University Press, 1950. Important for impact of intervention on civil war in Siberia.

Zeman, Z. A. B., ed., *Germany and the Russian Revolution, 1915-1918: Documents from the Archives of the German Foreign Ministry*. New York: Oxford University Press, 1958. Important collection; especially interesting references to German financial aid to Bolsheviks.

5

THE CONSOLIDATION
OF
SOVIET POWER
1921-1933

RETREAT AT HOME
AND ABROAD

In 1921 the Bolshevik regime was in danger of falling; foreign intervention and civil war were past; Allied forces—except for the Japanese—had left; the White opposition was beaten. But a new, potentially critical crisis was developing within Russia. The whole economic and social fabric of the society was on the verge of collapse. The people were exhausted, disillusioned and restless. Famine and disease were rampant: the results of over six years of war and civil war, Bolshevik blunders in attempting "communism" too soon, and the poor harvest of 1920. "Communism" itself was unpopular. Party leaders exhorting factory workers were shouted down. The party, moreover, was split internally. Rank and file members were disgusted at the luxuries enjoyed by certain party officials.

The most serious threat came from the countryside, still home for the great majority of Russians. The peasants, never overly fond of the Bolsheviks, were in rebellion. The Whites only seemed worse in the guise of a reincarnation of the hated Tsarist regime. With the Whites defeated, opposition in the countryside grew over the forced requisition of all surplus food to feed the Red Army and the city dwellers.

Discontent came to a head in the Kronstadt rebellion. The sailors at Kronstadt, a naval fortress on an island near Leningrad, had been among the strongest Bolshevik backers in November 1917. In late February 1921, rumors reached the fortress that striking workers had been fired upon in Leningrad. A mass meeting of 15,000 Kronstadt sailors and workers was held on March 1. In a definitely left-wing platform, the crowd demanded a loosening of party dictatorship, honestly elected Soviets "without the Bolsheviks," freedom for political prisoners of the working class and peasant origin, and greater economic freedom for the peasantry. The Bolsheviks crushed the revolt with carefully picked loyal troops. The garrison was butchered, and the movement labeled "counterrevolutionary" and part of a "great conspiracy" organized by the White opposition.

A New Economic Policy   Kronstadt did not go unnoticed. Lenin pushed through the first measures of what was later called the "New Economic Policy" (NEP) at the March 1921 Party Congress. The critical threat to the regime from the peasantry got first priority. Lenin insisted the Bolsheviks could make the transition to socialism in a peasant-dominated country such as Russia only if (1) the Bolsheviks were supported by a socialist revolution in one or several leading capitalist countries; and (2) they had the support of the Russian peasantry. A truce with the peasants was all the more necessary because revolution in Europe was not imminent. "Only an agreement with the peasantry can save the socialist revolution in Russia," said Lenin, "until the revolution has occurred in other countries." Ryazanov, a party theoretician, argued for a "peasant Brest," alluding to the first dramatic retreat of the Bolsheviks to save the regime in 1918.

The crucial concession of the Congress substituted a tax in kind from the peasantry in place of the forced requisition, leaving them free to sell any surplus on the open market. Some "capitalism" also was to be permitted in the trades and smaller industries. But all concessions would be temporary and partial. The party would keep ultimate control of the so-called commanding heights. It would continue to monopolize political power, and keep nationalized the larger industries, transportation system and foreign trade. In spite of such assurances, many party members grumbled over NEP and other Leninist policies as unnecessary, as a return to the capitalism they had shed so much blood to destroy. In response, Lenin demanded an end to opposition within the party.

A New Foreign Policy   But more than NEP was needed to build a strong Soviet state, a country able to hold its own in world politics. The Soviets had to import Western industrial goods to restore and develop their shattered economy. This meant trade between the Soviet state and the Western capitalist states. With trade went the need for credit. The Soviets did not have enough exportable goods—in this case raw materials—to cover the needed imports.

Trade and credit would only flow freely, the Soviets believed, if the Soviet government were recognized as the legitimate government of Russia by the Western powers. Could Western capitalists be enthusiastic about extending trade offers or credit to a country with whom their governments did not even exchange ambassadors? The *de facto* war between the Allies and Soviet Russia had ended. But peaceful relations between capitalism and socialism had not been automatic. The Bolshevik leaders still were treated as international criminals. They had to become members of the capitalist-dominated international club. And the key to the club door was diplomatic recognition by club membership. Western recognition of the Bolshevik government, thought the Soviets, also would be an additional safeguard against further capitalist intervention.

The man to make Soviet Russia respectable was Georgi Chicherin, who had replaced Trotsky as Soviet "foreign minister" during the final stages of the Brest-Litovsk negotiations in 1918. Chicherin was hardly a typical revolutionary, and never a member of the party "in-group" either before or during his job as Commissar of Foreign Affairs from 1918 to 1930. A Russian aristocrat turned Menshevik, then Bolshevik during World War I, Chicherin was a passionate idealist with a continuing vision of the millennium and the rightness of the Bolshevik cause. A man above petty intraparty fighting, he worked literally night and day.

The Commissar of Foreign Affairs also was hardly a typical diplomat. He was shy, retiring, a hypochondriac, and an aesthete whose greatest pleasure was playing Mozart on the piano. (For Chicherin, Mozart was the "world in extract and the incarnation of the beauty of life.") But these "undiplomatic" qualities were offset by a brilliant mind, a scholar's attention to detail, and an almost total recall of conversations and events which had occurred years before—qualities found in few, if any, bourgeois statesmen of the period. Chicherin's idealism, on the other hand, was coupled with a sensitive feel for Russia's traditional national interests, and he appreciated the need to protect these interests through traditional power politics at the nation-state level. Earlier, he had been a scholar in the Tsarist foreign office, studying Russian foreign policy from the Crimean War to the Congress of Berlin. His father and his grandfather had been Tsarist diplomats.

The Soviets could not have found a better man to handle formal relations with the capitalist world. But unfortunately for Chicherin, the Bolshevik leaders gave the Commissariat of Foreign Affairs responsibility for only part of the Soviet activity abroad. Chicherin never was in control of all Soviet foreign policy, even though formal diplomatic methods generally prevailed in achieving Soviet goals during the 1920's. The fundamental direction of Soviet foreign policy remained with the party leaders, first with Lenin and later Stalin. The leaders used formal Soviet diplomacy (Chicherin's domain), Comintern action, or both, depending on the promise of a particular technique at a given moment. And Comintern tactics continually threatened attempts of the Soviet foreign office to woo capitalist nations. The Comintern was openly dedicated to their destruction. Chicherin protested vehemently at Western insinuations that the Comintern might also be an instrument of Soviet foreign policy. But he was not always believed. Chicherin, on the other hand, could not avoid propagandistic overtones in his own speeches and writings. This was true even in formal confrontations with Western diplomats. (Note, for example, his opening speech at the Genoa Conference described later in this chapter.)

"PEACEFUL COEXISTENCE"— A NEW THEORY OF INTERNATIONAL RELATIONS

Communist theory had to change if the Soviet state were to exist for some time as a lone, socialist country in a hostile capitalist world. Since 1917 the Soviets had paid little attention to this possibility. Capitalism and communism were locked in a death struggle, and one or the other soon would win. At the height of the intervention in March 1919, Lenin told the Eighth Party Congress of the Russian Communist Party in an oft-quoted statement: "We are living not merely in a state, but in a system of states; and it is inconceivable that the Soviet republic should continue to exist for a long period side by side with imperialist states. Ultimately one or the other must conquer. Until this end occurs a number of terrible clashes between the Soviet republic and bourgeois states is inevitable." Lenin seemed to see continual wars between capitalism and the Soviet state, ending in a rather early victory for one side.

However, Lenin was a practical man, always attuned to international developments. Changing forces in international politics required a change in theory. Lenin began to see, much earlier than his colleagues, that the revolutionary wave in Europe was receding. And Lenin began to suggest that Soviet Russia might continue to exist *without* revolutions in other countries. Speaking on November 21, 1920, to a group of Moscow party functionaries, Lenin admitted asserting in 1917 that the October Revolution could not be a "firm" victory without revolution in the West, and that none of the Bolsheviks expected the "unequal struggle" between

Russia and the capitalists to last as long as three years. (Lenin here implies that the Allies did their best to sink the new regime.) But the struggle had lasted that long, and had ended in a draw. The capitalists had not destroyed the Bolshevik regime, but neither had the Bolsheviks brought down the capitalist edifice. In the meantime, there was "a little respite."

How long would the respite last? This could not be predicted. It was, according to Lenin, a "most unstable equilibrium." Lenin warned his comrades on December 21, 1920: "We do not for a second believe that this will be but a temporary interruption. The experience of the history of the revolutions, of large-scale conflicts, teaches us that wars, a series of wars, are inevitable. . . . The existence of the Soviet republic, . . . surrounded by capitalist states—is so inadmissible from the capitalist viewpoint that all these countries will seize the first opportunity to resume the war."

How would the new Soviet state protect itself from the ever-present threat of a capitalist attack? Previously, revolution in Europe was held absolutely essential for the security of Russia. But in July 1921, Lenin assured the group of European delegates to the Third Congress of the Comintern: "We in Russia can hold out not only five years but longer." European revolution was desirable, but not necessary for the continued existence of the Soviet state.

Soviet Russia's safety would depend on other factors. As long as the capitalist world was economically and militarily stronger than Russia (and Lenin acknowledged capitalism was a "hundred times" stronger) the Soviets had to exploit the contradictions *within* the capitalist world. The capitalists had to be kept occupied in struggling with each other, instead of with Russia. In the early 1920's, the Soviets saw several fundamental contradictions within the capitalist world. The basic contradiction described by Marx—the conflict between the bourgeoisie and the proletariat in each capitalist country—naturally was important. But recent events in Western Europe indicated the time was not ripe for revolution. In any case, this was the realm of the Comintern and not an "official" goal of Soviet foreign policy.

More important were other contradictions, and these would be exploited by Soviet diplomacy. There were (1) the continuing struggle among the capitalist powers to see who would reign supreme; the contest was now among the victors in World War I, specifically between the United States, at that time the richest nation, and Great Britain; and subsidiary struggles between the United States and Japan, France and Britain, etc.; (2) the contest among the victors and the vanquished, specifically between the Allies and Germany, potentially powerful in spite of defeat and needing an ally to fight the "injustices" of the Versailles

Treaty. (Lenin suggested in December 1920, that Russia might be this ally.); and (3) the growing conflict between the capitalist powers and their colonies and "semi-colonies" (countries controlled by the capitalists although not formally part of the mother country's empire). Lenin acknowledged the people in these countries, which comprised the "vast majority" of the world's population, were primarily interested in national liberation. But he prophesied that they would "turn against capitalism and imperialism, and will perhaps play a much greater revolutionary role than we expect." The Comintern, of course, would be active in the colonial areas. But the Soviet state itself would aid weak but independent Asian states in their struggle against the imperialist West. (Comintern activity in Europe and Asia will be discussed later in this chapter.)

While world imperialism was being split internally, the Soviets would build the economic and military strength of Russia—with the aid of the capitalist nations. Acquiring this aid would be the second major objective of Soviet foreign policy. But how could the Soviets aggravate antagonisms in the West and simultaneously strengthen Russia with the aid of Western capitalism? The answer would be to encourage capitalist competition to supply the manifold needs of the Soviet economy. Obviously the West would be "digging its own grave" by aiding Soviet Russia, the sworn enemy of all capitalism. But capitalist greed—the compulsive search for profits—would override second thoughts about future dangers. Capitalism needed Soviet trade, or so the Soviet party leaders thought.

Soviet diplomacy had a third objective, also designed to increase the security of the Soviet state. Any future intervention logically would come through countries bordering Russia. If these states could somehow be "neutralized," their use as staging bases by Western capitalism would be hindered. The obvious tactics, costing the Soviets little, would be treaties with the neighbors of Russia embodying three major principles: nonintervention, nonaggression, and neutrality.

Such were to be the tactics of Soviet foreign policy during the temporary "breathing space" in the conflict between the two systems of socialism and capitalism. And this breathing space would come to be known as a period of "peaceful coexistence." Whether Lenin first used the term is still debated. But the essence of the concept was Lenin's. Two irreconcilable systems—the capitalist and the socialist—had decided upon a temporary truce. The two systems, though fundamentally hostile, could trade with each other, could exchange ambassadors and follow diplomatic niceties. But relations could never become normal; peace never permanent. "Peaceful coexistence" for the Soviets was merely a new form of struggle. Because the tactics associated with peaceful coexistence were tactics of retreat, the concept was generally considered defensive in nature. But the concept definitely had offensive connotations. Retreats were only temporary, a means of preparing for the offense when conditions permitted.

The Soviets were not forsaking their aspirations for world revolution by politicking with international capitalism. Communism was unpopular in Russia, but it also was unpopular in Europe. An ebb period had begun in the revolutionary tide. Retreat and retrenchment were required to prepare for the next revolutionary wave. Communist parties everywhere, particularly the Russian Communist Party with its preeminent responsibility for the security of the revolutionary base, had to use defensive tactics. (If revolution beckoned in some sector of the globe, tactics naturally would be altered immediately.) "Peaceful coexistence" was the only answer in the face of internal and external reverses.

TRADE, CREDITS, AND RECOGNITION

The Soviets had theorized about something called "peaceful coexistence." But there were practical problems in its application. Russia faced great difficulties in acquiring trade, credits, and recognition —the expected fruits of "peaceful coexistence"—from the capitalist countries. The breakthroughs made in the capitalist wall during the next few years were minor punctures at best. The wall never collapsed and many of the holes were resealed.

Trade itself was not too difficult to arrange. Russia traditionally had supplied raw materials (timber, grain, flax, oil) to Europe, particularly to Germany and England, and had been a valued market for European manufactured goods. In the early 1920's, Europe was suffering from overproduction and resulting unemployment. Governments were pressured by manufacturers and workers to authorize trading with Russia.

The first tentative feelers from the West for trade appeared before the formal introduction of NEP and peaceful coexistence. And Western feelers met eager Soviet responses. As would happen repeatedly in Soviet foreign policy, the leaders were ready to experiment with new policies before their formal introduction or incorporation into the ideology.

Britain took the lead. Lloyd-George, the British Prime Minister, had been instrumental in lifting the Allied blockade of Russia in January 1920. But the Allied Supreme Council permitted trading only with Russian cooperative organizations, pre-war bodies now under Soviet control. The Allies thus could claim they had nothing to do with the Bolshevik government, a subterfuge the Soviets considered a huge joke.

In February 1920, the Soviets signed a treaty of peace with little Estonia, formerly an appendage of Tsarist Russia. Tallinn, the capital of Estonia, was a valuable, neutral port for trade destined for Russia. Lenin said "a window on Europe" had been opened. Chicherin, the Soviet foreign minister, called the treaty itself a "dress rehearsal" for future agreements with other powers, the "first experiment in peaceful coexistence with bourgeois states." All Soviet trade with the West for the next four months went through Estonia.

The Anglo-Soviet Trade Agreement   Later in the spring, British and Soviet representatives—the Soviet delegation ostensibly speaking for the Russian cooperatives—began talks on a trade agreement. Negotiations subsequently were hampered by the Soviet-Polish war in the summer of 1920. Lloyd-George wanted trade, but he did not want a Bolshevik Poland on the border of Germany. British trade unionists, on the other hand, were staunchly pro-Soviet. Dockers refused to load munitions bound for Poland. Labor leaders threatened the Prime Minister with "direct action" if Britain went to war on Poland's behalf.

Talks resumed in November 1920 after the end of the Soviet-Polish war. The Soviet delegation had not been idle during the fall. Krassin, the head of the delegation and the only leading Bolshevik formerly active in big business, dangled projected Soviet orders in front of British capitalists for the maintenance of Russian locomotives, the purchase of autos, textiles, and other goods. Krassin realized the support of at least some sectors of British industry for trade relations was especially important because most of the Conservatives considered the Bolsheviks an anathema. They obviously were against all the values Conservatives held dear —private enterprise, religion, tradition, thrift. Moreover, there were rumors that the communists had nationalized women.

Krassin's subtle enticements, together with cries in Parliament that the government had better move quickly or other countries would "pinch" the Russian trade, spurred negotiations. The Anglo-Soviet Trade Agreement was signed in London on March 16, 1921. Krassin later wrote that a contract with the Germans for delivery of 600 locomotives to Russia probably brought the British to heel.

The Soviets did not get all they wanted in the agreement. Their political aims had been mixed with their desire to lift restrictions on trade. The Soviets hoped for *de jure* recognition—to be acknowledged as the legitimate government of Russia. This the British refused. But they did recognize the Soviets as the *de facto* government—a government which existed and which one could deal with no matter how distasteful.

The British also had political aims. They wanted Soviet propaganda, directed at the peoples of the British Empire, to cease immediately. In the agreement, the Soviet *government* promised to stop stirring up "the peoples of Asia . . . especially in India and in the Independent State of Afghanistan" against the British. Nothing was said about Comintern activity; the British apparently thought this was covered by the pledge of the Soviet government. The British in turn agreed to refrain from anti-Soviet activity in those parts of the Tsarist empire now independent.

The real significance of the Anglo-Soviet Trade Agreement was much broader than the text indicated. Chicherin called it "a turning point" in Soviet foreign policy. (NEP, introduced a few days earlier, was a turning point in domestic policy.) Britain was still the hub of the imperialist system—although the United States was coming up fast. Britain's decision to trade with the Soviets, Krassin later wrote, was a "signal" to the majority of European states to do likewise. And they did. By the end of 1921 the Soviets had negotiated trade agreements with Sweden, Germany, Finland, the Baltic states, Poland, Norway, Czechoslovakia, Austria and Italy. Apparently there was something to the Soviet belief that capitalist competition for markets would override capitalist fear of the Bolshevik infection.

The recalcitrants were France and the United States. France was still the sworn enemy of the Soviet Union. If any move were to be made toward the Soviets, France wanted it carefully coordinated among the Western nations. The French were thus very upset at the Anglo-Soviet Trade Agreement. The United States on the other hand questioned whether the Soviet regime—a "non-representative government"—would last, and abhorred Soviet subversion through the Comintern. Secretary of State Colby declared in 1920 that "the existing regime in Russia is based upon the negation of every principle of honor and good faith, and every usage and convention, underlying the whole structure of international law." [1]

The Debt Question and Nationalization   Perhaps the central reason France and the United States would have nothing to do with Russia was the Soviet refusal to honor the debts of the Tsarist and Provisional Governments, and the Soviet nationalization of foreign-owned property. These actions of the Bolsheviks also became major stumbling blocks for other governments where *de jure* recognition and credits to finance Soviet imports were involved.

Primarily money, but also matters of principle, were at stake. On the eve of World War I, the Tsarist government had been the biggest international debtor. During the war, the Allies extended vast amounts of additional credit to the Tsarist and then Provisional Governments. Moreover, foreign firms or investors owned a healthy share of the Russian

[1] America did not ignore the Russian people. During the disastrous famine in the summer of 1921 when 25 million were starving in the Volga Valley alone, the American Relief Administration under Herbert Hoover gave more aid to Russia than any other organization or nation.

economy. The total amount of money and property came to around 14 billion rubles—approximately 20 billion dollars if valued at present rates.[2] France held most of the pre-war debt, much in the form of Tsarist bonds in the hands of French investors. The French also had lost the largest share of private property, although Britain, Germany and Belgium also were hurt. The United States held a sizable chunk of the war debt of the Provisional Government. But regardless of the amount, all countries wanted their money. Europe had to be rebuilt; and America, by then the world's chief creditor, wanted to be repaid for her wartime loans to the Allies.

The question of principle seemed almost as important. Here was a regime run by men who had flouted a basic tenet of capitalism—the sanctity of private property. Such a regime surely could not be recognized as a *normal* member of the international community, able and willing to carry out its obligations. The Soviets might give new guarantees to protect foreign investments in Soviet Russia. But was there any indication they could be trusted? Obligations assumed by a government composed of workers and peasants, the Bolsheviks countered, were "sacred."

The Soviets also said principle was at stake. Chicherin asserted "no people is bound to pay the cost of the chains which it has worn for centuries"—referring to Russia's "exploitation" by foreign imperialists. But the Soviets were practical. Some compromise might be necessary to achieve more important Soviet foreign policy objectives. In the first months after World War I, the Soviets announced their readiness to recognize obligations to foreign creditors—if the Allies would end the intervention. Chicherin later wrote this was the first Soviet appeal to the West "in the name of economic advantages." In October 1921, Chicherin promised the Soviets would assume responsibility for the Tsarist loans before 1914—if the Allies would recognize the Soviet government and conclude a final treaty of peace with Soviet Russia. (The Anglo-Soviet Trade Agreement had been a "preliminary agreement" to the conclusion of a "formal general Peace Treaty.") The logical vehicle for reaching agreement on these matters, Chicherin suggested, would be an international conference of all interested states.

The Road to Genoa   Chicherin's proposal couldn't have been more opportune. Western financiers and industrialists, spurred on by the French, had been wondering how to squeeze reparations out of a prostrate Germany. One suggestion was an "International Corporation" for the "economic reconstruction of Europe." A major effort of the corporation would be the exploitation of Russian resources. German in-

[2] George Kennan, *Russia and the West Under Lenin and Stalin* (Boston: Atlantic-Little, Brown and Company, 1960), p. 200.

dustry would participate to help pay German reparations. Conditions thus seemed favorable to settle all of Europe's economic problems at one stroke. The Russians wanted credit and recognition; the West wanted to invest and to assume the flow of reparations from Germany. Details, of course, might prove difficult. But many in the West thought these could be handled. Weren't the Russians rapidly lapsing into capitalism with NEP?

Lloyd-George took the initiative, hoping to bring off an international triumph before the coming British general election. At a meeting of the Allied Supreme Council in Cannes on January 6, 1922, he called for a general economic and financial conference in March at Genoa, Italy. The conference would discuss measures for "the economic reconstruction of Central and Eastern Europe," including German reparations. Soviet Russia and Germany, the bad boys of Europe and the chief problems facing the conference, were invited.

If the West was optimistic about the results of such a conference, so were some Bolsheviks. Radek thought the main task of the delegates would be to determine the size of the loans to Russia, who would make them, and how they would be raised. Chicherin and Lenin, however, were wary. The Cannes meeting in January acknowledged that no nation had a right to dictate the political or economic principles on which another nation should be organized. A "Bolshevik" government had a right to exist. On the other hand, the Allies asserted, governments had to recognize all foreign debts and compensate foreign investors for nationalized property. And this was made a prerequisite for the "official recognition" of the "Russian Government." Furthermore, the Cannes meeting approved the concept of the "International Corporation."

In reply, Chicherin said the Russians would never cooperate with the capitalist nations if cooperation took "the form of economic domination." Lenin stated that the Russians would go to the Genoa Conference "as merchants, because trade with the capitalist countries (so long as they have not completely collapsed) is absolutely necessary for us." But Lenin warned against any thought of imposing conditions on Russia as if she were a conquered country.

Two further developments altered the whole nature of the forthcoming conference. First, a new government came to power in France during the final hours of the January conference at Cannes. Poincaré, the French Premier, pledged a hard line against Germany. France would refuse even to discuss German reparations at Genoa lest this ease Germany's economic problems. Prospects looked bleak for German participation in the International Corporation, and as a result, for the Corporation itself. The only item now left on the agenda was Russia.

The second development was closely related. In the months before

Genoa, Germany and Russia secretly discussed a new bilateral treaty providing for the resumption of full diplomatic relations and the cancellation of their respective claims. Increasingly afraid of a united front of capitalists at the conference armed with impossible demands on Russia, the Soviets pressured the Germans to sign *before* Genoa. Such an agreement with Germany was now their main goal.

The German leadership, however, was divided on the wisdom of an agreement with Russia. Rathenau, the German Foreign Minister, still hoped to ease Germany's crushing reparations burden, and feared the effect on the Allies of a Soviet-German agreement. But if the Genoa Conference went against the Germans—as French intransigence indicated—Germany might have to sign. A "successful" Genoa conference thus looked doubtful.

THE SOVIETS
AT GENOA AND RAPALLO

In April 1922 delegations from 34 nations descended on Genoa, a delightful city on the Italian Riviera. The occasion was probably the most important international assembly since the Paris Peace Conference of 1919. (The United States was conspicuously absent, although an "observer" was on hand.) Some 700 news correspondents assured adequate coverage of the first formal confrontation between the Bolsheviks—objects of great curiosity—and leaders of the bourgeois West. The Russian delegation was quartered near Rapallo, a resort town some half-hour's ride east of Genoa. Lenin earlier had agreed to head the delegation because Lloyd-George desired that "big men meet big men." But the Soviet leader did not attend due to failing health and fear of assassination by Russian Whites. The honors thus fell on Chicherin.

The Soviets were on their best behavior. Members of the delegation had been lectured before leaving Moscow on the necessity of "good manners and exemplary conduct" at Genoa.[3] Top hats and cutaways were the proper uniform. The draft of Chicherin's opening statement at the conference supposedly was toned down after Lenin requested, "No terrible words, please." The Soviets apparently hoped the West would realize "business-like" relations were possible with proletarian "merchants."

The Conference opened on April 10, in the thirteenth-century Venetian palace, formerly the headquarters of one of the great Renaissance banks. (The Soviets thought this symbolic.[4]) Lloyd-George began the

[3] N. N. Lyubimov and A. N. Erlikh, "The 1922 Genoa Conference," *International Affairs* (Moscow), No. 6 (1963), p. 68.
[4] *Ibid.*

spectacle, reaffirming the principles laid down at Cannes. In particular, he insisted that "when a country enters into contractual obligations with another country or its nationals for value received, that contract cannot be repudiated, whenever a country changes its government, without returning the value." In other words, the Soviets and the Allies were still miles apart on the Russian debt question. (The Soviets had offered in October 1921 to pay the pre-war Tsarist debts, but no more.)

Chicherin's opening speech, intentionally mild, still caused a sensation. It was composed of reasonableness but also of propaganda, directed at the delegates but also at the world. Chicherin's style added to the sensation. He delivered it in flawless French, and then, rejecting an interpreter, repeated it in English—the performance of a diplomatic virtuoso. But he spoke with the passion of a revolutionary.

Chicherin began on a conciliatory note. The Soviets naturally remained faithful to communist principles, but they recognized that the present historical period permitted "the parallel existence of the old social order and the new one being created" and that "economic collaboration between the states representing these two systems" appeared "essential to world economic reconstruction." The Soviets would collaborate if Russia could "establish practical relations with the governments and with the commercial and industrial circles of all countries on a basis of reciprocity, equal rights and full recognition," and the "economically more powerful nations" did not attempt to crush Russia "under the weight of demands that not only are beyond her strength but are survivals of a past that is odious to her." For their part, the Soviets could offer concessions to foreign capitalists for the cultivation of millions of acres of "the most fertile soil in the world," for timber, coal, and mining. Everyone knew the "economic reconstruction of Russia, the largest state in Europe, with its incalculable natural resources, is an indispensable condition of universal economic reconstruction."

Chicherin had made the sales pitch—now for the propaganda. This particular part of the speech had been carefully planned much earlier. Lenin and Chicherin decided a "pacifist program" was called for, and Lenin prodded Chicherin to introduce it immediately since "they" (Lenin presumably meant the French) might break up the conference at any time.[5]

At the conference, Chicherin ticked off his program, urgently needed because "all efforts directed toward reconstructing world economy will

[5] Louis Fischer describes how the speech was written in *The Life of Lenin* (New York: Harper and Row, Publishers, 1964), pp. 570-73. Neither man, of course, was a pacifist. Lenin had enthusiastically approved Chicherin's draft program because it would appeal to the pacifists in "the bourgeois camp" and thus aid "the demoralization of the enemy." The Soviets, Lenin added, would be "venomous" as well as "friendly."

be in vain so long as threats of new wars . . . hang over Europe." To avert war, there had to be: (1) a general limitation of armaments, and abolition of the use of poison gas and aerial warfare against peaceful populations (this would appeal to all people); Russia would limit her arms if others did, and if she were given the "necessary guarantees against any kind of attack upon her or interference in her domestic affairs"; (2) more conferences like Genoa, enlarged to include all peoples, since "universal peace" could only be established when all peoples had "equal status" and the "right to determine their own destinies." (Chicherin had proposed this point to Lenin, arguing that all the "oppressed colonial peoples" should be appealed to because their growing movements for independence were causing the world powers "to crack at the seams.") Moreover, workers' organizations should be officially represented at future conferences; (3) the League of Nations should be reorganized to become "a true union of all peoples without the domination of some over the others, without the present division into victors and vanquished." (This point was bound to infuriate the French, and show the Germans who were their true friends.); (4) world gold stocks should be redistributed by means of long-term loans according to pre-war national holdings. (Chicherin had written Lenin that these stocks were now "lying unused in the vaults of American banks.") In addition, there should be a redistribution of industrial products. (Both of these measures would appeal to all except the rich nations, specifically the United States and Great Britain.)

Chicherin's speech almost broke up the conference. Barthou, the French foreign minister, vehemently protested bringing in the disarmament issue which was *not* on the agenda. Russia would be faced with France's "protest and absolute final and decisive refusal to discuss it." Luckily, Lloyd-George smoothed things over by an adroit reconciliation of the differing viewpoints. He was in favor of disarmament in general; on the other hand, Chicherin had not made disarmament a condition for further work at the conference.

The real negotiations began with a series of informal, secret discussions between the Russians, and the British, French, Belgians and Italians at Lloyd-George's temporary residence, the Villa Albertis. The Germans were excluded at French insistence. The Allies demanded repayment in full for all debts of the Tsarist and Provisional Governments. The Soviets had offered to repay the pre-war Tsarist debts—if they got credits in return. But they had been silent on the remainder. Now they trotted out a huge counter-claim against the Allies for damages done to Russia by the intervention and the blockade. The Allies were not about to accept liability for such damages, but they finally agreed on a mutual cancellation of war claims.

The main sticking point was over nationalized property. The Allies demanded that it be returned to the previous owners if they so desired, or paid for in full. The Soviets balked. They were prepared to lease nationalized properties to the former owners—to grant "concessions;" but, they were not ready to be exploited by foreign capital. The general concept of concessions was not new. The Soviets had suggested to the United States in 1918 the possibility of some such arrangement. Subsequently, the Soviets negotiated concessions with interested foreign companies—usually unsuccessfully.[6]

At first, the Soviets had offered concessions primarily for political reasons. They wanted to enlist the aid of foreign capitalists in getting recognition for Soviet Russia, and to increase the "contradictions" between capitalist nations. Thus an American named Vanderlip, whom the Soviets mistakenly took for a prominent banker of the same name, was offered a lease in the fall of 1920 to develop the mineral resources of the whole of Kamchatka peninsula—then controlled by the Japanese. In May 1921, Harry F. Sinclair, the well-known American oil pioneer, was given permission to develop the oil on Northern Sakhalin—also under Japanese control. Later, after NEP, the Soviets saw the economic benefits concessions might bring. Foreign capital and foreign technicians could help build Russia's industry as under the Tsars. A new principle was introduced: former owners of now nationalized property would be approached and offered leases on the *same* property, the lease or "concession" serving as compensation for any loss sustained by the former owners. Leslie Urquhart, the Chairman of Russo-Asiatic Consolidated, a company which had mined 60 per cent of Russia's lead in pre-war days, was offered the return of his firm's property. Royal Dutch-Shell also negotiated for a lease of its former holdings in Southern Russia and the Caucasus.

Such concessions still were being discussed at the time of the Genoa Conference. However, the French and Belgians at the Villa Albertis were unmoved. They insisted on full restitution. The British, on the other hand, appeared to be happy with 99-year leases. The impasse over what to do about such property was probably the main reason for the failure of the *formal* goal of the Genoa Conference—the integration of Russia into the world economy. A further meeting at The Hague in June 1922, to continue the Genoa negotiations, deadlocked on the same issue.

---

[6] The Soviets seem to have given contracts to less than 10 per cent of those companies applying for concessions from 1922 through 1924. German companies were most successful with 46 contracts; then England with 24; the United States, 18; France, 6; all others, 45. V. Butovskii, *Inostrannye kontsessii v narodnom khozyaistv SSSR* (Moscow, 1928), p. 41, cited by Stephan M. Horak in "Lenin on Coexistence: A Chapter in Soviet Foreign Policy," *Studies on the Soviet Union,* III, No. 3, 29.

The Rapallo Affair   While the Russians were closeted with the Allies at the Villa Albertis, the poor German delegates sat isolated in the Hotel Eden, expecting the worst. Rumors abounded that Russia would be offered German reparations—a possibility specifically provided for in Article 116 of the Versailles Treaty. This would enable Russia in turn to pay off her foreign creditors. The Soviets apparently did not plan to take advantage of such a scheme, but for some time they had carefully hinted at the possibility to the German foreign office. New reparations, after France had refused to discuss at Genoa the already crushing burden, would be more than the Germans could stand. The Germans especially were afraid when they heard on the evening of Good Friday—the second day of the secret talks at the Villa Albertis—that the Allies and the Soviets were close to an agreement. (Actually, they were approaching a hopeless deadlock.) Sometime after midnight on Easter Sunday morning, a member of the Soviet delegation telephoned the Germans, asking if they would drive down the coast to Rapallo that day to discuss a separate German-Soviet agreement. (The Soviets, as mentioned earlier, had attempted to get the German signature on such a document before Genoa.)

The whole German delegation turned out of bed to discuss the Soviet invitation. The meeting later became famous as the "pajama party." The lines were drawn, as they had been in Berlin, between the "Easterners" and "Westerners." Among German policy makers, a debate had raged for several years over how to restore Germany's position as a world power. The "Easterners," although they detested Bolshevism, said Germany should bargain with Russia independently. This would give Germany an alternative to collaboration with the West. The "Westerners" argued that Germany should emphasize cooperation with the West, and, in particular, follow Western policy in dealing with Russia.[7] The critical variable in determining which faction would win seemed to be Western policy—especially British and French policy—toward Germany at any one moment. The tougher the West became with the Weimar government, the more Germany leaned toward collaboration with Russia.

The "Westerners" held most of the high positions in the German government—President Ebert, the majority of his cabinet, and particularly important, successive German foreign ministers. The "Easterners" were lodged in the lower rungs of the German foreign office. But they drew support from German heavy industry, which needed Eastern markets and raw materials, and the General Staff with its ally, the armaments

---

[7] J. W. Wheeler-Bennett notes the continuation of this debate even among the unsuccessful conspirators against Hitler in 1944. See his introduction to Gerald Freund's *Unholy Alliance* (London: Chatto and Windus, Ltd., 1957), p. xviii.

industry. The General Staff was stifled by the restrictions on German rearmament in the Versailles Treaty. The army needed a sanctuary beyond Allied control where airplanes, tanks, and other forbidden weapons could be produced. Russia seemed an obvious choice. And so began one of the most curious episodes in Soviet foreign policy. During the 1920's clandestine military cooperation would develop between the Soviet Union and the German army—cooperation shrouded in such secrecy that the details still are not fully known, cooperation which during its first months was concealed even from the political leaders of the Weimar Republic.

As early as October 1919, General Hans von Seeckt, head of the new German "Peace Army," apparently attempted to contact the Soviets. Through the medium of Enver Pasha, an exiled Turkish nationalist, Seeckt suggested German arms could be built in Russia with the Soviets sharing in the production. (Seeckt had helped Enver get a ride on a new Junkers aircraft bound for Moscow, where Enver planned to discuss Soviet-Muslim cooperation against British imperialism.) However, serious negotiations between the German General Staff and the Soviets did not begin until December 1920.[8] For the Germans, only a few trusted staff officers were aware of the talks. In Berlin, meetings with Soviet representatives were held mainly in private apartments. Not until the fall of 1921 did Seeckt finally tell Wirth, the German Chancellor, of the negotiations, and then only because more money was needed to finance the Russian project than the army could lay its hands on. By the spring of 1922, planning for military cooperation between the Soviet Union and Germany had gone far. Formal *political* cooperation was still lacking, but this, as indicated, was the agenda of the "pajama party" early Easter morning in 1922.

Rathenau, the German Foreign Minister and a "Westerner," finally capitulated to the "Easterners" at three A.M. The principal German delegates arrived at Rapallo by noon; the treaty was signed by 6:30 P.M.—the date, April 16, 1922. The Allies were furious at this "immoral" and outrageous act by the trouble makers of Europe. The *Times* of London fumed at the formation of an "unholy alliance," which was "an open defiance and studied insult to the Entente Powers."[9]

Why were the Allies so upset? The treaty was hardly an alliance. Although rumors abounded to the contrary, there were neither secret clauses nor military applications. (On the other hand, the existing, clandestine military cooperation certainly was spurred on by the fact of

---

[8] All during this period, Zinoviev was working through the Comintern to bring revolution in Germany, a revolution which Seeckt and other members of the "bourgeoisie" were prepared to crush ruthlessly.

[9] Quoted in Kennan, *Russia and the West*, p. 221.

Rapallo.) The bland phrases of the treaty stated (1) full diplomatic relations between the two states would be resumed; [10] (2) each state would renounce its claims on the other, thus freeing Germany from fear of Russian reparations and Russia from German claims on property the Soviets had nationalized; (3) the two countries would work together to improve their trade relations on a "most-favored nation" basis.

Allied displeasure really stemmed from the significance of *any* agreement between Soviet Russia and Germany. Both countries had broken out of their isolation. They had been treated, if only by each other, as equals, not as defeated powers or cancerous growths on international society. The Soviets in particular considered Rapallo a signal victory. With the treaty they had (1) split Western capitalism, preventing a united Europe from exploiting Russia (a "contradiction" within the capitalist camp had been utilized); (2) made future cooperation with the Germans implicit; (3) set an important precedent—a capitalist country could resume trade and diplomatic relations with Russia if both simply cancelled their respective debts and claims.

THE CAPITALIST CAMP CAPITULATES

With Rapallo the Soviets rent a gaping hole in the capitalist ring encircling Russia. *De jure* recognition, trade, and credit from the West still were lacking. But Soviet confidence in the staying power of the new republic was growing. Agricultural production was on the upswing, the economy was reviving. Trade and long-term credit from abroad were important, but no longer critical for the survival of Russia. (Short-term credit eventually came through deals by the Soviet trading agencies with the German, Austrian and Italian governments.)

De jure recognition from the West to ease trade and credit still was desirable, but not if this meant compromising on the debt question or nationalized property. At the Second Congress of Soviets of the USSR in January 1924, Kamenev, a member of the Politburo, asserted Russia did not need "any legal anointment by the priests of capital." He quoted Lenin's statement of several years earlier that "the later the recognition,

---

[10] Recognition was not mentioned because the German Imperial Government had formally recognized the Bolshevik regime with the Treaty of Brest-Litovsk. During the rest of 1918, relations were rocky. The German ambassador, Mirbach, was assassinated in Moscow during July, presumably by "counterrevolutionaries" and not Bolsheviks. The Soviet ambassador to Berlin, Joffe, refused to present his credentials to the Kaiser, desiring instead to use the embassy as a clandestine revolutionary headquarters. But cooperation continued because both states were now fighting the Allies. Joffe, however, finally became too much for the Germans to stomach, and was thrown out of Berlin in the final days of the war. Diplomatic relations formally ended when the Kaiser abdicated on November 9, 1918, and the Soviets unilaterally annulled the Brest-Litovsk Treaty on November 13.

the harder our conditions." The Soviets apparently believed recognition would come no matter what they did.

The Bolsheviks were right in their forecast of recognition. In 1924, since labeled by Soviet historians the "year of recognition," most of the West fell into place behind Great Britain in recognizing the Soviets as the *de jure* government of Russia.[11] However, recognition was due to more than capitalist greed for the Russian market. A general improvement in relations between Germany and the Allies took place in the latter part of 1923, and a by-product was a lessening of the fear and hatred of the Bolsheviks. Against British objections and supported only by Belgium, France had marched into the Ruhr in January 1923 as a reprisal for the German failure to meet scheduled reparations payments. The general improvement in the European climate largely stemmed from the disgust of most of Europe with the French occupation. In addition, there was a wide desire on the part of European business for a return to economic normalcy with both Germany and Russia. Sentiment thus grew in Europe for those groups which favored a more conciliatory policy towards Germany. The same groups advocated more relaxed relations with the Soviets.[12] Even in France, there was uneasiness over Poincaré's intransigence.

Great Britain was the key country in the changing climate because of its critical role in European politics and finance. The key group in that country was the Labor Party. In February 1924, a newly-elected Labor Government gave full diplomatic recognition to the Soviets. The troublesome questions of debts and claims were simply deferred. The reasons were given above for this rather drastic change in handling the recognition problem. But the change in British policy was particularly remarkable because of the near rupture of Soviet-British relations in early 1923. A temporary high point had been achieved with the Anglo-Soviet Trade Agreement of 1921. Subsequently, the traditional struggle of both powers for influence in the Middle East had clouded the surface harmony.

The Soviet Union, Great Britain, and the Middle East
We have described Chicherin and his unique feeling for historic "Russian" national interests. Unfortunately for the Soviets, Chicherin found his match in Lord Curzon, the British foreign minister from 1917 to the end of 1923. Leo Kamenev, a contemporary Soviet spokesman, called Curzon the "typical representative of world imperialism and conser-

[11] Twelve countries actually had granted the Soviets *de jure* recognition before Britain, but only one, Germany, could be considered a major power. The rest were mainly immediate neighbors of the new regime. After Britain took the lead, Italy, Norway, Austria and others quickly followed. France capitulated in late 1924.

[12] Trotsky saw the resulting change in political leadership as heralding a period of rule by the "democratic-pacifist elements of bourgeois society."

vatism." Actually the British foreign minister was more interested in defending the British Empire than "capitalism," especially the Empire's Middle Eastern domain. Above all he valued India, the pre-eminent prize. In this general area, Britain's age-old rival was Russia, and Curzon, "the last authentic representative of the anti-Russian tradition of British foreign policy." [13] Chicherin in turn personified everything Curzon detested, standing "for Communist doctrine and the history of Russia—a combination which acted like a red rag on a bull." [14]

Russian Tsars had begun their penetration of Central Asia in the sixteenth century. A variety of motives provided the stimulus: at first the desire for exploring or subduing rebellious border tribes, later the need to acquire markets for Russia's developing industry. But in the nineteenth century, Russian attention focussed on one specific objective—control of the Turkish Straits. The Straits were an invasion route into Russia, and thus critical for state security. They also were important for economic development. Russian grain surpluses needed an exit from which they could be sold in the world market. Tsarist statesmen thus argued that the Straits were the "key" to the Russian house, which rightly belonged in the Russian pocket. For the Turks, of course, Russian control of this vital area meant Russian domination of Turkey.

Britain became increasingly uneasy, especially for the safety of India, as Russia moved ever southward. A duel between the two great nations for control of the Middle East began in the latter part of the nineteenth century, and lasted until British power declined after World War II. The Bolsheviks naturally had given a new twist to the duel's ground rules. Tsar Nicholas secretly had been promised the Straits and Constantinople (Istanbul) by the British and French as part of Russia's war booty. The Provisional Government of 1917 refused to give up such hard-won gains. But one month after coming to power, the Soviets issued a ringing "Appeal . . . to the Moslems of Russia and the East," including "Persians, Turks, Arabs, and Hindus." The secret agreements promising Russia the Straits and Constantinople were declared "null and void." The appeal ended with a stirring call for revolution. All Moslems were exhorted to "lose no time in throwing off the yoke of the ancient oppressors of your land."

The geographical facts of life for Russia had not changed. Even a Soviet Russia eventually would become concerned over who controlled the entrance and exit to the Black Sea. But the Bolsheviks now were busy

[13] E. H. Carr, *The Bolshevik Revolution 1917-1923* (New York: The Macmillan Company, 1953), III, 485.
[14] Louis Fischer, *The Soviets in World Affairs* (Princeton, N.J.: Princeton University Press, 1951), I, 401.

elsewhere. They did not even control their own country. The call for a Moslem revolt was primarily ideological lip service. The main hope for revolution still lay in Germany. An "Appeal" on the other hand cost the new regime nothing.

The Middle East—for reasons other than the "Appeal"—soon did become revolutionary and anti-Western. A new nationalist regime in Turkey, led by Kemal Pasha (later named Ataturk), rebelled against the harsh peace conditions imposed by the Allies on that country after World War I. In an attempt to crush the rebellion, British forces occupied Constantinople in 1920. The Greek army, subsidized by Britain, advanced onto the Anatolian plain.

Here was the first test case for Soviet foreign policy where a non-Western country was fighting its "capitalist oppressors." In theory, the Soviets would immediately come to the aid of any anticolonialist regime. The Second Congress of the Comintern had affirmed this in 1920.[15] In practice, there was some hesitation. The Soviets distrusted the "bourgeois" Kemal Pasha, and did not want to sabotage the commercial negotiations then underway in London. Stalin, a Georgian, was particularly worried about permitting a strong Turkey. In the spring of 1921, Russia finally signed a treaty of "friendship and fraternity" with Turkey. (The Turks had wanted a much stronger military alliance.) After the Greek advance had been checked in the fall of 1921 and British-Soviet relations were worsening, the Soviets furnished the Turks considerable military aid.

When it came, Soviet political and military support did not insure Turkish friendship. The Soviets distrusted Kemal, but he in turn was suspicious of Soviet motives. Russia openly had encouraged Turkish communists, although she was careful not to disrupt formal relations between the two governments.[16] Kemal rightly considered local communists potential enemies, and on occasion dealt with them ruthlessly. Seventeen Turkish communist leaders reportedly were thrown into the Black Sea in January 1921. Indeed, the period of cooperation and friendship had been possible only because both countries were under pressure from the West. When Western pressure on either nation slacked off—as it did in 1922 with Kemal's defeat of the Greeks and the withdrawal of the British —the old suspicions and particularly the latent rivalries over common border areas resurfaced. This general pattern would be repeated in Soviet-Turkish relations for the next several decades.

To return to the Anglo-Soviet duel for control of the Middle East, a

---

[15] See Chap. 4, p. 115.

[16] As would happen many times in Soviet dealings with other governments, local communists were expendable if Soviet state interests so dictated.

conference was called at Lausanne, Switzerland in late 1922 to write a definitive treaty between the new Turkish government and the West. The Soviets, not having been belligerents, were permitted to participate only in negotiations involving the Straits.

At the conference, the enduring principles of the contest for the Straits came into play. Russia, when strong, wanted the Black Sea exit kept open for her navy. The British at such times wanted the Russian navy bottled up. They argued for Turkish sovereignty over the Straits, closing the passageway to Russian warships. On the other hand, a weak Russia wanted Turkish control of the Straits to keep the British out. In 1922, Russia was weak. In a note sent to Western governments before the conference, Chicherin bluntly charged that "the freedom of the Straits which Great Britain has in mind means only the desire of a strong naval power to control a route vitally necessary to other states in order thereby to keep them under a constant threat. This threat is directed primarily against Russia and Turkey." (The Soviets were trying to plant fear of British in the Turks.) The British, having no fear of the puny Soviet navy, wanted the Straits demilitarized and open to all warships. Curzon quipped that the Soviets wanted "to convert the Black Sea into a Russian lake with Turkey as the faithful guardian at the gates."

However, Turkey did not rise to the Soviet bait. The major provisions of the British proposal were accepted. (The Turks sometime might like the support of other nations' warships against the Soviet navy in the Black Sea.) The Soviets had lost an important round in their duel with the British. Moreover, Turkey had been set free from threatened Soviet domination.

All through this period, the Soviets also supported other nationalist movements in the Middle East, particularly in Iran and Afghanistan. As with Turkey, complications arose in Soviet foreign policy because of the dual motivation behind that policy. The Soviets wanted friendly neighbors as a defensive barrier against Great Britain, and thus would cooperate with any anti-British leader. (They signed treaties of friendship in 1921 with Iran and Afghanistan.) But the Soviets also supported local leftists in Northern Iran until the latter part of 1921, though apparently with some misgivings. Conditions were not ripe for a true revolution in that country, and hardly worth provoking a British counter-move or sacrificing good relations with the anti-British nationalist government in Teheran. Subsequently, the Soviets seemed content with using economic pressure and intensive subversion to pursue their ends in Iran until 1939.

In any case, Lord Curzon considered all Soviet activity in the Middle East anti-British, and issued his notorious ultimatum to the Soviet government in May 1923. The memorandum contained a long list of British grievances, citing particularly Soviet actions in Asia, and demanded satisfaction on all counts within 10 days or else the British government would denounce the Anglo-Soviet Trade Agreement of 1921.

Some Soviet leaders sensed in the ultimatum an attempt to provoke Russia into a new war. But any worsening of political or economic relations would hurt. (Trotsky pleaded, "May this cup pass from us.") The Soviets swallowed their pride and capitulated on all points in the ultimatum, with the significant exception of Comintern activity in Asia. The Soviet government again reminded the British that it was not responsible for Comintern actions.

England and the Comintern   Although the crisis of the Curzon ultimatum blew over and the Labor Government gave the Soviets *de jure* recognition in February 1924, Soviet-British relations still had rough sailing until 1929. Comintern dabbling in British affairs—or what was assumed to be such dabbling—continually complicated official contacts. In October 1924, Parliament had been considering two new Anglo-Soviet treaties providing for normal relations. All "questions outstanding," meaning debts and claims, were to be deferred to a later conference. Suddenly, the sponsoring Labor Government found itself fighting for survival in a general election. In the midst of the campaign, the infamous "Zinoviev Letter" was published by the British press. Zinoviev, the Comintern head, gave advice in the letter to leading British communists on how to form the nucleus of a "British Red Army" in preparation for "an armed insurrection," and how to subvert the regular British armed forces. The letter—the original of which was never produced— apparently was a rather clumsy forgery by White Russian émigrés working with the Polish Secret Service. But it became a critical issue in the election and Labor was roundly beaten. Even if the Zinoviev letter was a forgery, the Comintern in other public pronouncements had left no illusions about its desire for revolution in Britain.

The incoming Conservatives dropped the proposed treaties. Subsequently, the Tory Government broke off all diplomatic relations with Russia as a result of the raid in 1927 on "Arcos," a branch of the Soviet trade delegation in London. The British government claimed to have found evidence on the premises of an extensive espionage network covering the British Empire as well as the Americas. Trade nevertheless continued, although at much lower volume. Arcos even was permitted to leave in England a "reasonable number" of persons to carry on "legitimate commercial operations."

Formal contacts were only resumed in late 1929 after Labor again came to power. This time the Soviets enjoyed normal diplomatic relations, including an exchange of ambassadors. (However, King George V still rebelled at shaking hands with the representative of a government "which, if it did not connive at, did not disapprove of, the brutal murder of his favorite first cousins.") [17] Moreover, there was no formal agreement even to consider the perennial "outstanding questions."

The United States Gives In   The only major power still withholding recognition was the United States. Secretary of State Colby's intransigent stance over Comintern activity and the Soviet failure to live up to the basic principles of international law was supplemented by the demand of subsequent Republican Administrations for satisfaction on debts and claims. Trade, however, gradually developed to a point at which the United States supplied roughly 25 per cent of Russia's imports in 1930—more than any other country. American journalists, businessmen, and technicians hired by the Soviets traveled to Russia. But, Russian purchases from the United States suddenly dropped in 1931 from 100 to 12 million dollars. Pressure for normal relations to restore the American share of Soviet trade understandably mounted. Franklin D. Roosevelt saw an even more urgent political reason in 1933. Japan was threatening America's position in the Far East. Healing the breach with Russia might help restrain the Japanese. The Soviets publicly acknowledged fear of Japan as the central reason they wanted diplomatic contact with the United States. In late 1933, diplomatic relations were formally opened. The Soviets gave an empty promise to abstain from propaganda, while debts and claims were reserved for later discussion. Negotiations on these continually troublesome questions dragged on until they were deadlocked in 1935.

In summary, the Soviets finally got the full diplomatic recognition they craved from the capitalist world—without paying the debts of the predecessors and the claims against the Soviet government. But until World War II the long-term loans never came. The Soviets still were not considered a normal government nor a responsible trading partner.

THE SEARCH FOR SECURITY

A Soviet drive for a state security system paralleled the Soviet attempt to get trade, credits, and recognition. The protection of Russia's western border was an incessant concern of the Soviet ruling elite. The pessimists saw new threats of intervention at every turning point; the optimists had confidence in Russia's growing strength. But all worked to insulate Soviet Russia from the West.

There were two key tactics in the erection of the Soviet security system: (1) The great capitalist powers had to be split so they could

[17] The King is quoted by Harold Nicolson in *King George the Fifth* (New York: Doubleday & Company, Inc., 1953), p. 441.

not form a united front against the Soviets—"contradictions" among the powers had to be utilized—and Germany was the logical wedge; (2) Russia's immediate neighbors had to be "neutralized" so they could never again serve as bases for intervention.

Germany The close relations Russia established with Germany at Rapallo in 1922 have been described. The period of harmony, however, would not last. A high point was reached with France's occupation of the Ruhr in early 1923. Russia condemned the French attempt to "enslave" Germany. The Soviets feared French power might advance to the Russian border through Poland, France's ally but Russia's enemy.

The informal German-Soviet alliance soon was given a difficult test. Moscow, through the Comintern, continually had been fascinated with German internal politics since Germany was still the hoped for spark of European revolution. Revolution in that harassed country seemed imminent in the summer and fall of 1923. Soviet leaders at first urged caution on the German communists, apparently fearing that a premature revolt would be crushed at once by France, placing Russia itself in danger. But after a new German government under Gustav Stresemann took power in August, even Soviet pessimists were sure conditions for the German revolution soon would be ripe. The only question was whether it would be tomorrow or in several weeks. In any event, there was no reason to prop up Stresemann; he seemed ready to throw over Rapallo for Western friendship. The Soviet leaders unanimously chose to give all-out support to the German revolution—short of sending in the Red Army.

To thrash out tactics and timing for the seizure of power, the Politburo brought the leading German communists to Moscow for what turned out to be six weeks of conferences—the very period during which the German leaders should have been on the spot in their homeland. This time, in contrast to earlier abortive communist revolutions in Germany, the Russians would be in charge. But before the date could be set for the revolutionary attempt, disaster struck. The German Army crushed the still meager force of "Red Hundreds," armed proletarians who had been organized under Soviet direction as the nucleus for the uprising.[18]

The German failure brought extended soul-searching and bitter recriminations among the Soviet hierarchy, particularly because this was the first foreign revolution its members had attempted to direct. Behind all the mud-slinging were several elementary facts. The Soviets and most of the leaders of the German Communist Party then in Moscow assumed

---

[18] As mentioned, the Soviets were now carrying on their clandestine cooperation with the German Army—an ironic example of the cross-purposes of Soviet foreign policy during this period. It also is of interest that the German Army thwarted Hitler's rightist "putsch" in Munich a few days later. This revolutionary attempt actually had posed a much more serious challenge to the Weimar Republic.

the desperate German workers would inevitably follow the communist call for an uprising. The German proletariat, however, was not ready for a communist revolution. Second, the Politburo, again with the advice of the German communists, considered the "working class elements" of the German Army sympathetic to a proletarian revolution. This also was not the case. The difficulty of assessing the situation from afar was further compounded by the Russian tendency to use the Bolshevik revolution as the model. Trotsky even insisted on November 7, the anniversary of the Bolshevik Revolution, as the date for the communist seizure of power in Germany. A fourth facet of the mud-slinging was the beginning of the struggle for power between Stalin and Trotsky over correct revolutionary tactics.

Relations between the German and Soviet governments were severely strained by the attempted revolution. But there was no formal break. Although Stresemann knew of Soviet complicity in great detail, he wanted to keep the Rapallo "alliance"—the Russian "trump"—to strengthen his hand with the Allies. Stresemann, a superb politician who had started life as the son of a beer salesman, did not want Germany a prisoner of the West any more than of the East. Germany had to be free to regain its place in the sun. The Eastern frontier of Germany imposed by the Versailles Treaty had to be revised. Stresemann would first neutralize Allied pressure in the West, and then press for changes in the East. Developments indicated success for Stresemann's strategy. In September 1924, Britain pressed for German membership in the League of Nations. Germany accepted the offer, but only if she did not have to take part in sanctions against League-designated aggressors. Stresemann did not want his country protecting Poland's boundaries. He hoped to change these, albeit peacefully. Nor did he want Germany used as a possible staging base against Russia.

The Soviets were sure Germany would become an Allied pawn against Russia if she entered the League. Consequently, Russia used every stratagem to keep Germany out, even threatening to guarantee with the French and the Poles the German-Polish border. But Stresemann was not deterred. As part of his plan to stabilize Germany's western border, the German statesman got Allied agreement in late 1925 to freeze the Rhine frontier in the Locarno treaties. In return Germany promised to join the League, with the rather vague concession that she (and the other signatories) would only take part in League sanctions to the extent that they were compatible with her "military situation" and "geographical position." This meant, Stresemann assured Chicherin, that no foreign troops would march through Germany to attack Russia.

Stresemann made a further attempt to assuage Soviet fears. On the very day of his departure for Locarno, October 2, 1925, he announced that Germany soon would sign a major trade treaty with Russia. Chicherin later proclaimed the treaty "a clearly expressed demonstration in favor of the Rapallo line." But he pressed Stresemann for an even stronger illustration. Germany finally yielded in the "Treaty of Berlin" signed in April 1926, promising its neutrality in case Russia were attacked by a third party. This document, in contrast to the Rapallo treaty, caused relatively little stir in London and Paris. There seemed nothing really new in the Soviet-German relationship. It appeared Rapallo merely had been reaffirmed. But the period of harmony was over; Germany was moving back into respectable society. She now had other friends beside Russia. The Soviets no longer could keep Germany isolated from the West; the major "contradiction" was malfunctioning.

The "Neutralization" of Russia's Western Neighbors   Soviet attempts to neutralize Russia's immediate neighbors in the West paralleled maneuvers to insure a friendly Germany. Eastern Europe could never again be permitted to serve as a staging base for intervention. However, the countries of Eastern Europe were just as worried about Russian intervention. Many had long suffered from Tsarist imperialism and indeed had been part of the Tsarist empire before World War I. Now they were the target of Soviet subversion and conquest. Temporary salvation had come from Soviet weakness. But Russia's peace treaties with the border states gave these countries little solace. Nagging territorial questions continually complicated peaceful relations. The Russians kept Eastern Karelia from Finland, and claimed Rumania's Bessarabia belonged to the Soviet Ukraine.[19]

Since the Soviets couldn't be trusted, mutual collaboration among the Eastern European countries seemed the only way to security. Poland, the key country in the area and thus Russia's chief rival, led attempts to forge a defensive bloc. Yet, in spite of the obvious threat from Russia, the border states had trouble getting together. They had their own little jealousies, and varying degrees of interest in mutual cooperation. Moreover, the Soviets used every opportunity to inflame territorial disputes between the East European states. (Russia's counter strategy aimed at isolating the border states from each other and from their Western European allies, particularly France and England.)

A minor victory for Soviet policy in Eastern Europe came with the Soviet-Lithuanian neutrality and non-aggression pact of 1926. One year earlier, the Soviets had signed the first such bilateral pact with their

---

[19] Eastern Karelia had not been part of the Grand Duchy of Finland under the Tsars, but about 60 per cent of the population was Finnish and even more would have decided to join an independent Finland. Jan Librach, *The Rise of the Soviet Empire* (New York: Frederick A. Praeger, Inc., 1964), pp. 44-45.

southern neighbor, Turkey. (Afghanistan and Iran soon followed suit.) During this era, two provisions were common to all such pacts between Russia and her neighbors: (1) each state pledged it would remain neutral if the other were attacked by a third state; (2) each state promised not to commit aggression against the other.

But real Soviet progress with her Eastern European security system did not come until 1928. That year the Kellogg-Briand Pact outlawing war was signed in Paris. The Soviets were not permitted among the fifteen original signatories. They might have used the formal ceremony for polemics on disarmament. Therefore, Chicherin labeled the pact "a constituent part of the policy of encircling the USSR." But after they accepted the invitation to join, the Soviet leaders decided that the pact contained a moral obligation that "obstructed, to some small extent, the psychological preparation for war." Russia shortly invited the border states to Moscow to sign the "Litvinov Protocol," putting the pact into effect immediately among Russia and her neighbors.[20] (Only Finland refused to adhere.) The Soviets had wanted to negotiate the Protocol only with Poland in keeping with their policy of isolating the Eastern European states. But they yielded to Poland's insistence on including the other border countries. Any increase in Russia's security in Eastern Europe apparently was then welcome.

The Soviet Union nevertheless continued to work for bilateral treaties on neutrality and non-aggression. Poland finally signed in 1932, after the Soviets first agreed to negotiate similar pacts with the other border states.[21] Poland's fears of Germany, combined with Russia's growing concern for Japanese designs in the Far East, had brought a mutual desire for security in Eastern Europe.

SOCIALISM IN ONE COUNTRY

In the early 1920's, political leadership in the Soviet Union began to change. This was to have a significant impact on both Russia's foreign and domestic policy. The most important change occurred when Lenin died on January 21, 1924. Long before his death, Lenin had been unable to handle the day-to-day business of government because of increasing illness. However, his policies still were the guidelines for Soviet action. No "Old Bolshevik" dared challenge the leadership of this brilliant and dedicated revolutionary. Yet Joseph Stalin already had begun his rise to power.

[20] Maxim Litvinov, Chicherin's assistant, was gradually assuming the duties of the Commissar. Chicherin was chronically ill in the later years of his service as foreign minister.

[21] Finland, Latvia and Estonia joined with Russia in short order. Only Rumania and Russia could not reach agreement. Talks repeatedly deadlocked over Bessarabia.

Stalin could not have been more different from Lenin. A comparatively minor figure in the Bolshevik Revolution, Stalin's talent lay in organization rather than in creative thought or dynamic leadership. He had little knowledge of the world outside Russia, while Lenin had lived abroad for years before the Revolution. Lenin ruled by the sheer force of his personality and his amazing power of persuasion. Stalin would rule through his domination of both the party organization and the secret police. Lenin felt secure in the company of devoted comrades. Stalin felt inferior to the brilliant, cosmopolitan leadership of the Revolution. Lenin was first among equals, the leader of the squabbling oligarchy. Stalin became the most powerful autocrat Russia had seen, surrounded by "yes-men."

But we must not push the contrasts between Lenin and Stalin too far. What we saw in the ensuing years was a different *style* in the conduct of foreign (and domestic) policy, not a radically different policy. There could be a difference in tactics, but not in the general goals of the nation's foreign policy.

Stalin's Style in Foreign Policy   Within these limitations, what was to be Stalin's style? Naturally cautious and pessimistic about the chances for revolution in other countries, Stalin would concentrate on building a powerful "socialist" Russia. Indeed, there seemed no other way. Stalin said in 1925: "What we at one time regarded as a brief respite after the war has become a whole period of respite." The revolutionary tide had receded indefinitely. Building "socialism in one country" was the only possible alternative to internal stagnation and defeat in foreign adventures. A socialist Russia in turn would be the "base" for world revolution when that time arrived.[22]

Stalin's theory, which he supported with a twisted interpretation of an article by Lenin in 1915, became the center of the foreign policy debate between Stalin and Leon Trotsky, his chief opponent in the struggle for power and generally considered Lenin's heir apparent. Both men, of course, agreed on the central tenets of Marxism. The debate was on tactics and timing. Trotsky argued that Russia's survival depended on "permanent revolution" abroad (as well as at home). Russia could not possibly become an economically self-sufficient "socialist" state unless socialist revolutions took place in other countries. (As late as 1924, Stalin accepted this thesis.) Stalin argued that socialism could and should be built in Russia, and then worry about the world.

The full story of how Stalin eliminated his opposition is beyond the

[22] See Chap. 2, p. 51 for a description of the "socialist" stage, and Isaac Deutscher's *Stalin* (New York: Oxford University Press, Inc., 1949), pp. 281-93 for a concise summary of "socialism in one country" and Trotsky's alternative of "permanent revolution."

scope of this book. It is sufficient to say that the major battle raged from 1924 to 1927. Stalin first joined Zinoviev, the Comintern head, and Kamenev, a close associate and assistant to Lenin, in isolating Trotsky. (The "heir apparent" was roundly disliked for his arrogance and resented for his power.) Then Stalin, through his growing domination of the party machinery, outvoted Zinoviev and Kamenev. Finally, Stalin defeated all three in 1927 when they had come together for a desperate last-ditch stand.

The residue from the power struggle had a lasting impact on Stalin's foreign policy. He continually had visions of his old opponents gathering support at home and abroad for his downfall. He seemed to feel this could be forestalled only by rigidly controlling communist parties everywhere, and periodically purging the dissident elements. Stalin especially feared a successful revolution abroad might become a base for his enemies. This fear reinforced his natural caution when possibilities for the seizure of power developed in other countries.[23] However, in the first few years after Lenin's death, the impact of Stalin's style on Soviet foreign policy was not evident. The struggle for power was absorbing most of the energy of the contenders, and Chicherin was running the foreign office—if not the Comintern.

Stalin Transforms Russia   The new Soviet leader's first major effort to create "socialism in one country" came in 1928, and this effort was to be the key to every major aspect of Soviet foreign and domestic policy until the rise of Hitler in 1933. Stalin was dragging all of Russia into a massive transformation of the society. (He later called it a "revolution from above.") The first of a series of five-year economic plans was introduced to turn backward Russia into a modern industrial nation, and particularly into a powerful military state. Simultaneously, the peasants—still the great majority of Russians—were herded into collective farms to give the Kremlin close control over agriculture. Food production had to be increased to feed the growing cities, while grain and raw materials had to be exchanged for needed imports from the capitalist countries. The immediate results of these two programs were catastrophic: famine, a general lowering of living standards, a serious break-

---

23 George Kennan believes Stalin's obsession with the protection of his personal position is the key to his diplomacy. Thus, right up to the attack on Russia in 1941, Stalin feared Trotsky and what he represented more than Hitler. This even though Trotsky had been exiled and then murdered in Mexico in 1940 presumably on Stalin's orders. If threats to state security corresponded with threats—or imagined threats—to Stalin's personal security, Kennan argues, both interests would be served. If not, personal protection came first even if the foreign policy of the Soviet Union was damaged. Kennan, however, is the first to admit it is still too early to definitively disentangle Stalin's motives—if we ever can. See Kennan's Chap. 17 in *Russia and the West* (Boston: Atlantic-Little, Brown and Company, 1960).

down of the transportation network—in effect a general disruption of the whole economic system.

All of this meant that Russia was militarily very weak for a few years. She desperately needed peaceful relations with the capitalist world. Moreover, the Soviets had to have outside assistance such as machinery and technical experts, to aid in the economic transformation. These could only come from the advanced capitalist countries, providing a second, compelling reason for peace with the capitalist world. Max Beloff remarks that Litvinov was merely being candid when he stated in 1930, "the larger the scale of our constructive work, the more rapid its tempo, the greater our interest in the preservation of peace." [24]

In the summer of 1927, the year before the internal upheaval began, Moscow suffered a severe case of war jitters. The British severance of diplomatic relations after the "Arcos raid" and other supposedly anti-Soviet moves led Stalin to charge that the Tory Government had "definitely and concertedly undertaken to organize a war against the Soviet Union." The "respite" he saw in 1925 was coming to an end. The British preparations for war—which the Soviets thought probably would be fought for England by the Poles or reactionary Chinese warlords—were designed to save decaying English capitalism.[25]

The Comintern's "Left" Policy in 1928   In a broader analysis, Stalin saw by December 1927 "all the symptoms of an intense crisis and growing instability in world capitalism." This meant not only "a phase of new revolutionary tendencies" but also "a revival of interventionist tendencies among the imperialists." Stalin's thesis became the central theme of the Sixth Congress of the Comintern in 1928, and dictated a "Left" or offensive turn in the tactics of all communist parties because of the anticipated revolutionary possibilities.

At the same time, foreign communists were forcefully reminded where their true loyalty lay. They always had had the duty of defending the Soviet state against counter-revolution and intervention. The program adopted by the Sixth Congress clearly implied that this obligation was now the *primary* duty of all communists in other countries. A special section of the program reads:

As the country of proletarian dictatorship and socialist construction, of tremendous working-class achievements, of the alliance of proletariat and

[24] Cited in Beloff's *The Foreign Policy of Soviet Russia* (London: Oxford University Press, 1956), I, 1929-1936, published for the Royal Institute of International Affairs, 27.

[25] Stalin wrote: "England always has preferred wars fought with the hands of others. And now and then, she has actually found fools to pick her chestnuts from the fire." Quoted in Louis Fischer, *The Soviets in World Affairs* (Princeton, N.J.: Princeton University Press, 1951), II, 740.

peasantry, as the country of a new civilization advancing under the banner of Marxism, the Soviet Union was bound to become the base of the international movement of all oppressed classes, the center of the international revolution, the most significant factor in world history. . . . The Soviet Union is the true fatherland of the proletariat, the strongest pillar of its achievements, and the principal factor in its emancipation throughout the world. This obliges the international proletariat to forward the success of socialist construction in the Soviet Union and to defend the country of proletarian dictatorship by every means against the attacks of the capitalist powers.[26]

Stalin had given an unmistakable indication of the complete subservience he would demand of foreign communist parties to the needs of Soviet foreign policy.

Whether Stalin really believed his prediction of a new phase in the development of capitalism is uncertain. Given his rather unsophisticated view of the world at this time, his naturally suspicious mind, and worsening relations with Great Britain and Germany, it seems possible. (The great American stock market crash in 1929 seemed to confirm the thesis, but it apparently was completely unforeseen by Stalin and other high-ranking Bolsheviks.)

We do know that Stalin was ready for a "Left" policy. He had begun a campaign to get rid of the "right" opposition led by Bukharin, formerly his chief ally against the "left"—Trotsky, Kamenev and Zinoviev. With these three out of the running, Stalin could adopt his own "Left" course to defeat the "right." He had adopted a Left policy internally with his "revolution from above." Foreign communist parties would also press for revolution, abandoning united front tactics of the previous period.

In any case, Stalin's Comintern program seemed unreal. Russian foreign policy continued to be defensive, pressing for peace with the Litvinov Protocol and the non-aggression pacts. Furthermore, there were no formal promises of Soviet aid to communist parties in other countries in the program. Stalin apparently permitted an offensive Comintern because he thought its activities inconsequential, and thus of little danger to Soviet foreign policy. Communism's real progress would come only from Russia's growth. Members of the Soviet hierarchy often quipped of the first five-year plan, "one Soviet tractor is worth more than ten good foreign Communists."

---

[26] Jane Degras, ed., *The Communist International 1919-1943: Documents* (London: Oxford University Press, 1960), Vol. II, 511-12. This policy apparently was not universally popular. Maurice Thorez, a member of the French delegation to the Congress and later head of the French Communist Party, reportedly disagreed in private with the new emphasis on the USSR. He admitted the Soviet Union was a platform, an example, a moral and material help—but not the basis or center of the world revolution. *Ibid.*, p. 454.

There was probably a second factor which helped at least to prolong the war scare. Stalin needed some excuse to offer his suffering populace as a result of the terrible hardships of the five-year plan and collectivization. In a series of mock trials, foreign as well as Russian technicians were charged with sabotaging the industrialization effort. Russia's capitalist enemies, the "obvious" organizers of the sabotage, were renewing their attempts at intervention. If some parts of Stalin's internal programs were bungled, it was the doing of these countries and not the fault of the Soviet Communist Party. The trials in turn made the war scare more creditable to the Russian people.

The Chinese Debacle   During Stalin's rise to power, we must note the one major revolutionary experiment in which he and the other contenders for leadership did participate—China. In the 1920's, repeated disasters in Germany had shattered the hopes for all but the most extreme optimists in Russia for immediate revolution in Europe. But the situation in China suddenly appeared on the verge of vindicating Lenin's prediction at the Second Congress of the Comintern of coming revolution in Asia. Lenin had argued that revolutions in Asia would be "bourgeois," directed against native feudalism and foreign imperialism—not capitalism. Local communist parties would form "temporary agreements or even alliances" with local national liberation movements. But local communists had to maintain their "independent character" so they could educate and organize the masses. A successful Asian revolution in turn would weaken Western imperialism.

The "national-liberation front" in China was the Kuomintang, founded by Dr. Sun Yat-sen. This party, with its headquarters in Canton, had broken with Peking, then recognized as China's legal government. Both centers of power pretended to speak for China, but neither had more than local authority. Meanwhile, Comintern agents had assisted in the birth of the Chinese Communist Party in 1921. The new party was composed of some 70 intellectuals, including a curious collection of "democratic socialists" and anarchists.

The Soviets wanted revolution, but they worried first of all about Russia's national interests in Asia, and about the security of her seemingly endless border across the middle of that continent. They particularly feared Japan, the only really powerful modern country in Asia, and her continual interest in Manchuria. The nations on the other side of this border, especially weak China, worried about Russia's designs because they had seen what Tsarist imperialism could do.

Upon assuming power, the Soviets condemned Tsarist designs on China. They even promised to give up the Chinese Eastern Railway, built by the Tsars across Northern Manchuria as a short cut to Vladivostok. (The Soviets later denied having made this statement.) But the old pattern of Sino-Russian relations soon reappeared. Taking advantage of a helpless Peking government, the Soviets set up a puppet government in Outer Mongolia—on paper, part of China. The alternative seemed to be a local government of White Russian remnants supported by the Japanese. And Outer Mongolia was too near the only thread holding Siberia together—the Trans-Siberian Railway.

Meanwhile, the Soviets prodded Peking for recognition. It came in 1924, but by that time Soviet interest centered on revolutionary possibilities in China. Sun Yat-sen had been casting about for Western aid for his revolution; rebuffed by the West, he turned to Russia. In 1923, Sun and Adolph Joffe, the Soviet emissary, agreed on guidelines for future Soviet-Kuomintang relations. Both agreed that China was not ripe for communism. Her "most pressing problem" was national unification and independence. The Soviets promised Sun money, and political and military advisors. Chinese, including Chiang Kai-shek, the future ruler of China, journeyed to Moscow for training. In addition, the Soviets organized and staffed the famous Whampoa Military Academy to train the future leaders of the Nationalist Army. Finally, Moscow pressured the tiny Chinese Communist Party to join the Kuomintang. (Many of the Chinese communists were hopelessly doctrinaire, and balked at surrendering to the "capitalists." Karl Radek chastized them for not wanting to leave their "Confucian study chambers.")

The working relationship between Moscow and Canton was destined for rough going since both sides desired domination. A Comintern chief of mission to China called Sun "an enlightened little satrap" who should be exploited but not trusted. And Moscow hoped that the Chinese communists could take over the Kuomintang from within. Michael Borodin, who had served as a Chicago school principal during his exile after the 1905 Russian Revolution, was the Comintern revolutionary expediter assigned this tricky task. Working as Sun's personal advisor, Borodin first moulded the Kuomintang according to the Bolshevik organizational pattern. A strong unified party had to be created for a successful revolution which would be followed by a Chinese communist take over.

Unfortunately, a strong Kuomintang turned out to be an excellent weapon against the communists. Sun had wanted the Chinese communists in his organization, because he was supremely confident that he could exploit their contacts and also control them. After Sun's death in 1925, Chiang Kai-shek, his successor, grew apprehensive about increasing communist influence in the Kuomintang organization. In March 1926, Chiang purged the political commissars—mainly communists—attached to his troops, removed a number of communists from influential party posts, and even placed his Soviet advisors under house arrest.

Chiang quickly apologized for the "inconvenience" he had caused the Russians, but placed even stricter limitations on the operations of the communist members of his party. Moscow nevertheless forgave all because it still felt Chiang could be manipulated. Besides, it appeared that a new alliance between Japan and Great Britain might threaten to sink the whole revolution. If the revolution failed, Soviet Russia itself would be in danger.

Soviet policy in China now had become an internal political football in Moscow. The Bolsheviks never really had understood China, and the revolutionary situation itself was exceedingly complex. But under the impact of the domestic power struggle, the debate in the Politburo lost all touch with reality; positions hardened. Under attack for his alliance with Chiang, Stalin merely defended the young warlord all the more, while Trotsky insisted that the Chinese communists should leave the Kuomintang.

In April 1927, Chiang's forces slaughtered the Shanghai communist leaders and their armed workers. The communists had recently led a victorious uprising against the local warlord while Chiang's troops camped outside the city gates. Stalin claimed he had foreseen such treachery; the nationalist leader had become a tool of the bourgeoisie. (In retrospect, Chen Tu-hsiu, the head of the Chinese Communist Party, was held responsible for tactical errors in handling the Kuomintang.) Moscow ordered the Chinese communists to break with the Kuomintang, but it was too late. By 1928, Chiang had extended Kuomintang power to most of China. Chinese communists in the urban coastal centers were crushed, or went underground. But Mao Tse-tung, leading a motley band in the hope of raising a peasant rebellion, escaped into the hinterland. And here began his long struggle with Chiang, in which he used the now classic Maoist strategy of guerrilla warfare.

SUMMARY

The overwhelming preoccupation of first Lenin and then Stalin from 1921 to 1933 was to rebuild a shattered nation into a modern and militarily powerful state. The Soviet Union had to "peacefully coexist" with capitalism—at least for the immediate years ahead. The Bolsheviks needed economic and technical assistance from the West if their plans to build "socialism in one country" were to succeed.

Almost as important to Stalin was the consolidation of his personal power, centering around his struggle with Trotsky. This contest inevitably complicated Soviet efforts to promote foreign revolutions, although actual hopes for imminent world revolution were dying. The only bright spots on the proletarian horizon had been Germany and China; but, in both cases the Bolsheviks had supervised and in both cases the revolutions failed.

Henceforth the Comintern would become a collection of subservient Stalinist parties owing first allegiance to the protection of the Soviet socialist motherland. The Comintern's "Left" turn in 1928 was not supported by Soviet foreign policy. Stalin clearly believed that "one Soviet tractor" was now worth more than "ten good foreign communists."

FURTHER READING

Beloff, Max, *The Foreign Policy of Soviet Russia, 1929-1941.* 2 vols. First vol., 1929-1936; second vol., 1936-1941. London: Oxford University Press, 1947, 1949. Published for the Royal Institute of International Affairs. Indispensable for the period indicated.

Brandt, Conrad, *Stalin's Failure in China, 1924-1927.* Cambridge, Mass.: Harvard University Press, 1958.

Carr, E. H., *German-Soviet Relations Between the World Wars, 1919-1939.* Baltimore, Md.: Johns Hopkins Press, 1951. Six lectures by British historian.

Deutscher, Isaac, *Stalin: A Political Biography.* New York: Oxford University Press, 1967, 2nd ed. Deals mainly with internal developments, but valuable sections on foreign policy.

Eudin, Xenia and Harold H. Fisher, eds., *Soviet Russia and the West, 1920-1927: A Documentary Survey.* Stanford, Calif.: Stanford University Press. Valuable collection of documents with introductory notes.

Eudin, Xenia and Robert C. North, eds., *Soviet Russia and the East, 1920-1927: A Documentary Survey.* Stanford, Calif.: Stanford University Press, 1957. Valuable collection of documents with introductory notes.

Eudin, Xenia and Robert M. Slusser, eds., *Soviet Foreign Policy, 1928-1934: Documents and Materials.* 2 vols. University Park, Pa.: Pennsylvania State University Press, 1966, 1967. Continuation of previous volumes on Soviet relations, 1920-1927.

Fischer, Ruth, *Stalin and German Communism: A Study in the Origins of the State Party.* Cambridge, Mass.: Harvard University Press, 1948. Study by former member of German Communist Party.

Freund, Gerald, *Unholy Alliance: Russian-German Relations from the Treaty of Brest-Litovsk to the Treaty of Berlin.* New York: Harcourt, Brace & World, Inc., 1957.

Hilger, Gustav and Alfred G. Meyer, *The Incompatible Allies: A Memoire-History of German-Soviet Relations, 1918-1941.* New York: The Macmillan Company, 1953. Firsthand account by former member of German foreign service.

Kochan, Lionel E., *Russia and the Weimar Republic.* Cambridge, Eng.: Bowes and Bowes, 1954. Covers diplomatic and military relations as well as relations between Comintern and German Communist Party.

McKenzie, Kermit E., *Comintern and World Revolution, 1928-1943*. New York: Columbia University Press, 1964. Comintern strategy and tactics from 1928-1943.

North, Robert C., *Moscow and Chinese Communists*, 2nd ed., Stanford, Calif.: Stanford University Press, 1963. Well-documented history of Chinese Communist Party from early years, and its relations with USSR.

Rosenbaum, Kurt, *Community of Fate: German-Soviet Diplomatic Relations, 1922-1928*. Syracuse, N.Y.: Syracuse University Press, 1965.

Schwartz, Benjamin, *Chinese Communism and the Rise of Mao*. Cambridge, Mass.: Harvard University Press, 1951. The formative period (1918-1931).

Von Laue, Theodore H., "Soviet Diplomacy: G. V. Chicherin, People's Commissar for Foreign Affairs, 1918-1930," in *The Diplomats, 1919-1939*, ed. by Gordon A. Craig and Felix Gilbert. Princeton, N.J.: Princeton University Press, 1953. Thoughtful, lengthy essay.

Whiting, Allen S., *Soviet Policies in China, 1917-1924*. New York: Columbia University Press, 1954. Soviet motives towards China.

6

THE NAZI MENACE
1934-1941

Hitler's grandiose plans for conquest inevitably became the central concern of Soviet Russia. From 1934, Stalin used every stratagem to delay or divert a German attack. When the invasion of the socialist motherland finally came in June 1941, he commandeered all the resources of the Russian people in a desperate attempt to halt the Nazi advance.

There are many strange aspects to the story of how Stalin attempted to preserve the land of socialism. Possibly the strangest is his initial blindness to the nature of Nazism.[1] Some even suggest that Stalin is responsible for Hilter's rise to power.

THE GERMAN COMMUNISTS
AND THE RISE OF HITLER

The world depression of 1929 dealt the youthful Weimar Republic a fatal blow. In the face of drastic unemployment, voters deserted parties of moderation for communists on the extreme left and Nazis on the extreme right. Both organizations promised the destruction of the existing political system, and both were unscrupulous.

[1] It could be argued that the leaders of other nations were just as blind.

158

Russian and German communists viewed Hitler's movement through the distorted Marxist-Leninist prism. There were two principal classes in Germany—the proletarians and the bourgeoisie. The communists fought with the German moderate socialists—their main enemy—for the allegiance of the proletariat.[2] The Nazi party represented the extreme right wing of the bourgeoisie and therefore was not revolutionary. How could the Nazis turn against the ruling class if they were part of that class? Communists saw no real difference between fascism and democracy.[3]

Communist hatred of the socialists was intense by 1931. They seemed to prefer a Nazi regime to any government containing socialists. In the horribly distorted communist view, this would complete the destruction of the socialists and pave the way for the proletarian revolution. In 1932, a Nazi government seemed imminent. Hitler received nearly 14 million votes in the July elections. Yet at the next election in November, Nazi voting strength unexpectedly declined. The communists thought their star was rising. For the first time they received almost six million votes; but then came the shock. On January 30, 1933, Hitler was given the chancellorship. The Nazis, bent on subverting the basic fabric of German society, had come to power through the democratic process.

Were Stalin and German communists to blame for this turn of events? Hitler had gained most of his support from the middle classes and the nationalists—not from the working class. The communist attack on German moderate socialism did not *directly* augment the Nazi voting strength. But in a broader perspective, Moscow and the German party must assume a great share of the responsibility for the fall of the Weimar Republic. They repeatedly had battered that shaky edifice since its birth in 1918. A democratic government in Germany, given the legacy of Versailles and the economic chaos of the Great Depression, could not hold off both the left and the right.

The Soviet Reaction The Soviets were not particularly worried about Hitler's sudden rise to power. The German communist revolution merely seemed nearer. Karl Radek wrote that every Nazi blow against the party organization rallied the proletariat. A party that received six million votes could not "be dismissed from the balance sheet of history." But Radek was proven wrong. Hitler immediately set out to crush the German communists.

[2] The "Left" Comintern program of 1928 had thrown over the united front tactics of previous years. Socialist leaders were called "social-fascists"—indicating they were no better than Hitler. In 1929, the communists pinned this label on all members of the socialist party as violent clashes grew between the two proletarian organizations.
[3] Fascism, which originated in Italy, was the general term used by communists for all right wing totalitarian movements.

Stalin saw no immediate or direct threat to Russia itself in Hitler's foreign policy. The Soviet leader still appeared to ignore the blunt forecast in *Mein Kampf*,[4] in which Hitler had warned that Germany's need for *lebensraum* could only be fulfilled at the expense of Russia. But Nazi Germany was militarily still impotent, and there seemed to be elements in Hitler's entourage favorable to the Rapallo policy. The Reichstag had extended the Treaty of Berlin in May 1933. Goering, Hitler's right-hand man, assured the Soviets that the "campaign for the extirpation of communism in Germany has nothing to do with German-Russian relations."

The Soviets became visibly concerned by 1934. In May of 1933, Hitler had promised a relieved world that Germany would destroy all her offensive weapons—if other nations did the same. In October, Hitler abruptly quit the Disarmament Conference and the League of Nations. He claimed Germany was not being treated equally; the Allies wanted eight years to bring their armaments down to Germany's level. The Nazi regime had started to rearm in defiance of the Versailles Treaty, although this would not be made public until March 1935. More ominous for Russia, however, was the increased anti-communism in Hitler's speeches.

Stalin finally commented on these disturbing trends at the Party's Seventeenth Congress in January 1934. The Soviet Union was "far from being enthusiastic about the fascist regime in Germany."[5] But this had nothing to do with Soviet foreign policy; Russia still could have good relations with Germany. On the other hand, Germany's policy toward Russia had changed. Stalin saw traces of German imperialism reminiscent of World War I.

A German flirtation with Poland increased Soviet uneasiness. In the month of the Seventeenth Congress, Hitler signed a ten-year non-aggression pact with Marshal Pilsudski. The Führer already had set his sights on Poland, but Poland first had to be cut loose from France, her Western ally. The Poles joined with Germany to block Hitler's plans for revising the German-Polish frontier. They knew that all German statesmen considered the worst crime of Versailles to be the separation of East Prussia from Germany proper by the Polish Corridor, and the creation of the Free City of Danzig. But the Russians suspected some dirty work behind the scenes. They were not very wrong. Beginning in 1935, the Nazi leaders tried to lure Poland deeper into the German web by playing on the Polish longing for the Soviet Ukraine. Goering even hinted at a joint crusade against Russia.

---

[4] Litvinov, on the other hand, reportedly had read *Mein Kampf* as early as 1928.
[5] Several months earlier, Litvinov had reassured the Nazis: "We of course sympathise with the sufferings of our German comrades, but we Marxists are the last who can be reproached with allowing our feelings to dictate our policy."

Trouble in the Far East A possible German-Japanese alliance against the USSR also contributed to Soviet discomfort. Russia long had worried in general about Japan, the most powerful modern state in Asia. But Japan's seizure of Manchuria in 1931 posed an immediate threat to Soviet Siberia. *Bolshevik*, the Party journal, labeled the Japanese aggression "a prelude to a war of intervention against the Soviet Union and to a new imperialist war for the hegemony of the world." The British and French, as usual, were thought to be secretly involved.

Meanwhile, the Japanese harassed Soviet personnel managing the Chinese Eastern Railway. In 1929 the Soviets had used a show of military force to forestall a Chinese attempt to get back the vital railroad. But Japan, unlike the Chinese, could not be bluffed. The Soviets therefore resorted to other tactics—they were too weak to risk a fight. In hopes of supporting China against Japanese pressure, the Soviets resumed diplomatic relations with Chiang Kai-shek's government in 1932. (Relations had been severed in 1929 after Stalin's clash with Chiang over the Chinese Eastern Railway.) And Stalin finally achieved American recognition of Soviet Russia in 1933, by playing on United States concern over her own Far Eastern interests. Finally, the Soviets asked the Japanese for a non-aggression pact. When this move failed, the Soviets tried appeasement. They sold the disputed railway to Japan's puppet regime in Manchuria in 1935 for approximately one-fourth the asking price.[6] Russia's relations with the West were improving, but Hitler now had to be taken seriously, and the possibility of a German-Japanese understanding had to be faced. With two fronts to defend, Russia's nightmare was a hostile Germany *and* a hostile Japan.

The ever-present threat of enemies in both the East and the West had constantly conditioned Soviet foreign policy, and would continue to do so. If the threat from both directions seemed overwhelming, obviously the Bolsheviks had to appease one, if not both, hostile parties. In 1935 they appeased Japan; later, Stalin would appease Nazi Germany.

COLLECTIVE SECURITY: DEFENSE
AGAINST AGGRESSION

In 1934, Stalin began a radical change in Soviet foreign policy to thwart Hitler. Russia's long alliance with Germany was scrapped for an alliance with the West, particularly with France and England.

---

[6] The Chinese reacted violently to this "unlawful transaction with an unlawful regime."

Versailles system, not, in alliance with Germany, its dedicated destroyer. Hopefully, this new alignment would add strength to the determination of the Western democracies to stop Hitler and prevent a new world war. If Stalin's policy failed, at least the direction of Hitler's thrust might be diverted toward the West, and not toward Russia. The Soviet leader still lived with the fear that the West might organize a new capitalist coalition against the Soviet Union, with Nazi Germany as the spearhead. Hitler had stressed the theme of Nazism as a bulwark against communism, and certain circles in the West were inclined to let Germany play the part.

To launch the new anti-Nazi coalition, Stalin had to obligate the Western powers, at least on paper, to come to the aid of any country attacked by Germany. He tried three tactics: (1) the Soviets would attempt to make the League of Nations function as a true collective security organization—its stated purpose; (2) the League could be buttressed with an "Eastern Locarno" system providing immediate mutual assistance to any victim of aggression in Eastern Europe (the 1925 Locarno treaties only guaranteed Germany's western borders), and the "Eastern Locarno" scheme could be supplemented with a bilateral treaty of mutual assistance between Russia and France; and (3) the Comintern would order communists in the West to join with liberal and even conservative groups in the democracies in the fight against internal and external fascism.

Maxim Litvinov, now foreign minister, was to carry out the new tactics, and may have played the major role in their formulation. A Western-oriented, Russian Jew with an English wife, Litvinov seemed the perfect Soviet emissary to negotiate the necessary security pacts and participate in the League debates. Chicherin, his brilliant predecessor, had been a recluse and a hypochondriac. Litvinov was ebullient, tempestuous, and he wanted Russia represented on the world stage. (The international correspondents loved his dripping sarcasm.) Chicherin had been fascinated with Russia's great duel with England over Asia. Litvinov placed first priority on Russia's relations with Europe. On the other hand, both foreign ministers intimated that Comintern activities hampered the promotion of Soviet interests through conventional diplomacy.

Litvinov's tactics to promote collective security, however, might not succeed. The final defense of the socialist motherland still hinged on the Red Army. All during the 1930's, Russia's ace in the hole was the great rearmament program begun with the first five-year plan in 1928.

The Soviet Union Joins the League   Soviet Russia had never trusted the League of Nations. The First Congress of the Comintern labeled it the "Holy Alliance of the bourgeoisie for the suppression of the proletarian revolution." The Sixth Congress in 1928 still charged that "the most shameless robber treaty of the last decade . . . cloaks the war-like work of its members by working out projects for disarmament." [7]

But in 1934 the USSR joined the League. The Soviet decision apparently had been triggered by Moscow's realization that she could get her bilateral pact with France—an essential component of the "Eastern Locarno" system—only if she became a League member. Once Russia joined, however, she became an enthusiastic supporter of the international security organization. Litvinov had castigated "European capitalism" and denigrated the League at the disarmament conferences. In his maiden speech at Geneva, the Foreign Commissar rapturously proclaimed that "the Soviet Government . . . could not but observe the increasing activity in the League of Nations of States interested in the preservation of peace and their struggle against aggressive militarist elements. . . . The organization of peace! Could there be a loftier and at the same time more practical and urgent task for the cooperation of all nations?" Litvinov also was realistic: "Far be it from me to overrate the opportunities and means of the League of Nations for the organization of peace. I realize, better perhaps than any of you, how limited these means are. . . . I am however convinced that, with the firm will and close cooperation of all its Members, a great deal could be done at any given moment for the utmost diminution of the danger of war. . . ." [8]

For once, the Soviet word was good. Litvinov ignored the obvious slight of his initial appointment to the Committee on Seaweeds, and set an example for other statesmen with his steadfast opposition to aggression. Litvinov's theme of cautious optimism guided Soviet policy toward the League for the next several years.

The "Eastern Locarno" and the Franco-Soviet Pact   The Soviets attempted to thwart Hitler with the traditional methods of diplomacy—pacts and alliances—before their entry into the League. The first overtures were to France. As late as July 1930, Stalin had characterized France as "the most aggressive and militarist country of all aggressive and militarist countries of the world." By 1932, the two countries had signed a non-aggression pact. The French were getting worried

---

[7] Beginning in 1927, the Soviet Union nevertheless took part in the League disarmament conferences. A militarily weak Russia had everything to gain. Even if the capitalist West didn't reduce its arms, the conferences were a splendid propaganda springboard. The Soviets paraded schemes for total disarmament as evidence of the superior moral character of their nation.

[8] For Litvinov's speech see Jane Degras, ed., *Soviet Documents on Foreign Policy* (London: Oxford University Press, 1953) III, published for the Royal Institute of International Affairs, 89-96.

about resurgent German nationalism. The Russians seemed more concerned about France herself than a Germany not yet Nazi. As we noted,
Stalin continued his official silence until 1934 on the disturbing trend
of German foreign policy. But sometime in the latter part of 1933, the
Soviets apparently talked with the French about a security system for
Eastern Europe as a bulwark against Nazi Germany. (In 1925, the French
had worked in vain to extend the Locarno guarantees to Germany's eastern borders.)

In June 1934, a pact was drafted calling for the USSR, Germany,
Poland, Czechoslovakia, Finland and the Baltic states to come to the
mutual assistance, in accordance with League requirements, of any member who might be the victim of aggression. A separate bilateral arrangement between France and the Soviet Union was proposed, guaranteeing
French aid if there were aggression against the "Eastern Locarno" members, and Soviet aid for the "Western Locarno" members. Unfortunately,
the whole grandiose scheme collapsed against a German brick wall.
Hitler, much more than Stresemann, refused to have his hands tied in the
east. To top off the failure, the Poles had just made peace with Hitler
in their own non-aggression pact, and refused to enter any other arrangement without Germany.

Their plans frustrated, Russia and France went ahead on May 2, 1935,
with a bilateral pact pledging to come to each other's aid in the case of
an unprovoked attack by another "European" state. (The French wanted
no part of a Soviet war with Japan.) The Soviets signed a similar treaty
on May 16 with Czechoslovakia; this latter document was to prove more
important. Czechoslovakia would soon be an object of Hitler's desire,
and a test of both Soviet and French resistance to Germany. A crucial
section of the Soviet-Czech pact stated that Russia would come to the
aid of the Czechs only if France did likewise. (The French had signed a
pact of mutual assistance with Czechoslovakia in 1925.)

The "Popular Fronts" The third arrow in the Soviet
quiver was the "popular" or "united" front policy for communist parties
in nations fighting fascism. The introduction of this policy is curious, and
at the same time revealing. Pierre Laval, the French foreign minister,
visited with Stalin in Moscow in May 1935 after the signing of the Franco-
Soviet pact. Upon his return to Paris, Laval announced that Stalin had
authorized him to say that Russia completely approved and understood
France's efforts to build up her defenses. Until this time, communist
deputies in the French Parliament had opposed all defense measures of
the "capitalist warmongers," and ordinary party members had spread
revolutionary propaganda among the armed forces. But Stalin's new instructions, however unorthodox their transmission, were not lost. The

French communists immediately dropped their opposition to the government's defense measures.[9]

As often happens in Soviet foreign policy, a period of experimentation had taken place before the formal change in tactics. The popular front concept was not officially introduced until the Seventh Congress of the Comintern in the summer of 1935. Georgi Dimitrov, the new head of the Comintern and a world famous anti-fascist, described the sweeping change: "How can fascism be prevented from coming to power and how can fascism be overthrown after being victorious. . . . The first thing that must be done is to form a united front, to establish unity of action of the workers in every factory, in every district, in every region, in every country, all over the world." Dimitrov reminded the faithful, of course, that the ultimate goals remained. Fascism had to be fought now so that the proletariat could create the "preliminary conditions for its final emancipation."[10]

But Dimitrov's promise to the faithful seemed mere lip service. The line had swerved sharply to the right. This was not the typical "united front" of yesteryear. The communists were ready to join *all* available groups, including the most conservative bourgeois parties, as long as they professed anti-fascism. Franz Borkenau, a skillful analyst of the Comintern, wrote about the new program: "It implied a wholesale overthrow of the basic principles of communism. Instead of the class struggle, cooperation with the bourgeoisie. Instead of the Soviet system, eulogy of democracy. Instead of internationalism, nationalism."[11] The Comintern truly had become an instrument of Soviet foreign policy, a sacrificial lamb on the altar of Soviet state security.

THE SOVIET SECURITY SYSTEM COLLAPSES

In 1936, the Soviet security system began to misfire. The collective security provisions of the League had proven empty

---

[9] Franz Borkenau dates the switch in policy even earlier. On February 6, 1934, the French Communists and a motley group of French fascists had caused the resignation of Daladier's democratic government. (The Germany of 1932 was being repeated.) But scared of fascist strength, and apparently without consulting Moscow, the communists joined with moderate trade unionists on February 12, in a general strike labeled as an anti-fascist demonstration. This was the first united action of communists and socialists in any country since 1929. Franz Borkenau, *World Communism* (Ann Arbor: University of Michigan, 1962), p. 383.

[10] Dimitrov, a Bulgarian communist, had won fame for making a fool of Goering at the celebrated Reichstag fire trial in 1933. Acting as his own lawyer, the future Comintern head refuted the Nazi charge that he had participated in a communist plot to burn the Reichstag. Later evidence indicated the Nazis had fired the building.

[11] Franz Borkenau, *World Communism*, p. 387.

against the rape of Ethiopia in the fall of 1935. Litvinov fought hard for strong action against Italy, but the Allies were too afraid of pushing Mussolini closer to Hitler. Moreover, the Franco-Soviet pact of May 1935 still had not been ratified by the French. Laval apparently was stalling in order to continue a flirtation with Berlin and Warsaw. The French right was bitterly attacking the whole concept of a pact with Bolshevism. Perhaps the most significant indication of the treaty's hollowness was the inability of France and the USSR to agree on specific military commitments in case of aggression.

The Rhineland   The first real blow to the Russian security system, however, came at dawn on March 7, 1936. Hitler, in brazen defiance of Germany's obligations under the Versailles Treaty and the Locarno Pact, ordered a token force of one division into the demilitarized Rhineland. Hitler claimed the Franco-Soviet pact, finally being ratified by the French Parliament, had introduced "an element of legal insecurity" into the Locarno arrangement. "In the interest of the primitive rights of its people to the security of their frontier and the safeguarding of their defense," cried Hitler, "the German government has reestablished . . . the absolute and unrestricted sovereignty of the Reich in the demilitarized zone!"

The French wanted to move; but, General Gamelin, Chief of their own High Command, warned that "any war operation, however limited, entailed unpredictable risks and could not be undertaken without decreeing a general mobilization." The French foreign minister flew to London and begged for British help, which the Locarno Treaty obligated Britain to give France if she in turn acted. The British were unenthusiastic. Lord Lothian, a prominent Tory, philosophized: "The Germans, after all, are only going into their own back garden."

We now know that *any* Western resistance would have forced the Germans to retreat, and probably would have meant the end of Hitler. But France and Britain were paralyzed, as Hitler had predicted to his frightened generals. And what was Stalin to think of his new ally— France? This nation, still possessing the most powerful war machine in Europe, had been the staunchest defender of Versailles. But France refused to stop the Germans on her own doorstep, and what would she do if Hitler turned his guns on Eastern Europe? The Rhineland was Hitler's last major objective in the West. All the rest of his stated demands lay in the East. Stalin may have thought the French and British "gave" Hitler the Rhineland for just that reason.

The Spanish Civil War   The value of League collective security and the Franco-Soviet pact had been compromised. A crucial test now came for the popular front policy. In July 1936, civil war erupted in Spain. With the aid of Italy and later Germany, Generalissimo Franco's fascist organization (the Falange) staged a coup against the Spanish Republican government. The ostensible reason—Spain was threatened with a communist revolution.

At first Stalin remained detached. He wanted to prove to the Western democracies that Russia no longer was playing with foreign revolution—the situation in Spain clearly had revolutionary possibilities—and that she could be a dependable ally.[12] A communist revolution was always desirable in principle, but not if it might impair the security of the socialist motherland. In August, Russia joined with France and the other powers in pledging not to intervene. The Soviets nevertheless insisted that all countries, including Germany and Italy, would have to abide by the agreement.

However, the two fascist powers continued to aid Franco, and the situation of the Republican government grew desperate. Sometime in September, Moscow decided it had to act to forestall a third fascist dictatorship in Europe. For with Nazi Germany on one side and a Falangist Spain on the other, France herself might succumb to a rightist coup. Stalin could not afford to lose France, his one major ally in the West, no matter how vacillating that ally might be. In short, the Soviets would intervene for compelling strategic reasons—not to bring off a communist revolution.[13]

Within a matter of weeks, Russian tanks were in action on the plains of Spain. The Comintern formed an International Brigade of communists and liberals from France, the United States and other nations. The Republican cause had aroused the profound sympathy of liberals and leftists everywhere.[14] Comintern agents assisted the Republicans in purchasing arms. However, the Soviets took pains to conceal their direct participation. Munitions were shipped in rebuilt freighters with false decks. The Russians in Spain, mainly political and military advisors, never exceeded a few thousand.

But the Soviet aid and the handful of advisors temporarily turned the tide. The communists threw all their organizational skill into building a centralized professional army. The raw material consisted of the enthusiastic but terribly undisciplined mob of workers which had come to

[12] In May 1936, Stalin gave a widely publicized interview to Roy Howard of the Scripps-Howard newspaper chain. Stalin assured the world that Russia never had planned or intended to export revolution. It was all a "tragi-comic" misunderstanding.
[13] For a discussion of Soviet motivations, see David T. Cattell, *Soviet Diplomacy and the Spanish Civil War* (Berkeley, Calif.: University of California Press, 1957), pp. 32-37.
[14] Louis Fischer in *Men and Politics* (New York: Duell, Sloan & Pearce, 1941), calls the Spanish Civil War "The Holy War."

the defense of the Republican government. Russian and Spanish communists fought all attempts of Spanish anarchists and socialists to turn the government left. The communist slogan read: "This is not a revolution at all; it is only the defense of the legal government." In their intense efforts to keep the semblance of a popular front, the Spanish communists under Soviet orders actually became the right wing element in the coalition—a strange development indeed.

In February 1937, Stalin must have taken a sober look at the situation. He had hoped that the Western democracies also would help the Republicans. If they had, Germany and Italy might have been scared off and the West finally would have been aligned against fascism. But the British and French had not budged. The Soviets could not afford to send the massive amount of aid necessary for victory. And this action might involve Russia in a full-scale war with Germany and Italy—the very thing Stalin was trying to avoid. Moreover, Japanese imperialism was threatening Russia's eastern frontier. The Soviet contingents in Siberia might need strengthening.

From then on Stalin sent just enough aid to prolong the war and keep the fascist regimes embroiled. (Hitler had the same goal for different reasons. War in Spain widened the breach between Italy and the Allies, and presented a superb illustration for his diatribes against Bolshevism.) Stalin also dispatched agents of his secret police to purge elements of the Spanish left resisting communist leadership. This witch-hunting, ostensibly to preserve the image of the popular front, paralleled the great purge trials then beginning in Moscow. It probably was part of Stalin's drive to eliminate all potential centers of opposition in the world socialist movement. As a result, Russia lost much of the good will generated in the early days of the civil war.

The popular front concept itself was an object of fear for many in the West. Every increase in the strength of the alliance in Spain (or in France) caused anxiety in the middle classes. The Republican government was called Bolshevist and Moscow-controlled. Communists, regardless of their intentions, could not live down decades of revolutionary slogans and attempted coups against democratic governments. Isaac Deutscher comments: "Thus, by a curious dialectical process, the Popular Fronts defeated their own purpose. They had set out to reconcile the bourgeois west with Russia; they increased the estrangement." [15]

Soviet intervention in Spain had failed to achieve its primary purpose —the strengthening of the anti-Hitler coalition. Instead, it increased the traditional distrust between the Soviet Union and the Western democracies. On the other side, Mussolini was driven into the clutches of Hitler

---

[15] Isaac Deutscher, *Stalin* (New York: Oxford University Press, Inc., 1949), p. 423.

through their mutual aid to Spain. The efforts of Britain and France to use Fascist Italy as a counterweight to Nazi Germany also had failed.

The Axis and the Anti-Comintern Pact   The cement for the new alliance between the fascist states was anti-communism. In the first months of the Spanish Civil War, Hitler renewed his propaganda attack on Russia. Germany had to lengthen the period of military service for conscripts because of the danger from communism. The official announcement of this measure warned, "History has taught us that it is better, if necessary, to make great sacrifices for external peace rather than to be overwhelmed in the Bolshevist chaos." Italy concurred. On October 21, 1936, the two dictatorships signed a secret protocol outlining a common foreign policy. Mussolini publicly admitted an "Axis" had been formed around which other European states interested in peace could gather. Count Ciano, Italy's foreign minister, spoke of "the supreme obligation assumed by Germany and Italy to defend the great institutions of Europe."

In November 1936, Hitler's net bridged the Asian continent. Germany and Japan signed the "Anti-Comintern Pact." (Italy joined one year later.) This was the more serious for Russia of Germany's new alliances. In the pact's text, the two states merely agreed to consult about Comintern activities and the necessary preventive measures each was taking. Hitler announced Germany and Japan (like Italy) had joined together to defend Western civilization. Ribbentrop pointed to Spain as "the latest victim of the desire for destruction shown by the Bolshevist virus."

The Soviets read a different significance in the agreement. Litvinov scoffed: "Well-informed people refuse to believe that in order to draw up the two meagre articles . . . which have been published it was necessary to conduct negotiations for fifteen months" in the greatest secrecy.[16] At the November meeting of the Congress of Soviets, the Prime Minister of the Ukrainian Republic charged Germany and Japan with preparing a "holy crusade" against the Soviet Union. Hitler was warned of his foolishness. "Our answer to the Nazi dream of invading the Ukraine is an old Ukrainian saying: Just as a pig can never look at the sky, so Hitler will never be able to see our cabbage patch. . . . If a Fascist army dares to approach the Soviet Union our army under Voroshilov will deliver such a blow as has never been seen before." [17]

The Soviets were right in charging the pact was other than it seemed. In a secret protocol, Germany and Japan agreed to safeguard their common interests in case of an unprovoked attack by Russia, and to avoid

[16] Jane Degras, ed., *Soviet Documents on Foreign Policy,* III, 224.
[17] Cited in Max Beloff, *The Foreign Policy of Soviet Russia, 1929-1941* (London: Oxford University Press, 1949), II, 64.

measures which might ease the situation of the Soviet Union. Each state also promised to make no treaties with Russia contrary to the spirit of the pact without first obtaining the other's consent. Germany soon would break this pledge with the Nazi-Soviet Non-Aggression Pact. In the meantime, it appeared that the most dangerous enemies of the Soviet state had banded together.

THE BEGINNING OF THE END

In the late afternoon of November 5, 1937, Hitler met secretly with his four ranking generals and the German foreign minister. William L. Shirer calls this meeting "the decisive turning point in the life of the Third Reich." [18] During the four-hour session, Hitler proclaimed that the time had come to enlarge the racial community—to gain *lebensraum*. Space could not come from colonial empires in Africa or Asia. It had to be taken from the heart of Europe. France and England stood in the way (*not* Russia). But they were weak, while Germany had almost completed her rearmament. Hitler realized that it was opportune for Germany to strike now before the rest of Europe had sufficiently rearmed.

Austria and Czechoslovakia were the first targets. Hitler was almost positive Britain, and probably France, had tacitly abandoned the Czechs. Russia probably would not intervene in view of Japan's attitude. Later, Germany would deal with Poland. A cold, carefully calculated plan of aggression had been outlined. In public, Hitler shouted about the danger of Bolshevism as justification for German rearmament. In private, he demonstrated Europe's nightmare would be German.

The Anschluss   Hitler moved quickly and ruthlessly to achieve his secret objectives now that preparations for war were ready —although he still hoped to avoid war. At Berchtesgaden, his palatial Alpine villa, Hitler launched a two-hour tirade against Kurt von Schuschnigg, the Austrian Chancellor, on February 12, 1938. Carefully arranging for the presence of several of his army generals, the Führer demanded the virtual integration of Austria into the Third Reich. Schuschnigg capitulated. But the Chancellor returned home to stage a

---

[18] *The Rise and Fall of the Third Reich* (New York: Simon and Schuster, Inc., 1960), p. 305. Alan Bullock disagrees. He believes Hitler's foreign policy had not changed since the publication of *Mein Kampf*—expansion eastward. Hitler was far too able a politician "to make an irrevocable decision on a series of hypothetical assumptions." He would continue to play the opportunist, in spite of the November "strategy" conference. The real significance of Hitler's meeting was his change of mood, the decision to increase the pressure and thus raise the risks. *Hitler: A Study of Tyranny* (New York: Harper & Row, Publishers, 1962), pp. 370-71.

last-ditch plebiscite. Hitler would be shown that the Austrian people didn't want the "Anschluss"—the joining together of Germany and Austria. The Führer was furious at Schuschnigg's treachery. Two days before the plebiscite, Hitler's tanks rolled south to take up positions on the Austrian border. The Austrian conservative-Catholic government gave up. Seyss-Inquart, front man for the local Nazi party, became Chancellor. Hitler's legions moved into Austria "to help it prevent bloodshed." The Anschluss was complete.

The West did nothing. Yet as late as 1932 France and England had forbidden an economic union of Germany and Austria to alleviate the effects of the depression. But Germany under Hitler was different. Neville Chamberlain, the British Prime Minister, told the House of Commons: "The hard fact is that nothing could have arrested what actually has happened—unless this country and other countries had been prepared to use force." But no one was. Wasn't this, after all, just self-determination? Hitler, Austrian by birth, merely had gone home.

During these first months of his diplomatic offensive, Hitler had reached new heights in his vitriolic attack on Russia. Several weeks before the Austrian crisis he stated: "There is only one State with which we have not sought to establish relations, nor do we wish to establish relations with it: Soviet Russia. More than ever do we see in Bolshevism the incarnation of the human destructive instinct. . . ."

Remarks such as this must have contributed to Stalin's growing feeling of isolation. On February 12, he wrote an open letter on the position of the Soviet state in "a capitalist encirclement." Stalin recalled Lenin's famous speech in March 1919 predicting that the continual existence of the Soviet Republic side by side with the imperialists was unthinkable. In the end one or the other would triumph after a series of the most terrible clashes.[19] Stalin saw Lenin's forecast coming true. "It would be absurd and stupid," Stalin argued, "to close our eyes to the fact of capitalist encirclement and to think that our external enemies, for example the fascists, will not try when the occasion offers to make a military attack on the USSR." In the meantime, the Soviet Union had to strengthen the ties of the working class of the USSR with the working classes of the bourgeois countries. The Soviet armed forces had to be augmented. The entire Russian people had to remain in "a state of mobilized readiness in face of the danger of military attack, so that no 'accident' and no tricks of our foreign enemies can take us by surprise."

Stalin seemed disenchanted with the prospects for collective security. He had not mentioned aid from the democracies as part of the Soviet defense strategy. It was left to Litvinov to make one of the final pleas

[19] See Chap. 5, p. 124.

for collective action. Five days after the Anschluss, the Soviet Foreign Commissar warned that international inaction in the face of the "armed invasion" of Austria had greatly increased the danger of new aggression. All states, the major powers in particular, had to take a firm and un-ambiguous stand to eliminate a new world massacre. The USSR mean-while would honor its obligations to Czechoslovakia—which Litvinov singled out as Hitler's next victim—if France did likewise. The follow-ing day, the USSR proposed that Britain, France, and the United States jointly consider measures to prevent further aggression.

The Road to Munich   Czechoslovakia was to be the key test of whether the Soviet Union and the West could ally to stop Hitler. And Czechoslovakia seemed quite a different case from Austria. That country had been a conservative, not terribly democratic remnant of a once powerful enemy state—the Austro-Hungarian empire. Czechoslo-vakia was a citadel of democracy, cut out of the same empire at the end of World War I. A strong supporter of the League, the East European state was allied by solemn treaties of mutual assistance with France and Russia. The Czech Army was a powerful, modern force, and the Czechs had built a version of the Maginot Line on their western border. They had taken Hitler at his word.

The British Conservative Government during this critical period was led by Neville Chamberlain. Anthony Eden, Chamberlain's one formi-dable counter-weight in the cabinet, had resigned as Foreign Secretary in February 1938.[20] The Prime Minister's years as a successful business-man had given him supreme confidence in his ability to understand and manipulate other men. But he did not comprehend the difference be-tween dealing with honorable and reasonable businessmen, and dealing with dishonorable and unreasonable dictators.[21] Hitler and Mussolini could not be bargained with like his former competitors in the world of commerce. But Chamberlain hoped to do just this by offering concessions in return for peace. And the bargaining would be done without Russia. On February 21, 1938, Chamberlain said that the peace of Europe de-pended on the attitude of the four major powers of Europe: Germany, Italy, France, and Britain.

The Prime Minister abhorred Russia, as did any good ultra-conserva-

[20] Eden finally got fed up with Chamberlain's refusal—or inability—to recognize the true character of Hitler and Mussolini. The Soviets lost a vital advocate of closer relations with Russia. Eden had journeyed to Moscow in March 1935, the first visit of a British cabinet minister to the Soviet capital since the revolution. Stalin personally presided over the reception and, against Bolshevik protocol, ordered "God Save the King" played.

[21] Lloyd-George, the great Liberal leader, said Chamberlain's outlook did not rise above that of a "provincial manufacturer of iron bedsteads."

tive Tory. He wrote to his sister a year later (March 1939): "I must confess to the most profound distrust of Russia. I have no belief whatever in her ability to maintain an effective offensive, even if she wanted to. And I distrust her motives, which seem to me to have little connection with our ideas of liberty and to be concerned only with getting everyone else by the ears." [22] With few exceptions, Chamberlain and the English establishment believed the USSR the real enemy of England—not the Third Reich.

Chamberlain's cold shoulder to Litvinov's call for a four-power conference therefore was hardly a surprise. The British government, he told the House of Commons, wanted no part of mutual undertakings in advance to resist aggression. England would choose between war and peace depending on the situation. Specifically, England would not agree beforehand to support France in her commitment to defend Czechoslovakia. The way was again cleared for the Nazi juggernaut. France was not prepared to act without Britain, in spite of her solemn promise to defend the Czechs.

Hitler's strategy was to demand autonomy for the some three million Germans in the Czech Sudetenland. But this was only to create an excuse for the destruction of the Czech state. Konrad Heinlein, the leader of the Sudeten Germans, was ordered to make impossible demands on the Czech government. Tensions would increase, and Germany would intervene in Czechoslovakia to prevent "civil war"—Hitler's pretext for entering Austria.

As Nazi pressure built up during the spring and summer of 1938, the Soviets repeatedly assured the Czechs, the French, and the world of Russia's readiness to fulfill her obligations. But the best the French could get from the British was a double negative: Britain promised to warn the Germans that she could *not* guarantee that she would *not* enter the conflict. Meanwhile, rumors abounded that the British Conservative leadership was considering cession of the Sudetenland—still the ostensible issue—to Germany. On March 22, the London *Times* had called for an international plebiscite in the contested area. Otherwise, Britain might be fighting against the principle of self-determination.

The September Crisis   The crisis came to a head in the late summer of 1938. Till then Hitler had been careful to keep Germany officially out of the conflict, maintaining it was between the Sudeten minority and the Czech government. In May, the Führer had confided to the key German generals his unshakeable will to wipe the Czechs off the map by force. The plan was to be executed no later than October 1.

[22] Keith Feiling, *Neville Chamberlain* (London: Macmillan & Co. Ltd., 1946), p. 403.

The foreign embassies in Berlin reported that the big September Party rally in Nuremberg probably would tell the tale. Hitler would choose either peace or war. They were disappointed. Goering muddied the water with a vicious charge that Czech stubbornness was due to Russia: "It is not these absurd pygmies [the Czechs] who are responsible. It is Moscow and the eternal grimacing Jewish-Bolshevist rabble behind it." In his final speech at Nuremberg, Hitler launched a bitter attack against Czechoslovakia's President Beneš. The Führer claimed that Beneš had humiliated Germany, a great power. He had ordered a partial mobilization in May, justifying the action with the lie that Germany had mobilized. But Hitler did not threaten war; he merely demanded justice for the Sudeten Germans.

The Czechs were worried, but they did not weaken. The dike broke in Paris, the day after Hitler's tirade. The French cabinet was hopelessly split over whether to aid Czechoslovakia, and believed a German attack imminent. The members asked Chamberlain to bargain with Hitler. This, of course, was what the Prime Minister wanted. Two days later he flew to meet Hitler at Berchtesgaden. After an hour or so with Chamberlain, the Führer was convinced Britain and France would not intervene. The British leader appeared to agree in principle to the detachment of the Sudetenland from Czechoslovakia. Hitler promised to take no military action until they met again.

At their next meeting on September 22, Hitler suddenly raised his price. Sensing he had the British and French on the run, the dictator demanded not the cession of the disputed area but its immediate occupation by German troops. This was too much even for Chamberlain. He and the French already had pressured the Czechs to accept the transfer without a plebiscite, and to cancel their existing pacts with Russia and France. Yet Chamberlain finally agreed to transmit Hitler's new ultimatum.

When the Czechs refused the fresh demands, Hitler at last made clear his course of action. At the Berlin Sportpalast on the evening of September 26, the Führer literally screamed: "The decision now lies in his [Beneš'] hands: Peace or War. He will either accept this offer and now at last give the Germans their freedom, or we will go and fetch this freedom for ourselves." September 28 was Black Wednesday: war seemed certain; the British and the French had begun mobilization; and, Hitler had been warned that Britain would support France.

In desperation, Chamberlain proposed one final conference to give Hitler what he wanted. The Führer had reassured him that the Sudetenland was Germany's last territorial demand in Europe. The Prime Minister broadcast to the British people on the evening of September 27. It would be horrible and fantastic to go to war, he said, "because of a

quarrel in a faraway country between people of whom we know nothing." Chamberlain would only feel the sacrifice justified if great issues
were at stake, if he were "convinced that any nation had made up its
mind to dominate the world by fear or force."

The so-called great powers—Britain, France, Germany, and Italy—
met in Munich on September 29. (Hitler refused to let Czechoslovakia
participate, and Chamberlain was not adamant on its presence.) It was
left to Britain and France to tell the poor Czechs about the "Munich
Agreement" to partition their country.[23] Upon his return to England,
Neville Chamberlain assured a thankful crowd outside Number Ten
Downing Street that he had brought "peace in our time." And Chamberlain had the support of the great majority. When a lonely Churchill rose
in the House of Commons to call Munich a total and unmitigated defeat,
there was a storm of protest.

Russia: The Outsider   But what had Russia, the other
"great power," been doing? During the months since the Anschluss, as
we noted, Litvinov repeatedly had pledged Soviet support of Czechoslovakia. However, as the crisis came to head and Chamberlain began
his negotiations with Hitler, Russian ambassadors in London and Paris
were given only the information released to the press. The West was not
interested in even discussing the Czechoslovakian problem with the USSR.
Pravda warned on September 17 of the fallacious belief the new concessions to Hitler would avert war. On the contrary, this only brought
war nearer. And Britain and France, said *Pravda*, might be the first to
suffer.

In the final days of the crisis the Soviets suddenly made a surprising
offer. Their ambassador in Prague, Alexandrovsky, told President Beneš
on the morning of September 21 that Russia would come to the aid of the
Czechs even if France didn't—provided the League branded Germany
the aggressor. Beneš quite rightly thought this an empty gesture; the
League had stood paralyzed in previous instances of aggression. The ambassador quickly checked with the Kremlin. According to Beneš' own
records, Alexandrovsky returned later the same day with the promise that
the Soviets would help the Czechs if they merely appealed to the League;
Russia would act regardless of what might happen to the Czech com-
plaint in the League machinery. Beneš later wrote he was extremely
grateful for the Soviet offer, but felt Czechoslovakia could not risk war
with the Soviet Union as its only ally. The Czech President also may

[23] This was not the end of Czechoslovakia's troubles. Egged on by Germany,
Poland and Hungary took those parts of the hapless country occupied by their
minorities.

have had in mind the anti-Soviet elements in his own government who were opposed to Soviet aid on principle.[24]

We probably never will know if this final Soviet offer was genuine, or even the earlier pledges to join Britain and France in the defense of Czechoslovakia. Soviet sincerity was never tested. The Soviet record, untarnished by Munich, still looks rather good when compared with that of the West. But if Alexandrovsky's second message to Beneš was in good faith, Russia must have decided to fight at the last minute. Before September, the Soviet leaders apparently thought they could promise the sky with no real fear of having to stand by their pledge. On May 11— the Czech crisis had begun—Litvinov had told Beneš' closest diplomatic aide that Russia would come to the defense of the Czechs if the French acted. "But Beneš is fundamentally wrong," Litvinov warned, "if he thinks that France will come to Czechoslovakia's help." [25]

Stalin must have rethought the whole concept of collective security long before Munich, and found it wanting. At least outwardly, Russia had gone as far as any nation to forge an alliance against Hitler. But her efforts had been rebuffed. Perhaps there was a more sinister plot behind Chamberlain's professed desire for peace. Possessing a suspicious mind colored by ideological preconceptions, Stalin saw evidence that Czechoslovakia was another sacrificial lamb to divert Germany eastward— toward Russia. Why else was Russian aid ignored, and the Russian presence prohibited at Munich? Certainly the combined military might of the West with Russia could have stopped Hitler in September 1938.[26] Stalin found it difficult to believe that Chamberlain and Daladier, the French Premier, could be sincere in their horribly mistaken belief that Munich would bring peace.

There is perhaps a more fundamental question than Soviet sincerity. Was there ever a real foundation on which to build an anti-Hitler alli-

---

[24] See Otakar Odlozilik, "Edvard Beneš on Munich Days," *Journal of East European Affairs*, January, 1957, XVI, 389-90, and J. W. Wheeler-Bennett, *Munich: Prologue to Tragedy* (New York: The Viking Press, Inc., 1964), pp. 127-28. A Soviet historian also claims that Russia, in the final hours of the crisis, offered the Czechs "military assistance" even if France wouldn't and Poland and Rumania refused passage to Soviet troops. There were only two obvious conditions: Czechoslovakia herself had to resist Germany and to request Russian aid. G. Deborin, *The Second World War* (Moscow: Progress Publishers, n.d.), p. 29. Other Soviet commentators assert that Stalin made a similar offer to Beneš through Klement Gottwald, the head of the Czech Communist Party, in May, 1938. See, for example, I. Zemskov, "New Documents on the History of Munich," *International Affairs* (Moscow), No. 10 (1958), p. 70.

[25] Quoted in *The Communist Subversion of Czechoslovakia* by Josef Korbel. (Princeton, N.J.: Princeton University Press, 1959), pp. 32-33.

[26] The German generals after the war unanimously testified that they would have been swamped. The French alone could muster 100 divisions against the 12 Germany could deploy in the West. After inspecting the Czech fortifications, even Hitler acknowledged that Germany had run a serious danger in threatening war.

ance of the West and Soviet Russia? George Kennan, for example, asserts that Stalinist Russia "was never a fit partner for the West in the cause of resistance to fascism." [27]

With great fanfare, the Soviets had introduced the Stalin constitution in 1936. The harsh, discriminatory measures of the early years were replaced by the most "democratic" regime the world had seen. But this change in the nature of the Soviet system soon proved superficial. Stalin began the first of the terrible purge trials the same year. Under the new constitution, the USSR proved an even more brutal and callous totalitarian state. It was distasteful for the West to ally with one dictatorship to fight another.

There was the legacy of 20 years of Soviet invective against the West, and almost 100 years of the communist movement—prophesying the revolutionary overthrow of the very governments the Soviets wanted as allies. Most Western statesmen knew about the *Communist Manifesto* if they hadn't digested *Mein Kampf*. Why should the Soviets be trusted? The popular fronts were only a phase in the program for world revolution; Dimitrov freely admitted this at the Comintern's Seventh Congress in 1935. There simply was too much history for the Soviets to live down, or the West to ignore.

Even if one assumed the Soviets were sincere and could be trusted, was their aid of any consequence? The great purge trials had indicated a monstrous fifth column in the Russian high command. How valuable was an army which had seen the majority of its senior officers, including three of its five highest ranking generals, charged with treason? (Some 30,000 officers may have been purged.) [28] Could a society which had seen countless thousands of its political and administrative leaders disappear have the ability or stamina to endure a war? (Estimates of the total purged range from three to nine million.)

Finally, there was the nagging question of how Russian forces could come to the aid of the Czechs. Russia at this time had no common border with Czechoslovakia. Her troops would have had to move through either Poland or Rumania. But these countries wanted Russian troops even less than German on their territory. The French foreign minister had questioned Litvinov about this technicality in May. The foreign commissar

[27] George Kennan, *Russia and the West* (Boston: Atlantic-Little, Brown and Company, 1960), p. 312.

[28] Key military figures, in particular Marshal Tukhachevsky, were accused of treasonable contact with unfriendly powers (Germany), sabotage of Soviet defense measures, and planning a coup to restore "capitalism" in the USSR. Contemporary evidence, including statements by Khrushchev, indicates the charges were fabricated. Stalin was merely bent on destroying the last source of *potential* opposition to his rule. See John Erickson, *The Soviet High Command, A Military-Political History, 1918-1941* (London: Macmillan & Co. Ltd., 1962), pp. 447-66.

said it was up to France to get the two East European countries to grant permission. She had the necessary treaties with each country.[29] Surely Chamberlain, Daladier—and Beneš—could have legitimate doubts about the wisdom of allying with Russia. Max Beloff concludes: "The collapse of the European system of security between the reoccupation of the Rhineland and 'Munich' cannot be dealt with merely as a series of diplomatic blunders." [30]

The Japanese Threat Increases   As 1939 approached, trouble grew for Russia in the Far East. The "plot" of the Western democracies to incite Japan, as well as Germany, against the Soviet Union continued. Russia's strategic position in Asia, however, was more critical. No protective belt of independent states existed as in Europe. Japan's penetration of Manchuria and Inner Mongolia had brought her troops face to face with the Soviet Autonomous Far Eastern Army along an ill-defined but vital border region. The Soviet press claimed war between the two states was only a matter of time.[31]

The year 1937, however, saw the Japanese involved in China proper; they had begun a full-scale invasion of the mainland that July. Until that year, Chiang Kai-shek had been preoccupied with his "bandit-suppression campaigns" against the Chinese communists. Under pressure from his supporters, Chiang finally formed a united front. After the renewed Japanese offensive in July 1937, he even signed a non-aggression pact with Moscow. Subsequently, the Soviets provided China with military aid and advisors until Hitler's attack on Russia in 1941. Significantly, the aid went only to Chiang's Nationalist Government. Stalin wanted Chinese resistance to Japan, not a new civil war. The local communists had to sacrifice revolutionary aspirations for the defense of the socialist motherland.

Soviet appeasement of Japan nevertheless was at an end. After the Japanese invasion of Manchuria in 1931, Russia had begun to turn her Far Eastern provinces into a veritable armed camp. She was now ready to fight. From 1937 until September 1939, a series of "incidents" occurred along the border. Most were minor; however, there were others, notably the two-week battle in 1938 at Changkufeng near the strategic Soviet port of Vladivostok, and the four-month campaign launched by the Japanese against Outer Mongolia in the summer of 1939, in which full-scale

---

[29] The German military attaché in Prague told George Kennan that it would have taken the Russians three months to move one division into Czechoslovakia over the primitive Rumanian railroad system, assuming that the Rumanians had given permission for the troop movement. Kennan, *Russia and the West*, p. 324.

[30] Beloff, *The Foreign Policy of Soviet Russia, 1929-1941*, II, 27.

[31] The Japanese, unlike Hitler, seemed truly worried about the "Communist menace" in Asia.

mechanized warfare involving hundreds of tanks and aircraft took place. On July 14, 1939, *Izvestia* casually announced that air engagements since May 28 of that year had resulted in 199 Japanese planes destroyed against 52 Soviet-Mongolian aircraft.

In other times and other places a formal war would have resulted; but in this case both sides had limited objectives. The Japanese seemed to be probing, not engaged in a full-scale invasion. The Soviets, in spite of decisive victories in the major battles, were only interested in halting the Japanese thrust. Russia's main enemy was still Germany. There was no sense in needlessly dissipating Soviet power in Siberia. However, a Soviet army had demonstrated what it could do in defense of the home-land—an illustration of military prowess ignored by Western military experts but not by the Japanese. Faced with stubborn Soviet military resistance, Japan wisely turned her attentions elsewhere.

The final blow to Japanese designs on Siberia was the Nazi-Soviet Non-Aggression Pact of August 1939. Germany, Japan's supposed ally, suddenly had become friends with Russia, her chief enemy.

THE NAZI-SOVIET
NON-AGGRESSION PACT

The stage now was set for one of the most coldly calculated deals in history—the notorious Nazi-Soviet Non-Aggression Pact. We shall investigate the negotiations for this pact, and its aftermath, in some detail. Much can be learned from this particular episode, about Stalin's style in foreign policy as well as the fundamental national interests of the Soviet state.

The fall of 1938 found Russia isolated in both the West and the East; Stalin had lost any faith he may have had in collective security. The Red Army couldn't stop a combined attack by Germany and Japan; it was even doubtful that the Soviets could repel Hitler's Wehrmacht. Some diplomatic arrangement was needed to turn the aggressors against the West—or at least delay the attack. Obviously the Soviets were not having any luck against the Japanese; the two countries had been locked in an undeclared war for some time. If a deal were to be made, it had to be with Hitler.

But how could one deal with this man who had been heaping abuse on Russia for years, and candidly hinting at Germany's need for Russian territory? What enticements could be offered Hitler to turn him away from the USSR? And how could one explain an agreement, assuming it could be negotiated, to the Russian people, the Comintern, and the world? Stalin faced these difficult questions after Munich.

The Origin of the Idea   Robert Tucker sees the germ of the Non-Aggression Pact in the great purge. He argues that Stalin used the purge trials, among other reasons, to eliminate all internal opponents to a future Russian alliance with Germany. These were the vehement "anti-fascists," of whom Bukharin was still the most eloquent spokesman.[32] Tucker also suggests that the evidence against the defendants was constructed to subtly communicate to the Germans the Soviet desire for collaboration. One of the guilty confessed, for example, to obstructing a "normalization" of Nazi-Soviet relations during his service in the Soviet Embassy in Berlin. This should have indicated to the Nazis that normalization was desired. Finally, the trials were to prepare Russia and the Comintern for the shock of such an alliance. There were blatant charges that the major defendants had conspired with the Nazis against Stalin and thus Russia. (The Germans knew these charges were false and thus would ignore them.) If these Old Bolsheviks could plot with Hitler against Russia while loudly proclaiming their anti-fascism, surely Stalin would be justified in later allying with Hitler in *defense* of Russia.[33]

Stalin may not have been quite as farseeing and calculating as Tucker suggests. But the Soviet dictator certainly had enough historical precedents to suggest an alliance with Germany as a defensive measure. Lenin had bought time with the Treaty of Brest-Litovsk in 1918. Germany and Russia had become unofficial allies at Rapallo. In the first months of the Nazi regime, the Soviets had hoped to continue the Rapallo spirit. When Hitler turned deaf ears to Soviet gestures for normal relations, Stalin gave Litvinov the go-ahead for collective security. But Stalin probably kept a deal with Hitler in the back of his mind in case other tactics failed.

First Overtures   The problem of how to approach Hitler remained. The overtures had to be handled delicately and slowly. What if Hitler turned down the Soviets after they had cut loose the Russian ship of state from the Western flotilla? Russia still had to string along with France and England. Stalin would cover his bets in this manner, and at the same time, up the ante. Sooner or later Hitler might decide to bid for Soviet aid. If he thought the West were also interested, he would pay more.

Stalin handled the tricky task of the first overture to Hitler. Intermediaries might not get through to the Nazi dictator. Stalin's opportunity came in his customary report to the Eighteenth Congress of the

---

[32] Robert M. Slusser cites the evidence for the intra-party dispute in the early 1930's over Soviet policy toward Hitler in "The Role of the Foreign Ministry," found in Ivo J. Lederer, ed., *Russian Foreign Policy* (New Haven, Conn.: Yale University Press, 1962), pp. 197-239.

[33] Robert C. Tucker and Stephen F. Cohen, eds., *The Great Purge Trial* (New York: Grosset & Dunlap, Inc., 1965), pp. iii-xl.

Soviet Communist Party on March 10, 1939. The new economic crisis, claimed the Soviet leader, was leading to a further sharpening of the imperialist struggle and a new redivision of the world between the aggressor and nonaggressor states. But the nonaggressor states, though more powerful, had rejected collective security. Their policy of "nonintervention" revealed an eagerness to embroil both Japan and Germany in a war with the Soviet Union. In fact, charged Stalin, the West was lying vociferously about Soviet weakness just to entice Germany eastward. Conversely, the concern in the Western press about German designs on the Ukraine was to incite the USSR against Germany—"to provoke a conflict by warmongers who are accustomed to have others pull the chestnuts out of the fire for them."

The speech was a masterpiece of indirection. Stalin had thundered against Nazism, encouraging the West that Russia still might be its ally. But the Germans got the more subtle innuendo, largely ignored in the West. If Stalin was hardly enthusiastic about German aggression, he also was disgusted with Western passivity and Western attempts to turn Hitler against Russia. However, there were no "visible grounds" for such a conflict, and Stalin was not going to be urged into a war with Hitler to save the hides of Britain and France.

Yet Hitler did not respond. He was preoccupied with gobbling up the rest of Czechoslovakia, upset that Munich had denied him the chance to crush the Czechs. In the middle of March, German troops occupied the remainder of the unfortunate country. The West made only token protests. But England finally decided that appeasement would not work.

Meanwhile, the Russians gave Hitler further hints. On April 17, Merekalov, the Soviet ambassador in Berlin, paid his first call on the German foreign office. He had been assigned to Berlin almost a year. The visit was to clear up certain economic problems. But Weizsaecker, the German State Secretary, later wrote that Merekalov soon "asked me point-blank what I thought of German-Soviet relations." The Soviet ambassador said Russian foreign policy always had followed a straight course. Ideological differences need not disturb Soviet relations with Germany. There was no reason, Merekalov concluded, why Russia and Germany could not live on a normal footing—"and from normal, the relations might become better and better."

A new signal appeared on May 3; a short announcement in the Soviet press noted that Litvinov had resigned because of ill health. The next day Moscow radio stated that this did not signify a change in policy. But there was obviously some significance to the move. The new foreign minister was Molotov, reportedly in charge of the subgroup of the Politburo dealing with foreign affairs. This was the first time a member of that august party organ had held the chief diplomatic post since 1918.

Perhaps something major was in the offing. The change could be interpreted another way. Litvinov was unfit to deal with Hitler because of his Jewish origin and his long attempts to thwart German territorial demands. Molotov was "Aryan," and a colorless if extremely efficient servant of Stalin. (Lenin supposedly thought Molotov the "best filing clerk in Russia.") A few days later the Soviet chargé d'affaires in Berlin asked Dr. Julius Schnurre, an economic expert in the German foreign office, whether Litvinov's dismissal would bring a change in Germany's attitude toward the Soviet Union.

Molotov soon entered the war of nerves. On May 20, he told the German ambassador in Moscow that economic negotiations between the two countries could be resumed if the "necessary political basis" were created. Apparently following exact instructions from Stalin, Molotov stubbornly refused to elaborate on what this pregnant phrase meant.

The careful Soviet overtures were beginning to take effect. Hitler's advisors, especially Goering and Ribbentrop, the foreign minister, were anxious to come to terms with Russia. The Führer, however, still was undecided. He was the supreme opportunist, but this step would make a mockery of his life-long diatribe against Bolshevism. Weizsaecker, Hitler's Secretary of State, cautioned that too eager a reply to Stalin might provoke "a peal of Tartar laughter." Nevertheless, on May 30, the German ambassador in Moscow was instructed to make "a certain degree" of contact with the Soviet Union.

Poland Becomes the Bait   The key to the changing German attitude was the Polish problem. After Munich, Hitler had tried again to tempt the Poles with the Russian bait. But there was a new catch in Hitler's offer to share the spoils of Russia. The Poles had to agree to the Free City of Danzig's becoming German. The Poles would have none of this; they didn't think the Führer's demands would end with Danzig. They certainly didn't want to become a German satellite in any anti-Russian campaign. Further complications for Germany arose when England and France announced on March 31 that they would come to the aid of Poland if she were attacked.

Hitler was not deterred. On April 3, he ordered his generals to prepare to invade Poland by September 1, 1939. By the end of May, the Führer had decided that war was inevitable. The Czech affair couldn't be repeated. Poland had to be crushed. Danzig as an issue was supplanted by the need for expanding living space in the east, securing food supplies, and settling the Baltic problem. Hopefully, an immediate war with England and France might be avoided, and Russia might stay out altogether.

There was one nagging problem. On April 16, Litvinov had made his last bid to the West. The foreign minister proposed that Britain and

THE NAZI MENACE 1934-1941   183

France join Russia in a tripartite mutual assistance pact, a military convention to carry out the pact, and a guarantee to defend the Eastern European states against aggression. On May 27, a reluctant Chamberlain finally agreed to discuss the proposal. Hitler was worried. Russia was the only major power able to aid the Poles immediately. In the West, Hitler might also face Britain and France. The dreaded spectre of the two-front war appeared. The negotiations had to be sabotaged, or better yet, a promise obtained of Soviet neutrality. But if both dictators at last were ready to negotiate, both still intensely distrusted each other. The war of nerves continued until the middle of July with no significant moves by either side.

A Matter of Urgency   On July 18, the Soviets asked the Germans for negotiations on a new trade agreement; the requirement was dropped for a "necessary political basis." Ribbentrop directed Dr. Schnurre, his East European economic expert, to wine and dine the head of the Soviet trade delegation and the Soviet chargé d'affaires. On the evening of July 26, in the private room of a plush Berlin restaurant, the obscure, second-rank diplomats laid the groundwork for the Nazi-Soviet Non-Aggression Pact. Schnurre assured the Russians that Germany was not menacing the USSR; her target was Britain. What could Britain offer the Soviet Union if they were allies—only war and Germany's hostility. Germany, on the other hand, could offer Russia neutrality, and, if Moscow wished, "a far-reaching arrangement of mutual interests with due consideration for vital Russian problems." The Russians warmly agreed that a *rapprochement* suited the vital interests of both countries.

Meanwhile, the British and French negotiators in Moscow had reached general agreement with the Soviets on the mutual assistance pact. But two difficult problems remained. The Russians primarily were concerned about "indirect aggression" by Germany in the Baltic area. Hitler had proven adept at staging internal coups—witness Austria. At the beginning of July, the Soviets demanded the right to intervene, with British and French permission, if German machinations threatened to turn the Baltic states into bases for an attack on the USSR. The Western Allies thought the Russian definition of indirect aggression too vague. The Russians could justify intervention even in the absence of a serious threat from Hitler. The professed Soviet fear seemed merely a scheme to extend Russian power in Eastern Europe. Secondly, the Soviets insisted that the military convention be brought into effect simultaneously with the political agreement. Stalin wanted to know what the West was prepared to do militarily before Russia committed herself. The Western powers wanted the convention after the political treaty had been signed. William Strang, the British negotiator, wrote his foreign office: "It is indeed extraordinary that we should be expected to talk military secrets with the Soviet Government before we are sure that they will be our allies."

In summary, the West and Russia also profoundly mistrusted each other; they could not forget history. Democracies, perhaps more than dictatorships, found it difficult to deal with a communist state. The Soviets wanted to nail down every loose end. Yet even at this late juncture Stalin might have signed with the West. He may not have been dragging out negotiations with Britain and France merely to keep Hitler interested. Britain, France and Germany were all fundamental enemies of the Soviet regime. There was only one important question for Stalin. Which alliance would give Russia maximum security?

Events of the next few weeks decided the issue. Although a definition of indirect aggression still had to be found, the Western powers agreed on July 25 to send a team of military and naval experts to Moscow to work on the military convention. The lukewarm attitude of the West toward the whole concept of the alliance was more than ever obvious. Rumors abounded regarding Soviet-German negotiations, although Molotov denied their existence. Time was critical. But the British and French military representatives took six days to get to Moscow, traveling by slow boat to Leningrad. (Chamberlain had journeyed by air when Hitler beckoned.) The British team itself was decidedly low level. The Russians were shocked to find out on August 12, that its chief somehow had not been given authority to negotiate. The Russian team, on the other hand, was headed by Marshal Voroshilov, the Soviet Commissar for War, and included the commanders-in-chief of the Soviet armed forces. They wanted answers to some awkward questions. How many British troops would go to the aid of the French? The British reluctantly revealed they had six divisions in being. More importantly, would Poland let Russian troops in if she were invaded by Germany? The Allied representatives said they couldn't handle this political question.

The British, if not the French, were stalling. Britain apparently still wanted the political pact first. Since this seemed doubtful, Chamberlain had decided to draw out the military discussions to somehow deter Hitler from war. These talks in turn may have been the clincher for Stalin. Three years later, Stalin told Churchill late one evening after Russia and Britain had become allies: "We formed the impression that the British and French Governments were not resolved to go to war if Poland were attacked, but that they hoped the diplomatic line-up of Britain, France and Russia would deter Hitler. We were sure it would not." [34] In short, Stalin was afraid the Western powers were neither willing nor able to come to the aid of Poland. Nazi Germany might then end

---

[34] Winston Churchill, *The Gathering Storm* (Boston: Houghton Mifflin Company, 1948) p. 391.

up on Russia's border. If Russia were allied with the West at that point, she could expect little or no military assistance from England or France, and certainly no mercy from Hitler. Russia would face the full weight of the Wehrmacht alone, while the Japanese nibbled away at the Soviet Far East. There now seemed no alternative to a deal with Hitler.

Hitler also had arrived at decision time. His plans were too far advanced to retreat. Poland was to be invaded no later than September 1. The German ambassador in Moscow told Molotov on the evening of August 15, that Foreign Minister Ribbentrop wanted to fly to Moscow. He would negotiate with both Stalin and Molotov a "concrete" settlement of all outstanding issues between the Baltic and the Black Sea. This was the bid Stalin had waited for. And Hitler was offering much more than Britain and France could pay. But still the Russians were distrustful. They wanted details, not vague promises. Molotov stressed the need for "adequate preparation" of the problems so that the conference could achieve results. Were the Germans ready to sign a non-aggression pact? Would they use their influence to stop Japan's campaign against the Soviet Far Eastern frontier? Were they ready to jointly guarantee the Baltic states? The next afternoon Ribbentrop wired Germany's acceptance of all three conditions. The German ambassador was to get an immediate reply from Molotov as to the date accepted for Ribbentrop's visit. (Hitler was approaching a state of panic.) Molotov again stalled. There first had to be the trade agreement which had been under discussion for some time.[35] Shortly thereafter the non-aggression pact could be signed with a "special protocol" defining the interests of the two powers.

In the late afternoon of August 19, Molotov, apparently on Stalin's direct instructions, finally told the German ambassador that Ribbentrop could come to Moscow on August 26 or 27. This date was too late for Germany. Hitler personally wired Stalin, and begged him to see Ribbentrop not later than August 23 because "the tension between Germany and Poland has become intolerable. . . . A crisis may arise any day." Stalin's reply was coolly formal: "The Soviet Government have instructed me to inform you that they agree to Herr von Ribbentrop's arriving in Moscow on August 23."

Ribbentrop in Moscow The rest was an anti-climax. The foreign minister landed in Moscow at noon on the scheduled day. The Non-Aggression Pact and the secret protocol were signed at the

---

[35] The Soviets probably valued the trade agreement as evidence of Germany's good faith. It also would soften the blow on opinion abroad of the political settlement. On August 21, *Pravda* stated the trade agreement, signed the day before, might be "a significant step towards further improvements not only of economic but also of political relations between the Soviet Union and Germany."

Kremlin that evening.[36] Stalin and Ribbentrop spent most of the night at a typical Russian banquet for visiting firemen. Their discussion was macabre because of its content, and incongruous because of the feigned friendship. The Soviet dictator and the Nazi foreign minister amiably dissected the world, nation by nation. In one of the innumerable toasts, Stalin remarked: "I know how much the German nation loves its Führer. I should therefore like to drink to his health." The usually humorless Ribbentrop was carried away. (He told Hitler later that he had "felt more or less as if he were among old Party comrades.") Ribbentrop assured Stalin that the Anti-Comintern Pact had been aimed not at Russia but at the democracies. In fact, quipped Ribbentrop, there was a joke in Berlin that Stalin might yet join the Pact. Stalin, however, may have had certain premonitions. As the foreign minister was leaving, the Soviet leader took him by the arm and emphasized: "The Soviet Government takes the new pact very seriously. I can guarantee on my word of honor that the Soviet Union will not betray its partner." [37]

The Non-Aggression Pact was published the next day. It was a bland document, each state merely promising neutrality if the other were attacked. But it was easy to read between the lines. Stalin certainly knew he had made war probable between Germany and Poland. However, he thought the war would have come in any event. Meanwhile, Russia had bought precious time to sit on the sidelines and increase her military power. The secret protocol, of course, was not published, and might still be unknown if it had not been found in the archives of the German Foreign Ministry after the war. This protocol would prove crucial for the future of the "alliance." In his haste for the Pact, Hitler had made some promises he would regret. The protocol contained a "delimitation" of the respective "spheres of interest" of the two countries in Eastern Europe. In plain language, the dictatorships were dividing the spoils before the war with Poland began. In case of a "territorial and political transformation" in the Baltic, Russia received Finland, Estonia and Latvia—Germany received Lithuania. Poland was split up along the rivers Narev, Vistula and San, giving Russia roughly the eastern half. Finally, Russia got Rumanian Bessarabia; Ribbentrop expressed Germany's "complete political disinterestedness" in this province.

A new era of Russian expansionism had begun. Certainly, the prime reason was to expand Russia's defensive perimeter—to create a buffer zone between Germany and Russia. Stalin was not yet interested in the

---

[36] The only real difficulty had been over the preamble. Stalin had objected to Ribbentrop's flowery prose declaring "friendly" relations had been established. The Soviet Government, said Stalin, "could not suddenly present to the public assurances of friendship after they had been covered with pails of manure by the Nazi Government for six years."

[37] Shirer, *The Rise and Fall of the Third Reich*, p. 540.

Balkans because Hitler was not. Bessarabia was the only territory not clearly of strategic importance. But this borderland had been part of Tsarist Russia. The Bolshevik regime never had recognized its annexation by Rumania in 1918.

The impact of the alliance on the Comintern was devastating. Since 1935, fascism in all its forms had been the official enemy. Foreign communists, kept completely in the dark about Soviet plans for Germany, now had to do an about face. After some initial floundering as the new line was formulated, Hitler became almost a friend. The democracies became responsible for the "imperialist war." It was obvious to all but the most thoroughly conditioned party faithful that foreign communists were merely tools of the Soviet state. As a consequence, party members and fellow travelers picked up during the united front era deserted the movement in droves.

STRAINS ON THE ALLIANCE

The next two years saw the collapse of the alliance and the beginning of Stalin's nightmare—the German attack on Russia in June 1941. Perhaps the attack had been preordained; if not, Stalin's actions helped make up Hitler's mind. The Führer had ranted and raved about Germany's need for Russian land since the 1920's. Stalin could never forget this, and worried as the Nazi juggernaut rolled through Europe. After August 1939, he used some of the most brutal devices in the arsenal of power politics to control or occupy every foot of land possible between Russia and Germany. The buffer zone had to be deep. Inevitably, Hitler began to wonder about the intentions of his new partner. Stalin's defensive moves seemed like sheer greediness. Both dictators attempted to show good faith and sincerity. But such demonstrations could not plaster over the basic immorality of the actors in the drama, and their fundamental antagonism.

The pitiful victims of the struggle between the two dictatorships were the peoples of Eastern Europe. In both cases they could be subject to death and imprisonment by the Gestapo and the S.S. or the NKVD. The only variation was in the targets of each dictatorship: the Germans were after Jews, while the Soviets were after "enemies" of the Party.

Russia and Poland   At daybreak on September 1, 1939, the Wehrmacht rumbled into Poland. On September 3, Britain and France declared war on Germany. In the next few weeks, the Polish defenses evaporated before the Blitzkrieg. Stalin was shocked. His calculations as to the course of the war were wrong from the beginning. He had thought the Western Allies would stand aside, but that the Polish

Army would give Hitler a hard fight. To insure Polish resistance, the Soviets actually had hinted to the Poles in the last few days before the war that Soviet aid might be forthcoming.

Stalin was suddenly faced with German troops overrunning his "sphere of interest" in Eastern Poland, and arriving at the Russian border. But how could he justify the occupation of his share of the booty? Russia couldn't be labeled Germany's partner in aggression. Stalin and Molotov told the German ambassador that Russia would announce she was coming to the aid of the Ukrainians and White Russians who were "threatened" by Germany. Ribbentrop wired that this excuse "was out of the question." The two partners couldn't appear as enemies to the whole world in view of the Non-Aggression Pact. Stalin deferred to Hitler's objections. On September 17, Russian troops entered Poland. The Polish ambassador in Moscow and the foreign press were told that the Soviet move was necessary because of "the internal bankruptcy of the Polish state." The government had ceased to exist. "Poland has become a suitable field for all manner of hazards and surprises, which may constitute a threat to the USSR." The Soviet government had to protect the life and property of the kindred Ukrainian and White Russian people living on Polish territory.

The strains on the alliance, which was not even a month old, were already showing. Stalin asked Ribbentrop to come to Moscow to arrange a definitive partition of Poland. His objective was to trade Russia's share of Poland lying east of Warsaw (inhabited mainly by Poles) for Germany's interest in Lithuania. This would make Russia's border with Poland more ethnically respectable, and it would give Hitler the headache of dealing with the native Poles. Hitler agreed largely because he had to worry about Britain and France in the West. But he didn't forget Stalin's opportunism.

Russia and the Baltic Countries   As Poland's fate was being decided, Stalin moved on Latvia, Lithuania and Estonia. On September 25, he informed the German ambassador that the Soviet Union, with Germany's consent, would at once "take up the solution of the problem of the Baltic countries." The Soviets moved quickly. One after the other, representatives of the three former Tsarist provinces made their pilgrimage to Moscow. (Ribbentrop heard Estonia had been threatened with "imminent attack.") Each signed a treaty of mutual assistance with Russia, provided naval and air bases, and agreed to have Soviet troops stationed in their countries. For the time being, each country kept its own government. But Hitler wasn't fooled; he had enough experience in such matters. On September 29, he ordered all inhabitants of German ancestry evacuated from Estonia and Latvia.

The Winter War with Finland   Finland's turn came next. She was a tougher nut to crack, and, in German eyes, an important test-case for Soviet friendship. Early in October, Molotov pressed Finland to send a representative to Moscow to discuss several "concrete political questions." When the Finnish delegate arrived a few days later, Stalin took charge of the negotiations. As in the case of the three Baltic countries, Soviet demands were strategic—a mutual assistance pact and bases. But there was an added detail. Stalin wanted "a few dozen kilometers" of Finnish territory adjacent to Leningrad. Finland would be compensated with twice as much territory from Russian Karelia.

The Finns rejected most of the Soviet demands. On November 3, Molotov warned the Finnish negotiators: "We civilians seem unable to accomplish anything more. Now it is up to the military to have their say." At the end of the month, Moscow charged the Finns with a "border provocation"—for which they promptly denied responsibility—and Soviet troops and aircraft were unleashed. The "winter war" had begun.

However, the Soviets did not formally declare war. They set up a puppet government headed by Otto Kuusinen, a Finnish communist who had been exiled in Russia since 1918. The Soviets apparently thought the Finnish proletariat would swarm to support the new regime. Instead, the whole Finnish nation united to repel the Red Army.

Sympathy poured in from all over the world for Finland. Russia was quickly expelled from the League of Nations—an ironic turnabout. Litvinov for years had tried to galvanize support against fascist aggression. Even German sympathy for the Finns was hard to conceal. The Soviets apparently had not consulted Hitler about their plans for their northernmost neighbor. And it was perfectly obvious that Stalin was worrying about possible German aggression through Finland. The Soviet propaganda machine, however, pictured Finland as a potential base for an Allied invasion. It turned out that the Soviet charges had some foundation.[38]

Militarily, the Russians got off to a slow start. The purges seemed to have taken their toll on the efficiency of the Red Army. The impression grew in the West, and also in Hitler's entourage, that Russia was truly a "paper bear." But Stalin had underestimated Finnish resistance. In February, a massive Soviet formation quickly pierced the front in the Leningrad area. The Finns sued for peace in March. The Soviet terms could have been worse; they were essentially the demands of the previous

[38] The Soviet invasion and the long history of Western hatred for Bolshevism reportedly spawned an incredible British and French plan. An Allied force would move across Norway and Sweden, cutting off Hitler's supply and then attack Russia from Finland. Simultaneously, the Allies, supported by the Turks, would hit Russia in the Black Sea area. If the plan had come off, Russia and Germany inevitably would have become closer allies.

October. Stalin probably felt he had strained Russian military and economic power enough. He had achieved security in this sector, and now had to worry about other areas. Stalin also may have been seriously concerned about an Allied expedition to Finland, involving Russia in a major war.

Russia Tightens the Noose in the Baltic   Stalin shortly saw another of his basic calculations proven wrong. Hitler ended the "phony war" in the West by invading Denmark and Norway in April 1940, and then France. In a few short months all of Western Europe was brought under Nazi control. France collapsed, and Britain retreated to her island bastion. Stalin had not believed that Britain and France would come to the defense of Poland. But he was almost certain the two democracies, if attacked, would keep Germany at bay in the West. Now Stalin faced the nightmare the Nazi-Soviet Non-Aggression Pact supposedly would forestall; Germany was free to turn her main force on Russia.

Ostensibly all was still amiable between the two dictatorships. Molotov, for instance, wished Germany "complete success in her defensive measures" against Denmark and Norway. But Stalin escalated his demands on Russia's neighbors. Before he had merely pressured the Baltic countries for military bases and security pacts, tactics frequently used by big powers against weaker neighbors. Now he forced the incorporation of Latvia, Lithuania and Estonia into the USSR, and moved to communize their societies. Russia's territorial aggrandizement had begun; Stalin's actions no longer could be justified strictly on Soviet security needs.

The incorporation naturally was "legal." In June 1940, the three states agreed to form governments able and willing to assure the honest application of their treaties with the Soviet Union, and permitted free entry of an unspecified number of Soviet troops. (Their foreign ministers had been summoned to Moscow and given 24 hours to accept these conditions.) In July, over 90 per cent of the qualified voters in each country put pro-Soviet "front" parties in power. (No opposition candidates had been allowed.) The next step was obvious. The new governments asked to have their countries made part of the USSR.

Russia and Southeastern Europe   With the Baltic region under wraps, Stalin turned to Southeastern Europe. In August 1939, Stalin had laid claim only to Bessarabia; Ribbentrop had indicated Germany's "political disinterestedness" in that province. Yet there was a general power vacuum in the whole area which couldn't remain, given the growing mutual suspicions and fears. And friction was bound to occur as Stalin and Hitler moved to eliminate the vacuum. As in the Baltic, each partner would pretend he was worried about the Allies. But it was obvious each partner was primarily worried about the other.

Stalin dispatched a 24-hour ultimatum to Rumania at the end of June demanding the cession of Bessarabia and Northern Bukovina. The latter was not mentioned in the secret protocol and had never belonged to Russia. The Germans, as before, were given little warning of the move. Yet Rumania was a much more sensitive area. Germany was integrating the Rumanian economy into the German war effort; her oil was particularly essential. Hitler reluctantly told the Rumanians to give in.

It was now Hitler's turn to check Russia. Hungary, her appetite whetted by Russia's acquisition of Bessarabia, demanded Transylvania from Rumania. Hitler feared instability in the area would give the Russians an excuse to intervene. In August, Germany and Italy forced a settlement by partitioning Transylvania with the Vienna Award. As insurance, Hitler moved German troops into Rumania and joined with Mussolini in guaranteeing Rumania's borders.

Stalin was upset. He had as much right to be interested in the Balkans as Hitler. Molotov complained to the German ambassador that the Vienna Award had violated that section of the Non-Aggression Pact which required previous consultation on questions of common interest. Ribbentrop countered that the territories involved were not of direct interest to Russia, and he implied that Germany merely had followed Russian procedure—meaning little or no consultation.

The Germans next countered Russia on the northern end of her security belt. In September, Finland agreed to let German troops move through her country to reach the isolated German garrisons in Norway. Ribbentrop explained this action was solely directed against the British. But Molotov got the message; the Soviets were not to push the Finns around any more.

Late the same month, Stalin's uneasiness was increased further. On September 27, Germany, Italy and Japan signed the Tripartite Pact, a mutual assistance arrangement. The German-sponsored pact was a warning to the "American warmongers"—Ribbentrop's term—to stay out of the war. But the Soviets couldn't ignore that the pact members also had formed the Anti-Comintern alliance. Molotov requested the full text of the new treaty, including the "secret protocols." Ribbentrop retorted there were no secret protocols and, in any case, Soviet-German relations were not involved. Ribbentrop nevertheless hoped that the new understanding between Germany and Japan would make Russia think twice about further moves in the Balkans.

THE ALLIANCE FAILS

The partners needed a nice, long talk about their spheres of influence. In the middle of October Ribbentrop wrote Stalin, covering the whole gamut of Nazi-Soviet relations since August 1939. It was time to discuss "the historical mission" of the four powers—the USSR, Italy, Japan and Germany. A long-range policy was required, Ribbentrop suggested, "to direct the future development of their peoples into the right channels by delimitation of their interests on a world-wide scale." Stalin agreed, and Molotov was readied for a journey to Berlin to help carve up the world. Or so Stalin thought.

The Collapse is Preordained   Hitler ordered a handful of his military staff in the summer of 1940 to begin planning the invasion of Russia. The attack was set for the spring of 1941. From the time of *Mein Kampf*, this had been the Führer's primary goal—expansion eastward. The only question had been the proper timing. On November 23, 1939, Hitler had warned his generals that Russia would adhere to the Non-Aggression Pact "only as long as Russia considers it to be to her benefit. . . . Russia still has far-reaching goals, above all the strengthening of her position in the Baltic. We can oppose Russia only when we are free in the West." [39] In the summer of 1940, Germany was still not free. Britain had been kicked off the continent, but the stubborn British would not surrender. Hitler made the fatal decision to turn the Wehrmacht's power on Russia. Britain, he thought, would probably fall as a bonus once hope of Russian resistance was lost. On the day Molotov arrived in Berlin, Hitler instructed his generals that "all preparations for the East which have already been verbally ordered will be continued." The discussions with the Foreign Commissar would clarify Russia's attitude "for the time being." Perhaps she could be stopped in the Balkans in the few months remaining before the invasion. The appearance of business as usual also would allay Russian suspicion of Germany.

Regardless of what Molotov did, Russia's destruction was being organized. It is doubtful whether almost total appeasement of Hitler would have changed his plans. Molotov's actions at the conference, on the other hand, certainly removed any lingering qualms the Führer may have had. Acting on the terribly erroneous belief that Hitler still needed Russia's assistance, Stalin had instructed Molotov to demand Russia's full share of the world. The record of the conference thus is an extraor-

---

[39] Shirer, *The Rise and Fall of the Third Reich*, p. 657.

dinary revelation of Stalin's aspirations—and possibly the aspirations of subsequent Soviet leaders.[40]

Molotov in Berlin   The deadlock between the two dictatorships was immediately obvious. At the first meeting on the morning of November 12, an optimistic Ribbentrop said the war was basically over. England was beaten.[41] It was time to divide the spheres of interest of Russia, Germany, Italy and Japan. The Führer reasoned the natural direction of expansion for each country was south. Germany would get her *lebensraum* in Central Africa. Russia would get her desired outlet to the sea. Molotov stunned the foreign minister by asking, "Which sea?" After attempting unsuccessfully to change the subject, Ribbentrop suggested the most advantageous access would be through the Persian Gulf and the Arabian Sea. Hitler's interpreter noted Molotov sat there "with an impenetrable expression."

That afternoon and the next morning, Hitler had his turn at luring Russia southward. And Molotov got down to details regarding his "exact instructions" from Stalin. Hitler's interpreter recalled later, "No foreign visitor had ever spoken to him (Hitler) in this way in my presence." Molotov demanded that German troops get out of Finland. Hitler asked what more Russia wanted from Finland. Molotov said she wanted "a settlement on the same scale as in Bessarabia"—meaning forced incorporation into the USSR. He then insisted that Germany revoke her guarantee to defend Rumania's borders; the guarantee was aimed against Russia. Furthermore, what was the significance of the Tripartite Pact? There also were issues to be clarified regarding Russia's interests in Bulgaria and Turkey. Molotov asked Hitler for "explanations."

Hitler was obviously getting nowhere. While sitting with Molotov in the air raid shelter of the German Foreign Ministry on the night of November 13, Ribbentrop tried a final ploy. Would Russia join the Tripartite Pact? The three signatories would recognize the present possessions of the USSR. In the secret protocols to the Pact, Russia's territorial aspirations would center south of the Soviet Union in the direction of the Indian Ocean. Molotov retorted that the USSR had to insist on effective guarantees, and paper agreements would not suffice. At that moment, said Molotov, the Soviet Union was interested in Europe and the Turkish Straits, and to know what the Axis powers planned for Yugoslavia,

[40] A fairly complete record of the conference was gained only after the war from captured Nazi documents. There is still no Soviet account for obvious reasons, although Churchill reports he received a summary of the talks from Stalin in 1941.

[41] The next night, the English bombed Berlin specifically to disrupt the conferees. In the air raid shelter, Molotov turned to Ribbentrop: "Why (if the English are beaten) are we in this shelter, and whose are these bombs which fall?"

Greece and Poland. Finally, what about Swedish neutrality, and the passages out of the Baltic Sea?

Stalin wanted in his zone—besides what Russia already had taken—Finland, Rumania, and Bulgaria. Two weeks later, he agreed to join the Tripartite group, provided a few additional requests were met. Russia desired control of the Turkish Straits and expansion toward the Persian Gulf, giving her Iranian and Arabian oil. Finally, Japan would have to renounce her coal and oil concessions on Northern Sakhalin. India was not mentioned.

A joint communiqué labeled the conference a success. But on December 5, Hitler approved "Operation Barbarossa;" the "life force" of Russia was to be destroyed.

Stalin Tries Appeasement   German troop movements into East Europe were obvious in the months before Barbarossa. Rumors multiplied in April and May of the impending attack. Numerous German aircraft penetrated the Soviet frontier on reconnaissance missions. Washington and London even warned the Soviets through diplomatic channels of the coming invasion.

Stalin's actions in the face of these facts still are a mystery. As late as June 13, *TASS* insisted that Germany was steadfastly abiding by the provisions of the Non-Aggression Pact. War rumors were "clumsily concocted propaganda of forces hostile to the USSR and to Germany and interested in the further extension and unleashing of war." Soviet deliveries under the 1939 economic agreement with Germany continued right up to the invasion.[42] A Soviet note on April 22, protesting the overflights was incredibly conciliatory, stating Soviet troops had been ordered "not to fire on German planes flying over Soviet territory so long as such flights do not occur frequently."

Why had Stalin switched to abject appeasement in the face of all the evidence? Shouldn't he have ordered full mobilization instead of the halfway measures he did take? Shouldn't the country have been put on a war footing? Some 15 years later, Khrushchev charged in his celebrated anti-Stalin speech at the Twentieth Party Congress that Stalin "took no heed of these warnings." Even after the invasion, Moscow ordered that German fire should not be returned. According to Khrushchev, Stalin thought several "undisciplined sections" of the German Army merely had resorted to provocations. A Russian reply might provide a pretext

---

[42] This agreement and subsequent arrangements involved the exchange of Russian raw materials (foodstuffs and oil), vital for the German war machine, for German military aircraft, naval armaments, and other strategic items.

for the Germans to start a real war.[43] As a result, Russian aircraft along the front were destroyed on the ground in the first hours of the war; Russian artillery did not even fire back. General Halder, Chief of the German General Staff, noted that the Red Army was "tactically surprised along the entire front."

Apparently Stalin believed what he wanted to believe. He assumed he had the diplomatic skill to cope with Hitler—witness the brilliant coup of the Non-Aggression Pact. Perhaps Molotov had gone too far at Berlin in November. But Russia's subsequent behavior should have convinced Hitler that she was a valuable ally. There were rumors of German preparations for an invasion. But surely military action would be prefaced by political demands. More concessions always could be made if necessary. If this was Stalin's thinking, he was wrong.

At 3:30 on Sunday morning, June 22, 1941, Germany attacked Russia. As dawn broke, Schulenberg, the German ambassador, delivered the familiar Nazi pretext for war to a stunned Molotov. Russia had indulged in "sabotage, terrorism and espionage" against the Third Reich, had frustrated Germany's attempt to set up a stable order in Europe, and had menaced Germany by concentrating "all available Russian forces on a long front from the Baltic to the Black Sea." It was Russia's turn to be on the rack, and it seemed so unreal. Molotov plaintively asked Schulenberg, "Can it really be that we have deserved this?"

SUMMARY

The central aim of Soviet foreign policy from 1933 was to turn Nazi Germany away from Russia. Every trick in the book was used, but all failed. It was now left to the Red Army and the Russian people to stop the Wehrmacht.

Stalin had tried to ally with the West. But the USSR—the self-proclaimed enemy of all capitalism—could hardly expect trust, let alone friendship, from the very countries it had sought to destroy since the Bolshevik Revolution. The alliance with Hitler failed because of mistrust —and a more basic reason. Hitler's whole life had been dedicated to making the Third Reich the great continental power through expansion eastward. He would not be deterred.

Given the historical setting, Stalin's one significant mistake was in

---

[43] Khrushchev's secret speech is printed in *The Crimes of the Stalin Era*, annotated by Boris I. Nicolaevsky (New York: *The New Leader*). Watered-down versions of the charges against Stalin can be found in such works as *History of the Communist Party of the Soviet Union* (Moscow: Foreign Languages Publishing House, 1963), p. 538. This is the first official party history since the famous "Short Course" history prepared under Stalin's close supervision in 1938.

judging how and when Hitler would attack Russia. For this he has been criticized by subsequent Soviet leaders. The more sordid aspects of Russia's territorial expansion in the wake of the Nazi-Soviet Non-Aggression Pact, however, call forth their approval. In these acquisitions was the germ of Russia's future greatness.

FURTHER READING

Armstrong, John A., *The Politics of Totalitarianism: The Communist Party of the Soviet Union from 1934 to the Present*. New York: Random House, Inc., 1961. Internal politics in the USSR since 1934.

Bishop, Donald, *The Roosevelt-Litvinov Agreements: The American View*. Syracuse, N.Y.: Syracuse University Press, 1965.

Browder, Robert P., *The Origins of Soviet-American Diplomacy*. Princeton, N.J.: Princeton University Press, 1953. Concentrates on period 1932-1938.

Cattell, David T., *Communism and the Spanish Civil War*. Berkeley, Calif.: University of California Press, 1956. Companion volume to his *Soviet Diplomacy and the Spanish Civil War*. Role of Communist Party in Spain.

Dallin, David J., *Soviet Russia's Foreign Policy, 1939-1942*. New Haven, Conn.: Yale University Press, 1942.

Davies, Joseph E., *Mission to Moscow*. New York: Simon and Schuster, Inc., 1941. Memoirs of American ambassador to Moscow during late 1930's.

Erickson, John, *The Soviet High Command, 1918-1941; a Military-Political History*. London: Macmillan & Co. Ltd., 1962. Standard source. Especially important for understanding status of Soviet Army before World War II.

Jakobson, Max, *The Diplomacy of the Winter War: An Account of the Russo-Finnish Conflict, 1939-1940*. Cambridge, Mass.: Harvard University Press, 1961. Clear and concise account by former Finnish journalist.

Litvinov, Maxim, *Against Aggression*. New York: International Publishers, 1938. His speeches from 1934-38, with texts of Soviet treaties of non-aggression.

Maisky, Ivan, *Who Helped Hitler?* London: Hutchinson & Co. (Publishers) Limited, 1964. Memoirs of Soviet ambassador to Britain during this period.

McLane, Charles B., *Soviet Policy and the Chinese Communists, 1931-1946*. New York: Columbia University Press, 1958.

Moore, Harriet L., *Soviet Far Eastern Policy, 1931-1945*. Princeton, N.J.: Princeton University Press, 1945. Based primarily on Soviet documents and Soviet interpretations.

Roberts, Henry L., "Maxim Litvinov," found in *The Diplomats, 1919-1939*. Ed. by Gordon A. Craig and Felix Gilbert. Princeton, N.J.: Princeton University Press, 1953. Perceptive essay.

Rossi, Amilcare, *The Russo-German Alliance, 1939-1941*. Boston: Beacon Press, 1951.

Scott, William Evans, *Alliance Against Hitler: The Origins of the Franco-Soviet Pact*. Durham, N.C.: Duke University Press, 1962.

Sontag, Raymond I. and James S. Beddie, eds., *Nazi-Soviet Relations: 1939-1941, Documents from the Archives of the German Foreign Office*. Washington, D.C.: Government Printing Office, 1948. Indispensable documentary record of secret Nazi-Soviet conversations.

Tanner, Vaino, *The Winter War; Finland against Russia, 1939-1940*. Stanford, Calif.: Stanford University Press, 1957. Best single source for diplomatic history of the war.

Wheeler-Bennett, John W., *Munich: Prologue to Tragedy*. New York: Duell Sloan & Pearce, 1948. Study of motivations, particularly of Western participants.

7

THE GREAT PATRIOTIC WAR
1941-1945

The "great patriotic war against the fascist invaders" brought the Soviet Union to the verge of extinction. In the first grim months, the heart of Russia crumbled under Hitler's legions. By November 1941, advance parties of the German Army were in the suburbs of Moscow. German troops occupied territory inhabited by 40 per cent of the Russian people, containing the predominant share of Russia's coal, pig iron, and aluminum.

On July 3, 1941, Stalin spoke to a bewildered populace. The cruel and implacable enemy, he warned, was out to seize the lands "watered by the sweat of our brows," to restore the rule of landlords and Tsarism, to germanize the Soviet people. This was no ordinary war, but a "great war of the entire Soviet people against the German fascist forces." The issue was of life or death for the Soviet State and for the peoples of the USSR. But the Russian people could find solace. Hitler's army was no more invincible than Napoleon's legions. Stalin ordered a scorched earth strategy in the face of the advancing enemy, as the great Russian general Kutuzov had done against Napoleon. In case of forced retreat, said Stalin, the enemy should be left not a single railway engine, a single pound of grain, a gallon of fuel.

Stalin's brave words may have concealed great personal fear. Khrushchev intimated in 1956 that the Soviet dictator thought the end had come. Stalin lamented: "All that which Lenin created we have lost forever."

THE GRAND ALLIANCE

Russia desperately needed aid. This could only come from the last strongholds of western capitalism—Great Britain and the United States. Before Hitler marched, Russia and the West had failed in their efforts to unite. Animosity and distrust were now plastered over in the face of the common menace. On the evening of the German attack on Russia, Churchill broadcast to the British people: "No one has been a more consistent opponent of Communism than I have for the last twenty-five years. I will unsay no word that I have spoken about it. But all this fades away before the spectacle which is now unfolding." The British Government, Churchill affirmed, had one single aim—the destruction of Hitler and every vestige of the Nazi regime. "Any man or state who fights on against Nazidom will have our aid." Hitler's invasion of Russia, the Prime Minister warned, was merely a prelude to an attempted invasion of the British Isles: "The Russian danger is therefore our danger . . . just as the cause of any Russian fighting for his hearth and home is the cause of free men and free peoples in every quarter of the globe." [1]

England and Russia signed a mutual assistance pact on July 12. America, still not at war, moved more slowly. Washington (and most of London) thought a Soviet defeat inevitable. Harry Hopkins, Roosevelt's confidential emissary, helped turn the tide of thinking after a visit to Moscow at the end of July. He was impressed with Stalin's optimism. The Soviet leader had exclaimed, "Give us anti-aircraft guns and the aluminum and we can fight for three or four years." But Stalin's desperate plight should have been obvious in his personal plea to Roosevelt. Stalin wanted American troops to serve anywhere on the Russian front under the complete command of the American army. In September, he even asked Churchill for 25 to 30 British divisions to fight on Soviet soil. Never again would the Soviet leader resort to such requests. From then on, he wanted all Allied troops in the West, away from the USSR and Eastern Europe.

At the end of September, W. Averell Harriman, the American Lend-Lease expediter, and Lord Beaverbrook, the British minister of supply, met with Stalin in Moscow. A Confidential Protocol was signed on October 1, promising Russia some 150 items ranging from tanks to army

[1] Winston Churchill, *The Grand Alliance* (Boston: Houghton Mifflin Company, 1951), pp. 372-73.

boots. The United States would provide the major share. The British themselves were heavily dependent on American aid. On October 30, Roosevelt wired Stalin that America would extend Russia one billion dollars in credit—interest free—under Lend-Lease provisions. Stalin quickly replied that this arrangement was accepted with sincere gratitude.[2]

On December 7, 1941, the Japanese attacked Pearl Harbor. The United States had no choice but to become the third full-fledged partner of the anti-fascist coalition. The Grand Alliance, in Churchillian terms, had been forged.

The grandeur, however, was a thin façade over a very shaky structure. None of the three partners had joined willingly. Stalin had done his best to stay out of the conflict. The only sturdy cement for the grouping was the common enemy and the need to crush that enemy. As defeat turned to victory, the cracks in the edifice loomed large. The pre-war enmity and distrust between the Western allies and Russia resurfaced. There is no convincing argument to demonstrate this might have been otherwise. Given a Stalinist Russia, the drift from World War to Cold War seemed endemic.

THE NATURE
OF THE WARTIME DIPLOMACY

Since we are investigating the foreign policy of the Soviet Union, our central task must be to sketch its general outlines during the war years. In effect, we will be watching the gradual disintegration of the alliance as Stalin's foreign policy goals clash with those of Roosevelt and Churchill. The main concern will be with the tedious fencing of the heads of state over the shape of the world to come. The locale will be the secret strategy conferences—Teheran in November 1943, Yalta in February 1945, and Potsdam in July 1945. But first, the general goals and perceptions of the coalition leaders must be discussed.

Stalin's Political Aims   Stalin's central concern was to keep what he had gained during the period of the Nazi-Soviet Non-Aggression Pact, and to acquire control over that territory which Hitler had denied him. The basic interests of the Soviet state had not changed, merely the men Stalin had to bargain with. These men, like Hitler, were capitalists. Temporary camaraderie, thought Stalin, could not conceal their fundamental antagonism toward the socialist motherland.

---

[2] By the end of the war, the United States had sent some nine billion dollars of supplies to Russia. Yet it was difficult for many Russians to feel terribly grateful. A disgruntled Muscovite told a Western correspondent in 1943: "We've lost millions of people, and they (America) want us to crawl on our knees because they send us spam." Alexander Werth, *Russia at War* (New York: E. P. Dutton & Co., Inc., 1964), p. 28.

Soviet interests, however, were not static. New vistas for Soviet expansion appeared as the war progressed, and Stalin, always the opportunist, was quick to exploit them. The pending collapse of Germany would leave a gaping hole in the heart of Europe. The defeat of Japan would put her Far Eastern empire on the auction block.

Two particular features of Stalin's approach to wartime politics should be noted. First, Lenin had preached that military force was part and parcel of the whole gamut of tools in the communist arsenal for achieving *political* objectives. Military strategy was a subordinate servant of political strategy. Even in the very darkest days of 1941, Stalin pressed Allied representatives to recognize Russia's territorial gains from the Nazi-Soviet Non-Aggression Pact. Stalin never forgot that he was fighting for more than just military victory.

Second, Stalin took great pains to picture his territorial desires as legitimate security needs of the Soviet state. Russia certainly deserved protection against a future Hitler. In some cases, he argued that areas had been traditionally Russian. A formula for Soviet security was found at the Yalta Conference. Russia's neighbors in Europe had to be friendly to the Soviet Union, and representative of all the democratic elements of the country. This meant Soviet domination internationally, and communist representation internally. Stalin bluntly warned his Western counterparts at the Potsdam conference: a freely elected government in any of the countries of Eastern Europe "would be anti-Soviet, and that we cannot allow." Of course, he was right. Eastern Europe had been anti-Russian for generations, if not centuries.

Meanwhile, Stalin played down communist internationalism. Ideological overtones could have ripped the alliance apart. The new nationalist phase of Soviet foreign policy was dramatically highlighted. The Comintern gave orders to communists to support the resistance movements in the occupied countries. Democracy, not proletarian dictatorship, received the allegiance of the world communist movement.

On May 22, 1943, an electric announcement came from Moscow. The Comintern itself was dissolved. A few days later, Stalin asserted that this action should put an end to the Hitlerite lie that Moscow intended to intervene in the life of other nations and "Bolshevize" them. Subsequent evidence indicated that Stalin merely had dropped an out-of-date intermediate link between the Soviet Politburo and the leadership of foreign communist parties.[3]

[3] Some observers believed that the Comintern apparatus merely had gone underground. But indications are that the organization itself was disbanded. See Gunther Nollau, *International Communism and World Revolution* (New York: Frederick A. Praeger, Inc., 1961), pp. 201-10. Dimitrov, the former Comintern head, together with Manuilsky, a Soviet functionary, reportedly directed the section of the Soviet Communist Party Central Committee responsible for collecting information and advising the Soviet leadership on foreign communist parties.

Perhaps the most heartening sign of Russia's apparent disinterest in exporting communism was the great upsurge of nationalism among the Russian people. This was a completely natural reaction of any invaded nation. But Stalin fanned the flames. He probably realized that the Russian people were much more ready to die for Mother Russia than for his oppressive communist regime. (The Ukrainians had welcomed German armies until they tasted Nazi brutality.) Stalin invoked all saints, Marxist and Russian Orthodox, and the memory of all Russian heroes to rouse the Russian people. As the Germans moved on Moscow in November 1941, the Soviet dictator castigated "these people with the morality of animals, who have the effrontery to call for the extermination of the great Russian nation—the nation of Plekhanov and Lenin, of Belinsky and Chernyshevsky, of Pushkin and Tolstoy, of Gorki and Chekhov, of Glinka and Tchiakovsky, of Sechenov and Pavlov, of Suvorov and Kutuzov!" If the Germans wanted a war of extermination, declared Stalin, they would have it. "Death to the German invaders," was Stalin's battle cry. What a change from 1917 when the Red Army was ordered to fraternize with its German working-class brothers!

Stalin did not stop with exhortations to nationalism. Army officers got back their epaulettes—banned in 1917 as part of the reactionary caste system. The army's political commissars were removed. Stalin awarded himself the rank of Marshal, rather good for his first hitch in the army. In September 1943, the Soviets even rehabilitated the Russian Orthodox Church; every gimmick had to be used to unify the nation. In addition, this would be a cheap sop to religious circles in the democracies. The church might later prove a useful tool in winning friends for Russia among Orthodox believers in the Balkans.

Some argue that Stalin himself had given up communism for nationalism, a trend supposedly started many years before with "socialism in one country." But even at the height of the nationalist fervor, he never seemed truly comfortable as the leader of just a nation-state, and not an international political movement. He apparently wanted to be both, and he rationalized that he was both.[4] Years before World War II, Stalin had made the cause of Russia the cause of world communism. Meanwhile, he assumed the nationalist role to avoid offending the Western Allies. Marxism-Leninism could resurface only after victory.

Yet even at the most congenial gatherings of the big three, communism remained an unstated curse on coalition unity. Stalin may not have talked like the leader of a world revolutionary movement. But he couldn't avoid decades of ideological conditioning. He couldn't forget the fundamental antagonism between the capitalist world and the social-

---

[4] Isaac Deutscher brilliantly analyzes this duality in Chaps. 12 and 13 of *Stalin* (New York: Oxford University Press, Inc., 1949).

ist motherland. Stalin's basic mistrust of the Western leaders was vividly evident in his conversations with Milovan Djilas, the Yugoslavian communist leader, in June 1944. Said Stalin:

> "Perhaps you think that just because we are the allies of the English that we have forgotten who they are and who Churchill is. They find nothing sweeter than to trick their allies. During the First World War they constantly tricked the Russians and the French. And Churchill? Churchill is the kind who, if you don't watch him, will slip a kopeck out of your pocket . . . . And Roosevelt? Roosevelt is not like that. He dips in his hand only for bigger coins."

Later the same evening, Stalin waved his hand over a world map with the USSR appropriately highlighted in red. Referring to his earlier characterization of the British and Americans, Stalin exclaimed: "They will never accept the idea that so great a space should be red, never, never!" [5]

As the war progressed, Stalin seemed to lack any "master plan" to communize Europe or Asia after the war. Marxism-Leninism was a highly flexible scheme for the acquisition of power. Stalin was Lenin's faithful, if heavy-handed, disciple. Tactics, including the use of "legitimate" nationalist goals, would be adapted to fit the political situation. The concept of the "people's democracies" of Eastern Europe, for example, was some distance in the future. Meanwhile, Stalin was feeling his way and doing things which made no sense if a master plan had been in existence. As we shall see, Stalin had a furious controversy with the Poles over their eastern border. But this was a needless irritant in his relations with the West if he planned to place a "friendly" communist government in Warsaw.

The Strategy of Stalin's Allies In sharp contrast to Stalin, President Roosevelt's central concern was to win the war as quickly as possible. Military victory came first; then political problems would be settled. This approach reflected the traditional American attitude that peace and war are two separate scenarios in the great drama of international politics. When war comes, all energy goes into fighting, and one does not speculate about a vague future which cannot be predicted. Herbert Feis suggests: "Roosevelt was trying to fight a coalition war without coalition politics, lest these hinder the conduct of the war." [6]

Roosevelt, of course, had Secretary of State Hull and his department doing some preliminary thinking about the world to come. But this planning focussed primarily on a new international system of collective

---

[5] Milovan Djilas, *Conversations With Stalin* (New York: Harcourt, Brace & World, Inc., 1962), pp. 73-74. British edition published by Rupert Hart-Davis, London.

[6] *Churchill, Roosevelt, Stalin: The War They Waged and the Peace They Sought* (Princeton, N.J.: Princeton University Press, 1957), p. 125.

security (the future United Nations), and an international "trusteeship" arrangement for colonial peoples. "Spheres of influence" or "territorial concessions" were considered sinister devices of power politics, sources of war, and contrary to the sacred right of self-determination of peoples. (This right had been written into the Atlantic Charter, a statement of war aims adopted by Roosevelt and Churchill in August 1941.) Unfortunately, these were the very security devices which attracted Stalin.

What made Roosevelt believe he could influence Stalin to postpone, and hopefully moderate, his demands? The President seemed to think that the surface harmony during wartime would continue in peace. He refused to be dissuaded by those who warned otherwise. Roosevelt thought Soviet security needs could be satisfied through a world jointly policed by the Grand Alliance. In the meantime, England and the United States should convince Russia that they would be friendly allies in peace, as in war. Western military strategy should give not the slightest suggestion that it might be designed to counter Russia in Eastern Europe. Stalin should have no reason to fear for Russia's postwar security.

The President was the prisoner of his considerable ignorance about communists and communism. He realized that good old "Uncle Joe" Stalin was sometimes difficult to approach. But he believed that Stalin and the Russians would change their stripes if only the West could show good will, patience, and forbearance.

Churchill was a different breed. He initially shared Roosevelt's optimism about future relations with Russia. But Churchill never forgot the centuries of struggle between Russia and England for the mastery of Asia, or the decades of British trouble with the Soviets in Europe. He could scarcely erase his own record of vehement anti-communism. Yet Russian resistance to Hitler seemed critical for the survival of England in the first stages of the war. The Prime Minister, therefore, was less reluctant than Roosevelt to give in to Stalin's territorial demands. And Churchill was ready to deal in spheres of influence—a concept which British statesmen understood. Soviet Russia, like Tsarist Russia, had to be checkmated with power to safeguard the interests of the British Empire. Finally, Churchill, much more than Roosevelt, understood the political implications of military strategy.

THE GREAT STRATEGIC DECISIONS

There is another question we must pursue before examining the political issues in detail. We must investigate the great problems of military strategy which had a profound influence on the political negotiations. For how the war was fought inevitably affected how the postwar world was constructed. The grand strategy determined the amount of real estate held by each nation at the end of the war, and this allocation tended to create the postwar spheres of influence. Victory or defeat on the battlefield also affected how far each nation could push its political goals at a given juncture. A Russia on the verge of defeat was much less demanding than a Russia flush with victory.

The Second Front   The paramount concern was to keep Russia in the war. Lend-Lease obviously was not sufficient. Hitler had thrown the great bulk of his forces against Russia—over three-fourths of his divisions were on the Eastern front. The pressure on Russia had to be relieved. In July 1941, Stalin asked Churchill to start a second front in Northern France and Norway. Churchill countered that any large scale invasion by Britain was then impossible.

By 1942, America was in the war. Stalin saw no reason for the Western Allies to stall any longer, particularly since the Wehrmacht had resumed the offensive in Russia that spring. The Russian front might collapse if Hitler suddenly decided to use all his force in the East. Molotov was sent to Washington in May to warn the President. In spite of the obvious hesitation of General Marshall and Admiral King, the chief American military leaders, Roosevelt told Molotov to inform Stalin that Russia could expect a second front later that year. The communiqué released to the press contained a pregnant phrase (drafted by Molotov): "In the course of the conversations, full understanding was reached with regard to the urgent tasks of creating a second front in Europe in 1942." Back in Moscow, the Soviet foreign minister acted as if his journey had been a complete success. An added reason for optimism was the 20-year alliance signed with Britain during Molotov's stopover in London. *Pravda* overflowed with happiness about the enemy's final rout in 1942.

Roosevelt, however, had not spoken for the British on the second front. Churchill and his War Cabinet balked at such a commitment. For one thing, the landing craft for a cross-channel operation simply were unavailable. Churchill warned Molotov that England could not promise a second front in 1942. The Prime Minister then flew to Moscow to explain to Stalin personally why the invasion could not be launched. (He thought this task a "somewhat raw job.") Churchill's legendary persuasiveness was lost on a grim Soviet dictator. Stalin couldn't understand why the British were so afraid of the Germans. He admitted the invasion of France would be risky. But one had to take risks to win. He was somewhat mollified by a promised invasion of North Africa later in 1942, and the rescheduling of the second front in Europe for 1943. Churchill thought the alliance was saved, and that Stalin in his heart knew the decision was right.

But 1943 also did not see the invasion of France. The American military planners had been lukewarm to the North African invasion. They now argued that this operation left the West still unprepared for the second front in Europe. Besides, there was the Pacific war to consider.

Stalin's pressure for the second front was unrelenting. Genuine relief for Russia, he insisted, could come only from an invasion of Europe. But once again Stalin received word from Churchill and Roosevelt. The invasion would be postponed yet another year. The strain on the alliance became intense. Stalin accused the Western leaders of deliberate bad faith. Churchill was enraged, and fired off an angry note in reply.

The salient point of this long story about the second front—finally launched in June 1944—is its interlocking relationship with Stalin's political demands on the Allies. Roosevelt had dangled the promise of the invasion of Europe in 1942 before Molotov to get the Russians to soften their territorial demands. (Even at this early date, Churchill was ready to recognize Russia's 1941 frontier as a condition for the 20-year Soviet-British alliance.) Yet the promised invasion proved impossible for the next two years. Allied resistance to Soviet political aims therefore began to crumble. Western military weakness generated Western toleration; Roosevelt and Churchill became much more sympathetic to Stalin's desires. Otherwise Stalin's distrust and bitterness over the second front question would have been further inflamed. And this might lead to a dreaded outcome of the war on the continent—a separate peace between Russia and Germany. Brest-Litovsk was a lively spectre.

Unconditional Surrender   The possibility of a separate peace, however, cut both ways. Stalin feared an agreement between the Western powers and Germany which would leave Russia completely at Hitler's mercy. The mutual assistance pact between England and Russia, signed a few weeks after the German attack, thus restricted separate negotiations with the enemy.

When the Red Army finally turned the tide in the summer of 1943, Stalin must have felt more secure. It was now the West's turn to fear a separate peace. Stalin seems never to have seriously considered this alternative. Before the tide turned in Russia, Hitler surely would have demanded unacceptable terms: namely, the destruction of the Soviet state. After 1943, Stalin saw victory in sight with a Red Army all over Eastern Europe. It then would have been foolish to sue for peace.

These mutual doubts led to the second great strategic decision which impacted on Russian political desires—the "unconditional surrender" formula. The origin of this concept is still somewhat vague. Roosevelt off-handedly announced it at a press conference at Casablanca in January 1943. Churchill claimed he had not been consulted, although evidence indicated he knew Roosevelt had toyed with the concept. Stalin, however, certainly was in the dark.

Among other things, Roosevelt hoped the formula would assure Russia of Western steadfastness, and thereby strengthen Soviet determination. Stalin realized the harsh terms indicated that the alliance would hold together to the last. But he argued that some conditions for surrender should be announced, no matter how harsh. Otherwise, the German people would have no choice. They could only unite behind Hitler for a fight to the bitter end. Stalin may not have sensed what a boon the formula would be for Soviet expansionism. Unconditional surrender almost guaranteed the presence of Soviet troops deep in the heart of Europe at the war's end. And possession is nine-tenths of the law, especially in international politics.

The Necessity of Soviet Aid in the Pacific   The third great military decision which affected Soviet political aims was the American determination to have Soviet troops enter the war against Japan. In the spring of 1941, Russia and Japan had signed a neutrality pact which suited Soviet interests perfectly. It prevented a renewed Japanese invasion of Soviet Siberia in case Germany attacked the USSR. The Japanese on the other hand were free to turn southward. Russia would not take advantage of Japan if she, in her pursuit of empire, ran head-on into the United States. When war finally came for both nations, the utility of the arrangement was confirmed. Both states maintained the temporary truce in their traditional rivalry.

But the United States was not satisfied with the Soviet reluctance to create a second front in Asia. Russia was preoccupied with the war in Europe. American military forces, however, had to fight a difficult war in two great theaters—Europe and the Pacific. It was understandable that American military planners wanted Russia to relieve some of the pressure on U.S. troops. We shall shortly take up the account of how the Soviets regained the former Asian holdings of Tsarist Russia—their price for entering the war against Japan.

RUSSIA GAINS AN EMPIRE

The strategic military decisions which helped Stalin regain most of the former empire of Tsarist Russia and extend Russia's effective control deep into areas never before under Russian domination, must be kept in mind as we begin our investigation. We must also remember that most of the political issues were raised at each of the great wartime conferences of the Allied leaders, and at numerous meetings of their foreign ministers and aides. Stalin incessantly pressed the Allies to accept his whole range of political objectives.

Poland   Poland was Stalin's central preoccupation in Europe. Naturally the Poles were interested in their future. Add the

Western Allies and you have a most difficult political issue, as well as a crucial indicator for postwar relations among the members of the Grand Alliance. The main question was whether Russia would keep Eastern Poland, which it had seized after the Nazi attack in 1939. Later, the character of the postwar Polish government became a critical point for discussion.

Stalin finally recognized the Polish government-in-exile in London, after the German attack on Russia. (Stalin had scorned this government when Poland had been partitioned in 1939.) In the recognition agreement, the Soviets promised to help establish a Polish army from some 250,000 Polish soldiers imprisoned in Russia, and to release the 1,200,000 Polish civilians interned in Soviet labor camps. But Maisky, the Soviet ambassador to Britain negotiating the agreement, insisted that Eastern Poland remain Russian: (1) ethnographically it belonged to Russia; (2) the British had recognized this fact in 1920 with the Curzon Line; and (3) the German attack had shown how vital this area was for the defense of the USSR.

General Sikorski, the Polish Prime Minister, was just as adamant that Poland should reestablish her borders of 1921. Under British prodding, the problem was postponed in order to complete the agreement on recognition. This document merely said that the Soviet-German treaties of 1939 providing for territorial changes had "lost their validity." *Pravda* quickly cleared up any misunderstanding of the Soviet position. It declared on August 3, 1941, that there was nothing immutable about Poland's 1921 border. This was "a matter for the future."

When Sikorski met Stalin in Moscow in December 1941, German advance parties were in the city's suburbs. But Stalin again brought up the border question. He intimated that Russia would settle for a "little" change in the pre-1939 frontier. Sikorski refused to discuss the problem. The Soviet state seemed on its last legs. Why should Poland agree to something which the Russians could not acquire later? Stalin never again would be so agreeable.

A few days later, Anthony Eden, the British Foreign Secretary, visited Moscow. Stalin asked for written recognition that Russia would get back all her territory as of the time of the German invasion. (The Soviet dictator suggested the matter be handled in a "secret" protocol to the pending British-Soviet treaty.) Stalin thought this settlement axiomatic in view of Russia's security needs and her war losses. In addition, he wanted air bases in Rumania, perhaps air and naval bases in Finland, and a slice of German East Prussia. Eden balked, inveighing the principles of the Atlantic Charter. Stalin retorted that it was beginning to look as if the Charter were directed at the USSR, and not the Axis powers. Eden smoothed the waters. Stalin's claims were not unjust. They merely had to wait. Moreover, Britain had promised to discuss all such questions with the United States.

Poland's big clash with Russia came in 1943. Stalin had agreed to the formation of a Polish army in Russia. But relatively few Polish officers trickled out of the Soviet prisoner-of-war camps. The Soviets could give no explanation for the over 8,000 missing men. On April 13, 1943, a German radio bulletin dropped a bombshell. The bodies of more than 10,000 Polish officers had been found in a mass grave in the Katyn Forest outside of the Russian city of Smolensk. The Germans claimed the officers were the victims of "Jewish-Bolshevik bestiality."

Three days later, the Polish exile government requested the International Red Cross to investigate the grisly discovery. On April 25, Stalin responded by severing diplomatic relations with Poland. The London government, according to the Soviets, had dealt "a treacherous blow" to the USSR. It had acted on the slanderous campaign of the German fascists without giving the Soviet government a chance to comment. Stalin charged the Poles with attempting to use the incident—the officers naturally had been murdered by the Germans—to wrest territorial concessions from the Ukraine, Byelorussia and Lithuania. Obviously the exile government was in league with the Nazis for this purpose.[7]

The Western Allies were disgusted with the exile government for disrupting the alliance. They also pleaded with Stalin to place Hitler's defeat above his quarrel with Poland. Stalin, however, probably had been looking for a pretext to dump the London Poles. They had steadfastly refused Russia's territorial demands. (A few weeks before Katyn, the Soviets had set up the nucleus of the future Polish pro-Soviet government—"The Union of Polish Patriots.")

On the other hand, it was both humanly and politically impossible for the London government to avoid searching out the truth of the massacre. The missing men made up almost 45 per cent of the Polish Army officer corps, including a large number of the intelligentsia serving in the reserves—an incalculable loss. The Poles initially suspected the whole thing was a macabre Nazi propaganda hoax. Later evidence proved beyond a reasonable doubt that the victims were executed by the Soviet NKVD in the spring of 1940. Some 4,500 bodies ultimately were recovered. The fate of 10,000 other officers and men is still unknown.[8]

The need now was to get the historic enemies back together before

[7] The exile government was hardly pro-Nazi. But many of its members were vehemently anti-Russian and anti-Communist. Moreover, Eden had complained to Roosevelt that the aspirations of the exile government for postwar Poland were utterly unreal. Poland supposedly would be much more powerful than before the war, and Germany and Russia much weaker.

[8] See J. K. Zawodny, *Death in the Forest* (Notre Dame, Ind.: University of Notre Dame Press, 1962).

the Russians formally created a Polish puppet government. Churchill, with Roosevelt's acquiescence, suggested to Stalin at Teheran that Poland be given a slice of German territory in the West as compensation for losing Eastern Poland. In effect, the Allies were proposing to make Poland a prisoner of Russia. The Poles would need Soviet protection if a future Germany attempted to regain its lost land in the East. Poland never again could attempt a neutral role in East European politics. Stalin accepted the formula; but, he refused to have anything to do with the London government unless it were also purged of its anti-Russian element. The London Poles, however, would not budge on either issue.

By January 1944, the Red Army was in Poland. The Soviet sponsored "Committee of National Liberation," composed of Polish communists and fellow travelers, took over the administration of Poland in the wake of Soviet troops.[9] Churchill and Roosevelt made a last ditch attempt to save what influence the London government still had. They insisted that Mikolajczyk, the Prime Minister, fly to Moscow to come to terms with Stalin.[10] Roosevelt flatly told the Prime Minister that the Allies were not going to fight Russia for the sake of Poland.

In Moscow, Stalin said he would only talk with a Polish government which accepted the Curzon Line. In effect, he would talk with the Committee of National Liberation. Stalin implied that the London Poles had better get together with the Committee if they wanted to participate in the governing of Poland. Mikolajczyk met with Committee representatives a few days later. He found to his distaste that they demanded 14 out of 18 cabinet posts in a coalition government. The Prime Minister understandably refused to take part in such an arrangement.

Another tragic event then occurred to inflame Polish-Soviet relations. At five P.M. on August 1, 1944, the day after the Prime Minister arrived in Moscow, over 35,000 men of the London-controlled Polish underground army rose in revolt against the Germans in Warsaw. Russian troops were shelling Warsaw's suburbs. On the evening of July 29, the communist-controlled Kosciuszko radio in Moscow had called on the people of Warsaw to revolt.

Intensely patriotic, the underground decided to act. It wanted to liberate Warsaw before the Red Army arrived. The Soviets (and the world) had to be shown that the underground army was not a fiction. They had to be given a demonstration of the will of the Poles to remain free. The uprising in essence was a political maneuver against Russia

---

[9] The Committee was the successor to the Union of Polish Patriots. It also is called the "Lublin government" because the Committee named that city as the temporary capital of Poland.

[10] Prime Minister Sikorski had been killed in a tragic air crash in 1943. Although able and relatively moderate, Mikolajczyk did not have Sikorski's persuasive power over the rebellious factions in the exile government.

and the rival Polish communist underground. (There was no compelling military reason for the revolt; the Germans were bound to lose Warsaw eventually.)

The Warsaw fighters only had supplies for a few days. But surely the Red Army would push through the German defensive perimeter in time. Instead, the Germans rushed up five Panzer divisions. Depending on the source, the Russian forces sat outside the city gates—or were stopped by the Germans—while the resistance army in Warsaw held out for 63 terrible days.

Before he left Moscow, Mikolajczyk pleaded with Stalin to aid the underground fighters. Stalin said he had expected to capture Warsaw on August 6, but had been stopped by German reinforcements. Anyway, he didn't believe there actually was a revolt in the city. (The insurrection had not been coordinated with the Soviets.) Perhaps there was some truth in Stalin's claims at this juncture.[11] But his further actions raised doubts. Churchill and Roosevelt planned exceedingly difficult air drops of supplies to the beleaguered defenders. Stalin refused to permit the Allied aircraft to terminate their long flights on Russian airfields. Stalin now seemed merely vindictive, charging that the Poles inferred Russia had abandoned Warsaw on purpose. And so it may have been. The Russians may have sensed a golden opportunity to discredit the exile government in the eyes of all Poland for the "purely adventuristic affair" in Warsaw. As a bonus, a major share of the anti-Soviet underground army would be destroyed.

In October 1944, a stormy meeting took place in Moscow. An irate Churchill and an unmovable Stalin confronted a stubborn Mikolajczyk. They told the Polish Prime Minister about their earlier meeting of minds (with Roosevelt) at Teheran on Poland's boundaries. The Polish Prime Minister finally consented to ask his colleagues in London to accept the new terms. They refused. The Lublin Committee proclaimed itself the provisional government on December 31, 1944. Moscow quickly gave it recognition.

At the Yalta Conference in February 1945, the Polish "headache" again consumed an inordinate amount of time. It was a subject in seven out of the eight plenary sessions and numerous tête-à-têtes. Churchill was now terribly upset about the situation, and Roosevelt was weary of the whole nagging question. The Western leaders finally agreed to the Curzon Line.

[11] A good case can be made that military factors dictated the initial pause outside Warsaw. The city wasn't taken by the Soviets until January 1945. For a summary of the complex affair see Samuel L. Sharp, *Poland: White Eagle on a Red Field* (Cambridge, Mass.: Harvard University Press, 1953), pp. 166-84. Alan Clark agrees with this analysis. See his *Barbarossa, The Russian-German Conflict, 1941-1945* (London: Hutchinson & Co. (Publishers) Limited, 1965), pp. 417-28.

Roosevelt first tried to have the city of Lvov—located east of the line —included in the reconstituted Poland. The President pleaded for this concession to placate the six or seven million Poles in the United States. Stalin, in a rare show of concern for public opinion, said he could not face his own people if he permitted this change in the Curzon Line. "Should we be less Russian than Curzon and Clemenceau?" he retorted. The drawing of the western boundary nevertheless was postponed. For Stalin, apparently now sure of a Russian-dominated Poland, attempted to push the Poles further into traditionally German territory. (Molotov admitted this territory had been Polish *very* long ago.)

The official question remained: Who would control this new Poland? Churchill and Roosevelt hoped Stalin would integrate Poles of all five Polish political parties into a new provisional government, and promise free elections as soon as practicable. Western acceptance of the Soviet border demands was supposed to ensure this. But Stalin harped that elections would be held in a month anyway. He secured Allied consent to a reorganization of the interim Lublin government on a "broader democratic basis." This was probably the best the West could get—as long as the safety of the Grand Alliance came first. The London Poles had wanted too much, been too anti-Soviet, and dreamed of an impossible future. But the Western leaders should have more clearly foreseen the end result of their policies—the death of an independent Poland.

Finland and the Baltic States   The other territorial problems in Eastern Europe paled in significance—and difficulty—beside the Polish question. We mentioned Stalin's demands regarding the future of little Latvia, Lithuania, and Estonia (and Finland) during Eden's visit to Moscow in December 1941, and Eden's refusal to discuss territorial questions. Churchill indeed was philosophically opposed to their forced incorporation into the USSR. The month of Eden's meeting with Stalin in 1941, the Prime Minister was sailing across the North Atlantic to meet President Roosevelt. Churchill told his shipboard companions that he would never be a party to countries such as Lithuania being given over to communism.[12]

In 1942, however, Churchill would not imperil the future of Britain for the sake of the Baltic. He asked Roosevelt to go along with Stalin's demands on his northern neighbors to show Allied sincerity to a beleaguered Russia. The President also was philosophically against the incorporation of these states into the USSR. But he seemed more interested in the impact of such a transfer on the voting attitudes of their minority groups in the United States. (Primarily to ease the impact on American public opinion,

[12] Lord Moran, *Churchill: The Struggle for Survival* (Boston: Houghton Mifflin Company, 1966), p. 9.

Roosevelt toyed with requesting a second plebiscite in the Baltic. He did ask the Soviets in 1942 to let dissatisfied persons leave the annexed areas. The Soviets refused.)

Roosevelt's second front proposal in 1942 let the Allies postpone the problem of the northern sector. In March 1943, however, the British became concerned about postwar political issues in general. During a discussion of the future world, Roosevelt and Foreign Secretary Eden agreed that they might have to give in to Russian demands on the Baltic states. Eventually they did and Latvia, Lithuania and Estonia stayed in the USSR with scarcely a whimper from the West.

Russia exacted her security needs from Finland in a peace treaty signed in 1947. (Finland had become embroiled with Germany against Russia.) The border was the same as that established after the "winter war" in 1940, with the addition of the strategic Petsamo area in the north and a new Russian naval base on Finland's Baltic coast. Things could have been worse. The Soviets neither occupied nor attempted to communize their Northern neighbor. Finland was left at least nominally independent. The Finns, as history had shown, would have been a tough people for the Soviets to digest. Moreover, a communist Finland probably would have driven the Swedes closer to the West. The Soviets decided to leave well enough alone.[13]

The Balkans There was more difficulty in the Balkans. Churchill wanted to check Russian expansion in that strategic area. At Teheran in November 1943, Churchill eloquently lectured Roosevelt and Stalin on the desirability of an invasion through the Adriatic. Churchill since has claimed that this proposal was put purely for military objectives —to dissipate German strength before the grand assault across the Channel in 1944.

The United States chiefs of staff were sure Churchill was trying to torpedo "Overlord" (the cross-channel invasion project) because of Britain's "Mediterranean ambitions." A cagey Stalin was perfectly content to let the Americans insist that nothing interfere with Overlord. Stalin merely reiterated that only the invasion of France could bring final relief on the Russian front. However, the eternally suspicious Soviet

---

[13] Yet this was not the end of Finland's difficulty. Local communists, who had infiltrated the government at all levels, appeared to be planning a coup in 1948 with the aid of external pressure from the USSR. This coup was averted at the last minute by cool and courageous President Paasikivi and the strongly anti-communist Finnish army. Recent Soviet pressure on Finland has been more subtle; the ultimate goal now may be the "peaceful" takeover of Finland by the indigenous communist party. See "Finland" by James H. Billington in *Communism and Revolution* (Princeton, N.J.: Princeton University Press, 1964), ed. by Cyril E. Black and Thomas P. Thornton, pp. 117-44.

dictator may have thought that Churchill was scheming to frustrate Soviet ambitions in Southeastern Europe.[14] Perhaps the Prime Minister was, and perhaps the strategy would have halted the spread of Soviet power in this area. We will never know. In any case, Churchill need not have apologized for thinking of political considerations in 1943.

We do know that Churchill was worried about the Balkans by 1944. He feared the whole area would be communized in the wake of the Soviet military steamroller. Moreover, rival communist and non-communist partisans in both Greece and Yugoslavia threatened civil war. Russia naturally would be inclined to ally with local communists, and Britain and the United States with the opposition. Churchill searched for some political arrangement to forestall such a catastrophe. The Prime Minister seemed ready to acquiesce in Soviet predominance in Rumania and Bulgaria as a *fait accompli*—but not in Yugoslavia and Greece. Churchill suggested to Roosevelt that Britain and Russia share the "management" of the Balkans pending the eventual peace conference. This smacked of spheres of influence to the President. He therefore, was against the idea in principle. At the same time, Roosevelt insisted America wanted nothing to do with the Balkans either during or after the war.

Churchill brought up the Balkan question with Stalin in October 1944 during the Prime Minister's visit to Moscow. (According to Churchill, "the moment was apt for business.") In blunt terms which Stalin understood, Churchill offered Russia 90 per cent "predominance" in Rumania and 75 per cent in Bulgaria. Britain (with the United States) would control 90 per cent of Greece, and share 50-50 with Russia in Yugoslavia and Hungary. In the light of future developments, this seems a curious, academic exercise. Predominance was not defined. Nothing was said about what kinds of governments might emerge. Stalin breathed no hint of his plans to communize the area, if he actually had such plans. Churchill and Stalin took pains to eliminate any taint of spheres of influence in a joint cable to Roosevelt. This really was not necessary. The President now seemed ready to accept some temporary arrangement to prevent possible conflict in the Balkans. And he was more eager than ever to wash his hands of the disagreeable prospect of policing the area.

The agreement, odd as it now appears, seemed to work for a while.

---

[14] G. Deborin, a Soviet author, claims Churchill's strategy was political: ". . . The British imperialists thought least of all about speeding the end of the war. The key purpose of their Balkan strategy was to establish British domination in South-East Europe, impose a colonial regime on its peoples and rehabilitate an anti-Soviet 'Cordon sanitaire' that would be a weapon of British foreign policy. After the Soviet Army won several major victories, Balkan strategy was meant to perform yet another task, that of blocking a Soviet offensive across the continent by occupying South-East Europe and subsequently moving the Anglo-American forces northward." *The Second World War* (Moscow: Progress Publishers, n.d.), p. 287.

Civil war broke out in Greece in December 1944. British troops crushed communist-led partisans. But the Soviet press uttered not one word in protest.[15] In return, Stalin assumed Russia would get completely free reign over its sphere. The 10 per cent interest of Britain in Rumania, and the 25 per cent interest in Bulgaria proved meaningless. Russian authorities systematically ignored local Allied representatives. Russia threatened to treat Hungary alike in spite of the promised 50-50 arrangement. Molotov bluntly told American and British representatives that they had better agree to Russian control. Otherwise, the Soviet Union might not even conclude an armistice with Hungary: ". . . The Red Army was practically master of that country. It could do what it wished."

The United States saw a "system of unilateral grabbing" developing in Eastern Europe. A tardy attempt was made to set things straight. The American delegation at Yalta obtained agreement to "The Declaration on Liberated Europe," essentially a repetition of the liberal ideals of the Atlantic Charter. The three states pledged to assist the liberated peoples in destroying the last vestiges of Nazism and Fascism, and in creating democratic institutions of their own choice. Interim governments would be broadly representative of all democratic elements in the population. Free elections of governments responsive to the will of the people would be held at the earliest possible moment. Stalin welcomed the vague phrases. He always had been for "democracy" and against "fascism." Time would demonstrate that only Western power, and not ambiguous and lofty declarations, could halt the spread of Soviet power.

Germany   The last major political problem in Europe was the fate of defeated Germany. This problem was extremely complex because it was heavily clothed in emotion. All Europe hated Germany for the millions slaughtered on the battlefield and the brutal treatment of innocent civilians. Stalin echoed a universal sentiment when he cried, "Death to the German invaders!" Among those with a longer perspective, there was the fear that the tragedy might someday repeat itself. Stalin told Mikolajczyk in August 1944:

> The Germans will rise again. They are a strong nation. From Bismarck's triumph in 1871, they needed forty years to undertake new aggression. After its failure twenty or twenty-two years of regeneration were sufficient to repeat that once more—this time almost successfully. Now who knows if after twenty or twenty-five years they will not be once more ready to fight.

[15] Stalin may have thought the Greek communists a waste of time, regardless of his agreement with Churchill. In the middle of 1944, a Soviet military mission in Greece reportedly told Moscow that the local communists were "just a rabble of armed men, not worth supporting." Edgar O'Ballance, *The Greek Civil War, 1944-1949* (New York: Frederick A. Praeger, Inc., 1965), p. 78.

Yes, Germany is a strong country even though Hitler is weakening it. But the German economic and military staff will survive Hitler. . . . I am for all possible and impossible repression of Germany. But in spite of this, they may rise again.[16]

Where was the great Stalin, friend and protector of the proletariat everywhere, including the German proletariat? It was hard to find Russian pity anywhere for the "exploited" classes of the Third Reich.[17] There had been curious Soviet broadcasts to the German people that only Nazis would be treated harshly, and urging revolt against Hitler. Even Stalin occasionally wavered, claiming it would be ludicrous to identify Hitler's clique with the German people. But Stalin seemed mainly bent on super-nationalistic revenge against *all* Germans. A communist "East" zone hardly seemed his preoccupation.[18] Stalin also did not want German territory except for part of East Prussia. He wanted blood money and insurance against a resurgent Reich.

Stalin's intentions were obvious in Allied planning for the postwar treatment of Germany. The foreign ministers of the three major powers agreed in October 1943 that every vestige of Nazism should be rooted out, the whole German army demobilized, and drastic changes made in German political life. A few weeks later at Teheran, Stalin called these measures very good but insufficient. He wanted 50,000, possibly 100,000, of the German commanding staff liquidated. This cold-blooded proposition was too much for Churchill. Moreover, the Prime Minister was beginning to see the necessity of a German counterweight to a victorious Russia. He didn't want to completely subjugate Germany. Roosevelt attempted to lighten the grim discussion. He suggested that only 49,000 German officers be executed. Stalin later joined Roosevelt in a proposal to break up the German state into seven pieces. One American at the conference predicted that Stalin, with this and other proposals, seemed

---

[16] Quoted in Edward J. Rozek, *Allied Wartime Diplomacy: A Pattern in Poland* (New York: John Wiley & Sons, Inc., 1958), p. 247. Even Roosevelt wrote in August 1944: "It is of the utmost importance that every person in Germany should realize that this time Germany is a defeated nation. I do not want them to starve to death, but, as an example, if they need food to keep body and soul together beyond what they have, they should be fed three times a day with soup from Army soup kitchens. . . . The fact that they are a defeated nation collectively and individually, must be so impressed upon them that they will hesitate to start any new war." Feis, *Churchill, Roosevelt, Stalin*, p. 366.

[17] One Russian worker commented to Alexander Werth: "It may be unMarxist to say so, but the Germans *are* a bad lot. . . . If there are any exceptions, I haven't come across any." Werth, *Russia at War*, p. 60.

[18] The calamitous communist revolutions in Germany apparently left Stalin very pessimistic. Mikolajczyk told Stalin in 1944 that German prisoners hoped for communism in their country after the war. Stalin was contemptuous, retorting that "communism fitted Germany as a saddle fitted a cow."

bent on making the USSR "the only important military and political force on the continent of Europe."

At Yalta in February 1945, Stalin was specific on the subject of Russia's economic vengeance. He wanted ten billion dollars in reparations. (Russia had proposed a total figure of twenty billion for all the allies.) These would be collected in kind from the Germans over a ten-year period. As the initial payment, the German military plant would be dismantled and shipped to Russia (and other countries), as well as 80 per cent of the remaining heavy industry. Stalin also repeated a demand made at Teheran for some two to three million Germans to serve for ten years to rebuild Russia.

At the Yalta Conference, all three leaders reserved the right to insist on the permanent dismemberment of Germany. But they could not agree on how this should be done. The decision was postponed for the more leisurely days of peace. However, a decision had to be made on areas of occupation. The big three planned the division of Germany into four occupation zones at the end of hostilities—Russian, American, British and French. (Stalin initially balked at giving the French a piece of the German pie.) Berlin, deep in the Soviet zone, was to be administered jointly. The critical question of Western access to Berlin was hardly touched upon.

In theory, the occupation soon would be terminated with a formal peace treaty. In fact, the occupation zones would be transformed into an enduring division of Germany, and the border of the "iron curtain." But neither Churchill nor Roosevelt seemed to consider this a possibility. Stalin gave no hint of any plans to communize his sector of Germany. The real quarrel was between Roosevelt and Churchill over whether the United States or Britain would occupy northwestern Germany.

The Far East   Stalin's last major territorial desires lay in Asia: the recovery of those pieces of the Tsarist empire lost to Japan in 1905: Here Stalin's foreign policy was strikingly nationalist. He was reaching back in time with demands for territories lost years before the Bolshevik Revolution. After Japan surrendered in August 1945, Stalin reveled in Russia's revenge. The defeat of Russian troops in 1904, he reminded the nation, had left "bitter memories in the mind of the people. It lay like a black spot on our country. Our people believed and hoped that a day would come when Japan would be smashed and that blot effaced. Forty years have we, the people of the older generation, waited for this day." [19] Forgotten was the fact that Old Bolsheviks—and Mensheviks—had rejoiced at the Japanese blow to Tsarism in 1904.

[19] Cited in Deutscher, *Stalin*, p. 528.

The report of the process by which Stalin regained the outposts of Russia's Far Eastern empire later became a celebrated issue in American politics. Vicious charges were leveled at President Roosevelt for the "giveaway" to Russia involved in the "Yalta Agreement." It was asserted that the Agreement contributed heavily to the later defeat of Nationalist China by the communist forces of Mao Tse-tung. The reality was far different.

Early in the war, American military planners pressed Roosevelt to get Stalin's approval for preliminary planning of a combined campaign against Japan. The Soviets wanted a second front in Europe just as the United States did in Asia. Stalin refused Roosevelt's request, citing Russia's difficult situation with the Germans. But the Soviet dictator dropped a pleasant bombshell in October 1943 at the big three foreign ministers' conference in Moscow. He told a delighted Secretary of State Cordell Hull that Russia would join in defeating Japan as soon as Germany was beaten. Stalin did not mention the necessity of political rewards.

A few weeks later, a political reward was made which must have started Stalin thinking. At the Cairo Conference in November 1943, Roosevelt, with Churchill's approval, announced the "Cairo Declaration." Japan was to be stripped of all the Pacific islands she had seized since 1914. The Chinese were to get back all their "stolen" territories, including Manchuria, Formosa, and the Pescadores islands. In marked contrast to Europe, the Western Allies were ready—even eager—to cut up an enemy empire without waiting for the war's end. And little thought was given to the sacred principle of self-determination. Formosa, for example, had not been Chinese for almost 50 years. No one bothered to reflect that the Formosans might prefer Japanese rule to Chinese.

For good or bad, America was now concerned about politics, not abstract principles. The United States was banking its whole Far Eastern policy on China's being the great power in that region after the war, and one of the "Four Policemen" of the proposed United Nations. This bit of wishful thinking was based on three highly questionable assumptions. First, American planners believed the Chinese could become a great power, given a chance for greatness, and would be friendly to the West. The Cairo Declaration was to help make this possible. The Chinese would be granted their territorial desires, and their sagging morale would be bolstered. Second, Chiang Kai-shek would finally win his feud with the Chinese communists. (Chiang and Mao still worried more about each other than about the Japanese.) Third, Russia would come to terms with the Nationalist Government, and resist the temptation to aid the communists.

There seemed some basis for the last assumption. Stalin referred to Mao and his comrades as "margarine communists," indicating doubts about the purity of their faith. The Soviet leader appeared unable to forget the bitter experience of the Chinese revolution in the 1920's. On the other hand, he had been rather cool to Chiang, accusing him of anti-Soviet propaganda. Apparently little thought was given to a future alternative to Chinese dominance—a powerful but peaceful Japan purged of militarism.

The Chinese were liberally taken care of. The Western Allies decided to sound out Stalin on what he might want in Asia. Here was a chance to show Russia sympathy for her burden in the West, and perhaps to speed her entry into the war against Japan. The three heads of state were lunching together one day during the Teheran Conference. Stalin had reaffirmed that Russia would enter the Pacific war upon the defeat of Germany. After some discussion of the recent Cairo Declaration, Roosevelt asked Stalin what could be done for Russia in the Far East. Stalin said the Soviets would like an ice-free port. The President suggested Dairen.[20] Subsequent discussions apparently touched on other territorial issues. Roosevelt later told the Pacific War Council in Washington that Stalin also wanted (1) the southern half of Sakhalin Island (lost to Japan in 1905), and (2) the Kurile Islands (which Russia had ceded to Japan in 1875—Stalin was really going back in history). Stalin, however, had agreed that the Chinese should get control of the foreign-built Manchurian railways.

At Teheran—not Yalta—the Soviet leader had forecast most of his primary wants in the Far East. Stalin later said that his only desire not mentioned at Teheran was to have the Chinese recognize the "status quo" in Outer Mongolia: in plain language, that this Asian borderland was a Soviet satellite.

Roosevelt seemed ready to grant Stalin's desires because he thought them reasonable—not as a cynical bargain simply to get Russia in the war. Stalin already had promised to do that.[21] Most important in the President's thinking was the promise of harmony between Russia and Nationalist China—a vital element in America's plans for the postwar Far East. Harmony would be promoted if territorial problems could be solved between the two nations.

[20] Russia had forced China to lease her the Kwantung Peninsula in Manchuria, containing Dairen and the magnificent harbor of Port Arthur, in 1898. Japan had taken possession in 1905.

[21] Kennan's comment is apt: "How he [Stalin] interpreted this disposition on the part of the Americans to reimburse him politically for something (namely, entering the Pacific war) which he had only recently stated his intention of doing anyway, without any reimbursement, we cannot know. I have a feeling there were many occasions when Stalin returned from discussions with our statesmen muttering to himself about the 'inscrutable Americans,' and assuring his associates that the motives of American policy were 'a mystery wrapped in an enigma'" (Churchill's classic description of Soviet foreign policy). *Russia and the West*, p. 354.

But Stalin dragged his heels in the coming months when it came to actual battle plans for Russia's entry into the Asian war. The Americans wanted air bases around Soviet Vladivostok in order to bomb Japan, and Soviet ports for the American fleet. Stalin pleaded lack of time, or professed worry that the Japanese might learn of the projected operations. Russia and Japan ostensibly were still neutral toward each other. In March 1944, they even completed a new fishing rights agreement. At that time, Japan also agreed to give up its concessions in Northern Sakhalin.

By late 1944, American military planners were frantic to tie down Russia's entry into the war. Japan's defensive perimeter was crumbling. But strategists predicted the Japanese would fight to the death on the home islands. They estimated the war in the Pacific would last 18 months beyond the war in the west. The United States and Britain wanted Russia in the war against Japan for one simple reason: to spread the terrible burden of dead and wounded.

Stalin was finally ready to talk business when Churchill visited Moscow in October 1944. The Soviet leader promised that Russia would be ready to move against Japan three months after Germany's defeat. Stalin talked of Soviet action on a grand scale. To the surprise and delight of the Americans, the Soviets suggested Red Army strikes into China itself to cut off the retreat route of the Japanese forces in Manchuria. But then, for the first time, Stalin clearly stated that Russia's political gains had to be granted before she entered the war. As Stalin delicately phrased it, "there were also certain political aspects which would have to be taken into consideration. The Russians would have to know what they were fighting for. They had certain claims against Japan."

Roosevelt, as we have seen, already had made territorial awards to China during the war. Why not to Russia? But he may have had a more pressing reason for some kind of agreement with Stalin's announcement of a major Soviet foray into China. Soviet forces might end up in control of strategic areas in China, and all of Manchuria. They would be in close proximity to communist-held areas. Roosevelt needed a meeting of minds with Stalin to limit Russian political gains—not to give away territory controlled by Chiang's government. A territorial agreement also would aid an understanding between Russia and Nationalist China *before* Russia entered the war. Chiang Kai-shek was known to be eager for closer relations with Stalin, and he had asked the President to serve as a middleman.

At Yalta, an agreement on the Soviet demands was hastily contrived in a series of side discussions between Roosevelt and Stalin, Molotov and Harriman. A weary Roosevelt—only a few months from death—gave in on seemingly insignificant issues. (The conference was dealing with the momentous questions of postwar Europe and the new international collective security organization.) Stalin wangled all he had asked for at Teheran, plus the "status quo" in Mongolia and the lease of Port Arthur for a Soviet naval base. Moreover, the critical railroad network in Manchuria was placed under a joint Soviet-Chinese company. The "preeminent interests" of the Soviet Union in this company were to be safeguarded. Finally, Roosevelt agreed in writing to get Chiang's concurrence to the provisions of the agreement. But this would be eased by a Soviet promise in the final paragraph of the agreement. Russia was ready to conclude "a pact of friendship and alliance" with China. The whole document, of course, was "top secret." (The American copy was locked in the President's White House safe.)

In August 1945, a new Sino-Soviet treaty was signed as Stalin had promised. China accepted the territorial provisions in the Yalta Agreement. In return, Russia promised to give moral support and military supplies only to the Nationalist Government. Chiang said that he was generally satisfied with the treaty. The Chinese apparently felt it was a better deal than they could have gotten if Roosevelt had not paved the way.

If United States policy makers had been wrong, it was on the larger questions. They had grossly overestimated the Japanese will to resist. But certainly there was strong evidence to support such a belief. Also, no one knew at this juncture what impact the yet untested atomic bomb would have against the Japanese homeland. Perhaps the more profound error was placing all American bets on a resurgent, unified China under Chiang's leadership. However, Stalin appeared equally wrong in his pessimistic estimate of what Mao Tse-tung might do if given the chance. The future of China was too complex for either the United States or Russia to grasp, let alone control.

AMERICA GAINS
AN INTERNATIONAL
SECURITY ORGANIZATION

Stalin's central political aim in World War II—the acquisition of territory and the creation of a new sphere of influence—has been analyzed. We must consider briefly Roosevelt's central political preoccupation—the creation of an international organization to banish war forever. Two distinct theories of postwar security were at issue. Stalin's was based on tangible defense in depth, Roosevelt's on the promise of collective action against aggression. In contrast, Churchill seemed to prefer a little of both schemes.

Stalin appeared bored with the whole UN concept. (Roosevelt was bored with the interminable wrangle over Poland.) It seemed obvious

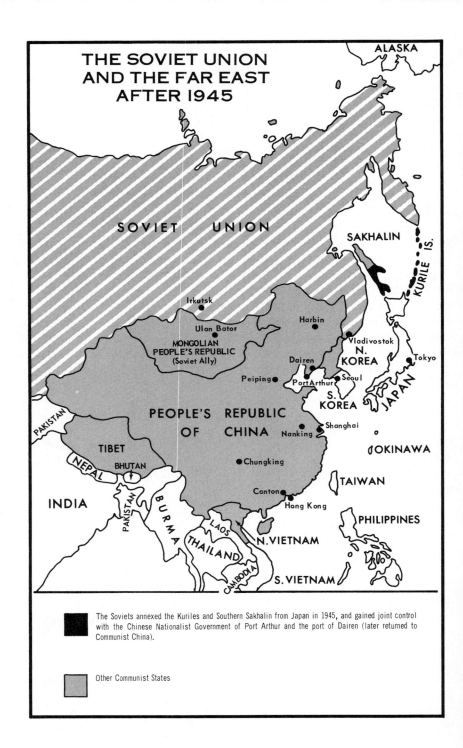

THE SOVIET UNION AND THE FAR EAST AFTER 1945

ALASKA

SOVIET   UNION

SAKHALIN

KURILE IS.

Irkutsk

Harbin

Ulan Bator

MONGOLIAN
PEOPLE'S REPUBLIC
(Soviet Ally)

Vladivostok
N. KOREA

Tokyo

Dairen

Peiping

Port Arthur

Seoul

S. KOREA

JAPAN

PAKISTAN

PEOPLE'S   REPUBLIC
OF   CHINA   Nanking

Shanghai

TIBET

OKINAWA

NEPAL

BHUTAN

Chungking

INDIA

PAKISTAN

BURMA

Canton

TAIWAN

Hong Kong

PHILIPPINES

LAOS

THAILAND

N. VIETNAM

CAMBODIA

S. VIETNAM

The Soviets annexed the Kuriles and Southern Sakhalin from Japan in 1945, and gained joint control with the Chinese Nationalist Government of Port Arthur and the port of Dairen (later returned to Communist China).

Other Communist States

at Yalta that Stalin had not even read a crucial American proposal on voting in the Security Council. Yet this had been submitted to the Russians 63 days earlier. Stalin's attitude clearly reflected the Soviet belief that a UN could provide little security for the USSR. There were sufficient grounds for this pessimistic attitude. Russia had tried to organize collective security through the League of Nations against Nazi Germany, and had failed. In turn, Russia had been kicked out of the League for warring against Finland. Yet the League had stood paralyzed against "capitalist" German, Japanese, and Italian aggression.

But Stalin agreed to go along with Roosevelt's pet project. Some kind of international organization seemed destined. It would be better to join immediately and have some influence on its character. All the other members would be capitalist, and thus fundamentally opposed to the USSR. Roosevelt, however, had talked informally about the three great allies, and perhaps China, becoming the "Four Policemen" of the world to come. They would act jointly to suppress trouble on all the continents. (Stalin was particularly attracted by the possible use of the UN to hold down Germany.) If action by the four had to be unanimous—and Russia would insist on this—the Soviets could block any collective effort against the USSR or its emerging sphere of influence. The fiasco over Finland would never be repeated.

At the same time, the Soviets would continue to rely on the naked power of the USSR. A collective security organization could never provide the safety of a militarily strong Russia buttressed by a protective belt of subservient states. Stalin would go along with Roosevelt's ambitious plan only if it complemented this primary scheme for assuring Soviet security. But some time elapsed before the Soviet attitude toward the UN became evident.

America and Britain initiated planning for the future UN in the summer of 1943. They hoped to take advantage of the momentum of wartime unity, and the longing of people everywhere for some new device to end war. Perhaps the Soviets also might moderate their territorial demands if an alternative method of national security were available. To the surprise of many, Molotov demonstrated unusual eagerness at the foreign ministers' conference in April 1943, to set up a commission to plan the new international organization.

But then Stalin and Molotov showed the extent of their interest. Stalin couldn't have cared less when Roosevelt suggested at Yalta that the UN should supervise international trusteeships for dependent peoples. (Churchill charged that this was a disguised attempt to dismember the British Empire.) At the Dumbarton Oaks Conference dealing specifically with the UN, the Soviet representatives argued against any economic and social functions for the new organization. The interest of the Soviets in the General Assembly also was limited. They felt it should be a power-less discussion group. Their only concern was to bargain for sixteen votes instead of one in the Assembly. All republics of the USSR should be accepted as members. The United States, the Soviets felt, had more than one vote because of her Latin American "satellites."

Soviet interest perked up only when UN security measures were discussed. The critical organ for handling the security function was to be the Security Council. On this the three heads of state agreed. But Stalin wanted Russia's position on the Council to be impregnable. All three leaders readily accepted the American proposition that a "permanent" member could veto any substantive decision of the Council. (The Americans seemed to think this would rarely happen, and then only where the use of force was contemplated.)

A more crucial question might arise if a small country brought charges against one of the permanent members of the Council. Roosevelt and Churchill argued that the body should at least permit discussion of the question. They were willing to grant a permanent member the right to veto any subsequent proposal for the use of force or sanctions. Stalin insisted on the power to veto the "procedural" question of whether such charges should even be discussed. There had to be unanimity on all matters. Certain influential circles, claimed Stalin, had ridiculous prejudices about the USSR. They were opposed to the unanimity rule because they wanted to constrain the Soviets. The Soviet government did not want to be outmaneuvered or isolated in a dispute to which it was a party.

The Soviets later accepted the Western voting formula for the Security Council. Perhaps they felt that the veto power was still sufficient to safeguard Soviet interests. (This would prove to be the case.) Russia also compromised by accepting three votes (the USSR, Byelorussia and the Ukraine) in the General Assembly rather than sixteen. Soviet basic disinterest in the whole UN concept was particularly obvious when Stalin refused to send Molotov to the UN's founding conference in San Francisco—pleading the necessity of the foreign minister's other official business in Moscow. Stalin only relented after Roosevelt's death as a tribute to his wartime partner.

Alexander Dallin neatly sums up the Soviet attitude toward the UN in 1945: "The Soviet Union signed the Charter with a more cynical but also more realistic assessment of the United Nations' capabilities and prospects than many of its fellow-members. Ideological and power-political considerations—and the experience of earlier years—combined to make the UN at best an ancillary instrument of Soviet foreign policy." [22]

[22] *The Soviet Union at the United Nations* (New York: Frederick A. Praeger, Inc., 1962), p. 25.

THE WAR ENDS

The German surrender to the Soviet forces on May 8 was announced in Moscow in the early morning hours of May 9, 1945. "VE Day" finally had come. The city went wild. People were so happy, writes Alexander Werth, that they did not even have to get drunk. That evening, two to three million Muscovites thronged the area around Red Square, dancing and singing, kissing every soldier in sight. Crowds outside the American Embassy shouted "Hurray for Roosevelt," although the President had died a month before.[23]

The war in the west was over—*the* war for the Soviet people. For them, it had been an unmitigated disaster. Some 20 million Russians had perished, the majority, innocent civilians. Of the seven million soldiers lost, perhaps three million had died in German captivity. Almost every Soviet family lost someone.[24] The people hated the thought that more men might be lost in a war with Japan. They felt Russia had done her share. They knew nothing of the Yalta Agreement and what Stalin planned in Asia.

The Soviet war in the east was an anti-climax. True to Stalin's promise, Russia declared war on Japan three months to the day after the conflict had ended in Europe—August 8, 1945. In a few short weeks, the Soviet forces overwhelmed the supposedly elite Kwantung Army in Manchuria and Northern Korea. Airborne troops occupied Dairen and Port Arthur, apparently in fear of an American landing. Southern Sakhalin and the Kuriles were taken in a Soviet combined operation. Japan formally surrendered on September 2 to all the allies on the U. S. battleship *Missouri.* The Soviet contribution to victory had been minor, her losses light. Moscow announced less than 10,000 Russian dead, and some 22,000 wounded. Later Soviet histories of World War II claimed Japan fell because Russia entered the war.

We now know Japan had been considering capitulation several months before the war ended, although she had hoped to get more favorable terms than "unconditional surrender." She had sent out cautious peace feelers to Russia in the spring of 1945 seeking Soviet mediation. Stalin mentioned two such overtures to Truman and Churchill at the Potsdam Conference in July 1945. But he emphasized that the Japanese were resisting unconditional surrender. (American cryptographers already had evidence of these communications.) In any case, Stalin was not ready for the war to end. He wanted to attack Japan so the promised gains at Yalta would not slip through his hands.

[23] Werth, *Russia at War*, p. 969.
[24] Only the Poles and Yugoslavs lost a higher percentage of their population.

The Western Allies on the other hand did not believe the Japanese collapse imminent. The Japanese press and radio were as uncompromising as ever. Churchill and Truman nevertheless were questioning the need for Soviet entry into the Pacific war. (Officially they still asked for Soviet aid.) At Potsdam, Truman got word on July 16 that the nuclear era had begun. A cryptic message arrived announcing the first atomic test at Alamogordo, New Mexico: "Operated on this morning. Diagnosis not yet complete but results seem satisfactory and already exceed expectations." In a few weeks the first atomic bomb would be ready for Hiroshima. Perhaps the dreaded invasion of the home islands would not be necessary.

One week after hearing of the successful atomic test, Truman privately informed Stalin of the new weapon. Stalin was delighted—what a bit of luck! Churchill thought Stalin hadn't understood the significance for he failed to ask one question about the experiment. Perhaps, as Molotov later claimed, Stalin understood this to be a "super bomb," the like of which had never been seen—but not an "atomic" bomb.[25] Perhaps Soviet intelligence already had briefed Stalin on the American project. We may never know.[26] The supreme irony, of course, is that Japan might have surrendered without either the atomic bomb or Soviet intervention.[27]

THE NEW BALANCE OF POWER

The twilight of World War II had seen the dawn of the nuclear era. The full implications of Hiroshima and Nagasaki could not be imagined. The hydrogen bomb, still to be developed, would have a hundred times the destructive force of the first atomic bomb. Yet the shape of the international political system had been changed by more conventional weapons—and the Russian foot soldier. Three basic alterations had been made in the international power structure. First, gaping holes existed in Europe and the Far East with the destruction of the Third Reich and the Japanese empire. After decades of worry about Hitler and the Japanese militarists, the Soviets and the Western Allies could concentrate on other problems. All the powers said their central

[25] Molotov's comment in 1946 to Werth, *Russia at War,* p. 1034.

[26] The Soviets apparently had a small-scale atomic research program at the end of the war. But it is still uncertain how much they had learned through espionage of Western efforts to develop the atomic bomb, and especially whether Stalin appreciated, or even had been told, the full significance of such information. See Arnold Kramish, *Atomic Energy in the Soviet Union* (Stanford, Calif.: Stanford University Press, 1959), Chaps. 5, 6, and 7.

[27] For a detailed account of the evidence, see Robert J. C. Butow, *Japan's Decision to Surrender* (Stanford, Calif.: Stanford University Press, 1954), esp. pp. 131-41.

concern was the prevention of resurgent Nazism or the Co-prosperity Sphere. But there was a scarcely concealed race to see who would fill the power vacuum in Europe and the Far East.

There was a second change in the power structure. After the collapse of Germany in World War I, Britain and France assumed the burden of maintaining the peace. Although Churchill was loathe to admit it, the end of World War II saw the sun setting on the British Empire. The French nation seemed to reside mainly in the obstinate and visionary General de Gaulle. Neither country could play the role—even in Europe —which it once had.

The third dramatic change was the emergence of the superpowers— the USSR and the United States. Before World War II, America had been isolationist, Russia had been isolated. Now their armies had met on the Elbe in Germany. Both had become world powers through the fortunes of war. Because of their new world interests, neither state could ignore the other.

At first glance, the USSR seemed unable to support her hard-won greatness. Russia's economic situation was "little short of disastrous." [28] Much of the progress of the five-year plans lay in ruin. The industrial power of the USSR was about half what it had been in 1941, her steel production was one-eighth that of the United States. We have mentioned the incalculable losses of Russia's most valuable resource—her people.[29] It is perhaps an understatement to say that the survivors were sick of war.

Economically and psychologically, Russia was relatively weak in 1945. But Stalin could still act like the leader of a great power, demanding Russia's fair share in running the world. The momentum of the Soviet offensive had carried Russian troops into the heart of Europe. And if Russia wasn't a superpower, she was as great as any other country except the United States.

Would the United States play the role she was capable of? Would she use her power to halt the Soviet advance? Or would America send the troops home and place all her reliance on a still untested United Nations? These were the critical questions. The beginning of the Cold War in 1946 was evidence that America had assumed that challenge.

[28] Werth, *Russia at War*, p. 1004.

[29] Russia also had lost the full allegiance of certain sectors of her population, especially the national minorities. The most striking evidence is the more than 500,000, possibly a million, ex-Soviet citizens who served in the Wehrmacht. Many had joined out of fear of what happened to Russian prisoners of war under the Germans. But there was a decided anti-Stalinist tinge to the whole movement. The Germans helped by labeling the motley collection the "Russian Army of Liberation." Red Army Lt. General Vlasov, a hero of the Battle of Moscow, was designated commander. He was hanged in Moscow in 1946. See George Fischer, *Soviet Opposition to Stalin* (Cambridge, Mass.: Harvard University Press, 1952).

The Road to Potsdam   The final days of the war saw no radical change in Soviet foreign policy toward the West. Stalin had pressed the Western Allies to grant his political desires since 1941. With the end of the conflict, his appetite merely increased. There was to be a vital difference, however, in the Allied response to Russia's pushy attitude.

During the war, bickering of the coalition members was kept secret. Open dissension at the top would have damaged Western morale and given false hope to the enemy. More fundamentally, Roosevelt still hoped that Allied forbearance would somehow negate the mistrust which had plagued Western relations with the USSR since 1917. Meanwhile, political controversies should not be allowed to trouble military operations. Different ground rules, however, could be used with the conflict nearing its end. The United States in particular could look more objectively at political questions. Military victory was assured regardless of coalition controversy.

Truman shouldered the heavy burden of leadership upon Roosevelt's tragic death in April 1945. His first impulse was to carry on the former President's policies, and to listen to Roosevelt's advisors. The United States supposedly still faced a cruel war in the Pacific. Truman, as had his predecessor, turned a deaf ear to Churchill's pleas to speed the Allied advance into Germany. Western armies, the Prime Minister argued, should "shake hands" with the Russians as far east as possible, and perhaps reach Berlin first.[30]

In May, Churchill begged Truman not to pull back the American forces which had advanced into the projected Soviet zone of occupation. Churchill wanted to hold these military spearheads until the West was satisfied about conditions in Eastern Europe. He wrote Truman on May 12: "Surely it is vital now to come to an understanding with Russia, or see where we are with her, before we weaken our armies mortally or retire to the zones of occupation."[31] None of the President's civilian or military advisors was ready to join Churchill in forcing Stalin's hand. American troops couldn't be left indefinitely in Europe; they had to be transferred to the Pacific, or, if possible, sent home. Anyway, Truman first wanted to try negotiations with Stalin.

The one move Truman did make was to cut off Lend-Lease aid to Russia (and Britain) on May 8, the day after the war ended in Europe for the allied forces. Talking with Hopkins a few weeks later, Stalin

---

[30] The American Joint Chiefs of Staff concluded on April 6, 1945: "Such psychological and political advantages as would result from the possible capture of Berlin ahead of the Russians should not override the imperative military consideration, which in our opinion is the destruction and dismemberment of the German armed forces." Feis, *Churchill, Roosevelt, Stalin,* p. 607.

[31] *Ibid.,* p. 636.

charged that the manner in which this decision was taken was "unfortunate and even brutal." If this were to pressure the Russians, "it was a fundamental mistake." Much could be done, said Stalin, if the Russians were approached frankly and on a friendly basis. But, "reprisals in any form would bring about the exact opposite effect." In retrospect, Truman's move was probably a strict interpretation of the wartime Lend-Lease Act, and nothing more.

Stalin's attempts to get an American loan to rebuild war-torn Russia also failed at this time. He thought capitalist America would face great unemployment in the postwar period as it changed from a war to peace economy. The United States would be eager to sell goods to Russia on any terms. Prominent American businessmen encouraged Stalin's thinking. In January 1945, Molotov asked for a thirty-year six billion dollar loan at low interest. But certain United States government officials in the spring of 1945 were becoming wary of Russia. They were not yet ready to stand up to Stalin; however, they wanted more evidence of Soviet good intentions before committing the United States to help rebuild Russia. The evidence, of course, never came.

In May, Churchill urged Truman to join him in a meeting with Stalin. The log jam of unsettled political problems had to be cleared up. As a result, the three heads of state traveled to Potsdam, a pleasant provincial city some 35 miles southwest of war devastated Berlin.

The Potsdam Conference   The last great wartime conference began on July 17, 1945. In a very real sense, it was destined to be the first peacetime conference. Germany was conquered. Japan's turn would definitely come. Russia's military aid against the home islands was desirable, but not vital. Military necessity no longer needed to dictate American foreign policy toward Russia.

Truman and James F. Byrnes, his new Secretary of State, were journeying for their first meeting with Stalin. (Truman thought the conference an unwelcome "chore.") The President wanted to test the Soviet leader before taking a harder line. Truman was aware of Russian chicanery in Eastern Europe, and elsewhere. But Stalin still might live up to such agreements as the Declaration on Liberated Europe, giving hope for postwar cooperation. Churchill was not so optimistic.

We have traced the great political issues up to the end of the war in Europe. Predictably, these held a prominent place on the Potsdam agenda. Poland again occupied the limelight. In accordance with the agreement at Yalta, the Lublin government had been reorganized. Most important was the promise of free elections in the near future. Fourteen out of twenty cabinet posts had gone to Lublin members. But Stalin had assured Harry Hopkins in Moscow at the end of May, that the Soviet system was not "exportable" to Poland. The United States and Britain had recognized the new government on July 5. It seemed the best that could be gained.

At Potsdam, the major question remaining was the nagging problem of Poland's western border with Germany. All elements of the new Polish government, including Mikolajczyk, now argued for a border along the Oder and Western Niesse Rivers. With Soviet backing, the Poles already had taken over this area. Molotov argued that their action was just retribution against the Germans. Truman and Churchill were bitter; they felt tricked. But Stalin and the Poles were immovable. The conferees deadlocked until the Western Allies found a bargaining point on German reparations.

By the time the Potsdam meeting took place, all three nations had decided against the permanent dismemberment of Germany. The Western policy makers worried about Soviet intentions toward the former Third Reich. They also feared a divided Germany bent on unification might be an even greater problem than a unified nation. We may only guess at Stalin's reasons for a change of heart. Perhaps he thought a unified Germany would be relatively weak with her loss of territory. He may have wanted to ease the German fear of Soviet revenge, and thereby lessen German resistance. The Germans were fighting desperately on the eastern front in April when the Soviet press suddenly dropped its hate propaganda. In any case, the Soviets had to look forward to some kind of Germany. They might as well be on speaking terms with a future German government.

The three powers readily agreed to treat the German people uniformly —although different kinds of "democracies" already were emerging in the Eastern and Western zones. A "Council of Foreign Ministers" of the big three, plus France and China, was organized to draft the treaties of peace with Germany's satellites and Italy. The former Third Reich would get its treaty after a German government "adequate for the purpose" was established. The three powers also agreed to keep Germany as a single economic unit.

The sticking point was over reparations. Stalin and Molotov insisted on the ten billion figure (out of a twenty billion total) requested at Yalta. The Americans thought the Soviets were callously ignoring the vital question of whether the Germans could meet this heavy demand. The United States was not about to support a prostrate Germany just so she could pay her Soviet reparations bill. The Soviets interpreted American obstinacy to mean that the United States was soft on Germany, and was refusing Russia just retribution for war damages.

Russia was upset about German reparations, the West, about Poland. Secretary Byrnes proposed a "package deal" in a spirit of compromise. The Western powers would agree to the *de facto* Polish-German border, with the face-saving proviso that the final decision could be made only at the eventual peace conference. There really was no alternative unless the West was prepared to be much more forceful against Russia. In turn, Russia would have to give in on reparations. The original plan specified that these would be drawn from all of Germany. The Western powers now said Stalin could have the reparations he was able to squeeze from Russia's zone, plus "excess" equipment the Allies might release from their areas. Molotov's proposal for four-power control of the great Ruhr industrial region, located in the British zone, also was turned down. (The Russians apparently hoped to cart off a major share of the Ruhr's industrial capacity.) After hard bargaining and recriminations on both sides, the deal was sealed. Perhaps none of the participants fully realized that Germany in effect had been divided.

Two other Russian ploys at Potsdam illustrated Stalin's growing appetite. The first was the perennial problem of the Turkish Straits. The Lausanne Convention in 1923 had been dictated to a defeated Turkey and a weak Russia. The Soviets had failed to have the Black Sea closed to foreign warships, and Turkey had been forced to keep the Straits demilitarized. At the Montreux Conference in 1936, the Soviets had strongly supported full Turkish sovereignty over the Straits region. Russia herself had won greater restrictions on the number and kind of foreign warships which might enter the Black Sea. But the USSR was not satisfied. It wanted complete control of Turkey's strategic area. In November 1940, Molotov had asked Hitler for Soviet military bases in the Straits as part of the long-range "spheres of influence" arrangement. This obviously came to naught.

During Churchill's visit to Moscow in October 1944, and at Yalta, Stalin had tried his Turkish demands on the Western leaders. He warned that Russia could no longer tolerate Turkey's "hand on Russia's throat." (Turkey had maintained a somewhat shaky neutrality through most of World War II.) It soon became evident what Russia wanted: (1) Soviet bases in the Straits—Molotov claimed World War II had shown the Turks couldn't defend the vital waterway; (2) Soviet-Turkish control of all traffic through the Straits—in effect, Soviet control; and, as a bonus (3) the return of the provinces of Kars and Ardahan which a weak Russia had been forced to yield to Turkey in 1921 by an "unjust" treaty.

The spirited Turks refused. Britain offered them support. The Americans at first counseled moderation; the Soviets had not actually threatened Turkey. But at Potsdam, Truman stood firm with Churchill in opposing any changes to the Montreux Convention. The only exception would be if the Straits were made a free passage for all the world, guaranteed by the wartime coalition. Stalin was blocked again. He curtly observed that the Soviets would talk later with the Turks.

The second indication of Stalin's expanding interests was more sur-

prising. In June 1945, the Soviet delegates at the UN founding conference seemed unusually interested in a trusteeship for their country.
Stalin and Molotov got down to details at Potsdam. Russia wanted to be
the UN trustee for one of the former Italian colonies. (At the first meeting of the newly formed Council of Ministers in September, Molotov
specifically named Tripolitania, the more prosperous western part of
Libya.) Russia deserved this opportunity because of the damages done
on the eastern front by the ten divisions and three brigades of Italian
Blackshirts. The West refused. Churchill seemed more shocked at this
evidence of Russian expansionism than at any other episode during the
conference.[32] Britain's vital interests in the Suez and the Persian Gulf
were at stake. Secretary Byrnes thought Stalin's demand a clear indication of a Soviet scheme to get a strategic point from which to threaten
the West. Libya hardly could be justified for reasons of Soviet state
security.

Russia had been thwarted on reparations, the Turkish Straits, and
Tripolitania. The Western Allies had been frustrated in their attempts
to influence the future of Eastern Europe. President Truman had been
impressed with Stalin as a man; his directness (so Truman thought), his
desire to do business quickly, and even by his occasional geniality. But
the President left for home determined to refuse Russia more information about the atomic bomb unless international control of atomic energy
could be assured. He would also keep Russia from sharing the occupation of Japan.[33] The United States had clearly drawn the line. The Soviet
challenge would be met. Yet it would be some months before the Cold
War was admitted, let alone formally recognized.

SUMMARY

World War II was a calamity for the Russian people—
but not for the Soviet state. The USSR had finally become a great power.
It held sway over more land and more people than had Tsarist Russia.
The sheer momentum of the Red Army's advance had brought Russian

---

[32] In the last days of the Potsdam Conference, the British electorate replaced their
great wartime leader with Clement Attlee and his Labor Government. But the Russians could take little solace from losing their most energetic political opponent.
Attlee was modest and unassuming. But Ernest Bevin, a one-time labor leader now
Foreign Secretary, soon won a reputation with the Russians as being a "very strong-
willed fellow." British policy toward Russia had not changed in the slightest.

[33] Two days after Russia's entry into the war in the Far East, Molotov asked that
a Russian general share the command of occupied Japan with MacArthur. Harriman,
the American ambassador in Moscow receiving the request, had gone through the
roof at Molotov's gall. Russia was given a seat—like the other allies—on the Far
Eastern Commission, a purely advisory body on occupation policy. The United States
was determined to run the show alone.

troops deep into Europe. But Stalin's tenacious, often brilliant, diplomacy had secured the Russian gains. In the darkest days of the war, Stalin never forgot what he was fighting for. It often seemed his were typically nationalist goals, but Stalin considered the cause of Russia the cause of world communism. This time he was right. Soviet armed power had done what decades of abortive local revolutions could not do. The Red Army had laid the foundation for the later communization of half of Europe.

FURTHER READING

Bialer, Seweryn, ed., *Stalin and His Generals: Soviet Military Memoirs of World War II*. New York: Pegasus (Publishers), 1968. Writings of Soviet military figures. Valuable for Soviet military preparedness before World War II, and Stalin's role in military affairs during the war.

Byrnes, James F., *Speaking Frankly*. New York: Harper & Row, Publishers, 1947. American Secretary of State at Potsdam.

Churchill, Winston S., *The Second World War*, 6 vols. Boston: Houghton Mifflin Company, 1948-1953.

Clark, Alan, *Barbarossa: The Russian-German Conflict, 1941-1945*. New York: William Morrow & Co., Inc., 1964. Study of military campaigns.

Dallin, Alexander, *German Rule in Russia, 1941-1945; A Study in Occupation Policies*. New York: St. Martin's Press, Inc., 1957.

Dallin, Alexander, *The Soviet Union at the United Nations: An Inquiry into Soviet Motives and Objectives*. New York: Frederick A. Praeger, Inc., 1962. Survey of Soviet attitude toward the UN from its founding.

Deane, John R., *The Strange Alliance: The Story of Our Efforts at Wartime Cooperation with Russia*. New York: The Viking Press, Inc., 1947. Head of U.S. military mission to Russia demonstrates difficulty of dealing with Russians in spite of formal cooperation.

Djilas, Milovan, *Conversations with Stalin*. New York: Harcourt, Brace & World, Inc., 1962. Indispensable for inside view of Stalin and his comrades during World War II and first years of Cold War.

Feis, Herbert, *Between War and Peace: The Potsdam Conference*. Princeton, N.J.: Princeton University Press, 1960. Continuation of *Churchill-Roosevelt-Stalin*.

Feis, Herbert, *Churchill, Roosevelt, Stalin*. Princeton, N.J.: Princeton University Press, 1957. Indispensable analysis of wartime diplomacy of the three leaders.

Kase, Toshikazu, *Journey to the Missouri*. New Haven, Conn.: Yale University Press, 1950. Insight into Japanese-Soviet relations during World War II by former member of Japanese foreign office.

McNeill, William H., *America, Britain, and Russia: Their Cooperation and Conflict, 1941-1946*. New York: Oxford University Press, 1954. Comprehensive treatment.

Sherwood, Robert E., *Roosevelt and Hopkins.* New York: Harper & Row, Publishers, 1948. Vital for American policy making.

Snell, John L., ed., *The Meaning of Yalta; Big Three Diplomacy and the New Balance of Power.* Baton Rouge, La.: Louisiana State University Press, 1956. Contains essays on political problems treated at Yalta.

Stalin's Correspondence with Churchill, Attlee, Roosevelt and Truman, 1941-1945. New York: E. P. Dutton & Co., Inc., 1958. Basic documentary source.

Stettinius, Edward, *Roosevelt and the Russians; the Yalta Conference.* Garden City, N.Y.: Doubleday & Company, Inc., 1949. American Secretary of State at Yalta.

Werth, Alexander, *Russia at War: 1941-1945.* New York: E. P. Dutton & Co., 1964. Massive work. Vital for impact of war on Russia.

8

THE COLD WAR
1946-1953

The Cold War was a strange war. The main opponents were the emerging superpowers—the United States and the USSR. But Russian and American troops never exchanged fire. The two states never broke off diplomatic relations. We call it a "war" because each great power was using every technique at its command, short of frontal attack, to thwart the objectives of the other: economic warfare, military alliances, military aid, propaganda, limited war—even the threat of a general war. The United States and the USSR acted in this manner because each believed the other was out for world domination, and might start World War III if it sensed victory.[1]

Neither the United States, nor the USSR as far as we can tell, seriously contemplated a major attack on the other. America had the atomic bomb, and Russia had a great army. Each felt insecure. But once the two powers started up the escalation ladder, each nation considered the moves of the other "offensive." Consequently, each power tightened control over its sphere of influence.

A vicious, ascending circle of move and counter-move had begun, fed by the distorted perceptions of the leaders and peoples of each country.

[1] Some argue that the "Cold War" still exists. Yet the sustained, intense fear and suspicion which characterized the years 1946-1953 largely ceased after Stalin's death. For this reason, only the designated period in this Chap. is labeled the "Cold War."

Soviet blinders resulted from years of communist indoctrination. But many in the West now wore some rather badly fogged glasses. They had swung from popular affection for Russia to hysterical anti-communism. Americans in particular were angry because they felt betrayed by Russia; guilty, because of what was happening to Eastern Europe and China; and frustrated, because nothing much could be done. Every move of the USSR was interpreted as part of an elaborate scheme to dominate the world. With the advantage of hindsight, Stalin's objectives during this period seem to have been much less ambitious.[2]

Who Started the Cold War?   The Soviet Union must assume the major share of guilt for the Cold War. It was Stalin's growing appetite for territory and power which finally aroused the West to action. The Soviets had legitimate security needs, and Western leaders were ready to grant these. But Stalin did not stop there. At a certain point his demands began to look "illegitimate"—control of the Turkish Straits, Libya, and Iran (which we will soon discuss). In addition, Stalin's techniques for controlling those areas the Red Army had occupied looked questionable. Perhaps Stalin began to communize the East European nations just to make them "friendly" to Russia. This may have been necessary, given the fear of Eastern Europe for Russia, Tsarist or Bolshevist. Perhaps Stalin was not simply pushing Marxism-Leninism. But to the people involved—and to the West—communism was communism regardless of why it was imposed.

Why didn't Soviet Russia put its faith in the United Nations? Why was Stalin's concept of security so different from that held by Roosevelt? True, Russia had seen the League fail to stop Germany. But Roosevelt had offered to merge American and Russian might with that of the other Western Allies to preserve world peace. Stalin was unmoved.

It has been argued by "revisionist" historians that Stalin's mistrust of the West and its international organization stemmed basically from his difficulty with the Western powers during World War II: the second front problem and Truman's abrupt termination of Lend-Lease. Certainly there could have been some cause for suspicion in Allied handling of such issues, but this hardly could have justified the belief that the West was determined to destroy the USSR. Roosevelt actually had gone out of his way to treat Stalin decently, and even magnanimously. Moreover, America's boys were being rushed home from Europe. What was Stalin afraid of? [3]

---

[2] For a thoughtful analysis of the character of the Cold War, see Marshall Shulman, *Beyond the Cold War* (New Haven, Conn.: Yale University Press, 1960), esp. Chap. 1.

[3] For a good survey and bibliographical guide to the "revisionist" literature see Christopher Lasch, "The Cold War, Revisited and Re-Visioned," *New York Times Magazine,* January 14, 1968. Also see Arthur Schlesinger, Jr., "Origins of the Cold War," *Foreign Affairs,* XLVI, No. 1 (1967), 22-52, and the bibliography for this Chap.

We must delve deeper for the source of Stalin's mistrust of the West. Stalin feared the Western Allies the day the war began—*and long before.* Stalin's ideological conditioning, abetted by personal insecurity, led him to believe that *all* capitalist statesmen were fundamentally opposed to the very existence of the USSR. (Stalin in turn was bent on destroying capitalism.) The Soviets would hardly rely on an international security organization which consisted of a solid phalanx of capitalist states arrayed against one socialist state—the USSR.

There wasn't much the West could do to stave off the Cold War—except appeasement. And there is no reason to believe that appeasement would have worked with Stalin any more than with Hitler. The Führer was opportunist by nature, Stalin was opportunist by creed, and he was a disciple of Lenin, the greatest opportunist of them all.[4]

THE COLD WAR BEGINS

In the fall of 1945, the first great postwar crisis was brewing between Russia and the West. Iran was the unlucky subject.[5] In the early days of World War II, Soviet and British forces had occupied Iran to keep the supply line open to Russia. (The weak, pro-Nazi government in Teheran, the capital, was not dependable.) Both powers agreed to withdraw their forces six months after the war.

Meanwhile, the Soviets were up to their old tricks. They boosted the strength of the local communist Tudeh party, kept the central government in Teheran out of the northern area, and set up a Soviet style "autonomous" republic in Iranian Azerbaijan headed by a known Comintern agent. A "Kurdish People's Republic" also was created, drawing on the Kurdish tribes in eastern Turkey and western Azerbaijan.

The Iranians naturally feared the later incorporation of the two republics into the Soviet Union. But Stalin's main goal apparently was an oil concession in the northern provinces. He hoped to pressure Teheran to grant Russia her wish. (This was "just"; the West had concessions in

---

[4] At a reception given by Molotov on Red Army Day in February 1947, Litvinov, the old foreign commissar, poured out his heart to Western correspondent Alexander Werth. Litvinov was very unhappy about the Cold War. At the end of World War II, Litvinov said, Russia could have cashed in on the goodwill she had accumulated with the United States and Britain. But "they"—meaning Stalin and Molotov—thought "security" was the only thing that really mattered. "Goodwill" could not be a lasting basis for any kind of policy. Therefore, said Litvinov, they grabbed all they could while the getting was good. Litvinov never again appeared at a public reception. *Russia at War,* p. 938.

[5] In 1920, Soviet troops had forged into Northern Iran in pursuit of Denikin's White Guard forces. In temporary control of the area, the Soviets set up a shaky Persian Soviet Socialist Republic. The Russians withdrew the next year under British pressure. But they did not forget their lost beachhead. One of Stalin's demands on Hitler was for Soviet free reign in the direction of the Persian Gulf.

southern Iran.) The Soviet leader's excuse for not withdrawing the some 30,000 Russian troops from Iran was ludicrous; he was afraid the Iranians might take hostile action against the Baku oil fields in southern Russia.

Late in 1945, Teheran sent a column of 1500 soldiers to halt the formation of the two new people's republics. The Soviets used their 30,000 men to block the pitiful Iranian force from entering the northern provinces. The Iranian government appealed to the UN on January 19, 1946, protesting Soviet interference in its internal affairs. The brand new Security Council at once became the debating ground for a widely publicized clash between Russia and the West. Secretary Byrnes had informed Stalin in December that America would have to take Iran's side.

Under the harsh light of the world forum, the Soviets agreed to negotiate with the Iranians. (They first gave a preview of the obstructionist tactics they would later make famous in the UN.) After several months of hard bargaining, Stalin withdrew his troops. He apparently thought the USSR had gained its real aim. The Iranian government had consented to a joint company for the development of the national oil reserves, and had given limited autonomy to Azerbaijan. These concessions, and perhaps growing American pressure, had led Stalin to pull out.[6] "World public opinion," in spite of the claims of UN enthusiasts, seemed to play a subsidiary role in the actual removal of Soviet troops.

However, the Iranians had the last laugh. In October 1947, the Iranian parliament refused to ratify the Soviet oil concession. The Teheran government by then was receiving United States military assistance. The two people's governments also faded away. The Soviets stoically accepted both defeats.

Two Speeches During the Iranian crisis, speeches by Stalin and Churchill marked a critical turning point in the postwar relations of Russia and the West.

Stalin spoke on February 9, 1946, the eve of elections for the Supreme Soviet. It was his first public message since the end of the war in September 1945, and thus the first official indication of the postwar party line. The Soviet dictator had a profoundly disturbing message for the Soviet people, and the world. When Japan surrendered, Stalin had said the conditions necessary for the peace of the world had been won. Now he implied that the defeat of the Axis powers had not eliminated the danger of war. World War II had been the inevitable result of the second

---

[6] Some 13 years later, Citizen Harry Truman told a group of Columbia University students that he sent a secret "ultimatum" to Stalin during the Iranian crisis. The President threatened to send the U. S. fleet up the Persian Gulf and even use American troops unless the Red Army units withdrew from Iran. Unfortunately, we have no other record of this critical document.

crisis of world capitalism. (World War I resulted from the first.) And the capitalists still were at each other's throats over raw materials and markets. Stalin insinuated the West could easily foment a new global conflict.

The war-weary Soviet people had to be prepared for any eventuality. This meant a tremendous increase in production to protect the USSR against a new invasion. (Stalin set new goals to bring Russia close to American production figures, but acknowledged this might take at least three five-year plans.) The Soviet dictator had signaled that Marxism-Leninism was "in," and the superficial wartime harmony between capitalism and socialism was "out." Nationalism also was downgraded. Stalin credited the Communist Party and the Soviet system with making victory possible, not just the great Russian nation.

On March 5, 1946, Winston Churchill spoke at Westminster College in Fulton, Missouri. President Truman was at his side. The former Prime Minister warned the American people about the ever-present threat of war and tyranny. Then he got down to the distasteful details. Britain admired Stalin and the valiant Russian people. Britain understood Russia's need for security on her western frontiers. But Churchill felt it his duty to present certain facts about postwar Europe: "From Stettin in the Baltic to Trieste in the Adriatic, an iron curtain had descended across the Continent." All the peoples in this area were under Soviet influence and increasing control from Moscow. The former Prime Minister concluded: "This is certainly not the liberated Europe we fought to build up."

However, war was neither inevitable nor imminent. Russians did not desire war, said Churchill, but the "fruits of war and the indefinite expansion of their power and doctrines." What was the proper answer for the West? Certainly not appeasement. Churchill was convinced the Russians admired strength, while they had no respect for weakness. Security could be assured if the Western democracies stood together and continued their wartime alliance.

The Soviets were most upset about the "iron curtain" speech. Stalin claimed on March 13: "Mr. Churchill and his friends bear a striking resemblance to Hitler and his friends." Hitler started his warmongering with a racial theory; Churchill was doing the same, asserting that the English speaking nations must rule over the other nations of the world. But Stalin stopped short of openly attacking the United States.

Washington reacted to Churchill's warning with a stony silence. American officials were not yet ready to admit the necessity of an Anglo-American alliance against the USSR. But privately, President Truman and his advisors agreed with Churchill. George Kennan, the relatively unknown American chargé d'affaires in Moscow, had cabled a secret analysis of Stalin's new party line and the needed American response to the State Department. Kennan's reasoning would soon form the theoretical underpinning of America's "containment" policy.[7]

The speeches of Stalin and Churchill, in conjunction with the Iranian crisis, had clarified positions on both sides. The surface harmony of the Grand Alliance had concealed fundamental discord, now revealed to all the world. Obviously there had been tension before between Russia and the West. (Some date the Cold War from 1917.) Obviously there would be instances of harmony after the spring of 1946. But at this point, conflict became the dominant factor in East-West relations.

THE WEST RESPONDS

The two speeches did not lead immediately to hardened positions on each side. The United States and the USSR still were reluctant to admit that the war had begun. In the remaining months of 1946, treaties of peace were even drafted for Italy, and Germany's wartime satellites—Rumania, Hungary, Bulgaria and Finland. They were signed in February 1947. (The treaties yet to be concluded in Europe were with Germany and Austria, once part of the Third Reich.)

Molotov, however, had been cantankerous during the drafting sessions. He demanded the right to veto clauses not to Russia's liking. The Soviet foreign minister capitulated only after Secretary of State Byrnes threatened to abandon the whole treaty drafting project. The Soviets had little to lose by signing. They already were doing as they wished in Bulgaria, Hungary and Rumania, and had secured what they wanted from Finland. Western goodwill, nevertheless, was rapidly evaporating. And Soviet probing around the perimeter of the USSR had not ceased. It was a matter of time before the West reacted dramatically to Soviet expansionist policies.

The Truman Doctrine   Trouble over Greece and Turkey finally brought about America's decision to halt Soviet expansionism publicly and unmistakably.[8] In 1946, civil war broke out between Greek communist guerrillas and the reactionary and corrupt central government.[9] Stalin had hung back during the December 1944 round of the Greek civil war, apparently because of his bargain with Churchill placing

---

[7] For the reasoning behind the "containment" policy see p. 29. Kennan's lengthy cable—he apologized for burdening the telegraphic channels—is printed in full in *The Truman Administration: A Documentary History*, Barton J. Bernstein and Allen J. Matusow, eds. (New York: Harper & Row, Publishers, 1966), pp. 198-212. He later expanded his argument in "The Sources of Soviet Conduct," *Foreign Affairs*, XXV, No. 4 (1947); he used the pseudonym "X."

[8] The material for this section and the following section on the Marshall Plan is largely taken from *The Fifteen Weeks* (New York: The Viking Press, Inc., 1955), an excellent case study by Joseph M. Jones, the drafter of the Truman Doctrine.

[9] The Athens government, of course, was relatively democratic when contrasted with the regime the insurgents hoped to set up.

Greece in the British sphere of influence. From what little we know of the origins of the 1946 communist uprising, it appears that Stalin was also lukewarm toward this second stage of the Greek civil war.[10] The Yugoslavs seem to have been the prime engineers of the 1946 phase, promising Greek communists military aid in exchange for their later membership in a proposed Balkan federation. This Yugoslavian and Bulgarian scheme was enough to upset Stalin. Moreover, the uprising could complicate Soviet relations with the United States. Moscow, which claimed to be the fountainhead of communism, would get the blame for the revolution regardless of the facts.

The plight of the Athens government was desperate by the end of 1946. The United States had to act or Greece would slip behind the Iron Curtain. The British were supplying military and financial aid, and 16,000 troops. But these measures were not stemming the tide.

Meanwhile, a tenacious Stalin reopened the Turkish Straits question. In August 1946, Moscow demanded from Turkey what the Allies had refused to permit at Potsdam—in effect, Russian control of the strategic waterway. To punctuate the Soviet demand, 25 Red Army divisions paraded along the Turkish border and the Soviet Black Sea fleet held summer "maneuvers." The United States replied with a 25 million dollar loan to Turkey. Ships of the U. S. fleet, headed by the new aircraft carrier *Franklin D. Roosevelt,* visited the Eastern Mediterranean for courtesy calls. The Turkish Army also quietly mobilized. Stalin let his demands die.

But Turkey still needed economic aid—the economy was badly strained in order to support the army. Greece was even more hard pressed. On February 21, 1947, the First Secretary of the British Embassy in Washington delivered two diplomatic notes to the State Department; Britain no longer could afford to support either Turkey or Greece—both formerly in her sphere of influence. Would the United States assume the responsibility and pick up the tab?

Since World War II, a bankrupt Britain had relinquished her historic commitments to maintain the stability of Iran, South Asia, and the Southern Mediterranean. Greece and Turkey were merely the latest countries to be crossed off her list. The United States had publicly shunned Britain's attempt to pass the burden of world leadership. American counter-moves to Soviet expansionism—considered the prime threat to international peace—had been through formal and usually highly secret diplomatic channels.

President Truman and his advisors, however, now had to bring the

[10] R. V. Burks, "Eastern Europe," *Communism and Revolution,* ed. by Cyril E. Black and Thomas P. Thornton (Princeton, N.J.: Princeton University Press, 1964), p. 97. In any case, Stalin told the Yugoslavian and Bulgarian communists in February 1948 to stop the Greek uprising as quickly as possible since it had no chance of success in the face of American intervention. Djilas, *Conversations with Stalin,* p. 182.

Cold War out in the open. (Truman called the situation the most serious any President ever had faced.) Money—lots of it—was needed for aid to Greece and Turkey. There would be problems because Congress would have to be consulted, and it was Republican-controlled, economy-minded, and still somewhat isolationist. On the other hand, liberals would be upset if the UN were bypassed.

The American public also had to be convinced of the need for aid; it paid the taxes. Americans had assumed the UN was the answer to international peace and the security of the United States. Congress and the public had to be told that the UN was not enough. The United States had to play the dirty game of power politics to stop the Soviets, and in an area where she never really had been involved before. Furthermore, this critical area might be the first of many trouble spots. A fundamental revolution in peacetime American foreign policy was required.

Some fast talking was needed to bring about this basic change in America's attitude toward international politics. Senator Vandenberg, a staunch Republican supporter of a bipartisan foreign policy, advised the President to "scare hell out of the country." On March 12, 1947, Truman spoke to a joint session of Congress: "I believe that it must be the policy of the United States to support free peoples who are resisting attempted subjugation by armed minorities or by outside pressures." Although the President did not mention Russia by name, it was obvious where the outside pressure came from. "Aggressive movements" were forcing totalitarian regimes on peoples of a number of countries, including Poland, Rumania and Bulgaria. Turkey and Greece were only two recent targets. The United States, said Truman, had to prevent these two countries from losing their freedom. They had no one else to turn to. If America didn't act, Greece and Turkey would be lost to the free world, and then other countries around them would fall. Truman drew the line sharply: there were only two ways of life in the world—one based on the will of the majority with freedom, the other on the will of the minority with terror and oppression.[11]

The immediate measures Truman asked from Congress were mild in contrast to later Cold War requests: 400 million dollars in economic and military aid for the two besieged countries, to promote economic stability and orderly political processes.[12] The foreign policy implications of the "Truman Doctrine," however, were vast. America had taken the first public

[11] George Kennan, the author of "containment," strongly objected to this part of the speech, and also to the promise of military aid. He was afraid the Russian reply might be a declaration of war. Jones, *The Fifteen Weeks*, p. 155.

[12] The Greek communists finally admitted defeat in November 1949. American aid for the Athens government had been vital. But Tito's feud with Stalin resulted in less aid from Yugoslavia for the rebels, and also split the leadership of the Greek party. Finally, the Greek communist leaders made serious tactical errors in their revolutionary strategy. See Edgar O'Ballance, *The Greek Civil War, 1944-1949* (New York: Frederick A. Praeger, Inc., 1966).

step to contain Russia. And Truman clearly implied the United States would defend *any* country, regardless of political complexion, threatened by communism.[13] (Truman admitted Greece was not a model of democracy.)

For good or bad, the Truman Doctrine was cast in the form of an anti-communist crusade. The Soviets naturally were disturbed by this aspect, though they claimed to see through the American smoke screen. *Izvestia* next day labeled the Truman Doctrine a fresh example of the "growing appetite" of the United States for imperialist expansion. America's excuse was a familiar one, often used by Hitler: the United States was saving Turkey and Greece from expansion by the "totalitarian states."

The Marshall Plan   In the midst of the drafting of the Truman Doctrine, an inter-departmental study group in the American government investigated other areas which might need similar aid, either immediately or over a long term period. The drastic situation of postwar Europe was given first priority. The economic recovery of Western Europe had come to a sudden halt in the winter of 1947. Unless Europeans got food, coal, raw materials and machinery, conditions might soon be ripe for communism. One-third of the electorate in both France and Italy was voting communist; general strikes were threatened almost daily. Secretary of State George Marshall, the former American Army Chief of Staff, came home from a meeting of the Council of Foreign Ministers in Moscow convinced that immediate action was necessary to save Europe for the free world. The Council had deadlocked on the German problem. Stalin appeared to be stalling for time while Europe disintegrated.

On June 5, Secretary Marshall launched a plan for European economic reconstruction, later to bear his name, at the Harvard commencement exercise. The emphasis in this second American response to the spread of communism was different from the Truman Doctrine. There had been growing concern in America and abroad that the Doctrine was justified in terms which were too anti-Soviet and militaristic. Marshall restored the balance. America was ready to provide economic aid to Europe to relieve hunger, poverty, desperation, and chaos. Her help was not directed against any country or ideology. (Churchill called the Marshall Plan "the most unsordid act in history.") In fact, Marshall refrained from defining "Europe." The Administration wanted to give the USSR another chance. America was offering to join Russia in aiding the reconstruction of all of Europe, including the Eastern sector under Soviet control. Administration planners still considered the continent an interlocking eco-

---

[13] There was considerable variation, of course, in the later application of the Truman Doctrine. The promise to fight "communism" was selectively applied, especially in Asia. In short, America did not immediately take up the defense of "free" nations everywhere. See Hans Morgenthau, "Globalism: Johnson's Moral Crusade," *The New Republic*, CLIII, No. 1 (1965), 19-22.

nomic unit. They did not want to solidify the Iron Curtain by offering aid only to the Western half.

Europe quickly responded. Britain and France asked Russia to meet in Paris on June 27, to discuss the machinery for administering the promised American aid. The USSR came. Marshall's offer was sufficiently vague to be tantalizing. There might be the possibility of getting American money for Eastern Europe, perhaps even Russia. (The Soviets had tried in vain to get a loan from the United States at the end of the war.) At the same time the Russians were wary. Would this turn out to be a Truman Doctrine for Europe?

The Soviet delegation stayed in Paris only a few days. In the midst of a debate on the third day of the conference, Molotov was handed a telegram from Moscow. Dean Acheson, the American Under Secretary of State, noted that the foreign minister turned pale and the bump on his forehead swelled. (Acheson said this always happened when Molotov was under an emotional strain.) Apparently the foreign minister had been instructed to pull out of the conference.

It was clear what the Russians had wanted: American aid given directly to each country with no strings. But the first few discussions had shown that the aid would be administered through a new regional organization—not bilaterally. The UN Economic Commission for Europe was also bypassed. (The Soviets had some influence on that body. All European countries except Albania were members.) Finally, there was talk of a grand scheme for integrating the economies of the various countries, presumably keeping Eastern Europe as the granary for the Western half, and of joint committees to survey the resources of each country.

In the Soviet view, these moves foreshadowed intolerable interference in Eastern Europe, which Moscow hoped to industrialize and integrate into its own economic plan. Second, the Soviets saw the plan as an attempt by the United States to avert a coming economic crisis, and to stabilize Western Europe in the process. The Soviets seemed convinced that the United States needed the Soviet market to help avoid this crisis.[14] Why should the Soviet Union help bail out Western capitalism from its impending depression by cooperating in a plan for European recovery?[15]

---

[14] Stalin reflected this analysis in his election eve speech of February 1946. Eugene S. Varga, a highly respected Soviet economist, published a book the following September (*Changes in the Economy of Capitalism Resulting from the Second World War*) which contradicted Stalin; Varga suggested economic planning might defer the crisis up to ten years. He was roundly criticized for his thesis in May 1947, and eventually recanted.

[15] The Soviets erred if they stayed out of the plan primarily to frustrate economic recovery in the West. Their best chance to sabotage the program was to stay in. Truman had just warned America of the communist menace. The money for the Marshall Plan might have been difficult to get from Congress if Russia and Eastern Europe had been on the list of recipients.

A few months later, the Soviets charged that the Marshall Plan was basically a variant of the Truman Doctrine. The United States was assuming direct political and economic control of Western Europe, splitting Europe into two camps. The Western bloc was hostile to the interests of the "democratic countries" of Eastern Europe, and above all to the interests of the Soviet Union.

The Marshall Plan nevertheless surged ahead. The French and British foreign ministers invited the 22 European states to Paris on July 12 to set the machinery in motion. Sixteen nations came; Eastern Europe stayed home. The Czechs at first had accepted the invitation. They thought the Soviets would agree, and Poland said it was going to attend. But the Czech viewpoint proved incorrect. Klement Gottwald, the Czech communist prime minister, and Jan Masaryk, the democratic foreign minister in the coalition government, were in Moscow on July 9, negotiating a new trade agreement. That evening Stalin ordered them to reject the Western offer. Stalin said the Marshall Plan was directed against the USSR; Czech participation would be considered a hostile act against the Soviet Union. Masaryk was humiliated. After landing in Prague, he told friends: "I left for Moscow as Minister of Foreign Affairs of a sovereign state; I am returning as Stalin's stooge." [16] Yet Czechoslovakia, in contrast to the rest of Eastern Europe, was still relatively free. Less than a year later, this would not be true.

RUSSIA TIGHTENS HER GRIP

The United States at last had formalized and institutionalized its response to Soviet expansionism and the trend toward communism in Eastern Europe. It was Russia's turn to feel the heat.

Until the summer of 1947, the Soviets had avoided a full scale confrontation with the United States. Such a clash would have made their aims more difficult to achieve. Now Stalin could act openly; the Cold War was on. He moved quickly to tighten control over the Russian sphere of influence, and he attempted to sabotage America's efforts to build an anti-communist alliance in Western Europe.

In the West, it seemed the Soviets merely had put their offensive into high gear. But it is entirely possible that Stalin and the party elite thought their moves essentially *defensive*. During the war, Stalin had justified Russia's western territorial acquisitions and her need for friendly neighbors as vital for state security. The potential enemy was a resurgent Germany. Yet in the background lurked the fear of all capitalist countries.

---

[16] Korbel, *The Communist Subversion of Czechoslovakia*, pp. 181-83.

Stalin had predicted a new imperialist crisis and danger to the USSR in his speech of February 9, 1946. It seemed his predictions had come true with the Truman Doctrine and the Marshall Plan. Instead of a Germany bent on revenge in the distant future, Russia had a new and much more powerful enemy in the present—the United States.

Stalin must have thought it doubtful that the West had challenged Russia only for defensive purposes. The disparity in power between the United States and Russia seemed too great for America to be afraid. The USSR, of course, still had an impressive land army. But the United States had overwhelming superiority in long-range bombers and naval craft. Moreover, America had the "bomb," which Stalin apparently respected very much. He confided to Yugoslavian communists in January 1948: "That is a powerful thing, pow-er-ful!" [17]

There seemed no doubt in Stalin's mind that the United States was Number One in world politics.[18] Indeed, the impelling need to catch up with the United States was a basic theme in his speech to the Soviet people in February 1946. And Stalin must already have given top priority to the secret development of nuclear weapons and rocketry. The Soviets always placed first reliance on their own national power.

Until Soviet military and economic power could begin to equal that of the United States, Stalin feared an imperialist attack. Meanwhile, he had to use whatever means existed to make the USSR secure. Stalin's personality, the methods he had found successful in the past, his ideological conditioning—all pointed in one direction. Russian security hinged on tighter control of the Soviet sphere of influence, aided by disruptive feints in the enemy camp. Within the next year, the Soviet dictator decided to impose the Stalinist model on Eastern Europe. This would insure loyalty to the USSR. Moreover, forced industrialization, an integral part of Stalinism, had helped save the Soviet Union in World War II. It might also save Eastern Europe, and aid Soviet security. Second, Stalin ordered Western European communist parties to adopt militant tactics to thwart Europe's economic recovery. Third, Stalin blockaded West Berlin to stop the creation of an independent West Germany. These tactics, defensive or not, merely generated another round in the escalation of the Cold War. For heightened tension was inherent in the tactics chosen.

[17] Djilas, *Conversations with Stalin*, p. 153.

[18] Stalin told a group of Yugoslavian and Bulgarian communists in February 1948, while discussing the Greek civil war: "What do you think, that Great Britain and the United States—the United States, the most powerful state in the world—will permit you to break their line of communication in the Mediterranean Sea! Nonsense. And we have no navy. The uprising in Greece must be stopped, and as quickly as possible." *Ibid.*, p. 182.

Eastern Europe: Many Paths to Communism During World War II, Stalin seemed to have no master plan for the communization of Eastern Europe. Even at the end of the war there was no timetable or rigid program laid down in Moscow for the countries on Russia's western border. Stalin did not want to excite the West over developments in his new sphere of influence. The security of the USSR might be at stake.

On the other hand, Stalin had impressed on the Western Allies Russia's need for friendly governments on her borders. (Roosevelt and Churchill generally had accepted his argument.) In addition, the former German satellites in Eastern Europe were to be tapped for reparations. The whole area was to be exploited economically to help rebuild Russia. These objectives required some fundamental changes in the internal political structure of each country. Otherwise, the prewar hostility against Russia inevitably would reappear. As a minimum, there had to be coalition regimes with communist membership. And different tactics would be needed to achieve this initial program. The political situation varied in each country at the end of the war. From the outset, the Russians had to be flexible in their approach.

Yugoslavian and Albanian communists had fought civil wars with rival partisan groups during World War II, and emerged victorious. We traced Stalin's bitter conflict with the Western Allies over Poland, and their reluctant acceptance of a communist-dominated coalition. East European communists, exiled in Russia until the end of the war, followed the Red Army into the remaining countries—Rumania, Hungary, Bulgaria and Czechoslovakia. The first three states had been German satellites. Their social and political structures, therefore, were left largely intact. On the other hand, the Czech middle class had been far too strong for Hitler to destroy. Genuine coalition governments thus could be formed at the end of the war in all four countries, as was done. But communists gained control of the critical levers of power—the secret police, the army, and the propaganda organs.

Occasionally, the Soviets had to apply a little pressure to get the desired coalition. Soviet Deputy Foreign Minister Vyshinsky got results in Rumania after threatening the King, in early 1945, with extinction of his country as a sovereign state. (After his audience with the King, Vyshinsky slammed the door so hard that the plaster cracked on the wall.)

Once "friendly" governments were established, local communists went their own way. They had one objective: to take over the coalition and consolidate power—the aim of communists everywhere. Each communist party quickly jumped on the popular bandwagon. It demanded reforms to which no progressive group could object—a purge of all fascists, land reform, long-needed social and economic reforms. If local communists had their way, these measures would be only a stage stop on the road to Soviet style socialism. But there was no prescribed timetable. The new "people's democracies"—the theoretical label applied to the curious blend of communist and non-communist elements—might last for an indefinite period.[19]

Local autonomy relieved the Soviet Union of the need to maintain control over Eastern Europe with naked force. It also permitted internal changes in each country to have a pseudo-democratic character. The USSR's role was limited to moral support and guidance for the local communists. (Russia, of course, had a big stick in case the local parties became involved in deep trouble.) On the international level, the USSR kept the West from interfering with internal developments.

Diplomatic relations between the Soviet Union and each country in Eastern Europe were correct: mutual respect for the principles of independence and noninterference in internal affairs. No hint was dropped of incorporating any of the states into the USSR.[20] Local communist leaders, in fact, became ultra-nationalists. Before the war, they had been adamantly opposed to nationalism—a bourgeois anachronism. Proletarian internationalism now would have drastically hurt their popularity; it would suggest subservience to Moscow.

Genuine coalitions soon were transformed into bogus coalitions, the second stage of the seizure of power in Hugh Seton-Watson's terminology.[21] Peasant and middle class parties were kicked out of the government, and their meetings harassed by communist strong-arm men. The third and final stage, the monolithic communist regime, had been achieved only in Yugoslavia and Albania by the summer of 1947. The rest of Eastern Europe, with the notable exception of Czechoslovakia, was somewhere in stage two. All told, it had been a cheap and low-risk way for the USSR to achieve friendly, communist-controlled neighbors.

At this point, however, Stalin stepped in. The West had moved to halt

---

[19] See p. 51 for the theoretical basis of the "people's democracies."

[20] After positions hardened in 1947, Stalin considered federations for Bulgaria and Yugoslavia, Rumania and Hungary, and Poland and Czechoslovakia. In private, the Soviet leaders may have toyed with a more extreme means of control—the reorganization of the USSR to permit the Soviet Ukraine to join with Hungary and Rumania, the Soviet Byelorussia to join with Poland and Czechoslovakia. Djilas, *Conversations with Stalin,* p. 177.

[21] The first stage was the establishment of the genuine coalition. For an excellent analysis of the take-over process see Hugh Seton-Watson, *The East European Revolution* (New York: Frederick A. Praeger, Inc., 1956), Chap. 8. For another interesting classification scheme of communist takeovers in Eastern Europe see R. V. Burks, "Eastern Europe," *Communism and Revolution,* ed. by Black and Thornton, pp. 77-116.

Soviet expansionism. Stalin decided the process of communizing Eastern Europe had to be accelerated. He was worried because, given a relatively free hand in guiding the internal transformation, local communist leaders began to lose sight of the broader international considerations as seen from Moscow. First things came first for East European communists—the consolidation of their own power. Thus the Czechs (and at first the Poles) accepted the invitation to participate in the July 1947 conference to discuss the implementation of the Marshall Plan. Wouldn't this help build socialism? Moreover, the old nationalistic quarrels over territory broke out among the East European states: the Czechs versus the Poles, the Hungarians versus the Rumanians, and so on.

The Cominform   Stalin's formal device to bring Eastern Europe under closer Soviet control was the Cominform (the Communist Information Bureau). Marshal Tito of Yugoslavia—his country would soon be excommunicated from the socialist brotherhood—had suggested to Stalin in 1945 the need for a new international communist organization. Tito wanted an exchange of views and experience among the various parties. Stalin seemed interested, but undoubtedly thought a new "comintern" would scare the West. Eastern Europe was in a delicate transition stage. In June 1946, however, he asked Tito to take the initiative in founding the organization. This would veil Moscow's obvious dominance in any international communist grouping, and give Eastern Europe another country as a developmental model.[22] (Yugoslavia already was far along the road toward a Stalinist type society.) Stalin emphasized that decisions of the new body would not be binding.

The founding conference nevertheless was postponed until September 1947. Stalin apparently judged the time had not been ripe in 1946. It was obvious from the start who was calling the shots. Invitations went to East European communist parties in the Soviet sphere of interest. Albania was missing, perhaps because it was considered unimportant. In any case, it was supposedly under Yugoslavian control. The Greek communists were not asked, although they were risking their lives in a violent revolution. The Chinese party also was ignored. Only the powerful French and Italian parties were invited from Western Europe. The Soviets were concerned over the recent tactics of these two parties. Their programs were not sufficiently militant in view of the intensification of the Cold War.

The delegates gathered at a small spa in southwestern Poland for the seven-day meeting. Andrei Zhdanov, ranked by many as second after

[22] The Yugoslavians later suspected Stalin had given them the initiative to bind Yugoslavia closer to the new body, making their country easier to deal with.

Stalin in the Soviet hierarchy, immediately prescribed the line.[23] His speech marked a critical turning point in Soviet foreign policy, as well as that for Eastern Europe. For Zhdanov made explicit what Stalin had intimated in his election eve speech some 18 months before. Zhdanov said the postwar world had solidified into two camps—the imperialist, anti-democratic camp headed by the United States, and the anti-imperialist democratic camp headed by the USSR. The United States had come out on top in the imperialist camp because of World War II. Fundamental changes had been wrought on the international scene. Three of the great imperialist powers had gone down in defeat—Germany, Japan and Italy. The other two, Britain and France, had been gravely weakened.

Zhdanov repeated the now familiar prediction: America, the new leader, faced a severe economic crisis. To avoid this calamity, the United States had embarked on a "frankly predatory and expansionist course" to establish its world supremacy. "The cardinal purpose of the imperialist camp," Zhdanov warned, "is to strengthen imperialism, to hatch a new imperialist war, to combat socialism and democracy, and to support reactionary and anti-democratic pro-fascist regimes and movements everywhere."

In view of the worsening international situation, the communist parties of Europe had to resist American aims. The French and Italian parties—the only parties at the conference not from Eastern Europe—were ordered to take up the flag of defense of national independence. (Imperialist America was bent on extinguishing French and Italian sovereignty.)

Obviously, coordination was needed to plan the defense of the democratic camp. The dissolution of the Comintern, said Zhdanov, had quashed once and for all the slanderous allegation that Moscow was interfering in the internal affairs of other states, that communist parties in other countries were acting "on orders from outside." Now things had gone to the other extreme. "Some comrades," Zhdanov remarked, "understood the dissolution of the Comintern to imply the elimination of all ties, of all contact, between the fraternal Communist Parties. But experience has shown that such mutual isolation of the Communist Parties is wrong, harmful and, in point of fact, unnatural." Mutual consultation and "voluntary" coordination of policy were necessary. Continued isolation might lead to a slackening of mutual understanding and even serious blunders.[24]

Only Yugoslavia seemed overwhelmingly in favor of the new Comin-

---

[23] Zhdanov and his faction may actually have taken the lead in establishing the militant, hard line at home and abroad. Zhdanov, who died in 1948 at age 52, seems to have been in contention with Malenkov for the position of heir apparent to Stalin. Marshall Shulman, *Stalin's Foreign Policy Reappraised* (Cambridge, Mass.: Harvard University Press, 1963), pp. 47-50.

[24] For the text of Zhdanov's speech, see *Readings in Soviet Foreign Policy* (Boston: D.C. Heath & Company, 1961), ed. by Arthur E. Adams, pp. 244-56.

form. Gomulka, the Polish party head, actually objected to its establishment. On the other hand, some of the hard-line Stalinists in Eastern Europe may have welcomed the promise of greater Soviet participation. They were having difficulties in seizing power, and had smarted under the restrictions of coalition government. They may not have realized the extent to which the Cominform would exceed its information function. It was destined to become a tool of Soviet foreign policy, a new, if more subtle version of the Comintern. The superficial equality of the organization's membership was a cover for the total coordination of the domestic and foreign policies of the USSR and Eastern Europe. Soviet national interests would determine the common foreign policy. The Soviet road to socialism would be the mandatory guide for internal development. Local variants on this model were now out of the question.

Soviet control of the new organization was at once obvious. Zhdanov became Secretary-General. The conference delegates chose Prague as its headquarters. After Zhdanov called Stalin long distance, the site was changed to Belgrade. Paul Yudin, a servile Soviet ideologist, was put in charge of the Cominform bulletin.[25] (In the Soviet Union, the joke ran that he was the best philosopher among the NKVD men, and the best NKVD man among the philosophers.) The bulletin was printed in Belgrade. But the first copies were flown by special aircraft to Moscow for censoring before the main printing run. Sometimes there were so many changes that the whole edition had to be made up again. Perhaps the most striking example of Soviet control is that the Cominform held only two significant meetings over the next several years. Both times, it chastised the Yugoslavians who had fallen from Soviet grace.

Russia and Eastern Europe: A Monolithic Bloc   Zhdanov had not specifically touched on the necessity of following the Soviet socialist model in his Cominform speech, or on Soviet leadership in international affairs. But the Cominform bulletin soon carried articles unmistakably pointing the way. Local communist leaders who had "antiquated" ideas were castigated. Gomulka of Poland, for example, had fought the collectivization of agriculture. The Polish party also implied he had an inadequate understanding of the role of the USSR in directing the foreign policy of the democratic camp. (The really violent party purges began in 1949.)

Simultaneously, communist parties in Eastern Europe speeded up the elimination of the democratic opposition. Non-communists who were

---

[25] Stalin personally devised the ungainly title for the Cominform house organ: "For a Lasting Peace—For a People's Democracy." He said the capitalist press would have to repeat the title (a nice little bit of peace propaganda) each time it quoted something from the new publication.

flexible were allowed to join a communist-dominated front. Others either fled or were arrested for "espionage" (usually American directed). By the summer of 1948, communists were firmly in control of Hungary, Rumania, Bulgaria, Czechoslovakia, and Poland. The Western powers had made repeated protests at each stage in the seizure of power. Moscow ignored the diplomatic notes; she would not interfere in the internal affairs of other countries.

Czechoslovakia had been the one dramatic exception to the gradual take-over practiced in other parts of Eastern Europe. A genuine coalition government was still functioning in the summer of 1947. Elections had been honest. Yet the communists had won over a third of the votes—mainly from the working class and certain sections of the peasantry. Debates in parliament were free, if bitter, and the democratic press courageously exposed communist excesses.

Stalin apparently had been satisfied with the *status quo*. The Czech government-in-exile during the war had maintained good relations with Moscow. In 1945, the new regime in Prague had ceded Ukrainian speaking Sub-Carpathian Ruthenia to Russia.[26] Finally, many Czechs accepted Soviet friendship as a shield against a revived Germany after their betrayal by the West at Munich.

The situation changed radically after Czechoslovakia's unseemly show of independence in accepting an invitation to join the Marshall Plan, and after the formation of the Cominform. The transition stage which the other countries of Eastern Europe had undergone was compressed into less than eight months—from July 1947 through February 1948.

The final political crisis arose in February when twelve non-communists resigned from the cabinet. Gottwald, the communist Premier, publicly accused them of serving foreign reactionaries. Carefully co-ordinated communist mass demonstrations and telegram writing campaigns demanded that President Beneš appoint a new government headed by Gottwald. (On paper, he still led a minority party.)

In the middle of the crisis, Valerian Zorin, a Soviet deputy foreign minister, landed at Prague. Apparently, the government knew nothing of his coming. Zorin's mundane mission, obviously a shallow cover story, was to supervise Soviet grain deliveries to Czechoslovakia. In fact, he spent the next few days in mysterious visits to important officials. Thinly veiled threats were passed that Moscow would not remain passive in the face of the "extravagancies" of Czech political parties. With communists firmly in control of all organs of power, including the army,

[26] Stalin promised President Beneš in late 1943 that this easternmost segment of Czechoslovakia would remain Czech. At the end of the war, however, a communist-led separatist movement in Ruthenia asked for incorporation into the USSR. Stalin said he couldn't ignore the will of the people.

Beneš reluctantly accepted a communist-controlled "National Front." The dreaded spectre of Soviet intervention overshadowed all. Beneš, the victim of Munich, knew the West would not help.

The coup d'état shocked the West, possibly more than any event thus far in the Cold War. Czechoslovakia had seemed the last outpost of democracy in Eastern Europe. Its sudden demise removed lingering doubts about Stalin's plans for Russia's sphere of influence.

Yugoslavia is Excommunicated   In June 1948, a second dramatic event highlighted the Soviet effort to consolidate control over Eastern Europe. The Yugoslav Communist Party was expelled from the Cominform. In the rest of Eastern Europe, communist leaders and communist parties had been given their start by Moscow and the Red Army. Their paths to power often had been rocky, and the Soviet presence had helped at crucial moments. Tito and the Yugoslav party, however, owed their power to no one—least of all Stalin.[27] Soviet forces helped liberate Yugoslavia in the final days of the war, but Tito's forces already had largely beaten their local opposition.

Stalin had been downright unsympathetic to Tito's plea for Soviet recognition of his movement. The Soviets did not want to frighten the British with a communist regime in the Balkans even before the war ended. In September 1944, Stalin insisted to Tito that King Peter of Yugoslavia be reinstated. (He added that this need be only a temporary arrangement—"you can slip a knife into his back at a suitable moment.") Tito refused. The King, who had fled the country, was a traitor.

Stalin, in concert with Churchill and Roosevelt, then forced a coalition government on the Yugoslavs. The King was replaced by a regency.[28] Tito's party, however, retained control of 23 out of 28 cabinet posts. By November 1945, communist terrorism had destroyed what opposition remained. In the next few months, the country moved far toward Stalinism. It seemed that Tito's regime ruled a model satellite. The Soviet and Yugoslav parties were on the same ideological track.

Evidence of a smouldering conflict between Russia and Yugoslavia erupted during March through May of 1948 in an extraordinary bit of secret correspondence between Stalin and Tito.[29] We will start with the

[27] Albania was the only other communist regime in Europe to win power independently of the Soviet Union. In this case, the Yugoslavs gave the necessary advice and aid.

[28] Stalin and Churchill had divided Yugoslavia on a "50-50" basis in October 1944. See p. 214.

[29] The Yugoslavs published the letters after the formal break with Moscow. See *The Soviet-Yugoslav Dispute: Text of the Published Correspondence* (London: Royal Institute of International Affairs, 1948). Also see *The Soviet-Yugoslav Controversy, 1948-58: A Documentary Record*, ed. by Robert Bass and Elizabeth Marbury (New York: Prospect Books, 1959).

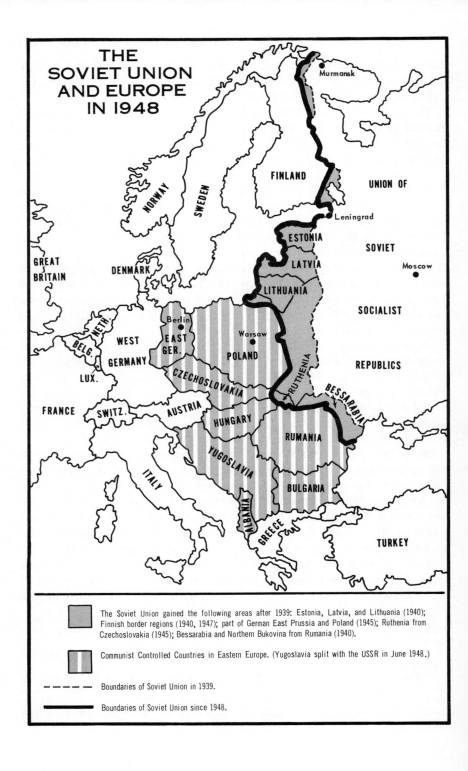

THE SOVIET UNION AND EUROPE IN 1948

NORWAY
SWEDEN
FINLAND
Murmansk
UNION OF
Leningrad
SOVIET
ESTONIA
LATVIA
Moscow
LITHUANIA
SOCIALIST
GREAT BRITAIN
DENMARK
NETH.
BELG.
WEST GERMANY
LUX.
Berlin
EAST GER.
Warsaw
POLAND
CZECHOSLOVAKIA
RUTHENIA
REPUBLICS
BESSARABIA
FRANCE
SWITZ.
AUSTRIA
HUNGARY
RUMANIA
YUGOSLAVIA
ITALY
BULGARIA
ALBANIA
GREECE
TURKEY

The Soviet Union gained the following areas after 1939: Estonia, Latvia, and Lithuania (1940); Finnish border regions (1940, 1947); part of German East Prussia and Poland (1945); Ruthenia from Czechoslovakia (1945); Bessarabia and Northern Bukovina from Rumania (1940).

Communist Controlled Countries in Eastern Europe. (Yugoslavia split with the USSR in June 1948.)

– – – – – Boundaries of Soviet Union in 1939.

——— Boundaries of Soviet Union since 1948.

Yugoslav case against the Soviets. According to Tito, the Russians had supplied military advisors, but suddenly withdrew them in March 1948. The Russians had falsely charged the Yugoslavs with "hostility" toward the advisors. The Soviet intelligence service had attempted to recruit Yugoslavs as spies against Tito's government. Tito charged that the Soviet ambassador even had been snooping around the Yugoslav party. (Stalin retorted that his ambassador not only had this privilege, but was obligated to do so.) Yugoslavia had the right to economic assistance from the USSR because it was in the interest of the Soviets for Yugoslavia to be strong. (Instead, the Soviets had attempted to set up "joint" stock companies to exploit the local economy for the benefit of the USSR.)

The Soviet case against Yugoslavia contained even stronger charges. Yugoslav military leaders thought the Soviet army advisors too expensive, Soviet military expertise of no use. (Yugoslavia had been required to pay these officers four times the going rate for its own commanders.) Yugoslav security agents were spying on Soviet government representatives. "Leading comrades" in Yugoslavia circulated rumors that "great-power Chauvinism" was rampant in the USSR, the Cominform was a means for Soviet control of other communist parties, and Yugoslavia alone had "revolutionary socialism." The next Soviet insinuation was particularly galling. "Trotsky also started with accusations that the CPSU (Communist Party of the Soviet Union) was degenerate, was suffering from the limitations inherent in the narrow nationalism of great powers." When Trotsky was exposed, he crossed over into the camps of the sworn enemies of the Soviet Union. "We think that the political career of Trotsky," wrote Stalin, "is quite instructive." Finally, there was no democracy in the Yugoslav party. Leaders were not elected but chosen by the ruling clique. There was no freedom of criticism. This party could not be considered a Marxist-Leninist organization.

In the last letters of the bitter exchange, Stalin decided to put Tito and his comrades in their place. The unwillingness of the Yugoslav Politburo to admit its errors was due to the "unbounded arrogance" of the party leaders. In contrast, the leadership of other East European parties behaved "modestly." Yet the services of the other parties in Eastern Europe were just as significant as those of the Yugoslav party. The Yugoslavs boasted about their coming to power. This really was due to the Red Army. No accusation could have hurt the proud Yugoslavs more.[30]

[30] Stalin was particularly upset by one example of independence shown by Tito, not mentioned in the secret exchange. Soon after the war, Tito proposed a Balkan federation. When Dimitrov of Bulgaria publicly commented on the possibility of some such arrangement, Yugoslav and Bulgarian leaders were summoned to Moscow to answer for this and other machinations. Stalin was furious. He was learning about their foreign policy initiatives in the newspapers. Stalin humiliated the head of the

Moscow demanded that Yugoslav behavior be discussed at a Cominform conference. Tito refused. He knew Stalin had mobilized all the other parties against him. The Yugoslav leaders also feared Tito might not return from such a meeting. The conference went ahead as scheduled in June 1948. Tito was accused in absentia of being an imperialist spy. A shocked world heard for the first time of the deep cleavage between Russia and her model satellite. In the published resolution of the Cominform, Tito's government was labeled a "purely Turkish terrorist regime." Its "nationalist line" was turning Yugoslavia into an ordinary bourgeois republic and an imperialist colony. The Yugoslav leadership in effect had become anti-Soviet, had placed Yugoslavia "outside the family of the fraternal Communist Parties, outside the united Communist front and consequently outside the ranks of the Information Bureau." However, the excommunication was not irrevocable. The resolution called for Tito's removal by the party rank and file. "Healthy elements" in the party should compel the present leaders to recognize their mistakes openly and honestly and then rectify them. If not, a new internationalist leadership should be created.

Stalin had made several fatal errors in handling the Yugoslavs. He had greatly overestimated his own power when dealing with a communist leadership which had come to power independently. He reportedly told Khrushchev: "I will shake my little finger—and there will be no more Tito." However, Tito did not fall. An internal revolution did not bring Yugoslavia into the fold.[31]

Stalin's more fundamental error lay in his refusal to permit any trace of independence in Eastern Europe—any vestige of nationalism. If Stalin had accepted something less than total subordination, Tito probably would have accepted Soviet leadership. All through the secret correspondence the Yugoslavs pledged their loyalty to the cause of communism. They held Stalin's charges, which shocked and hurt deeply, to be the result of misinformation. To the last, they hoped the quarrel would be patched up. But Tito and his Politburo would not subordinate every facet of their national life to Moscow's direction. Early in the secret correspondence, they warned: "No matter how much each of us loves the land of socialism, the USSR, he can, in no case, love his country less. . . ."

Yugoslav delegation by forcing him to sign an agreement for "mutual consultation" on matters of foreign policy. The message was clear. In the future, the Soviets would prohibit the slightest show of independence by Yugoslavia or any other government in Eastern Europe.

[31] Subsequently, the Soviets and their satellites applied political and economic warfare to bring the Yugoslavs to heel. Trade, for example, was drastically limited. To encourage "Titoism," the West provided the struggling outcast with economic and military aid. No strings were attached. Tito insisted on his country's neutrality.

Yugoslav communists had to look out for Yugoslav problems, as well as the cause of international communism. Tito felt the Yugoslav national interest was not served by making his country an economic and political satellite of the USSR. Stalin, however, would not grant that other communist states might have legitimate national interests. He was blind to the malaise of nationalism which eventually would affect the whole communist system.

Militant Communism in Western Europe   Stalin's second major tactic to thwart the West was to order the powerful French and Italian Communist Parties on the warpath. These parties had gained enormous prestige for their work in the wartime resistance movements. Since the war, they had been necessary elements in all coalition governments.[32] The French party's participation in the postwar regimes was of particular interest to the Soviets; the USSR was attempting to wean France away from the United States.

In May 1947, however, the French Communist Party was expelled from the reigning coalition. The French government had abandoned its attempt to build a bridge between East and West. The Marshall Plan was introduced a few months later. The Soviets decided France was fully enmeshed in the American net. The Italian party, twice the size of the French, was also expelled in May 1947 from the coalition government in power.

With both parties out of government, Zhdanov ordered a Left turn in their tactics in his Cominform speech.[33] The Marshall Plan had to be stopped. In November 1947, communists in France and Italy launched massive strikes to paralyze the economic and political life of their countries. The class struggle was intensified. Communists denounced moderate socialists, their former coalition allies, as well as middle class parties. More strikes followed in 1948.

Temporary chaos resulted. But the new militancy could not halt the Marshall Plan. Communist subservience to Moscow again was emphasized. The two communist parties were pushed far to the left and further isolated from the basically unrevolutionary working class of

[32] The French communists, who had the strongest political following in France, saw participation in coalition governments as an "evolutionary" path to socialism. Stalin was not so optimistic. In the secret correspondence with Tito, he explained that the French and Italian parties had achieved less success than the Yugoslavs because the Soviet army could not and did not aid the parties in Western Europe. In short, Stalin thought communism depended on the Red Army clearing the way.

[33] On October 29, Thorez, the French party leader, confessed to the Central Committee of his party that he had erred in not recognizing sooner the character of the international situation. Specifically, he failed to sense that the communists had been kicked out of the coalition "on the express order of American reaction."

Western Europe. Economic recovery was on its way, and this seemed more important to the average man in France and Italy.

The First Berlin Crisis Stalin's third tactic in the first years of the Cold War was the Berlin Blockade. This dramatic gambit was designed primarily to block the integration of an independent West Germany into the imperialist camp.

The division of Germany between Russia and the West was foreshadowed in the decision on reparations at the Potsdam Conference. In the next few years, the division became a fact. Russian greediness had provided the spark—the attempt to drain the Eastern zone, and the Western zones if possible, of ten billion dollars in reparations. Allied countermoves set off a chain reaction. The problem of Germany inevitably became a part of the Cold War. The occupation zones were natural extensions of the spheres of influence of Russia and the Western powers. As the Cold War developed, each side worked to control its sphere— and this included such zones. The Iron Curtain soon clanged down through the middle of the defeated nation.

The few German communists who had escaped Nazi Germany for Russia, returned to the Eastern zone on the heels of the Red Army. The German communist party was formed immediately. Other parties were allowed to organize if they were "anti-fascist" and "democratic." But the Soviet plan was soon evident. Stalin now had decided to build up the power of a communist-controlled East Germany instead of pauperizing it.

The Soviets forced the Social Democratic Party to merge with the local communists in early 1946. The resulting Socialist Unity Party (SED) came to power late that same year. The Soviet authorities also nationalized the larger industries and began land reform. By 1948, the Eastern zone was in essence a separate state and further along the road to communism than Czechoslovakia.

The three Western zones (American, British, and French) developed differently. The central concern of the Western Allies was to ease the dreadful economic situation. The Eastern zone traditionally had been the breadbasket of Germany. The Soviets thus could live off the land and also feed the people. The Western zones were largely industrial, and always had imported food. At the end of 1947, Secretary of State Marshall calculated that America and Britain were spending some 700 million dollars a year to provide food for West Germany.

A revitalized German economy seemed the only way out. German recovery also was essential to the health of Western Europe. As a first move, the United States and Britain merged the economies of their zones on January 1, 1947. The door was left open for the Russians and French to join. Simultaneously, the West began plans for a long overdue currency reform to halt the runaway inflation. The Russians balked at all measures aimed at economic integration or reform, although it had been decided at Potsdam to treat Germany as a single economic unit. The Soviets seemed bent on maintaining economic chaos in Western Germany while building up the Eastern zone.

Attempts to write a German peace treaty inevitably fell by the wayside. The Soviets would not risk having a united Germany fall into the Western camp. They apparently decided to delay any general settlement unless unification could bring about a communist front government in all of Germany. This the Western Allies would not permit. In February 1948, they resolved to organize a German federal republic, internationalize the Ruhr without Soviet participation, and include the new German state in the Marshall Plan.

The Soviets replied by walking out of the Allied Control Council in Berlin on March 20. With Soviet obstruction gone, the vitally needed currency reform was put into effect on June 18, 1948. That night the Soviets suspended railroad passenger service out of Berlin. By August 4, all land and water routes in and out of West Berlin were blocked because of "technical difficulties." Two million West Berliners faced starvation.[34]

What could the West do? For several months East-West tension had been growing. The February coup in Czechoslovakia had caused great alarm. There were indications that a blockade of Berlin might be coming. But few in the West believed the Soviets really would use such a tactic. Starvation was not the way to win friends and influence the German people. If the Soviets did begin a blockade, the West was uncertain whether it should—or could—stay in Berlin. It seemed an impossible task to defend the isolated city if the Soviets chose to use force, and everyone dreaded a showdown. For the first time since World War II, a major war seemed possible.

When the blockade started, indecision still was rife in Washington. America's course was not determined until June 23. President Truman told a White House gathering that we were in Berlin by agreement and the Russians had no right to force us out by either direct or indirect pressure.[35] Truman's advisors temporized; no one in Washington even at this date had thought through the consequences of American firmness. The total reinforcements immediately available were four squadrons of B-29 long-range bombers. Two of these were dispatched to Germany.

---

[34] On the first Berlin crisis, see the excellent case study by W. Phillips Davison, *The Berlin Blockade* (Princeton, N.J.: Princeton University Press, 1958).

[35] Ernest Bevin, the truculent British Foreign Secretary, made an even stronger public statement to the House of Commons on June 30: the Western Allies would not retreat from Berlin even if it meant war.

(The Soviets had overestimated actual American military strength in the late 1940's.)

General Clay, the American military governor in Germany, proposed sending an armed convoy to Berlin. Washington refused. Meanwhile, Clay had begun the amazing Allied airlift of food and coal to West Berlin. This was considered a stopgap measure. A few more supplies might give the West a bargaining point with the Russians. The airlift went through unscathed. The Soviets complained about "irregular" flights over the Eastern zone or failure to observe safety regulations in the air corridors. But they would not use force to stop the Allied transports, just as the West would not send an armed convoy to Berlin. Russia was no more eager than the United States or Britain for a showdown involving naked military power. The Soviets thought the blockade, a skillful application of indirect pressure, should do the job.

The Soviets soon clarified what they wanted. In public, the Soviets had prated about the Western currency reform as the main irritant. But this was only a facet of the larger German problem. The three Western military governors met with Marshal Sokolovsky, their Soviet counterpart, on July 3. The Marshal blandly stated that the technical difficulties would continue until the Allies gave up their plans for a West German government. Sokolovsky wasn't even interested in discussing currency.

If the Allies wouldn't give in on the main issue, the Soviets had a consolation prize—West Berlin. The Allies couldn't defend the city militarily without a major war. The Soviets were certain (as were many in the West) that the airlift could provide only temporary relief. Russia could not lose.

Instead, the American and British airlift became more efficient, involving some 277,000 flights over more than a twelve month period. The magnificent spirit of the West Berliners enabled them to get along with a minimum of necessities. The West had stumbled on its own indirect technique to frustrate the blockade.

During the fall of 1948, Allied negotiators tried direct bargaining with Stalin. The issue also was carried to the UN Security Council. The Soviet representative vetoed a resolution urging that the blockade be withdrawn as a first step toward settlement. Neither side was ready to capitulate. The struggle over Berlin had become a matter of prestige.

But in the spring of 1949 the Soviets were ready for a settlement. The blockade had brought about the very things it was designed to prevent. The Allies had not given in on the formation of a German state. Perhaps more important was the change of opinion in Germany. West Germans had been less than enthusiastic about the Allied offer to permit the creation of a federal republic. Too many strings were attached; the military government still would retain great veto powers. But Allied resistance to Soviet pressure on Berlin forcefully demonstrated to the West Germans where their real interests lay. Plans for the new government moved ahead.[36]

The Soviets saw the blockade accelerating an even more ominous threat to Russia's security. The expansion of Soviet power in Eastern Europe and Soviet aggressiveness over Berlin brought fear of a Soviet attack on Western Europe. The Red Army, according to published intelligence estimates, was over ten times stronger than the forces of the Western European nations.[37] Europe could only be defended with American atomic power. Moves were soon afoot to guarantee this. Less than a month after the Czech coup, Britain, France, and the Benelux countries pledged their solidarity against the Soviet threat with the Western European Union. After the blockade began in the summer of 1948, the five countries initiated secret military talks with the United States. These talks led to the establishment of the North Atlantic Treaty Organization (NATO) in April 1949. The military power of the Western world, including the all-important bomb, had been set against the USSR.

The United States soon put teeth into NATO with a billion and a half dollars of military aid for Western Europe. General Eisenhower became the commander of the Allied forces in Europe—a symbol of the unprecedented peacetime commitment of American military might on the continent.

The new alliance had an unsettling effect on the Soviets. It was clearly labeled a defensive measure to frustrate Soviet aggressive designs on Western Europe. But the Soviets claimed they did not intend to attack anyone. NATO was only a cover for the aggressive aims of the Anglo-American grouping of powers which laid claim to world domination. It was clearly designed to intimidate the states which refused to obey the dictates of the Western coalition.

The Soviets had lost hope of achieving their main objective—blocking the creation of the Federal Republic. They had speeded up the formation of NATO. They were even losing the consolation prize—West Berlin. It was time to stop the blockade. After secret negotiations between the Soviet and American UN delegates, technical difficulties ceased with the land and water routes into Berlin on May 12, 1949.

---

[36] The Federal Republic of West Germany came to life on May 23, 1949. Soviet plans for the reunification of Germany on Soviet terms had been dealt a heavy blow. Somewhat reluctantly, Russia set up the German Democratic Republic in the Eastern zone in October 1949. The Western powers and the West German government refused to recognize the new Russian satellite.

[37] The Soviets supposedly had some four to five million men under arms. In 1960, Khrushchev said the Soviet strength in 1948 was under three million.

THE PEACE CAMPAIGN

The Soviet advance into Western Europe had been halted. Further probes after 1949 would encourage a threatened war with the NATO powers. During his remaining years, Stalin had to be satisfied with the *status quo* in Europe. The USSR simply was not strong enough to change the situation. Yet the future held promise. President Truman announced on September 23, 1949 that an atomic explosion had been detected in the Soviet Union. The Soviets played down the event. There was no sense in talking about Soviet nuclear power until a supply of bombs and a delivery capability were in being. Bragging would increase the danger of war. And the danger seemed imminent with NATO and Western rearmament underway. The addition of a Red China to the camp of peace in October 1949 was very encouraging for the future of communism. But this also did not negate Western military superiority.

New tactics were necessary to supplement Soviet power until parity could be gained in nuclear weapons and their delivery systems. More tactics of the militant variety would not work. These had merely brought war nearer. A soft line was needed, and one gimmick fit the bill—a peace campaign. This would have two objectives. First, America's atomic capability would be neutralized with "ban the bomb" appeals.[38] Second, Western rearmament and NATO would be frustrated by appeals to pacifism and neutralism, and warnings about the danger of a rearmed Germany.[39]

Appeals to peace always had been part of the Soviet propaganda arsenal. The first foreign policy statement of the Bolsheviks in November 1917 was the Decree on Peace. The war-weary working classes of Britain, France, and Germany were exhorted to rise against their capitalist governments.

Even during the first years of the Cold War, appeals for peace were an integral part of Soviet foreign policy. (In aggressive or Left periods, peaceful tactics usually appear as a mask to cover predominantly militant tactics.) During the Iranian crisis in 1946—caused by the Soviet refusal to withdraw Russian troops—Stalin appealed to public opinion and the ruling circles of all states to organize counterpropaganda against the advocates of a new war (American and British statesmen). Zhdanov amplified the peace theme at the Cominform founding conference in

---

[38] In an interview with Western journalist Alexander Werth in September 1946, Stalin indicated the atomic bomb did not create a threat because the Western capitalists would not have a monopoly on the bomb for long, and its use would be prohibited.

[39] This section on the peace campaign draws heavily from Marshall Shulman, *Soviet Foreign Policy Reappraised*, especially his Chaps. 3, 4, and 5.

September 1947. The peoples of the world did not want war. The forces for peace, claimed Zhdanov, were big and influential. The plans of the aggressors could be halted if the peace forces were staunch and determined, displayed fortitude and firmness.

In 1948 the Soviets apparently decided more could be done with the peace theme. They may have been impressed with the spontaneous enthusiasm in France for a non-communist peace movement early that year. The Poles experimented with a World Congress of Intellectuals for Peace in September 1948. Alexander Fadeyev, head of the Soviet Writer's Union, bitterly attacked American policy at the conference. Prominent Western liberals in the audience, made up of writers, artists, scientists and professors, were being used.

In an October 29, 1948, *Pravda* interview, Stalin exhorted the social forces in favor of peace to unseat aggressive American and British leaders through political action. In effect, Stalin had ordered communists everywhere to begin a massive peace campaign based on a broad coalition of all anti-war forces.

The indigenous French movement was taken over by local communists. The Women's International Democratic Federation, an old-time communist front, joined with the International Liaison Committee of Intellectuals for Peace (set up at the Polish conference) in sponsoring the Cultural and Scientific Conference for World Peace. The conference was held at the Waldorf Astoria Hotel in New York City, the heart of the aggressor's camp, in March 1949. (The Soviet delegation had 23 members, including composer Dimitri Shostakovitch.) In order to attract the broadest possible following, the leaders fought off specific resolutions condemning NATO and United States policy. The conference announced its support for the UN and the defense of cultural freedom in America— in jeopardy because of the Cold War.

More peace conferences were held in Moscow, Mexico City, Tokyo, Budapest and Bucharest in 1949. But the important meeting convened in Paris shortly after the NATO agreement was signed (April 1949). Moscow radio claimed that the delegates to this "World Congress for Peace" had been elected by 300 million people. The French government nevertheless had restricted participation from communist countries. Only eight of the 52-member Soviet delegation were given visas (including the peripatetic Shostakovitch).

Picasso's famous Dove of Peace greeted the delegates. Paul Robeson sang. Metropolitan Nicholas of the Russian Orthodox Church gave his blessing. The Congress chairman was Frederic Joliot-Curie, French High Commissioner for Atomic Energy, and a well known fellow-traveler. Dependable communists, however, held the vital behind-the-scenes jobs. Louis Aragon, the French communist writer, carefully guided the drafting of the resolutions to assure wide appeal. The delegates of 50 nations condemned war, colonialism, the atomic bomb, violations of the UN Charter, and, specifically, the rearmament of West Germany and Japan. (The resolutions avoided identifying the aggressor by name.) A Permanent World Peace Committee was organized, and National Councils of Partisans for Peace were established by each delegation.

The USSR, aided by the Cominform, finally had given the peace movement an international foundation. *Izvestia,* the press organ of the Soviet government, candidly revealed the link between the Paris congress and Soviet foreign policy. According to *Izvestia,* the Soviets hoped popular resentment against war would cause the Western governments to modify their programs. This would create the prerequisites for new high level efforts to resolve world tensions.[40] In plain language, the USSR was hoping that public pressure, feeding on the potent appeals of anti-Americanism, neutralism, nationalism, would force the French government to pull out of NATO. Perhaps the peace movement also could halt the creation of an independent West Germany and German rearmament, a very sore point all over Western Europe. At a November 1949 meeting of the Cominform, the Soviets directed all communist parties to make the peace movement the pivot of their entire activity. Peace had become a major Soviet tool to negate Western defense efforts.

The Soviets, however, had not switched to a basically defensive foreign policy as in 1921 or 1933. The line laid down by Zhdanov in 1947 still held. The militant tactics of the first two years of the Cominform merely were replaced by militant peace mongering.[41] Soviet Foreign Minister Vyshinsky was extremely amiable at a Paris meeting of the Council of Foreign Ministers in June 1949. But he wouldn't budge an inch on Soviet opposition to the Federal Republic of West Germany. The USSR was not ready to retreat just because it was in favor of peace.

The Stockholm Peace Appeal   For some time the Soviets had been casting about for a way to neutralize America's nuclear monopoly. In June 1946, Bernard Baruch, the grand old man of American

---

[40] The official *History of the Communist Party of the Soviet Union* (Moscow: Foreign Languages Publishing House, 1963, p. 597) says about the peace campaign begun in 1949: "The peace movement is the biggest socio-political movement in the history of mankind. It by no means infringes the social and economic systems of states. But it helps to expose and isolate the most aggressive imperialist circles and thus undermine and weaken the position of reaction in general. The struggle for peace was the main aspect of the activity of the Communist Party and the Soviet state in the sphere of foreign policy" (in the early 1950's).

[41] Molotov warned in March 1950, that the supporters of lasting peace "must not be passive, must not turn into empty pacifists engrossed in phrases, but must wage a daily, obstinate, and ever more effective fight for peace. . . ." Cited in Shulman, *Stalin's Foreign Policy Reappraised,* p. 118.

business and a presidential advisor, had presented the "Baruch Plan" for international control of atomic energy to the UN Atomic Energy Commission. He proposed an international authority to control the production of fissionable materials, perform world wide inspections, and promote the peaceful use of atomic energy. The United States would cease manufacturing atomic bombs and dispose of its stockpile—once the authority was functioning.

The Soviets were hardly enthusiastic over an international authority which obviously would be Western-dominated, and would roam around the USSR on inspection trips. They also objected to the American proposal that no nation should have a veto over the authority's actions. Gromyko, the Soviet spokesman on the Commission, countered with an international treaty to prohibit the manufacture and use of atomic weapons. Once the treaty had been ratified, the United States would be asked to destroy its weapons. The Soviet proposal was unacceptable to the United States. America was not ready to destroy its stockpile in return for a paper pledge.

Stalin later agreed in principle to international inspection and to suspension of the veto in the day-to-day operations of an inspection commission. But a major stumbling bloc remained. The Soviets still insisted on the right to veto punitive actions against violators. The Atomic Energy Commission's work was deadlocked. The nuclear arms race could not be stopped.

The Soviets switched their efforts to overcome the temporary American nuclear monopoly to the peace campaign. In late 1949, a novel way had been found in France to mobilize popular sentiment for peace. Seven million Frenchmen signed a "peace ballot" to mark World Peace Day (October 2). The members of the communist-dominated Permanent World Peace Committee, meeting in Stockholm in March 1950, knew a good technique when they saw it. An international campaign was launched to collect signatures for the Stockholm Peace Appeal. This propaganda document was brilliant, calling all people of good will to put their names to three simple and unimpeachable sentiments: 1) the unconditional prohibition of the atomic weapon as an instrument of aggression and mass extermination of people; 2) strict international control over this decision; and 3) the government which first used the atomic weapon would be labeled a war criminal. By the end of 1950, 600 million signatures were claimed. The vast majority came from the communist zone. But 15 million were gained in France, almost 17 million in Italy, and two and a half million in the United States.

Yet the peace movement in general seemed to be having limited success. The NATO powers agreed in the spring of 1950 to construct an integrated defense system of the entire North Atlantic area. Preliminary planning had begun on the delicate question of how to include West Germany in the alliance system. And a Soviet blunder was about to put in question the validity of the whole peace campaign. Soviet expansion had been halted in Europe since 1949, but the Soviets still nibbled away at the Western sphere of influence in the Far East. In June 1950, Russia went too far. The Korean invasion dramatically demonstrated the hypocrisy of communist pleas for world peace, and called forth Western rearmament on a grand scale.

COMMUNIST EXPANSION IN ASIA

As World War II drew to an end, Stalin's main interest in Asia was to secure the territorial gains promised Russia at the Yalta Conference. This was done with Soviet entry into the war with Japan. From then until the Korean war, Russia seemed more an observer than an active participant in promoting Asian communism.

Stalin gave first priority to the consolidation of Soviet power in Eastern Europe. The primary threat to Russian security seemed to come from that direction. Stalin continued to equate the progress of communism with the Soviet military presence. (He was pessimistic about the French and Italian communists' coming to power without a boost from the Red Army.) But Soviet troops held no foreign territory in the Far East except during the initial occupation of Manchuria and North Korea. There was perhaps a third reason for Stalin's pessimism about indigenous revolutions in Asia. His fingers had been badly burned in attempting to direct the Chinese revolution of the 1920's. He was left with lingering doubts about the purity—or reliability—of Asian communists. The course of events in Asia in the late 1940's would show how wrong Stalin could be. The first major communist revolution since the Bolshevik victory in 1917 was about to take place in China.

The Chinese Revolution and the Soviet Union   In order to further legitimize Russia's Far Eastern booty, Stalin signed a treaty of friendship and alliance with Chiang Kai-shek in 1945. In return, Stalin agreed to deal only with the Chinese Nationalist Government—a boon to Chiang in his struggle with Mao Tse-tung. Other signs soon appeared indicating that the interests of the Soviet state came before those of international communism. Without consulting the Allies, the Soviets carted off some two billion dollars worth of industrial equipment and machinery from Russian-occupied Manchuria. (This would hardly have been necessary if Stalin was anticipating a communist revolution in China.) Then the Soviets delayed their promised withdrawal from Manchuria—the date had been initially set for December 3, 1945. They wanted joint Sino-

Soviet control of the main industrial and mining enterprises, and of the principal airfields.

The Nationalists refused. In effect they would be relinquishing control of this vital industrial area. Luckily for Chiang, Stalin was not prepared to force the issue. Russia might find herself face to face with the citadel of world capitalism, since the United States was getting rather heavily involved in China's smouldering civil war. Fifty-five thousand American marines had landed in China. United States aircraft were ferrying Nationalist troops to critical sites before the Chinese communist forces could arrive on foot.

Stalin, however, seems to have hit upon another tactic in early 1946 to pull Manchuria into the Soviet orbit. The Red Army had helped set up communist regimes on the USSR's western borders. Perhaps Soviet forces could perform the same task in Manchuria. The Red Chinese might be able to hold this area, giving Russian Siberia security in depth. Whatever Stalin's reasons, Nationalist troops entered Manchuria in the spring of 1946, only to find Chinese communists in control of much of the territory. Moreover, the communist forces had appropriated invaluable caches of Japanese arms. But this appeared to be the extent of Soviet aid to Mao's armies.

We now know that Stalin apparently had little faith in Chinese communist success in China, and possibly even in Manchuria. After their excommunication, the Yugoslavs revealed some intriguing details of a meeting in Moscow between Stalin and certain Chinese communist leaders sometime after the war. Stalin bluntly told the Chinese that their uprising had no prospect. They were to seek a *modus vivendi* with Chiang, and dissolve the Red Army. The Chinese communists undoubtedly felt betrayed. They had been fighting the Nationalists for almost two decades. The Soviets had deserted the cause when victory seemed possible.

On the political level, the Chinese communists seem to have made a superficial attempt to carry out Stalin's directive. After the Japanese surrender in August 1945, they agreed to negotiate with the Nationalists on the future of China. But Mao's true intentions came through—as did Chiang's. Years of mistrust and hatred generated a race between Nationalist and communist forces to occupy those parts of China formerly held by the Japanese.

In 1946, the Nationalists seemed on the road to victory. They had occupied important sectors of Manchuria. The former Chinese communist capital of Yenan fell in March 1947. But even when the tide turned against the communists, Mao refused to heed Stalin's advice. The Red forces fought back. And the corrupt, inefficient and unpopular Nationalist regime began to totter. By the end of 1947, its soldiers who had not already surrendered or deserted offered token resistance to the Reds. Yet Stalin continued his correct relations with Chiang.

By January 1949, the Chinese Reds had taken North China and Manchuria. In April, the Soviets tentatively climbed on the bandwagon, asserting that the reactionary rule of the Kuomintang was at an end. (Stalin had admitted to a Yugoslavian delegation in February 1948 that he had been wrong and the Chinese comrades right—the Reds were beating Chiang's army.) In May, the Soviets nevertheless were negotiating with the "reactionary" Kuomintang to increase the Russian sphere of influence in Sinkiang. Did Stalin still doubt that Mao's forces could conquer all of China, or was he trying to present his comrades with a *fait accompli* when they won full control? In any case, the Soviets finally broke relations with the Nationalist Government after the Chinese People's Republic was formed in October 1949.

Mao Tse-tung and his comrades, against Stalin's advice and with little Soviet aid, had persevered in their struggle with the Nationalists. At one stroke, some 550 million people were brought into the socialist camp. World communism had been given an enormous boost.

The Soviets seemed to gain new confidence. They had been blocked in Europe. But the great colonial empires of the imperialists finally were awakening, and China provided the most dramatic evidence. However, nationalist rebellions also had been underway in Southeast Asia since World War II. At first, local communists had cooperated with nationalist groups in united fronts. But after the Cominform was organized and aggressive (Left) tactics adopted, Asian communists pulled out of coalition movements.[42] (Communists traditionally do not serve in united fronts during Left periods.) In 1948, they adopted or speeded up terrorism and insurrection in Indonesia, Indochina, India, Pakistan, Burma, Malaya, and the Philippines.

The turn to the Left in Southeast Asia was generally a blunder. If Stalin ordered this change in tactics, he had made another mistake in his analysis of Asian communism. He had grossly underestimated the appeal of nationalism in Asia, and overestimated the appeal of communism. Local communists, still weak, had been ordered to attack the much stronger and more popular local nationalists. These men were now

[42] We do not know definitely whether the Zhdanov line was transmitted in the form of specific instructions for action from Moscow to Asian communist parties. (Asian communist parties were not invited to join the Cominform.) However, the new line was discussed early in 1948 in Calcutta at a communist-sponsored Youth Conference for countries of Southeast Asia, and a few days later at the Congress of the All-India Communist Party. Asian communists then may have acted on their own initiative. Charles B. McLane, *Soviet Strategies in Southeast Asia* (Princeton, N.J.: Princeton University Press, 1966), pp. 351-71. Later, the Permanent Liaison Bureau of the World Federation of Trade Unions, a communist front, appeared to have coordinated communist movements in Asia.

labeled "traitors" to the people. (Stalin refused to believe that Asian nationalists could be truly independent and anti-imperialist. The Philippines, for example, were referred to as a model American colony.) The result—with the exception of Indochina—was a temporary catastrophe for Asian communism.

However, the Soviets had a more pressing problem in Asia than organizing revolutions in small countries. They now had to deal with the gigantic country on their border which already had gone communist. Could Stalin adjust his foreign policy style to treat the first major communist state outside of Russia with respect and rough equality? He had failed miserably in handling Yugoslavia, the only other significant communist country which had come to power independently.

The Chinese were not yet showing signs of Titoism. They loudly proclaimed their loyalty to the USSR and the inviolable friendship of the Chinese and Soviet peoples. (In turn, the Soviets bubbled over with enthusiasm for the great Chinese people.) The Chinese also were destined to be economically and militarily weak for some years to come. But the Chinese communists were deservedly proud of their achievements. (Theirs were far more impressive than those of Yugoslavia.) The Chinese Reds also were hardly upstarts. They had been fighting as an organized army and governing a large area in the Chinese hinterland for decades. Moreover, the Chinese communists reflected the xenophobia and expansionism—"great nation chauvinism" in Leninist terms—of a people with a culture stretching back thousands of years. Finally, they had to pay attention to Chinese national interests—the basic security needs of the country—just as the Bolsheviks had to protect Russian national interests.

It was soon apparent that the Chinese Reds were not abject supplicants to the Socialist Motherland. Mao Tse-tung journeyed to Moscow at the end of 1949, apparently his first visit to Russia, to meet Stalin. The Soviet dictator was now 70; Mao was decidedly his junior at 56. But Mao was just as tough and shrewd as Stalin. Their immediate task was to establish a working relationship between the two major communist states.

Many Western observers were surprised at the outcome. They were sure Stalin would force more concessions from Mao than he had wrung (with American assistance) from Chiang Kai-shek. Instead, some hard bargaining apparently took place. (Mao stayed in Moscow for nine weeks.) The Chinese received Stalin's promise to return not later than 1952, most of the war booty given to Russia in 1945—the Manchurian railways, Port Arthur, and the facilities at Dairen. On the other hand, the USSR granted China only 300 million dollars in credit to buy Russian industrial equipment. (This was a niggardly sum—the Soviets had removed two billion dollars worth of goods from Manchuria in 1945. A year earlier, they had loaned the Poles 450 million.) Finally, the two nations signed the Sino-Soviet Treaty of Friendship, Alliance, and Mutual Assistance. This 30-year military alliance ostensibly was directed against Japan. In fact, it was aimed at "any state allied" with Japan—meaning the United States. Mao may have felt the promise of Soviet protection from American imperialism was the most important achievement of his long stay in Moscow.

Molotov announced: "A lasting anti-imperialist alliance was formed between the Soviet and Chinese peoples, between the two largest States on earth." The treaty had transformed Soviet-Chinese friendship into "a mighty force for consolidating universal peace such as has no equal and never had an equal in human history." Neither side, however, could be completely happy with the agreements signed in Moscow. But this was as it should be between two great powers, even if they were "fraternal" states. Stalin seemed to have learned a lesson from the failure of his imperious treatment of Tito.

Korea   When the Soviets attacked Japan in August 1945, arrangements still had not been made for the occupation of Korea. To keep Russian troops from overrunning the whole peninsula, the United States secured Soviet agreement on a temporary division of the country along the 38th parallel (38 degrees North latitude). The partition soon became permanent, a consequence of the Cold War.

By 1950, the Soviets had turned the Democratic People's Republic of Korea ("North Korea") into a Russian satellite. Soviet citizens of Korean ancestry, aided by Russian advisors, penetrated all levels of government. The North Korean army, which had undergone an accelerated buildup, was Russian trained and equipped.

There seems little doubt that the Soviets planned and directed the North Korean invasion of South Korea, destined to be launched in June 1950. Yet we still lack a definitive answer as to what Stalin hoped to achieve by the invasion. At the time, many in the West thought Korea signaled the beginning of a new aggressive period in Soviet foreign policy on a world-wide basis. Korea might be designed to test American reaction before the launching of attacks on Western Europe, Iran, or Yugoslavia. Another theory saw Korea as a device to absorb United States military power, thereby hampering American resistance to communist aggression elsewhere.[43]

In retrospect, none of these interpretations seems valid. Soviet objec-

---

[43] The various American interpretations of Stalin's motivations are analyzed in Alexander S. George, "American Policy-Making and the North Korean Aggression," *World Politics* (January 1955).

tives probably were much more limited. The first objective was simply to conquer South Korea. The North Korean army was definitely superior in equipment to the American-trained South Korean force. And American military might in general seemed very weak in the Far East. Most important, General MacArthur in 1949, and Secretary of State Acheson in January of 1950, had described the American "defense perimeter" in Asia as running through the Philippines, Okinawa, Japan and the Aleutians—Korea was not mentioned.

The second objective may have been to forestall Japan's resurgence as a powerful force in the Far East. In 1950, Japan was still unarmed and occupied by the United States. But the USSR—and China—undoubtedly saw danger in the American decision in 1948 to rehabilitate Japanese industry. (Marxists traditionally associate capitalist industrialism with military expansionism.) In 1949, the Western Allies discussed writing a peace treaty for Japan without Soviet participation. (The treaty was signed in September 1951—in spite of Soviet objections.) Rumors circulated about long-term leases for United States bases in Japan. All these developments may have led the communists to an ominous conclusion: an aggressive American military alliance directed against the communist sphere of influence in the Far East.[44] NATO, together with rumors of West German rearmament, demonstrated a similar trend in American policy toward Russian-controlled Europe.

If communism were triumphant in Korea, Japanese neutralism and opportunism might force the pro-American government to stay out of the Western camp. If not, the Soviets at least would have tidied up their own defense perimeter with the inclusion of South Korea in the communist orbit.

It still is unclear what part the Chinese played in the initial decision. Stalin probably told Mao of his plans during the negotiations in Moscow for the Sino-Soviet Treaty. But there is no definite evidence of Chinese participation in the planning process. The Chinese, of course, would be happy to see American prestige in Asia suffer. And they shared Russia's hopes that a communist victory in Korea might keep Japan out of the American camp. But Peking's main military objectives centered on conquering Taiwan (Formosa) and Tibet. Indeed, there is evidence that China planned an invasion of Taiwan for the summer of 1950.[45]

---

[44] In January 1950, the Japanese Communist Party was ordered to switch from united front tactics to revolutionary struggle involving an attack on imperialism. This may have been part of the overall Soviet strategy to frustrate Japan's inclusion in the American alliance system.

[45] See Alan S. Whiting, *China Crosses the Yalu* (New York: The Macmillan Company, 1960). Marshall Shulman disagrees with this ranking of Chinese objectives. He suggests that the Chinese may have wanted to round out their victory on the mainland with an attack on South Korea. The Soviets thus had additional reasons to push

The North Korean army attacked South Korea at dawn on June 25, 1950. South Korean military forces were surprised, and quickly overrun. (Even today, the Soviets claim that the South Korean army attacked North Korea on this date.) The desperate South Korean government immediately appealed to the UN Security Council. Before the day was over, the Council met in emergency session. An American resolution was adopted calling for a cease-fire and the withdrawal of North Korean troops. When this had no effect, a Security Council resolution on June 27 sanctioned the dispatch of United States military forces—land, sea, and air—to support the South Koreans. The United States Seventh Fleet also was moved to the Formosa Straits in case the Chinese decided to invade Chiang's island outpost.

The Russians must have been shocked; they probably had expected a quick victory. The United States supposedly was not interested in defending Korea. Soviet contempt for the UN itself was obvious. The Russian delegate on the Security Council had boycotted that body since January 1950, protesting the Council's refusal to recommend the admission of Red China to the UN. The Soviets apparently thought the UN would be powerless to help South Korea. The Council might pass some inane resolution expressing its distaste for the invasion—but no more. When the Council did act, the USSR asserted that the resolution was illegal. The Soviet delegate and the delegate from Communist China (the true representative of "China") had to be present. Their absence meant no substantive decisions could be made because the Soviet Union and "China" were "permanent" members of the Council. The Council, however, ruled that absence equaled an abstention, not a veto.

By September, the tide had turned against the North Korean forces. The Soviet problem now was to keep control of just North Korea. The communist-controlled world peace movement had been mobilized to condemn "the bloody intervention of the United States imperialists in Korea." But this tactic proved ineffective in stopping the United States. Jacob Malik, the Soviet Security Council delegate, returned to the Council on August 1 to launch a month long indictment of American intervention in the "civil war" in Korea. However, Malik's filibuster came too late to halt the already functioning UN command in Korea.

By the end of October 1950, UN forces had crossed the 38th parallel under the authorization of an ambiguous UN resolution. They soon reached the Yalu River, the boundary between North Korea and Man-

---

the invasion: to keep their influence over China, and to maintain their dominant position in North Korea—traditionally part of the Chinese sphere of influence. Shulman, *Stalin's Foreign Policy Reappraised*, p. 141. Harold C. Hinton, on the other hand, argues in *Communist China in World Politics* (Boston: Houghton Mifflin Company, 1966), pp. 205-11, that Mao persuaded a reluctant Stalin to support the invasion plans of the North Koreans.

churia. Korea was about to be unified through UN military power. The North Koreans had to get help or their defeat would be certain. The use of Soviet forces might lead to a world war. Chinese "volunteers" of the Fourth Field Army assumed the burden, launching a massive counter-attack in late November.

Our evidence is fragmentary regarding the means by which this decision was made. China probably entered the war of her own free will, though surely encouraged by the USSR.[46] The Chinese communists saw vital national interests at stake. China was just as worried as Russia about facing an American-dominated anti-communist coalition in Northeast Asia. Total UN victory in Korea could influence Japan to swing to the West and form the center of this coalition. Moreover, China herself now seemed threatened. There was talk in America of preventive war. General MacArthur, commander of the UN troops in Korea, and Chiang Kai-shek might order their forces to invade the mainland. (This might galvanize the latent opposition to Peking, present in much of China.) The doctrinaire and parochial Chinese communists were ready to believe the worst.

Chinese intervention stemmed the UN advance. For a few weeks, UN forces were driven back across the 38th parallel. However, the war soon stalemated along this boundary line. Both sides fought bitterly, but could not gain territory. The first clear communist peace feelers appeared when it became obvious that the UN forces could not be pushed off the peninsula. On June 23, 1951, Malik, the Soviet Security Council representative, saw hope for settling the Korean conflict. The first step should be a cease-fire and an armistice providing for the withdrawal of troops from the 38th parallel. The Chinese press agreed to the proposal two days later. Negotiations began in July. Because of the Soviet disclaimer of any responsibility for the war, only Chinese and North Korean representatives took part. The truce talks, however, soon bogged down, and were repeatedly interrupted by violent clashes along the border. The armistice was not signed until July 1953—some four months after Stalin's death. It had been left to his successors to finally ease tension in Korea.

The Korean conflict was a mixed blessing for the USSR. The Soviets had failed to extend their sphere of influence. The United States started to rearm on a massive scale after the near defeat in Korea. Truman asserted on June 27, 1950, that the attack on Korea made it clear that communism had passed beyond the use of subversion to conquer independent nations. It now would utilize armed invasion and war. Soviet aggressiveness in Asia also had increased American concern for Europe.

[46] David Dallin believed a reluctant Mao agreed to enter the war only after Stalin promised to furnish all kinds of military aid for the Chinese forces. *Soviet Foreign Policy After Stalin* (Philadelphia: J. B. Lippincott Co., 1961), p. 88.

In 1952, the United States pressured her Western allies to accept West German soldiers as part of an integrated European army. This worried Russia, as well as Eastern Europe.

But there were some Soviet gains. China was now completely isolated from the West. Chinese Titoism had been forestalled. The Chinese Reds had to rely more than ever on Soviet economic and military aid.[47] In addition, American strength had been sapped by the Korean war without the sacrifice of one Soviet soldier.

The Soviets saw another gain from the Korean war. Marxist-Leninists always considered a cardinal source of socialist strength to be the divisive forces within the imperialist camp—the internal contradictions. There was no doubt that these had been intensified with Korea. America's Western allies were especially worried about General MacArthur's march into North Korea in the fall of 1950. They feared a new world war. Truman casually remarked at a press conference in December 1950 that the use of the atomic bomb had to be considered because of the Chinese entry into the war. Britain's Prime Minister Clement Attlee flew at once to Washington, apparently to get a clarification of Truman's offhand comment. Europe was nervous.

Tensions among the powers grew over other issues. America demanded that her European allies accept a greater share of the rearmament burden. The United States then threatened to cut American aid to Western countries engaged in shipping strategic goods to communist nations. (Europe wanted to use trade to relax tensions, and she needed trade to live.) The United States next began stockpiling scarce raw materials. Prices inevitably shot up, making recovery even more difficult for the struggling economies of Western Europe. Most of all, American insistence on West German rearmament caused bitter political debates in Britain, and especially France. The French were more worried about a revived Wehrmacht than about the threat of Soviet aggression in Europe. Fear of the Soviet Union had reached a high point with the Berlin blockade and the initial attack on Korea. It was now receding in Western Europe. Many thought America was preoccupied with the Soviet military threat to the exclusion of the economic and political contest.

STALIN'S LAST WORD

The aging Stalin made his last major pronouncement on foreign and domestic policy in "Economic Problems of Socialism in the USSR." This dull, pedantic essay was published on the eve of the Nine-

---

[47] The Chinese also had gained. They achieved new world respect for their military prowess. In particular, they had demonstrated to the United States that China was a force to be reckoned with in Asia. Finally, the Chinese Reds finished the war with a completely re-equipped army and a first rate jet air force—compliments of the USSR.

teenth Party Congress in October 1952. (A congress was long overdue; the last one had been held in 1939.)

Stalin's whole foreign policy after World War II had been built on one premise: a coming war between the USSR and the capitalist West, headed by the United States. In his essay, however, Stalin made a curious about-face. He now wrote that only "mistaken" comrades held such a view of world politics. It was theoretically true that the contradictions between capitalism and socialism were stronger than the contradictions among capitalist states. But war was much more likely between capitalist states, claimed Stalin, than between the camps of socialism and capitalism. War between the two great economic systems threatened the very existence of capitalism. War between capitalist states only challenged the supremacy of certain nations within the capitalist camp. As proof of his thesis, Stalin cited history: World War II had begun between capitalist states, not with an attack on the USSR. Second, the capitalists shouted for propaganda purposes about Soviet aggressiveness. But they really were aware of the USSR's peaceful policy and knew that it would not attack their countries. In 1952, Stalin saw signs—internal contradictions—of impending conflict in the West:

> Outwardly everything would seem to be "going well": the U.S.A. has put Western Europe, Japan and other capitalist countries on rations: Germany (Western), Britain, France, Italy and Japan have fallen into the clutches of the U.S.A. and are meekly obeying its demands. But it would be mistaken to think that things can continue to "go well" for "all eternity," that these countries will tolerate the domination and oppression of the United States endlessly, that they will not endeavor to tear loose from American bondage and take the path of independent development . . . . Would it not be truer to say that capitalist Britain, and after her, capitalist France, will be compelled in the end to break from the embrace of the U.S.A. and enter into conflict with it in order to secure an independent position and, of course, high profits? . . . . Let us pass to the major vanquished countries, Germany (Western) and Japan . . . . To think that these countries will not try to get on their feet again, will not try to smash U.S. domination and force their way to independent development, is to believe in miracles.

Stalin appeared to be modifying the "two-camp thesis" which had guided Soviet foreign policy since the beginning of the Cold War. War between the capitalist states was still inevitable, and indeed more probable than war between capitalism and socialism.

Yet we can only speculate on the further significance of Stalin's apparent change of heart. Stalin died on March 5, 1953. His directive was not translated into dramatic changes in Soviet foreign policy during the remaining few months of his life. Perhaps the Soviet director had decided on a major shift in strategy, involving collaboration with European capitalist nations in an attempt to isolate the United States. Perhaps he had recognized the sterility of militant communism in the underdeveloped area in the face of indigenous nationalism. There was a tantalizing hint. The communist-sponsored Asian and Pacific Area Peace Conference held in Peking during October 1952 did not even mention the need for armed struggle against local non-communists. All classes in the small states of Asia were encouraged to combine against the United States.

It may be, as Marshall Shulman suggests, that Stalin had decided upon a defensive shift in Russia's foreign policy.[48] Perhaps he had realized that Soviet militancy during the Cold War had further increased Western fear of the Soviet Union, and had led to Western rearmament. Yet "peaceful coexistence"—which Malenkov talked about at the Nineteenth Party Congress in 1952—was ambiguous. Western leaders still were accused of following Hitler's footsteps and of being imperialist warmongers. It would take Stalin's successors to relax the tensions of the Cold War.

SUMMARY

Stalin began the Cold War with his tactics for making the Soviet Union secure. The United States, leader of the West, replied in kind: economic and military aid to its allies. Later, the Grand Alliance of World War II was replaced with NATO, a coalition directed against the USSR. Stalin's answer to the West soon came: tighter control over Russia's sphere of influence and disruptive feints in the enemy camp.

The super powers were reluctant to meet on the battlefield. Korea, the one violent clash, apparently was a Soviet miscalculation. But even in Korea, American forces did not face Soviet soldiers.

In fact, Stalin's tactics generally were cautious, and in his view, defensive. Stalin's problem was that his tactics seemed aggressive to the West, and generated great fear of the Soviet Union.

Russia needed leadership with more flexibility, subtlety, and understanding of the new world, especially of the vast underdeveloped areas pregnant with change. Perhaps Stalin was about to make the necessary adjustments in Soviet foreign policy when he died. We do know it was left to his successors to bring Soviet foreign policy more in tune with the times.

FURTHER READING

Alperovitz, Gar, *Atomic Diplomacy: Hiroshima and Potsdam.* New York: Simon and Schuster, Inc., 1965. Documents case made by Williams in *The Tragedy of American Diplomacy.* (See below.)

---

[48] Shulman, *Stalin's Foreign Policy Reappraised*, especially Chap. 10. For the view that Stalin would have continued the Cold War, see Robert C. Tucker, *The Soviet Political Mind* (New York: Frederick A. Praeger, Inc., 1963), Chap. 2.

Barghoorn, Frederick C., *The Soviet Image of the United States; a Study in Distortion.* New York: Harcourt, Brace & World, Inc., 1950. Soviet view of U. S. during early years of Cold War.

Beloff, Max, *Soviet Policy in the Far East, 1944-1951.* London: Oxford University Press, 1953.

Black, Cyril E. and Thomas P. Thornton, eds., *Communism and Revolution.* Princeton, N.J.: Princeton University Press, 1964. Contains essays on communism in Eastern Europe, Finland, Southeast Asia, Indochina, and Korea after World War II.

Borkenau, Franz, *European Communism.* London: Faber & Faber Ltd., 1953. Commentary by old Comintern hand on Soviet policy, in particular on post-World War II period.

Brzezinski, Zbigniew K., *The Soviet Bloc,* Revised and Enlarged Edition. Cambridge, Mass.: Harvard University Press, 1967. Detailed discussion of developments in Eastern Europe since 1945, and of Soviet relations with this area.

Davison, W. Phillips, *The Berlin Blockade: A Study in Cold War Politics.* Princeton, N.J.: Princeton University Press, 1958. Case study of 1948 blockade.

Dedijer, Vladimir, *Tito.* New York: Simon and Schuster, Inc., 1953. An "official" biography by a Yugoslavian journalist. Much valuable material on Yugoslavian relations with Russia.

Fleming, D. F., *The Cold War and Its Origins, 1917-1960.* 2 vols. Garden City, N.Y.: Doubleday & Company, Inc., 1961. Massive study by "revisionist" scholar placing blame for Cold War largely on the West.

Ingram, Kenneth, *History of the Cold War.* New York: Philosophical Library, 1955. Concise and readable, but debatable treatment of Soviet motivations.

Kautsky, John H., *Moscow and the Communist Party of India.* New York: John Wiley & Sons, Inc., 1956. Study of Indian party line after 1945.

Kennan, George F., *Memoirs, 1925-1950.* Boston: Atlantic-Little, Brown and Company, 1967. Particularly useful for 1945-1950 period when Kennan played an important role in forming American foreign policy toward Russia.

Korbel, Josef, *The Communist Subversion of Czechoslovakia, 1938-1948.* Princeton, N.J.: Princeton University Press, 1959. Analysis of events leading to coup in 1948.

Kousoulas, D. George, *Revolution and Defeat: The Story of the Greek Communist Party.* London: Oxford University Press, 1965.

Laqueur, Walter Z., *Communism and Nationalism in the Middle East.* New York: Frederick A. Praeger, Inc., 1956. Analysis of growth of communist movements in this area.

Laqueur, Walter Z., *The Soviet Union and the Middle East.* New York: Frederick A. Praeger, Inc., 1959. Collection of essays on Soviet policy toward this area from 1917-1958.

Lenczowski, George, *Russia and the West in Iran, 1918-1948: A Study in Big Power Rivalry*. Ithaca, N.Y.: Cornell University Press, 1949. Historical and political treatment.

Lukacs, John, *A New History of the Cold War*. Garden City, N.Y.: Doubleday & Company, Inc., 1966. Concerned primarily with Soviet-American relations in Europe. Well-written summary, but questionable treatment of Soviet motivations.

Mackintosh, J. M., *Strategy and Tactics of Soviet Foreign Policy*. New York: Oxford University Press, 1963. Analytical treatment of Soviet foreign policy from 1945-1962.

MacVicker, Charles P., *Titoism: Pattern for International Communism*. New York: St. Martin's Press, Inc., 1957. Developments in Yugoslavia after the break with Russia.

McLane, Charles B., *Soviet Strategies in Southeast Asia*. Princeton, N.J.: Princeton University Press, 1966. Soviet strategy toward this area from 1917-1953. Very important for post-World War II period.

McNeal, Robert H., ed., *International Relations Among Communists*. Englewood Cliffs, N.J.: Prentice-Hall, Inc., 1967. Forty-five selections from communist sources dealing with relations among communists since 1943, together with an introductory essay.

Mikolajczyk, Stanislaw, *The Rape of Poland: Pattern of Soviet Aggression*. New York: McGraw-Hill Book Company, 1948. Memoirs of leader of Polish Peasant Party.

Nagy, Ferenc, *The Struggle Behind the Iron Curtain*. New York: The Macmillan Company, 1948. Personal account of communist takeover by noncommunist Minister President of Hungary (1946-1947).

Seton-Watson, Hugh, *The East European Revolution*. New York: Frederick A. Praeger, Inc., 1951. Analysis of the communization of this area.

Shulman, Marshall D., *Stalin's Foreign Policy Reappraised*. Cambridge, Mass.: Harvard University Press, 1963. Stalin's foreign policy in his later years.

Traeger, Frank, ed., *Marxism in Southeast Asia; a Study of Four Countries*. Stanford, Calif.: Stanford University Press, 1959. Essays on communism in Burma, Thailand, Vietnam, and Indonesia.

Ulam, Adam B., *Titoism and the Cominform*. Cambridge, Mass.: Harvard University Press, 1952. Study of Tito's break with Stalin.

Whiting, Allen S., *China Crosses the Yalu: The Decision to Enter the Korean War*. New York: The Macmillan Company, 1960. Chinese motivations for entering the Korean War.

Williams, William Appleman, *The Tragedy of American Diplomacy*. Cleveland, Ohio: The World Publishing Company, 1959. Seminal work in the "revisionist" school. Argues Cold War mainly due to American "globalism."

Wolff, Robert Lee, *The Balkans in Our Time*. Cambridge, Mass.: Harvard University Press, 1956. Historical treatment of Yugoslavia, Rumania, Bulgaria, and Albania, emphasizing events since World War II.

Xydis, Stephen G., *Greece and the Great Powers, 1944-1947: Prelude to the "Truman Doctrine."* Thessaloniki: Institute for Balkan Studies, 1963. Analysis of the Greek crisis.

Zinner, Paul E., *Communist Strategy and Tactics in Czechoslovakia, 1918-1948.* New York: Frederick A. Praeger, Inc., 1963.

9

THE INTERREGNUM
1953-1957

Joseph Stalin died on the night of March 5, 1953. But the objectives of Soviet foreign policy underwent no basic change. The men who assumed the burden of leadership were communists—and Russians. They accepted Stalin's main goals and his general conception of international politics. The United States was still the primary enemy, and the German problem was still a problem.

New tactics, however, were needed. A change in the style of Soviet foreign policy was long overdue since this policy had stagnated. The USSR had lost the initiative. Its advance had been thwarted while the capitalist countries were reaching new levels of power. Clearly a temporary retreat was needed—a deescalation of the Cold War—before a new communist offensive could be launched. A pause in the global conflict would permit the flowering of Stalin's programs for nuclear and missile development and a general increase in Soviet economic power. And the new weapons and new industrial strength promised to change the world balance of power.

The prime requirement was to relax tensions between the capitalist and socialist camps. Stalin's heavy-handed policies in Europe and Asia, especially Korea, had caused great fear in the West and stimulated Western rearmament on a grand scale. The new Federal Republic of Germany was being integrated into the capitalist "offensive" system. There was not even a dialogue between West and East. The Korean truce talks were deadlocked. Negotiations for a peace treaty with Austria had not progressed satisfactorily. Finally, Yugoslavia was a continual thorn in the side of the USSR.

There was another reason for a relaxation of tensions. Stalin had left his political house in disarray. The Soviet system did not provide for orderly succession to a supreme post; in fact, the system provided for no such position. This very lack of fixed responsibility for leadership generated a struggle for power among Stalin's heirs. It remained to be seen whether one of the contenders would strive for the ultimate position of dictator. In any case, the last thing the contenders wanted was more trouble with the capitalist world. This would only complicate the inevitable machinations during a power struggle.

Although Malenkov seemed the logical successor, Stalin had avoided so designating him. Malenkov had to do battle with Beria, head of the dreaded secret police, and Khrushchev, a late bloomer and second in importance in the party organization after Malenkov. Finally, Molotov, the Old Bolshevik who had served so long in foreign affairs, was still very much in evidence.[1]

Stalin's successors at once moved to insure continuity of leadership and prevent, according to a public announcement, "disorder and panic." Malenkov was made Premier and Secretary of the Party; he represented a "collective leadership."

This first distribution of power had been an emergency measure. On March 14, the Communist Party's Central Committee "granted" Malenkov's request to be relieved of his job as Party Secretary. Khrushchev assumed the post. On June 26, Beria, who had been made Deputy Premier in charge of internal security, was arrested. Beria apparently was suspected of plotting to seize power through his control of the secret police. Obviously the collective leadership was an uneasy equilibrium.

MALENKOV'S FOREIGN POLICY— A THAW IN THE COLD WAR

During the next two years Malenkov was thrust into prominence in international politics because of his position as Premier. And Malenkov had the public backing of most of the top members of

[1] Andrei Vyshinsky had replaced Molotov as Foreign Minister in 1949. Molotov apparently had been kicked upstairs to the increasingly powerless Politburo. Evidence indicated that Stalin may have been preparing to purge Molotov, Beria and other members of the hierarchy shortly before his death. There is some evidence that even Malenkov was on his list. (The Politburo had been replaced by a larger "Presidium" at the Nineteenth Party Congress in 1952.)

the new hierarchy for his foreign policy. The fragmentation of power meant that some degree of collective leadership had to be practiced. Surface harmony nevertheless concealed a growing struggle between Malenkov and Khrushchev and their factions for control of the party, and thus the government.

Malenkov's foreign policy was characterized by a relaxation of tensions which affected all the major areas of conflict between Russia and the West. The cumulative effect of the relaxation led many in the West to believe that the Soviets finally were ready to compromise on the major issues of the Cold War.

Asia   The first major evidence of a change in Soviet foreign policy came in Korea. Negotiations for an armistice had deadlocked for months over the forced repatriation of prisoners of war. Large numbers of Communist Chinese and North Korean soldiers refused to return home and UN representatives would not force them. Chou En-lai, Mao's man at Stalin's funeral, apparently discussed Korea during his stay in Moscow. Shortly after his return to Peking, the Chinese and North Korean governments agreed to exchange wounded prisoners, and two days later, they agreed to the principle of voluntary repatriation of all prisoners. The armistice was signed on July 27, 1953. It contained a proposal for a conference on the unification of the shattered country. The West was heartened. Optimism grew when the Soviets announced that they were ready to hold the promised conference at Geneva in the spring of 1954 to discuss Korea and also the hot war in Indochina between the French and the communist-led Viet Minh. Over the protests of American Secretary of State Dulles, Communist China was placed on the invitation list. (Many Americans considered China to be the aggressor in Korea and Indochina, and Peking was not recognized by Washington.)

The negotiations at Geneva lasted from April 26 through July 21. No progress was made on the Korean problem. Each side proposed a unification scheme which would place a united Korea in its camp. Indochina was a different story. France had suffered a painful defeat with the fall of its jungle fortress of Dienbienphu in May 1954. Total victory seemed near for Ho Chi Minh and his Viet Minh forces. Yet in the final hours of the conference the participants agreed to partition Vietnam along the 17th parallel. Laos and Cambodia, the other sectors of French Indochina, were neutralized. (The United States did not sign the agreement but promised to view any violation with grave concern.)

Why did the Soviets and Chinese sacrifice Ho's chance for victory in all of Indochina for the consolation prize of North Vietnam? Here we must speculate.[2] The new Eisenhower Administration talked about pos-

---

[2] My speculation is largely based on the excellent study of the Geneva Conference and related events by Melvin Gurtov, *The First Vietnam Crisis* (New York: Columbia University Press, 1967).

sible American intervention, although in private there was great reluctance to do so. And talk was buttressed by the "New Look" in American military strategy announced on January 12, 1954, by Secretary of State Dulles: for reasons of economy and to avoid another Korean-type ground war, the United States would rely on "a great capacity to retaliate instantly, by means and at places of our choosing." Dulles later indicated that he had in mind a whole range of possible retaliatory responses and not an instant and automatic nuclear strike ("massive retaliation"). But the Soviets and the Chinese apparently thought that the United States might use nuclear weapons in every local war—meaning Indochina. Moreover, "massive retaliation" might be directed against the Soviet and the Chinese homelands.

The Chinese had other reasons for ending the conflict in Indochina. The Korean war had been costly for the Chinese economy. Peking was now interested in playing a major role in world politics at Geneva, and in continuing the diplomatic offensive begun with the Korean armistice. The use of the "peace" line seemed to promise greater gains than wars of national liberation for China's new program to lead the developing nations of Asia. Meanwhile, all would not be lost in Indochina. Ho's territorial gains would be consolidated without further risks, and the new people's democracy would be the first step in the eventual absorption of all of Indochina into the communist bloc.

The USSR also had other reasons for wanting a Geneva settlement.[3] Malenkov's overall program to reduce world tension would be enhanced. But perhaps most important, the Soviets were ready to pressure Ho Chi Minh (and the Chinese) to give the French the peace they desperately wanted in Indochina. In return, the Soviets expected French procrastination on the proposed European Defense Community (EDC) described below. The Soviets still gave first priority to weakening Western defense plans for Europe. In this respect, it seems significant that partition was quickly achieved after a new French government under Pierre Mendès-France, a known opponent of EDC, came to power in the latter stages of the Geneva Conference. (The new Premier had promised to resign if he did not obtain a truce in Indochina within five weeks.) [4]

Western Europe Soviet foreign policy's new look also appeared in Europe. On May 30, 1953, the Soviets informed the Turks that Russia was dropping its demand for a revision of the Montreux Con-

---

[3] Dulles' speech and the Geneva negotiations came at the very time of a "great debate" among the Soviet leadership, described later in this chapter, on the future course of Soviet defense policy. The debate hinged on the possibility of nuclear war and how to prepare for it, and disagreement in the Presidium on this basic issue probably made it difficult for the opposing factions to agree on a strong Soviet commitment to China and Ho Chi Minh.

[4] Dallin, *Soviet Foreign Policy After Stalin*, pp. 153-54.

vention and its claims on Turkey's eastern provinces of Kars and Ardahan.

But the limits surrounding the relaxation of tensions were soon apparent. As might be expected, the test case was Germany. In May 1952, the United States, France and Britain had negotiated a series of agreements which, in effect, granted West Germany its sovereignty. Germany, France, and Britain then joined Italy and the Benelux countries in signing a 50-year treaty providing for an integrated European army—the European Defense Community (EDC) just noted in relation to the Geneva agreement on Indochina. Malenkov's reply was the old Stalinist line: German militarization was the greatest danger to Europe; reunification of Germany would be impossible if EDC were ratified.

The Soviet position was spelled out at a meeting of the Council of Foreign Ministers in Berlin during the first two months of 1954. The very fact of the meeting was encouraging. It was the first time the foreign ministers had discussed the German (and Austrian) problem since 1949. The dour Molotov, again the Soviet Foreign Minister, was unusually courteous. His program for Germany, however, was completely unacceptable. The West wanted free elections in all of Germany to choose a government for the whole country and then a peace conference. This, of course, would mean the end of communist influence in Germany. Molotov therefore demanded the merger of the governments of East and West Germany—and then free elections. Moreover, Germany had to be neutralized. The Soviets would not chance a united Germany aligned with the West. The conference also deadlocked over a peace treaty for Austria. The Soviets would neither withdraw their troops from that country nor sign a treaty until peace was made with Germany.

Molotov then proposed an alternative to NATO which was so preposterous that the Western delegates laughed as he read it. The Soviets wanted a collective security arrangement for all of Europe. The members would agree not to join any alliance contrary to the aims of this treaty. Molotov in essence was proposing the dismantling of NATO and the proposed EDC, and the elimination of American ties with Europe. This naturally would mean the end of American troops and bases on the continent. (In March the Soviets agreed to let the United States join the proposed European organization. The Soviets, on their part, would join NATO.)

Malenkov's general soft line, however, soon scored a significant success. The German Bundestag had ratified EDC in March 1953, but, the French parliament rejected the proposed West European army in August 1954. The spectre of a revived Wehrmacht was more frightening than the supposed menace from the East. Prominent French politicians indeed hoped for a new understanding with Russia. Moscow hailed the French action as an important event in the political history of Europe.

Soviet jubiliation was short lived. The United States and Britain sponsored a new series of conferences in October 1954 to bring West Germany into NATO. The Federal Republic would have an autonomous army instead of forces integrated in the abortive EDC. France went along with the plan.

The Soviets were obviously worried. They threatened to renounce their wartime treaties of friendship and alliance with Britain and France. Molotov invited all the European states on November 13 to a conference in Moscow to discuss the safeguarding of European security. The conference was clearly designed to block ratification of the October agreements on Germany's entry into NATO.

The conference met on November 29. But only the East European states came. The delegates, including a Chinese observer, fulminated for three days against American imperialism and German militarism. The conference declaration insinuated that a Soviet bloc "NATO" might be necessary if a rearmed Germany entered the Western alliance.

The Soviet threat failed. Germany officially joined NATO on May 6, 1955. The Soviets retaliated the next day by renouncing their treaties with Britain and France. On May 14, the USSR and its satellites signed the 20-year Warsaw Pact—an Eastern NATO with a unified high command and a Soviet marshal as commander. Yet the Soviets had not changed the balance of power. They already controlled the military might of Eastern Europe. The Warsaw Pact recognized the obvious.

Many in the West saw Soviet militancy over Germany as a return to Stalinism in foreign policy. This seemed the result of Malenkov's resignation as Premier on February 8, 1955, because Malenkov was thought to be the force behind the relaxation of tensions. (He apparently had been voted out of office for "a bad style of leadership.")

The West was in for a shock. Khrushchev, Malenkov's replacement, would be a much more vociferous proponent of "peaceful coexistence." And Khrushchev would make major changes in Soviet strategy where Malenkov had merely refined Stalin's tactics.

The Great Debate   During this period, Malenkov and Khrushchev and their factions on the Presidium debated the great issues of Soviet politics. (Stalin and Trotsky had fought a similar intellectual duel for power some thirty years before.) The debates were crucial for the contestants because the winner could become top man in the Soviet hierarchy. The debates are important in our study because of their ramifications for Soviet foreign policy.

The major issue was the future direction of the Soviet economic system. Malenkov wanted more consumer goods for the people, while acknowledging that the development of heavy industry was still vital.

(Economic concessions for the populace obviously would make Malenkov popular.) Khrushchev, on the other hand, saw the issue of economic priorities as a golden opportunity to gather support from the more conservative members of the Presidium (Molotov in particular). These men still wanted first emphasis on heavy industry—an article of faith for strict Stalinists. Khrushchev reasoned that more heavy industry was needed to fill defense requirements because of the imperialist threat. This argument in turn was based on a major overhauling of Soviet military strategy then under way. The basic question was the impact of nuclear weapons on military strategy and international politics.[5]

Malenkov predicted in 1954 that a new world war, given modern methods of warfare (nuclear weapons), would mean the end of civilization. In effect, he was arguing that the sheer destructiveness of nuclear weapons ruled out the possibility of general war between the Soviet Union and the West. Malenkov had announced on August 8, 1953, that Russia had developed the hydrogen bomb. (The less powerful atomic bomb was revealed in 1949.) In line with this policy, the Soviets reduced their defense budget in 1953 and 1954.

Khrushchev and his faction took the opposite view: the advent of nuclear weapons did not rule out war between the capitalist and socialist camps. The Soviets had to go all out in the development of this new spectrum of very costly weapons. At the same time, the large Soviet conventional forces had to remain in being. Khrushchev had the support of most Soviet military leaders and strategists, headed by Marshal Zhukov, the hero of World War II—an important source of strength in the power struggle with Malenkov and his followers.

Official military doctrine still reflected the thinking of that great military strategist—Joseph Stalin. The late dictator asserted that five constant factors gave Soviet conventional forces ultimate superiority in any war: stability of the home front; morale of the troops; quantity and quality of the divisions; weapons of the armed forces; and abilities of the Soviet commanders. Stalin's strategic dogma could not be publicly challenged in his lifetime. Yet Stalin wisely had begun the development of nuclear weapons and their delivery systems (aircraft and missiles)—even if he had not fully understood their significance.

Stalin's theory of warfare obviously left the Soviet armed forces in a difficult position if faced with a surprise nuclear attack on the homeland. Soviet military power could be paralyzed before the "constant factors" had a chance to operate. Soon after Stalin's death, military strategists therefore began to challenge his analysis. Pressure grew for a full arsenal

---

[5] For the debate see Herbert S. Dinerstein, *War and the Soviet Union* (New York: Frederick A. Praeger, Inc., 1962), and Raymond L. Garthoff, *Soviet Strategy in the Nuclear Age* (New York: Frederick A. Praeger, Inc., 1962).

of conventional and nuclear weapons including the ability to hit the enemy before he could launch his nuclear attack (the doctrine of pre-emption). In order to pre-empt, an up-to-date warning system was needed to give advance indications of enemy plans to commit "surprise aggression." More than a deterrent nuclear capability—which Malenkov asserted the USSR already had—was necessary. And the ability to wage a general nuclear war and provide a defense against nuclear attack was a very expensive proposition.

In summary, Khrushchev and his generals doubted whether Malenkov's rather skimpy deterrent would always work. Malenkov was accused of complacency. In March 1954, Khrushchev asserted that the capitalist states were still preparing for war regardless of nuclear destructiveness. He accused Malenkov of being defeatist in his assertions that all of civilization would be destroyed in a nuclear war. Khrushchev agreed that capitalism would be destroyed, but he implied that communism would emerge victorious.

Khrushchev, of course, won the debate. But the special significance for our narrative concerns what the outcome meant for the future course of Soviet foreign policy. By winning approval for a massive program of nuclear weapons, Khrushchev had laid the basis for his future offensive against the West. The nuclear-tipped ICBM was to be the vital hardware underlying "offensive" peaceful coexistence. It might even tilt the world balance of power in favor of the socialist camp.

KHRUSHCHEV FORMS
A FOREIGN POLICY: 1955-1957

Khrushchev had not won his final battle for power with Malenkov's resignation. The struggle had only entered a new stage. Malenkov still was lodged on the Party Presidium, and had powerful support. Molotov, basically a Stalinist, would have to be isolated. In recognition of this partial victory, Khrushchev retained his old job as First Secretary of the Party. Bulganin, a front man, was named Premier. Marshal Zhukov became Minister of Defense.

But Khrushchev began to act as the official spokesman of the Soviet state in world affairs even though he lacked a formal governmental office. Most impressive was the overall tone of reasonableness which suddenly imbued Soviet foreign policy. Khrushchev had talked about the ever-present danger of war and ordered a great buildup of Soviet nuclear power, but Soviet foreign policy became inordinately peaceful and conciliatory after his preliminary victory with Malenkov. Khrushchev—not Malenkov—was about to make the decisive break with Stalinism in Russia's world affairs.

Yet Khrushchev seemed to be feeling his way toward a new orientation for Soviet foreign policy. He was not a great strategist with a carefully thought out master plan, but an innovator addicted to large-scale, crash programs to solve complex problems in domestic as well as foreign policy: the Virgin Lands scheme to advance agricultural production in one gigantic stroke; the frontal attack on Stalin's image; the installation of missiles in Cuba to shift the world balance of power by one dramatic move. Some of these innovations backfired, but Khrushchev always exuded great confidence. Some of his tactics in foreign affairs would bring the USSR close to war with the West: they involved much more risk than the cautious, carefully planned policies of Stalin. Yet Khrushchev seemed basically less aggressive than Stalin—or the Chinese. It was his style of leadership which got him (and Russia) in trouble. It was the way he attempted to solve problems—not his major foreign policy line which we will later characterize as "offensive" peaceful coexistence.

Soon after his temporary victory over Malenkov, Khrushchev set out to solve three general problems facing Soviet foreign policy. First, the Soviets had been stopped in Europe since 1949. Khrushchev could make no major changes there. Like Stalin and Malenkov, he was prepared to accept the *status quo*. But the West still had not acquiesced to Soviet control over Eastern Europe, particularly East Germany. Russia needed this acceptance or the communist zone could never be secure. Perhaps tensions could be eased further. New methods might be found to protect the Soviet sphere of influence in Europe.

Second, there was a crying need for a new look at Soviet policy toward the vast underdeveloped areas. The Soviets might be able to ally with the non-communist but violently anti-colonial governments of the emerging nations in a great united front against the imperialist West.

Third, something had to be done about Soviet relations with other communist states. Stalin had made a mess of things with Tito, and the Chinese were getting restless. A formula was needed combining local autonomy with ultimate Soviet control.

Détente in Europe   Khrushchev's hand was soon evident in Soviet relations with Western Europe. The USSR had balked for years at drafting a peace treaty for Austria. But in April 1955, Moscow agreed to sign a treaty and quit its occupation in return for Austria's neutrality and 150 million dollars of reparations.

The Soviets apparently had grown concerned that the Allied sector of Austria, like West Germany, might be incorporated into the Western defense network. Khrushchev probably considered it more sensible to accept a unified and neutral Austria, even if this meant giving up the Soviet zone. Russia, moreover, was not really losing anything. The Soviet sector had not been turned into a people's democracy. Yet Khrushchev had thrown over a basic principle of Stalinist foreign policy: any retreat from territory gained is a loss.[6] Soviet propaganda organs later gave the USSR full credit for the treaty, maintaining the West was opposed to neutralization.

Khrushchev's relaxation of tensions seemed to augur well for Russia's relations with the imperialist camp. Pressure had been building up around the world for the Western Allies and the Soviets to sit down together and ease the Cold War tensions. Moscow's new leaders accepted a Western invitation in late May to a summit conference—the first meeting of the heads of state of the great powers since Potsdam in 1945.

The conference was held in the Geneva headquarters of the defunct League of Nations in July 1955. World attention was riveted on the proceedings; thirteen hundred reporters assured adequate press coverage. President Eisenhower, British Prime Minister Eden, French Premier Faure, Soviet Premier Bulganin and Khrushchev, listed as a member of the Presidium of the Supreme Soviet, parlayed for six days. Soviet Marshal Zhukov also was present, probably because of his wartime camaraderie with President Eisenhower. The Soviets were on their best behavior, toasting everyone in sight at the many formal receptions and buffet dinners, talking freely with all comers—and disagreeing politely. Eisenhower's goodwill in turn impressed the Soviet delegation.

The "spirit of Geneva" lent a mellow glow to East-West relations for the next few months. The Soviet press even claimed that the Cold War had ended. But the hard questions had not been touched—merely relegated to a subsequent second level conference of foreign ministers. (This conference, held three months later, also deadlocked.)

The American delegation had gone to Geneva on the mistaken assumption that the Soviets were ready to make real concessions. Their economy supposedly was in dire trouble, forcing them to buy from the West. Secretary of State Dulles therefore wanted to discuss Eastern Europe and the activities of "International Communism." Bulganin, the official head of the Soviet delegation, refused to permit either issue on the agenda: the countries of Eastern Europe had freely chosen their governments; the conference was convened to discuss inter-governmental problems, not the activities of political parties in various countries.

The West, on the other hand, vetoed the Soviet request to discuss the ending of the Cold War, neutrality, Asia, and the Far East. The only

[6] Another retreat soon made news. The Soviets voluntarily returned Porkkala Naval Base to the Finns in September 1955. Russia had exacted a 50-year lease on Porkkala, located on the Baltic 12 miles from Helsinki, in the 1947 peace treaty. The base had now lost much of its importance. But the Soviets pictured their magnanimous action as part of the Soviet campaign to abolish military bases on foreign soil—an example for the United States and its allies to follow.

real issues left were Germany and disarmament. The Soviets agreed to German reunification by free elections "in conformity with the national interests of the German people and the interests of European security." Khrushchev soon demonstrated that the USSR intended no concession. He told the East Germans on his way back to Moscow that Russia was sure the East German government would never agree to a solution which put Western interests above those of the German Democratic Republic. In effect, the Soviet leader had pledged that the USSR would not permit all-German free elections if they threatened to sink the communist regime of East Germany.[7]

The Soviet disarmament plan at Geneva revived ideas advanced by the Allies since 1947: gradual reduction of nuclear weapons inventories leading to complete prohibition of their use; a ceiling of 1,500,000 men for the armed forces of the United States, USSR, and China, 650,000 for Britain and France, and 200,000 for other nations (German rearmament would be severely limited). Russia proposed an international control system to supervise the disarmament program. But the Soviets balked when it came to details. And Bulganin objected to the only original contribution on disarmament made at Geneva. Eisenhower had proposed an "open skies" scheme whereby the USSR and America would exchange blueprints of their military installations and check on further developments with aerial photography.

Khrushchev seemed genuinely to desire a détente in Europe. He had made concessions to Austria and Finland. But he was just as unmovable as Stalin and Malenkov when it came to fundamental interests: the refusal to permit German reunification except on Soviet terms. And Khrushchev, like his predecessors, was suspicious of all capitalists—witness the Soviet rejection of the open-skies plan. Finally, he was about to launch a new onslaught against the West in the vast underdeveloped area, a supposed victim of imperialist exploitation.

A NEW POLICY
FOR THE UNDERDEVELOPED COUNTRIES

Militant communist revolutions in Asia, with the notable exceptions of China and Vietnam, had failed. Asians in general were

---

[7] Khrushchev's intent to keep East Germany in the Soviet orbit was reemphasized in September 1955. Encouraged by the new Soviet reasonableness, Chancellor Adenauer of West Germany traveled to Moscow to discuss the establishment of diplomatic relations with the USSR. Adenauer managed to "normalize" relations. But he got nowhere on reunification. Khrushchev accepted that West Germany was now solidly a part of NATO. In return, he wanted recognition that East Germany was there to stay, and that reunification could only occur on Soviet terms. On September 22, the Soviets announced that East Germany would be granted full sovereignty. Adenauer's government, they indicated, would now have to deal with the German Democratic Republic on the reunification question.

stirred by nationalism—not communism. It is difficult to say whether Stalin recognized this fact. In any case, Mao's successful "National Front" strategy soon was held up to Asian communists as their model for the seizure of power. The official endorsement came at a regional conference in November 1949 of the World Federation of Trade Unions (a communist front) in Peking.[8]

The essence of Mao's strategy was a broadly based coalition uniting all elements of the society who were working for national independence. The inclusion of the "national bourgeoisie" in the front was particularly significant. This grouping includes local capitalists, but also intellectuals, landowners, even local nobility. During the struggle for liberation they are considered "progressive." Ultimately, of course, they become "reactionary" as the society moves toward communism.

Yet the Soviets still seemed doubtful of Mao's formula, as indicated by Moscow's official analysis of the national bourgeoisie until 1955. Two years after Stalin's death, Soviet sources continued to label prominent Asian nationalists as "obedient executors of the will of the British-American imperialists." Gandhi, for instance, was "the principal traitor of the mass national liberation movement" in India. Asian nationalists supposedly were still in league with their former imperialist masters—their vaunted national independence was a sham. (Moscow ignored the difficult fact that these same men often had spent years in imperialist prisons for their beliefs.)

Soviet distrust of the bourgeois rulers of the newly independent countries also was evident in formal Soviet relations with such countries. Since 1951, Moscow had made vague offers of trade and technical aid to the underdeveloped areas at international conferences. But no agreements were concluded while Stalin lived.

Stalin's heirs showed signs that they were testing his thesis about the "unprogressive" nature of the national bourgeoisie. On July 15, 1953, the Soviet representative on the UN Economic and Social Council suddenly reversed the long history of Soviet opposition to the UN technical assistance program for the underdeveloped countries. In the middle of a speech, he announced that the USSR would contribute four million rubles to the program for 1953. Malenkov made friendly references to India and Burma in a speech to the Supreme Soviet on August 8, 1953. He gave special praise to the Indian government's mediation in the touchy Korean prisoner of war issue. In September, the Soviets signed a five-year trade agreement with the Indians. The most spectacular Soviet overture then came in February 1955: an agreement to construct the

---

[8] See Bernard S. Morris and Morris Watnick, "Current Communist Strategy in Nonindustrialized Countries," in *Political Change in Underdeveloped Countries,* John H. Kautsky, ed. (New York: John Wiley & Sons, Inc., 1962), pp. 282-92.

over one hundred million dollar Bhilai steel mill in central India. For the first time, Moscow had promised investment capital to non-communist governments—a function traditionally reserved for the imperialist powers.[9]

Later in 1955, the official Soviet line on the national bourgeoisie began to change. A full scale debate on their character developed among Soviet scholars and ideologists. It was now admitted that Gandhi had never been an ally, let alone an agent, of British imperialism. Gandhi, on the contrary, was "progressive." The responsibility for such errors in analysis was placed squarely on J. V. Stalin.[10] The debate, of course, merely revised the ideology to bring it in line with a developing offensive tactic in Soviet foreign policy.

It is difficult to say what part Khrushchev had played in the initial development of the new policy toward the underdeveloped areas. Given his flamboyant nature, Khrushchev may have urged greater emphasis than Malenkov on a fresh approach to the newly independent nations. It is significant that Soviet relations with these countries really flowered after Malenkov's resignation as Premier in February 1955. Prime Minister Nehru of India received extraordinary attention when he visited the USSR for 16 days in June 1955. The Indian leader addressed 80,000 people in Moscow's Dynamo Stadium, a privilege never before accorded a foreigner. Premier U Nu of Burma followed Nehru's route in October 1955.

In return, Bulganin and Khrushchev left in November for a triumphant month-long tour of India, Burma, and Afghanistan. "B and K's" reception in India was especially enthusiastic. Perhaps ten million people heard the Russian leaders. Khrushchev demonstrated signs of his flair for politics: riding elephants, wearing an Indian cap, and embracing Indian dancers. Promises of Soviet economic aid were liberally sprinkled along the way. At the same, Khrushchev blasted colonialism, and boasted of Soviet achievements. (His claim that the USSR had exploded the most powerful hydrogen bomb misfired, however, with the sensitive Indians.)

The Soviet pilgrimage to Asia was clearly designed to impress Asians with Soviet power and Soviet sympathy for Asia, and to separate that continent from the West. The Russians had some success. Joint communiqués issued by Soviet and Asian leaders during 1955 stressed Soviet-Asian friendship, applauded Asian neutrality and condemned "regional

---

[9] For an analysis of Soviet economic aid, see Marshall I. Goldman, *Soviet Aid and Trade to the Less Developed Countries* (New York: Frederick A. Praeger, Inc., 1967).

[10] See W. W. Kulski, *Peaceful Coexistence* (Chicago: Henry Regnery Co., 1959), pp. 216-22.

military pacts," called for the admission of Communist China to the UN, and for the prohibition of testing and production of nuclear weapons.

The Soviets developed a somewhat different approach toward the Middle East. In contrast to Southern Asia, Russian security interests were at stake. Turkey and Iran were the only pro-Western governments on the borders of the USSR in 1953. The hole had to be plugged.

Malenkov made favorable references to the Middle Eastern governments on August 8, 1953. (As in Asia, Stalin had been castigating the bourgeois leaders of these states.) In 1954, East European countries agreed to take Egyptian cotton in barter agreements. Khrushchev then introduced a new element in the Soviet approach to the underdeveloped areas with the sale of arms to Egypt in September 1955. (The weapons, including jet fighters and bombers, officially came from Czechoslovakia.) The West was shocked. A few weeks earlier at Geneva, the Soviets had talked about relaxing tensions. With one inexpensive stroke, the USSR had upset the balance of power in the Middle East and had become a significant factor in the affairs of that region.

Russia's new venture might have been foreseen. The British were preparing to withdraw from the Middle East. They had agreed in October 1954 to evacuate their troops from the Suez. The Soviets were sure that the United States would step in. The organization of the Baghdad Pact in 1955 was evidence. This arrangement, like NATO, was strictly a defensive alliance uniting Turkey (already in NATO), Iran, Pakistan, and Iraq—Egypt's chief rival for the leadership of the Arab world. Only Britain joined for the West. But Moscow could see the American hand of Secretary of State Dulles running the show. The United States already was allied with Turkey and Pakistan. These countries, plus Iran, were receiving American arms.

The Soviets were scared. A new "aggressive" coalition had been formed with outposts on the border of the USSR. One defensive tactic held promise—the creation of a counter force of Arab states with Egypt at the center. Communist arms would help Egypt play the leading role. (The USSR later offered arms to Syria, Saudi Arabia, Yemen and Sudan.) Egypt in turn wanted arms because of her running feud with Israel, and she was not adverse to becoming the major Arab power in the Middle East. Egyptian President Nasser was especially happy to show the West that he could deal with whomever he chose—in this case, Russia. The West had offered to sell Egypt arms, complained Nasser, only if she joined a "security pact."

The Peace Zone   Khrushchev developed the full ideological significance of the new policy toward the underdeveloped areas at the Twentieth Congress of the Soviet Communist Party in February

1956. He talked about the emergence of a vast "Peace Zone" of nearly one and a half billion people—the majority of the world's population. The countries in this zone were the socialist and nonsocialist peace-loving states of Europe and Asia. In the second category, the Soviet leader listed India, Burma, Indonesia, Egypt, Syria, Lebanon, and Sudan. These countries, while not socialist, had won genuine political independence. (This means that they were not part of an "aggressive" American bloc— NATO, SEATO, the Baghdad Pact.) The Peace Zone reflected a postwar development of historic significance: the collapse of the colonial system. Lenin had predicted that the peoples of the East would some day play an important part in deciding the destinies of the world. This period, claimed Khrushchev, had arrived.

Khrushchev noted that these countries still had to win *economic* independence from the West. In this struggle, however, they would have the help of the "socialist world system." It was no longer necessary to beg for up-to-date equipment to build "independent national economies" from former colonial oppressors. The socialist states would furnish the economic requirements of the newly independent states—without political or military conditions.

With one ideological stroke, Khrushchev had added some 700 million people to the forces opposing imperialism. But these people hardly were under Russia's thumb. The Soviet leader merely had thrown out Stalin's two-camp thesis for a much more realistic appraisal of world politics. Stalin's rigid categorization held that a country not communist was capitalist or capitalist-controlled. There was no room for neutrality. After several years of experimentation and his eye-opening visit to India, Burma, and Afghanistan in 1955, Khrushchev realized that genuine neutrality existed in the underdeveloped area. And on two vital issues—the desire for peace and anti-colonialism—the Soviets could unite with neutralists against the imperialist West.[11]

What were the Soviets after? First, they were not just for the independence of the underdeveloped countries. Ultimately, the Soviets hoped each country would move toward communism. Meanwhile, Soviet strategy had one basic aim: splitting the underdeveloped area from the West. Khrushchev's promise of economic aid—and, as it developed, military aid—was designed for this purpose.[12] A Leninist article of faith held that the imperialist mother countries would be gravely weakened if they no longer could exploit the colonies (or former colonies) for markets

[11] As a result of their new approach to the developing countries, the Soviets showed new enthusiasm for the UN. Here was a ready-made forum in which to mobilize the Peace Zone in the defense of peace and the anti-colonial cause. See Alvin Z. Rubinstein, *The Soviets in International Organizations: Changing Policy Toward Developing Countries, 1953-1963* (Princeton, N.J.: Princeton University Press, 1964).

[12] On the purposes of Soviet military aid, see Stephen P. Gibert, "Wars of Liberation and Soviet Military Aid Policy," *ORBIS*, X, No. 3 (Fall, 1966), 839-58.

and sources of raw materials. The West therefore was still the main enemy and thus the main target. The USSR's frontal attack on the West through Europe had been stalemated since 1949. Now the Soviets would attack the West through its back door—the underdeveloped sector of the world.

Naturally the Soviets would not shout about their real aims. The image the USSR projected was that of benevolent "big brother," the altruistic champion of the world's underprivileged in their struggle for nationhood. The Soviet Union had several points in its favor in this propaganda campaign. First, imperialism in the underdeveloped area was Western, not Soviet. The Soviets had solved their colonial problem by forcefully incorporating the Tsarist colonies into the USSR. Eastern Europe, obviously Soviet dominated, seemed far away from Asia—and the East Europeans were "white." Asians thus had little fear and few second thoughts about Soviet motives. Second, the communists had vehemently opposed Western colonialism for decades. The ambivalent attitude of the United States, ally of the former great imperialist powers, was in sharp contrast. Many leaders and intellectuals in the underdeveloped countries moreover accepted the Leninist explanation of imperialism. Third, the bourgeois leaders of the new nations appreciated Soviet aid and trade. It gave them an alternative to Western aid, and was offered without obvious strings.[13] Fourth, the statesmen and intellectuals of the new nations were impressed with the planned economic progress of Russia, particularly the rapid advance of the Soviet republics of Central Asia. All the modernizing elites of the underdeveloped countries wanted rapid economic development, and the Soviet model seemed more applicable than the long haphazard path of Western capitalism.[14]

Suez A test case soon came for the new alliance between the communist bloc and the underdeveloped area. On July 26, 1956, Egypt nationalized the Suez Canal. The British and French, major owners of the canal company, had two options: they could accept Egypt's act and work out a plan to compensate the shareholders while assuring freedom of navigation through the canal; or they could use force to regain control of the canal and possibly topple Nasser's government in the process. The second course also might block further Soviet penetration of the Middle East. After several months of futile attempts to regain control through negotiations, the British and French turned to force.

On October 29, Israeli forces attacked Egyptian units in the Sinai

[13] Almost all Soviet "aid" consists of long-term (12 years), low interest (2.5 per cent) loans, generally for large, showy projects. Outright grants are few, consisting mainly of symbolic gifts.

[14] In fact, the USSR is not a particularly relevant model for the underdeveloped countries. See Alex Inkeles and Oleg Hoeffding, "The Soviet Union: Model for Asia?" *Problems of Communism,* VIII, No. 6 (1959), 30-46.

Peninsula and the Gaza Strip. Israel had been very worried about the rapid buildup of Egypt's military strength after the Soviet arms deal, and Nasser's plans for Israel were well-known. Britain and France at once gave Egypt and Israel an ultimatum to withdraw their forces ten miles from the canal. Israel agreed, but Egypt refused. On October 31, British and French planes attacked Egyptian air bases.

This bit of gunboat diplomacy rocked the world. The Soviets were handed a splendid chance to champion a poor, helpless country against its former imperialist master. But the crisis held dangers. If a full scale war developed, the Soviets might have to put up—or shut up. Was Egypt worth a war? As tension grew during the autumn of 1956, Russia stoutly defended Egypt's right to nationalize the canal. Soviet canal pilots were sent to help run the strategic waterway. (At the same time, the Soviets insisted that they should share in any international arrangement to manage the canal.) In August, Khrushchev even hinted at Soviet "volunteers" to aid Egypt if she were attacked.

But when the hostilities began, the Soviets apparently refused to let the Egyptians use their Czech-supplied IL-28 jet medium bombers—the most effective weapon the Egyptians had. Russia merely called on the UN to take strong measures against the colonial powers.

On November 4, the British and French agreed to cease operations if UN troops occupied the canal zone. The pressure on the two powers had become enormous. The other Western nations, led by the U. S., opposed the use of force at Suez. The underdeveloped countries naturally were enraged. The Soviet UN delegation found itself voting for American resolutions to ease the crisis. Only when a solution to the crisis was in sight did the Soviets finally make a dramatic—and ominous—gesture.

On November 5, the Soviets dispatched notes to the British, French, and Israelis with an indirect but clear threat of nuclear retaliation. Premier Bulganin reminded the British: "In what position would Britain have found herself if she had been attacked by more powerful states possessing every kind of modern destructive weapon? Yet there now are countries which would not even need to send their naval and air forces to British shores, but could use other means, such as rockets. . . . We are fully determined to crush the aggressors and restore peace in the Middle East through the use of force." Bulganin simultaneously made a preposterous suggestion to President Eisenhower that the United States and the USSR team up to "curb aggression" in the Middle East. The U. S., of course, refused and warned the USSR that attacks against Britain and France would bring American retaliation against Russia.[15]

---

[15] A few weeks later, Khrushchev claimed that the Soviet offer of joint action was designed to show the Arab world that America did not really want to stop the British and French intervention.

The nine-day war ended on November 6. The Soviets claimed their clear and firm position had a sobering influence on the British and French ruling circles, and played a decisive role in the cessation of hostilities. Actually the USSR had been upstaged by the United States. The European allies were much more worried about American opposition. (The British government also faced bitter criticism in Parliament and the press.) Even Nasser considered the Soviet ultimatum against the three powers of secondary importance in ending the war.

Why had the Soviets waited until the conflict was almost over to intervene? The Hungarian Revolution, soon to be discussed, was at a critical stage during the Suez crisis. Some suggest this paralyzed the Soviets in Egypt.

The Soviets undoubtedly worried more about Hungary. But a better explanation for Presidium paralysis is that Moscow realized the American role in the Suez crisis was critical. If the United States supported Britain and France, Soviet intervention could lead to a major confrontation. And Moscow did not think Nasser's government worth a war.

When America clearly came out against her allies, the Soviets could threaten nuclear retaliation with little risk of having their bluff called.[16] This resolute, if tardy, stand paid off. Nasser may not have been awfully appreciative of Soviet efforts, yet the rest of the underdeveloped world seemed impressed with Russia's defense of the Peace Zone. The Soviets also claimed that the "contradictions" among the imperialists grew as a result of Suez—the Soviets were right.

Russia's pretended role as protector of the Arab world during the Suez crisis quickly gave birth to the Eisenhower Doctrine in January 1957. The Truman Doctrine of military and economic aid for governments threatened by communism had been extended to the Middle East, with the added promise to use American military power where necessary. Soviet Foreign Minister Shepilov predictably blasted the Eisenhower Doctrine; here was new proof that the United States had become the "main bulwark of the system of colonial oppression."

A NEW APPROACH
TO FRATERNAL STATES

A third basic problem nagged Khrushchev: something had to be done to repair Soviet relations with the other communist states. This problem had been growing for some time; its crux was simple. The

---

[16] For a well-reasoned defense of this explanation see O. M. Smolansky, "Moscow and the Suez Crisis, 1956: A Reappraisal," *Political Science Quarterly*, LXXX, No. 4 (1965), 581-605.

Soviets could not run other states in the socialist system forever as an extension of the USSR. Tito's defection had been the first danger sign. Mao Tse-tung, while outwardly professing loyalty, would be no puppet. The "satellite" peoples of Eastern Europe would not stay quiet indefinitely.

Stalinist controls, although subtle, could not conceal Soviet dominance. Soviet attempts to relax tensions with the West had a hollow ring while Stalinism reigned over—and in—Eastern Europe. Most of all, Stalin's heirs had to abandon his methods because they could not assure the loyalty of other peoples to the USSR. As long as Stalin's hand-picked yes-men ruled Eastern Europe, communist regimes would be unpopular. If their subjects revolted, the West might intervene, threatening the Soviet state itself. In addition, unpopular regimes hardly inspired productivity. Yet greater economic wealth in the satellites was vital if the strength of the communist bloc were to increase.

The first requirement was to make the East European regimes tolerable, if not popular. The police state apparatus could be relaxed. (This had been done in the Soviet Union after Stalin's death.) Local leaders could be given more autonomy. Individual paths to socialism could evolve, permitting an outlet for nationalism.

But then came the rub. Where could Khrushchev find local leaders who would exercise the "proper" degree of autonomy? It would be difficult to bring change through local Stalinists; they were too inflexible. Yet other communists who might prove popular and welcome autonomy, also might prove Titoists. Malenkov, then Khrushchev, faced a dilemma: how to have decentralization without disintegration? For no Soviet leader was ready to free Eastern Europe from the Russian sphere of influence. Indeed, an additional reason for de-Stalinization in the satellites was to entice Tito back into the communist camp. Finally, the special relationship with China needed constant attention. If China ever broke with Russia, the Yugoslavian schism would look like child's play.

The revolution in Soviet policy toward fraternal states proceeded slowly, and haltingly. Stalin's heirs were experimenting, and there still was no general recognition that a new policy was needed.

In April 1953, Malenkov's government ordered the East German regime to ease its pressure on the people. (Under Stalin's orders, East Germany had gone all out to build socialism.) In June, the regime stopped the forced collectivization of peasants, set free thousands of prisoners, and ended its campaign against religion. The people thought Stalinism finally was on the way out. The East German government, confused by the new course dictated from Moscow, then raised work norms—in effect cutting wages. Workers went on strike in East Berlin. The strike quickly spawned a full-blown revolt. Uprisings flared in 60 East German cities. In

Berlin, workers attacked communist officials. Members of the government fled to buildings guarded by Soviet troops.

Malenkov and the Presidium must have seen that Eastern Europe was a powder keg. A little de-Stalinization had triggered a major revolt, and unrest could spread quickly. The new Soviet rulers immediately demonstrated that de-Stalinization did not mean freedom. Three Soviet divisions moved in to East Berlin to save the shaky Ulbricht regime. The rioters were helpless against Russian tanks and the revolt ended. The Soviets wisely did not reinstitute Stalinism in East Germany. On the other hand, Malenkov's government seemed reluctant to permit further major changes in the satellites.

It took Khrushchev to make the major break with Stalin's foreign policy toward Eastern Europe. His first move was an attempt to heal the rupture with Tito. This obviously would not be easy. Both sides had slung too much mud since 1948 to permit normal relations immediately. And Tito was wary of losing his country's hard-won independence and neutrality.

Molotov had taken the first step in June 1953, with a proposal to resume diplomatic relations with Yugoslavia. This tactic, of course, merely put Yugoslavia's relations with the Soviet Union back on the same plane as those between the Soviet Union and any capitalist state. Khrushchev, against Molotov's advice, also wanted to resume close contact between the Soviet and Yugoslav communist *parties*—the proper, intimate relationship between fraternal states.[17] Such a move required concessions to Tito, which Khrushchev was prepared to make. He referred to the Yugoslav leader as "comrade" in November 1954 during a speech celebrating the Russian Revolution, and he invited Tito to Moscow.

Tito insisted that Khrushchev first come to Belgrade to eat humble pie. And Khrushchev went. Speaking at the Belgrade airport in May 1955, the Soviet leader charged Beria and his secret police with making all the trouble between Yugoslavia and Russia—Stalin was not mentioned. Khrushchev then proposed that party relations be renewed.

Subsequent developments indicated that Khrushchev had to go much further to succeed with Tito. The Soviets were forced to dissolve the Cominform.[18] But most important, Tito revealed that the "new leaders" of

[17] Khrushchev's reconciliation with Tito may have been partly designed to isolate Molotov, Khrushchev's major opponent on the Presidium after Malenkov's demotion. Conquest, *Power and Policy in the U.S.S.R.*, p. 264.

[18] The official dissolution was delayed until April 17, 1956, apparently to minimize Khrushchev's concession. The Soviets probably would have eliminated the organization in any case. The Cominform had never been a very effective instrument of Soviet foreign policy. Khrushchev seems to have been considering an alternative: a new, less rigid version of the old Comintern embracing all communist parties and permitting some measure of national autonomy.

the USSR agreed it was impossible to subject all nations in the world to one developmental pattern (the Soviet). Yugoslavia would build a social system in her own way, and the USSR in its own way. Khrushchev had sanctioned "national paths" to communism—a crucial step in the de-Stalinization process.[19]

The floodgates to de-Stalinization were really opened at the Twentieth Party Congress in Moscow during February 1956. In a closed session, Khrushchev astonished the assembled delegates with a long and shocking revelation of Stalin's crimes against the party and the Soviet people. Khrushchev apparently was trying to further isolate his Stalinist opposition in the Party Presidium. Those who did not applaud his attack on Stalin became implicit accomplices of the dead dictator—now shown to be a monster. Those who approved were obviously Khrushchev's followers.

Khrushchev spent little time criticizing Stalin's foreign policy in the secret speech. He was not making a foreign policy statement. More important, Khrushchev obviously approved of the general direction of Stalinist foreign policy. The main charges leveled at Stalin's handling of foreign policy dealt with his blindness to the German attack in 1941—it apparently was correct to sign the Non-Aggression Pact with Hitler in 1939—and his mistreatment of Tito.

If Khrushchev did not treat major issues of foreign policy, he apparently intended for the secret speech to shake Stalinism in Eastern Europe as well as in Russia.[20] In this he suceeded—far beyond his expectations.[21] Coming after the gradual de-Stalinization in the USSR and Eastern Europe since 1953 and the approval of "national paths" to socialism, the speech lit the fuse on a gigantic time bomb of popular unrest. Khrushchev implicitly had condemned Stalin's henchmen in Eastern Europe, and the main targets of the people were the dictatorships led

[19] Khrushchev expanded the many roads to communism at the Twentieth Party Congress in 1956. He foresaw *peaceful* transitions to communism as possible for many capitalist and former colonial countries. Local communists and their allies could make "fundamental social changes" by winning power through parliamentary majorities. Khrushchev apparently had two goals in mind with this new line: first, to give hope to West European communists who had almost no chance of coming to power through the traditional violent revolution; and second, to quiet the fears of the bourgeois regimes of the underdeveloped countries who continually worried about their local communist opposition. However, Khrushchev (and Mikoyan) carefully stipulated the conditions under which a "peaceful" revolution might be possible—in a small country which had powerful "socialist" neighbors.

[20] Zbigniew K. Brzezinski, *The Soviet Bloc* (New York: Frederick A. Praeger, Inc., 1966), p. 179.

[21] Copies of the speech were secretly passed to the communist elite in Eastern Europe. *Borba*, the Yugoslavian party paper, published excerpts in March. The American State Department apparently had obtained a copy of the speech from a foreign communist party, and released the complete text on June 2, 1956.

by such men.[22] But an undercurrent of hatred for Russia—the supposed cause of their misery—was obvious. Certain communists also shared the popular passion for independence from the USSR. Explosions soon came in Poland and Hungary. We must analyze Soviet reaction to each revolt because two different kinds of challenges faced the Kremlin.

Poland The Polish crisis exploded with a strike in Poznań, a manufacturing city in the western sector, on June 28, 1956. At issue were low wages and the poor standard of living. The citizenry soon joined the workers, and the strike turned into a mass demonstration against the government. The demands of the mob also broadened. Signs appeared: "Down with Dictatorship"; and "Down with the Russkies!"

It took the Polish army to quell the uprising, leaving 44 demonstrators dead and over 300 injured. The Russians, as usual, blamed "hostile agents" of "international reaction" for Poznań. The Poles were more candid. In clear disagreement with the Soviets, the First Secretary of the Polish party admitted that the strike was "a warning signal testifying to the existence of serious disturbances between the party and various sections of the working class." In the next few months, a group of Polish party leaders decided radical reforms were needed to save the regime. And these reforms had to be made regardless of what the Soviets might think. The Polish communist elite had set out on its tortuous path to national communism.

In October 1956, the challenge to Soviet control came to a head. Moscow got word from pro-Soviet members of the Polish Politburo that the leader of the "nationalist" faction, Wladyslaw Gomulka, was about to be elected First Secretary. Moreover, the new Politburo membership would not include Soviet Marshal Rokossovsky (foisted on the Poles in 1949 as their military commander). Moscow was shocked at this brazen defiance of the rules of the game: Polish party leaders always should consult the Soviets on such vital decisions.

Khrushchev was not yet ready to use force against a "people's democracy." Neither was he ready to permit a "Titoist" regime on Russia's western border. He decided to bluff the Poles. Soviet army units in Poland and East Germany received orders to move on Warsaw. Meanwhile, Khrushchev and other Soviet leaders, accompanied by a coterie of Soviet generals, descended on Warsaw on October 19. During a ninety-minute tirade, Khrushchev demanded that Rokossovsky and the Polish

---

[22] To carry further the de-Stalinization process in Eastern Europe and also to placate Tito, Stalinists were removed from power and "national" (Titoist) communists rehabilitated during the spring and summer of 1956 in Bulgaria, Hungary, Poland, and Czechoslovakia.

Stalinists be kept in the Politburo. The "traitor" Gomulka could be elected to membership in that body, but not to the post of First Secretary. Khrushchev reportedly threatened to crush the Poles if they refused his ultimatum; "I'm going to show you what the road to socialism looks like! If you don't obey us, we will crush you. We are going to use force to kill all sorts of uprisings in this country." [23]

Gomulka, now backed by a majority, would not bend. The Poles threatened war if the Soviet army did not halt its advance on Warsaw. At the same time, Gomulka promised that Soviet-Polish "friendship" would continue on the vital issues of international politics. Poland would not leave the Warsaw Pact to join the imperialist camp. The Soviets seemed mollified, although certainly not happy. A few days later Khrushchev telephoned Gomulka to apologize for his outburst, and promised to return Soviet troops to their bases. Moscow apparently was ready to permit Poland autonomy because that country would still be communist, and in the Soviet sphere of influence. It was not worth a war merely to assure a malleable party leadership.

Hungary   The challenge was more serious in Hungary. Here the Soviets clearly faced the loss of a socialist state to the West. Here the opposition was clearly anti-communist as well as anti-Soviet.

Hungarian unrest, already articulated by the intelligentsia, reached new heights with news of Gomulka's victory over the Russians. On the evening of October 23, more than 200,000 citizens of Budapest demonstrated in the streets. The huge statue of Stalin—a despised symbol of Soviet control —was pulled to the ground. Without warning, the hated Hungarian secret police then fired on the crowd. Sympathetic police and soldiers passed weapons to the rioters. Some even joined the demonstration.

Next morning, Radio Budapest announced that the Central Committee had named a new premier: Imre Nagy, a popular Hungarian "Gomulka." Meanwhile, Erno Gero, the ruthless First Secretary of the Hungarian party and a Stalinist, had taken another desperate step to preserve party control. He apparently called Moscow and asked for Soviet military assistance, justifying the request by painting a picture of disastrous rioting and imminent danger to the regime. Shortly after midnight on October 23, Soviet tanks moved into Budapest.

Mikoyan and Suslov, Soviet Presidium members, arrived in Budapest on October 24 to reconnoiter the situation. Mikoyan reportedly castigated Gero for having "stampeded" Moscow into an unnecessary military intervention. The Presidium representatives then replaced Gero with Janos Kadar, previously imprisoned by the local Stalinists. Finally, they agreed

[23] Raymond L. Garthoff, *Soviet Military Policy* (New York: Frederick A. Praeger, Inc., 1966), p. 157.

that Soviet troops would be withdrawn from Budapest as a "concession" to the people. The Soviets apparently hoped the crisis, "fomented" by the United States, was over. They had seriously misjudged the situation.

Intoxicated with their apparent victory over Russia and Stalinism, the revolutionaries pressed for other concessions. Nagy, swept along by the tide, announced he would seek the withdrawal of Soviet troops from all of Hungary. Meanwhile, the proletarian dictatorship had collapsed. The communist party had ceased to exist as an organization. Nagy announced a cabinet with non-communist members, proclaimed the restoration of the multi-party system, and promised free elections.

This critical situation faced Mikoyan and Suslov when they returned to Budapest on the evening of October 30. The Presidium representatives now offered to withdraw all Soviet troops except those stationed on Hungarian soil under terms of the Warsaw Pact. The local party leaders, however, demanded immediate withdrawal of all Soviet forces and threatened to repudiate the Warsaw Pact regardless of what the Soviets did.

Surprisingly, Mikoyan and Suslov agreed to organize a joint commission to discuss the Soviet withdrawal. They then left for Moscow. Apparently, the Presidium members were only buying time to prepare a second intervention. Moscow seems to have decided at this juncture to crush the revolution. The alternative was a humiliating blow to Soviet power and prestige and the defection of Hungary from the bloc.

Fearing that Soviet troops were massing, Nagy formally announced on November 1 that Hungary would withdraw from the Warsaw Pact and adopt neutrality. The regime then appealed to the UN for assistance in maintaining its shaky independence. It was too late. Soviet armor and troops, now heavily reinforced, attacked strongholds of the Hungarian army and the "Freedom Fighters" at daybreak on November 4. (Khrushchev later admitted that the decision was taken after agonizing soul-searching.)

The defeat of the Hungarians was inevitable in the face of overwhelming Soviet power. Almost three thousand Freedom Fighters were killed; some 180,000 fled the country. Nagy sought asylum in the Yugoslav embassy, but was arrested a few weeks later by the Soviets as he was leaving the embassy on a "safe conduct" pass. (In 1958, Nagy was tried for high treason and executed.)

The West offered sympathy to the Hungarians—but no more. The Suez crisis, occurring at this exact moment, had gravely split the Western camp. Britain and France were isolated from the United States. Even without Suez, Western intervention would have been doubtful. The Soviets obviously considered their vital interests at stake. Hungary, perhaps more than any crisis since 1945, might have triggered World War III if the West had acted. And the Western powers could not ignore what the bloody demonstration signified for Soviet foreign policy.[24] Russia would fight to maintain the *status quo* in Europe. Khrushchev's "relaxation of tensions" had a rather hollow ring.

1957: KHRUSHCHEV TRIUMPHS

The most pressing problems for Khrushchev in 1957 came from within the communist orbit: first, he had to repair the Hungarian damage to Soviet relations with the fraternal states; second, he had to consolidate his power on the Presidium.

Repairs for the Bloc   Soviet repression in Hungary had soured Soviet relations with Yugoslavia and Poland, and had disenchanted those groups in the rest of Eastern Europe looking for greater freedom. Somehow, the USSR had to patch together its fallen empire. "National communism" obviously had gone too far. (The most extreme deviations from the accepted path of social and economic development—notably the Yugoslavian experiment—were chastized as "revisionism.")

The Soviet Presidium realized that Stalinist control could not be reinstituted. The search was still on for a middle way permitting local autonomy, but assuring Soviet control on vital international issues. The Soviet press emphasized individual paths to socialism within the "community of socialist nations." In short, communist societies could experiment as long as they stuck together under Soviet leadership. Most of Eastern Europe seemed ready to accept this proposition. There really was no alternative; Hungary had shown it was futile to expect aid from the West against the USSR.

Khrushchev failed to advance his pet project for a new Comintern. Poland, Yugoslavia, and particularly important, China, adamantly opposed any formal, coordinating body obviously under Soviet leadership. They wanted *ad hoc* bilateral or multilateral meetings with no formal rules of procedure or organization. Khrushchev capitulated, apparently satisfied with a declaration in November 1957 of the 12 communist parties in power that the Soviet Union was the leader of the communist world. Mao Tse-tung humbly admitted at the meeting in Moscow that China was not worthy of the mantle of leadership.[25]

---

[24] Western European communists and fellow travelers also were shocked at the brutal Soviet repression of the revolutionaries, who obviously were not all agents of American imperialism.

[25] In March 1958, the Soviets finally secured agreement from the other parties to the publication of a "theoretical and information monthly," the *World Marxist Review*. The Poles, Italians, and Yugoslavs had stalled action on the Soviet project, certain the new periodical was designed to combat their "revisionism." This soon proved to be the case.

The Rout of the Anti-Party Group   Meanwhile, Khrushchev had met the second, pressing challenge in 1957: Malenkov, Molotov, and Kaganovich (like Molotov, a good Stalinist) had led a last-ditch attempt to unseat him on the Party Presidium. Khrushchev's opponents garnered a majority of that body against their boss at a meeting in June 1957. With the backing of the army and the secret police, Khrushchev managed to transfer the question of his continued leadership to the much larger Central Committee of the party on which he had built up powerful support. Zhukov, the army head, used air force planes to fly Central Committee members to Moscow for the meeting. The "anti-party" group (a later nickname) was roundly defeated. According to subsequent reports, not one member of the 309 man augmented Central Committee supported the losers.[26]

Khrushchev's opponents apparently had questioned his major initiatives in domestic and foreign policy, which in turn reflected his basic style of leadership. "Stalinists" and "liberals" on the Presidium were upset over their leader's passion for ill-conceived projects on a grand scale and general lack of prudence. (Khrushchev would be deposed in 1964 for similar reasons.) Opposition had coalesced over immediate issues: the unfortunate results of de-Stalinization in Eastern Europe; the unproductive flirtation with Tito, and Khrushchev's new scheme for a drastic reorganization of the economic system. However, the anti-party group, it later was revealed, had long been snipping at Khrushchev's whole foreign policy. They supposedly were against economic and military aid to the underdeveloped countries, "national roads" to communism, the Austrian peace treaty—and the basic concept of "peaceful coexistence."

A Forecast of Khrushchev's Grand Strategy   Khrushchev had proclaimed "peaceful coexistence" as the basis of Soviet relations with states having different social systems at the Twentieth Party Congress in 1956. There was actually nothing new in this doctrine; Lenin had developed the theory in the early 1920's.[27] But Khrushchev gave it a new twist with a corollary thesis: peaceful coexistence *could* continue between socialism and capitalism until the communist millennium. Khrushchev claimed that war was no longer "fatalistically inevitable," despite Lenin's prediction that war would continue as long as imperialism existed. Powerful social and political forces now could prevent the imperialists from "unleashing war and, if they try to start it, to give a smashing

[26] Malenkov was made manager of a power station in Siberia; Molotov, the ambassador to Outer Mongolia. Their fate might have been much worse under Stalin. Bulganin was relegated to the anti-party group after Khrushchev assumed Bulganin's position of Premier in March 1958. Khrushchev retained his post of First Secretary.

[27] See p. 124.

rebuff to the aggressors and frustrate their adventurist plans." Indeed, peaceful coexistence was the only way; the alternative, Khrushchev warned, would be the most destructive war in history.

The struggle against capitalism, the Soviet leader stated, would be relegated to the ideological plain. Peaceful competition would show that the socialist mode of production was superior to the capitalist. Precisely because of this superiority, the ideas of Marxism-Leninism would capture the minds of the broad masses of workers everywhere. There was no need for the socialist countries to use "armed interference" in other countries to bring communism. The establishment of a new social system, said Khrushchev, was the internal affair of the people concerned.

Khrushchev was implying that the balance of power had begun to change in favor of the socialist camp. The West no longer could dominate the world. On the contrary, capitalism was surely doomed. The progressive people of each country would gradually see the superiority of socialism, and act to change their political and economic systems.

Khrushchev could not launch "offensive" peaceful coexistence—as we shall call his revision of the Leninist doctrine—in 1956 or 1957. He first had to put the communist bloc and his own house in order. Soviet military power, a vital foundation for his scheme, also was not obvious. Marshal Zhukov had boasted at the Twentieth Party Congress of "diverse atomic and nuclear weapons, mighty guided missiles, among them long-range missiles." In November 1956, Khrushchev then threatened to use "rockets" against France and England because of their invasion of the Suez. But few in the West were ready to grant the Soviets a serious nuclear capability in long-range strategic weapons.

Two dramatic events in the last half of 1957 finally gave teeth to Khrushchev's claim that "powerful" socialist forces existed to prevent imperialist aggression. On August 26, Moscow released a terse communiqué: the Soviets had successfully tested an intercontinental ballistic missile (ICBM). Even yet, many in the West were skeptical. On October 4, however, the world could no longer doubt Soviet technological—and thus military—progress. Russia leapfrogged America into space by orbiting the first artificial satellite—the famous Sputnik. If the USSR could hurl a satellite around the earth, surely it could launch an ICBM. Insult was added to injury when the Soviets launched a second Sputnik one month later, six times the size of the first. There was no longer reason to believe that Western military power would always be superior to that of the socialist camp.

SUMMARY

The years 1953 through 1957 saw the death of one ruler, Stalin, and the rise of another, Khrushchev. Stalin had achieved total control of party and society through ruthless suppression of all opposition. Times had changed. Khrushchev inherited a party which would resist a new dictator, and a society which thirsted for relief from Stalinism. Eastern Europe, on the other hand, wanted relief from Russian domination.

Khrushchev came to power through his dynamic leadership of shifting party majorities. In both domestic and foreign policy, he was the innovator. Whether Khrushchev would continue to rule would depend on the success of his innovations.

Khrushchev had shifted the Soviet grand strategy. The West, in particular the United States, was still the main enemy. But the main attack on the capitalist states would be through the imperialist backdoor—the emerging nations in Africa, Asia, and Latin America. The lands of socialism and the new nations were natural allies, forming a vast zone of peace. The West would be isolated. Meanwhile, Soviet experiments in nuclear weaponry promised a long awaited shift in the world balance of power. At least this was Khrushchev's plan.

FURTHER READING

Barghoorn, Frederick C., *The Soviet Cultural Offensive*. Princeton, N.J.: Princeton University Press, 1960. Emphasis on period since 1953; survey of Soviet goals for "guided culture contact."

Barghoorn, Frederick C., *Soviet Foreign Propaganda*. Princeton, N.J.: Princeton University Press, 1964. Emphasizes period since 1953.

Blackmer, Donald M., *Unity in Diversity: Italian Communism and the Communist World*. Cambridge, Mass.: The M.I.T. Press, 1968. The relationship of one of the most powerful and important non-ruling parties and the international communist movement since 1956.

Conquest, Robert, *Power and Policy in the U.S.S.R.* London: Macmillan & Co. Ltd., 1962. Kremlinological study of power struggle from last years of Stalin's rule to 1960.

Dallin, David J., *Soviet Foreign Policy After Stalin*. Philadelphia, Pa.: J. B. Lippincott Co., 1961. Soviet foreign policy from 1953 to 1960.

Kennan, George F., *Russia, the Atom and the West*. New York: Harper & Row, Publishers, 1957. Lectures given in 1957; treats "disengagement" in Central Europe.

Pistrak, Lazar, *The Grand Tactician: Khrushchev's Rise to Power*. New York: Frederick A. Praeger, Inc., 1961. Particularly good on Khrushchev's early career.

Swearer, Howard R. with Myron Rush, *The Politics of Succession in the U.S.S.R.* Boston: Little, Brown and Company, 1964. Documents from 1953 to 1958 relating to Khrushchev's rise to power with interpretive notes.

Vali, Ferenc A., *Rift and Revolt in Hungary; Nationalism vs. Communism.* Cambridge, Mass.: Harvard University Press, 1961. Comprehensive and well-documented.

Zinner, Paul E., ed., *National Communism and Popular Revolt in Eastern Europe: A Selection of Documents on Events in Poland and Hungary, February-November, 1956.* New York: Columbia University Press, 1956.

Zinner, Paul E., *Revolution in Hungary.* New York: Columbia University Press, 1962. Study of 1956 revolution.

10

OFFENSIVE COEXISTENCE

1958-1964

For decades, the USSR had been in constant danger of "capitalist encirclement." On March 19, 1958, Premier Khrushchev asserted that this dictum was out of date: "At present it is not known who encircles whom." His confidence came from the USSR's new military might and from its supposed leadership of the "Peace Zone."

Khrushchev claimed that Soviet military power was equal (and by 1960, superior) to that of the West. But there is no real indication that he was planning a surprise attack or preventive war against capitalism. Khrushchev probably realized that the American Strategic Air Command could still deliver a crushing blow to the USSR. His main object was to impress the West, particularly the United States, with the fact that the USSR now had "parity"—and even superiority—in strategic nuclear weapons. America could no longer threaten Russia with massive retaliation and expect safety.

Because of the mutual deterrent, general war between the socialist and imperialist camps was ruled out. On the other hand, Khrushchev would take every advantage of the favorable balance of power—or a balance which he *claimed* was favorable. The USSR had been on the defensive since 1917, now the scale was changing in favor of Soviet Russia and the socialist camp. The USSR at last could mount a grand offensive against the West, confident that Western retaliation against Russia was effectively discouraged.

The first use of Soviet nuclear power was to protect the socialist motherland as the offensive moved into high gear. In 1959, Khrushchev promised that the Soviet deterrent also would be used to defend Eastern Europe. Later the People's Republic of China was brought under the nuclear shield.

But the hard won and very expensive Soviet ICBM's would serve for more than the ultimate sanction. They were to provide the muscle behind Russian *political* demands on the West. (Khrushchev would discover this was a dangerous game.) Peaceful coexistence meant the absence of general war between the two systems, but it permitted intense competition on all other levels. For example, the Soviet nuclear capability would provide an omnipresent umbrella for "just" wars of national liberation, and it would serve to protect the newly independent underdeveloped countries from the imperialist West.[1]

Soviet optimism during the period 1958-1962 is nicely illustrated in an article from the Moscow journal *International Affairs*. A few excerpts give the flavor of the official view of the new balance of power and its impact on international politics:

> The change in the balance of forces in favour of Socialism and the application of the Socialist principles of international relations on an ever wider scale have made for an entirely new presentation of the *problem of war and peace*. . . .
>
> Having achieved unsurpassed successes in the economic field, science and engineering, the Soviet Union and the other Socialist countries have created defence facilities of such a high level as to pre-condemn any imperialist aggression to inevitable failure. . . .
>
> *For the first time the advantage of overwhelming strength is not with the exploiting classes and social groups using it to the detriment of society . . . but with the peoples building Socialism and Communism and utilizing this strength in the interest of peace and international justice.*
>
> The result of this is the *crisis of imperialism's foreign policy*. Its most striking symptom is the failure of all attempts by world reaction headed by U.S. imperialism to "roll back" Communism, to suppress the national-liberation and democratic movements and to revive the all-embracing system of imperialist plunder and violence, on which international relations in the past were based.

The article also stresses the *offensive* nature of peaceful coexistence after the change in balance of power:

[1] See L. Glavolev and V. Larionov, "Soviet Defence Might and Peaceful Coexistence," in the Soviet journal *International Affairs* (Moscow) No. 11 (1963), pp. 27-33. The article cites the various uses of the Soviet missile forces in Soviet diplomacy.

Peaceful co-existence not only does not preclude, but, on the contrary, pre-supposes revolutionary changes in society, accelerates the revolutionary process and intensifies the decline and collapse of capitalism.[2]

A warning must now be inserted about the general Soviet strategy during the period from 1957-1962. Khrushchev's policies were not all militant as the official line described above might suggest. There were moves to collaborate with the West in arms control, a unilateral reduction of the Soviet armed forces in 1960, the Rapacki Plan to neutralize Europe. These proposals helped the Soviets to appear reasonable and peaceful. More important, a reduction of tension would lessen the possibility of nuclear war and permit the other aspects of peaceful coexistence to work.

In part, the apparently contradictory tactics of peaceful coexistence reflected increasing Soviet sophistication in combining traditional Right and Left tactics in the same period. (Peaceful coexistence in the past had been defensive.) In part, they may have resulted from Khrushchev's personal style in foreign policy—often erratic and sometimes impromptu —and disagreement or indecision in the Presidium. Time would show that Khrushchev had improved, but not solidified, his political power in 1957.

In any case, Khrushchev's grand scheme had "come a cropper" by the end of 1962. The final blow was the Cuban missile crisis. To give a preview. Khrushchev ran head-on against the reluctance of the United States to accept its assigned role as the leader of a deteriorating coalition. Instead, the Eisenhower and Kennedy Administrations began a major program of missile building. By 1962, Khrushchev apparently thought that the balance of power was again turning against the USSR. His placement of missiles in Cuba late that summer seemed a calculated attempt to redress the balance. Another blow to Khrushchev's grand strategy was the indifferent success of the Soviet Union in uniting the under-developed countries in the Peace Zone against the West. Finally, the unity in the communist camp achieved in 1957 proved temporary and superficial. Khrushchev may have considered the rebellions in Eastern Europe a headache. Now he would face the wrath of the most populous nation in the world. The seeds of the Sino-Soviet schism had been latent since the birth of the People's Republic of China. In the late 1950's, the seeds began to flower. China's later defection from the Soviet bloc would shake the socialist camp to its roots, and split the camp beyond repair.

[2] Note: the italicized portion above is in italics in the original. For the full text see "The Nature and Specific Features of Contemporary International Relations," *International Affairs* (Moscow), No. 10 (1962), pp. 93-98. The article is the abridged "preface" from a new work on international relations since World War II. The Editorial Board of the journal believes that the preface is an attempt to make a "profound theoretical generalization of the laws governing modern international life."

THE OFFENSIVE AGAINST THE WEST BEGINS

Khrushchev's offensive had been incubating since 1955. The main objectives now would merely be pursued with more enthusiasm —backed by more muscle. Khrushchev wanted: 1) the solidification of Russia's sphere of influence in Europe—as a minimum, Western recognition of communism in Eastern Europe as the *status quo;* better yet, the elimination of the American presence in Europe and the neutralization of West Germany. The Soviets still considered NATO an American-controlled dagger aimed at the heart of Russia, and they feared an American supported neo-Nazi regime might attempt the reunification of Germany by force: 2) the detachment of the underdeveloped areas from the imperialist powers, leading to the ultimate defeat of the West. The final goal for each underdeveloped country, of course, would be a communist society. In the interim, the Soviets would collaborate with any regime having anti-colonialist (read anti-Western) tendencies.

Khrushchev's foreign policy goals were intimately related to his domestic policy. He had defeated Malenkov in 1955 by heading a temporary coalition of Presidium conservatives against Malenkov's reform proposals—particularly the former Premier's objective of reorienting the Soviet economy toward greater production of consumer goods with an attendant reduction of the defense budget. Khrushchev would now take over Malenkov's old line because in reality he was much more the reformist than the deposed Premier.[3] Khrushchev wanted to drag the whole Soviet economy, especially Soviet agriculture, into the Twentieth century. He was searching for efficiency and productivity. His grandiose plan to reorganize the economic system in the spring of 1957 was part of this scheme, as well as the earlier gamble to develop the "virgin lands" of Central Asia. Khrushchev probably hoped a dynamic domestic program would finally consolidate his personal political power.

Economic reorganization and increased production, however, demanded a reallocation of always scarce resources; something had to give. The massive arms budget, which dictated the continual development of heavy industry, was an obvious place to cut. Yet Khrushchev needed to keep tension with the West below the boiling point in order to keep arms expenditures level, let alone bring about the reduction. Peaceful coexistence therefore was an absolute necessity if the Soviet leader's domestic reforms were to succeed.

At the same time, Khrushchev had to demonstrate that peaceful co-

[3] On Khrushchev's reformist tendencies see Carl A. Linden, *Khrushchev and the Soviet Leadership: 1957-1964* (Baltimore, Md.: The Johns Hopkins Press, 1966), Chap. 2.

existence would produce international victories for the USSR and the socialist camp. Otherwise, he would face criticism at home and abroad (especially from Mao Tse-tung) that the USSR under his leadership had forsaken the cause of international communism. Khrushchev had to walk a tightrope: he would press the West for concessions and demonstrate Soviet support of the non-Western world—but stop short of provoking foreign crises endangering domestic programs.

Khrushchev in Europe   Khrushchev used both hard and soft lines over the next several years in attempting to gain his objectives in Europe, an indication of the subtlety and flexibility with which peaceful coexistence would be pursued. In the first months of 1957, he tried to capitalize on the temporary chaos in the Western alliance caused by the Suez fiasco. The USSR made individual offers of trade, and cooperation in disarmament and collective security to Britain and France. At the same time, the Soviets dispatched diplomatic notes to other NATO countries (including Norway, Denmark and West Germany): the USSR was concerned at their "lack of independence under United States' domination" and it warned of the danger of underestimating Soviet military might.

President Eisenhower and British Prime Minister MacMillan brought their countries together again at the Bermuda Conference in March 1957. The NATO Council then decided in May to equip the alliance forces with nuclear weapons—a very serious development in Soviet eyes. Perhaps worse, the Council agreed in December 1957 to permit American intermediate range ballistic missile (IRBM) bases on the soil of NATO's European members.

The Soviets now stepped up threats of retaliation. ICBM's would not be needed against Turkey, wrote Premier Bulganin, since "simpler rockets" would do. And then the Soviets played the peace theme. TASS announced a unilateral reduction in the Soviet armed forces. Some Russian troops were withdrawn from Germany and Hungary. The Supreme Soviet passed a resolution on December 21, 1957, proposing a suspension of nuclear tests and other pacific gestures. (The Soviets later scored a propaganda coup by voluntarily suspending their testing of all hydrogen and atomic weapons on March 31, 1958. They just had finished a series of tests, while the United States was about to start.)

In another ploy to block NATO's increased fire power, Khrushchev held up the vision of a neutral belt of countries stretching from Scandinavia (including NATO members Norway and Denmark) through West Germany, Austria, and Eastern Europe to the Balkans. The Soviet leader indicated a neutralized Germany would be one solution to the German problem. Khrushchev's scheme in turn was tied in with Polish

Foreign Minister Rapacki's plan presented to the UN in October 1957, for a nuclear-free Central Europe. Rapacki had proposed that no nuclear weapons be stockpiled, based, or manufactured in East Germany or West Germany, Poland, or Czechoslovakia. Later, all conventional arms and troops could be withdrawn from the area. The West was hardly enthusiastic about the Rapacki Plan. NATO was asked to give up its superiority in nuclear weapons, leaving West Germany at the mercy of superior Soviet and East European conventional forces.

The Second Berlin Crisis   So far Khrushchev had been fighting a rearguard action against NATO with little success. Now he launched a major offensive to change the *status quo* in Europe. Predictably, the target was West Berlin—the vulnerable outpost of freedom in the Soviet sphere of influence.[4] For over a decade, West Berlin had been a constant irritant for the Soviets and the East German regime. The Western sector of Berlin was a prosperous showcase and almost the only feasible escape route left for disenchanted East Germans. If Khrushchev could force the Allies out of West Berlin, he would show the socialist camp that "peaceful coexistence" could win bloodless victories for communism. Second, neutralist trends in Western Europe would be encouraged—hampering NATO's nuclear rearmament. Finally, the whole world would see a dramatic demonstration of Soviet power.

Khrushchev opened the campaign in November 1958; West Berlin, he asserted, should become a free and demilitarized city. The USSR would hand over the control of access routes into the Western sector to the East German regime at the end of six months (May 27, 1959)—regardless of what the Allies did. Khrushchev further escalated tensions in February 1959, threatening to sign a separate peace treaty with East Germany. (Russia and the West still had not written a definitive peace settlement with Germany as a whole.)

All during these tense months, the now familiar Soviet theme of nuclear blackmail was played as a constant refrain. On December 19, 1958, the Soviet commander in East Germany warned that the United States would face "annihilating defeat" if it used force to hold West Berlin. Communists would use tanks and "more powerful weapons" if the West attempted to keep the access routes open. In January 1959, Soviet Minister of Defense Marshal Malinovsky claimed that the USSR had begun to manufacture ICBM's in quantity. On June 23, 1959, Khrushchev

---

[4] Hans Speier, *Divided Berlin* (New York: Frederick A. Praeger, Inc., 1961), provides an excellent analysis of the continuing Berlin crisis from 1958 through the summer of 1961. A broader treatment of this period is Arnold L. Horelick and Myron Rush, *Strategic Power and Soviet Foreign Policy* (Chicago: University of Chicago Press, 1966).

made the point clear in an interview with Averell Harriman: "Your generals talk of maintaining your position in Berlin with force. That is bluff. If you send in tanks, they will burn and make no mistake about it. If you want war, you can have it, and remember it will be your war. Our rockets will fly automatically . . ."[5]

The Allies read Khrushchev's campaign as an ultimatum to abandon West Berlin to "socialism"; a "free city" could not long exist deprived of Western support. In addition, the Allies would have to recognize the East German regime, a slap in the face for Chancellor Adenauer's West German government. The United States, Britain and France refused to be forced out. They had a legal right to be there, and they had been committed since 1954 to go to war if West Berlin were attacked.

Yet the three powers were not particularly eager to fight. Khrushchev's ultimatum thus generated continuous diplomatic exchange over the next several months, including an unproductive foreign minister's conference in Geneva during the summer of 1959. The Western states were unwilling to budge in principle, and they hoped to convince the Soviets of this. (Khrushchev in turn hoped to heighten the "contradictions" among the capitalists by means of the Berlin issue.) The West seemed temporarily successful: Soviet spokesmen set the time limit for handing over East Berlin to the East German regime further and further into the future.

Khrushchev was not going to get West Berlin in 1959. But his offensive was not a complete failure. The West had been forced on the defensive. It had agreed to negotiate on Berlin and the German question; the Soviets had another chance to discuss their plan for a nuclear-free Central Europe. Khrushchev also wangled a presidential invitation to visit the United States—a considerable boost for his prestige. In return, Eisenhower would visit Russia.

Khrushchev's triumphal transcontinental tour of America in September 1959, ran the gamut: from the UN, where he introduced a grandiose proposal for universal disarmament, to a Coon Rapids, Iowa corn farm and a glance at the can-can on a Hollywood sound stage. After talking with Eisenhower at Camp David, the presidential hideaway, the Soviet leader seemed convinced that the United States was softening up. He promised to withdraw the "ultimatum" on Berlin. In return, Eisenhower agreed to a summit conference in Paris during spring 1960. (The Soviets had pressed for a summit meeting since December 1957.) Khrushchev appeared hopeful that this conference might finally give him the former German capital.

To emphasize and promote the new relaxation of tensions, Khrushchev

[5] Harriman, "My Alarming Interview with Khrushchev," *Life,* XLVII, No. 2 (July 13, 1959), 33.

talked as if the Cold War had ended at Camp David. On January 14, 1960, he noted the disappearance of the "bankrupt" positions-of-strength policy, brinkmanship, containment and deterrence. (The Soviets associated these policies with Secretary of State John Foster Dulles, who had died in May 1959.) However, Khrushchev gave no indication that the Soviets would soften their own demands on West Berlin.

The Allied position on Germany began to stiffen as May 1960, the date for the summit, drew near. Khrushchev had journeyed to France in March to soften up de Gaulle, playing constantly on the danger of revived German militarism. This was usually a good theme to worry the French, but de Gaulle would not budge. He insisted on absolute respect for the *status quo* in Berlin. West Germany's Adenauer was not to be an official conference participant, but he also was against any change in Berlin's situation. The new American Secretary of State Herter then made it clear that Khrushchev would get no major concessions. The West was interested in talking about disarmament, a nuclear test ban, and a general lessening of East-West tension—but not the surrender of West Berlin.

The U-2 Affair Now came the thunderbolt. The Soviets downed an American U-2 high altitude photo-reconnaissance aircraft inside the USSR at 5:36 A.M. Moscow time on May 1.[6] Washington, at first knowing only that the U-2 probably was down, announced that one of its "weather" planes was missing. Khrushchev then revealed the details at sessions of the Supreme Soviet on May 5 and 7: the plane was brought to earth 1200 miles inside Russia and the Soviets had captured the pilot complete with assorted spy gear. The United States, he charged, was trying to torpedo the summit. But Khrushchev gave Eisenhower an out; he was prepared to grant that the President had no knowledge of the U-2—a spy project of the American "militarists."

On May 9, Secretary of State Herter admitted that the President had authorized such flights, and claimed that the United States had a responsibility to make the reconnaissance runs to prevent a surprise attack on the Free World. News reporters—and probably the Russians—assumed from Herter's statement that the flights would continue. Two days later, President Eisenhower, like a good commander, accepted responsibility. He and the whole administration probably should have kept silent—an unwritten rule of spying.

Meanwhile, Khrushchev refused to participate in the coming summit conference unless the United States would denounce the U-2 flights,

---

[6] For the dramatic story, see David Wise and Thomas B. Ross, *The U-2 Affair* (New York: Random House, Inc., 1960).

promise never to repeat them, and punish the responsible parties. It was too late, of course, for this. The President couldn't punish himself, although he did agree to stop the flights—hardly a concession at this juncture.

Khrushchev nevertheless went to the Paris summit. However, the conference aborted after one tense confrontation between Khrushchev and Eisenhower on May 16. As a result, the Soviet Premier requested that the President's visit to Russia be postponed. The Soviet people no longer could show him the "proper cordiality."

Why did Khrushchev even journey to Paris? More basically, why did he decide to provoke an international crisis over the U-2? Khrushchev certainly was not surprised at the overflights, which the United States admitted had been going on for four years. (He may have been surprised that the Soviet armed forces finally had shot down a U-2.)

Obviously, Khrushchev had picked the U-2 incident to heighten tension. But for what end? Here we can only speculate. The Soviet leader must have known that his chances for success on West Berlin at the summit were fading. Yet there might be certain pay-offs for going to Paris. If he could extract an abject apology from the President of the United States for "spying," this would demonstrate Russia's power. In addition, Eisenhower might be put on the defensive at the conference because of the U-2 fiasco. Some concessions might be gained from the West.[7] But once the President assumed full responsibility, Khrushchev virtually was forced to rant and rave against the United States and Eisenhower. The Soviet ruler no longer could claim before the communist world (and the Soviet Presidium) that Eisenhower was a man of peace. Khrushchev had to be just as "tough" as the American President.[8]

Yet the Soviets became relatively conciliatory during the rest of 1960. Khrushchev did not seem prepared to push his claims against the West while international tension remained high. In addition, he probably was waiting to see whether the new American President would represent that section of the "Western bourgeoisie" favoring peaceful coexistence.

Perhaps there was a deeper reason for Soviet caution. Khrushchev may have feared that the U-2 and other American intelligence sources had uncovered a closely guarded secret: the USSR did not have quite the ICBM force Khrushchev had claimed. Arnold Horelick and Myron Rush have the intriguing theory that Khrushchev in fact had been engaged

---

[7] The Kennedy Administration reportedly found that Eisenhower had been ready to make concessions at Paris. Arthur M. Schlesinger, Jr., *A Thousand Days* (Cambridge, Mass.: Houghton Mifflin Company), p. 348.

[8] Conquest believes the U-2 affair produced a definite, though perhaps not major, crisis in the Presidium. *Power and Policy in the USSR*, pp. 390-91.

in a grand and elaborate deception since 1957 to convince the West of Soviet strategic superiority.[9]

Khrushchev had been relatively successful, irrespective of whether his claims represented a carefully conceived plan or bombast—or both.[10] Agonizing cries arose in the United States during the late 1950's about the "missile gap," demonstrating that many in and out of the government were truly worried about Soviet claims. West Europeans also seemed to believe that Russia had surged ahead in missile strength. The USSR was commonly thought to have around 200 ICBM's. The United States Department of Defense finally set the record straight in 1964: The Soviets had deployed only a "handful" of ICBM's as late as 1961.[11]

The Vienna Conference   Khrushchev's opportunity to take the measure of newly elected President Kennedy came at Vienna in June 1961. He caught the President somewhat off balance. Kennedy's first major experiment in East-West politics had been the Bay of Pigs disaster —the attempted invasion of Castro's island on April 17 by CIA trained and sponsored Cuban refugees. American interests also had suffered a setback in Laos. Khrushchev apparently thought the time ripe to renew the pressure. At the second day of the informal Vienna meeting, the Soviet leader trotted out the old demands to make West Berlin a free city and to write a peace treaty with Germany—the deadline now was the end of 1961.

Kennedy left Vienna a sober man. He had been shocked at Khrushchev's blunt insistence on how the game of world politics should be played.[12] The Soviet leader wanted the United States to keep hands off "wars of national liberation"—to accept revolutionary change as the *normal* order of things. Change indeed was the *status quo*, not "peace" or "stability." Kennedy agreed that change was inevitable. But this change had to be peaceful—not led by communist minorities which might upset the world balance of power and affect the vital interests of the USSR or the United States. Khrushchev, however, refused to accept the blame for the expansion of communism in other countries; he was so busy at

---

[9] See Horelick and Rush, *Strategic Power and Soviet Foreign Policy*, particularly Part Two.

[10] Another factor muddied the water: traditional Soviet secrecy always made it difficult to arrive at accurate intelligence estimates.

[11] The Soviets have given one relatively precise figure for their ICBM strength during this period—but the reference is ambiguous. Khrushchev revealed in a speech on January 19, 1963, after the Cuban missile crisis that the United States was still covered by "80, probably 120" missiles—presumably ICBM's—after the Soviet missiles were withdrawn from Cuba. See V. D. Sokolovski, ed. *Soviet Military Strategy*, eds., H. Dinerstein, L. Gouré, and T. Wolfe (Santa Monica, Calif.: RAND, 1963), p. 24.

[12] For this remarkable confrontation, see Schlesinger, *A Thousand Days*, pp. 358-74.

home that he did not even know the leaders of foreign communist parties.

Yet Kennedy did not give way before the verbal onslaught. In March 1961, he had accelerated the Eisenhower-initiated program to install 800 solid-fuel Minuteman ICBM's. After the Vienna meeting, the President requested three and one-half billion dollars from Congress to increase the American capability to fight conventional (non-nuclear) conflicts. Kennedy had in mind the need to meet communist-sponsored national liberation wars in all areas of the globe.[13] But he singled out Berlin: "I hear it said that West Berlin is untenable. So was Bastogne. So, in fact, was Stalingrad. Any dangerous spot is tenable if brave men will make it so. We do not want to fight—but we have fought before."

Meanwhile, Khrushchev's fulminations over Berlin had scared the East Germans. They were afraid the gates to freedom might be closed forever if West Berlin became a "free city." The number of refugees pouring into West Berlin shot up dramatically in July, reaching more than one thousand a day. On the night of August 12, construction crews, protected by Soviet and East German troops, began the infamous Berlin Wall to seal off the eastern sector of the city. The justification for the Wall was ridiculous: Western agents supposedly were entering East Berlin and thereby threatening the security of the socialist states. The Western powers, apparently taken by surprise, protested this strictly illegal closing of the border. Force was needed, however, to remove the wall, and few in the West seemed eager to use force.

With the Wall, Khrushchev had eliminated the continuing drain on East Germany's vital manpower. He also had demonstrated Soviet power to change the *status quo*. But the larger German problems remained: West Berlin was still free, and Western Germany was rearmed and in the Allied camp. And the ultimate Soviet goal still existed: the elimination of the American presence in Europe, specifically, the destruction of NATO.

Khrushchev now seems to have made a critical decision: he would not try to achieve Russia's major goals in Europe until the USSR could pull off a dramatic piece of "one-upmanship" truly altering the world balance of power. He had tried to snuff out independent West Berlin since 1958. He thought—or at least gave the impression—that the USSR had the

---

[13] Part of the Administration's concern over the need to prepare for communist inspired "counter insurgencies" was due to Khrushchev's famous speech of January 6, 1961, dealing with future war. Washington thought Khrushchev was promising increased Soviet support of "national liberation wars." Actually the Soviet leader was developing his position that nuclear war was the only possible outcome if the superpowers both got overly involved in a local conflict. Therefore, the two powers should avoid such direct confrontations. The Chinese, by the way, correctly understood Khrushchev's cautious position.

power to do so. But his tactics failed. Khrushchev could not afford to fail again. His leadership of communists everywhere would be seriously compromised.

Khrushchev had other foreign policy problems which might be eased if the offensive against the West could get rolling again. There was trouble in the "Peace Zone." Contrary to his prediction at the Twentieth Party Congress in 1956, the underdeveloped and anti-colonial world had not flocked to join the camp of socialism in a grand alliance against the West. More dangerous for the USSR was the growing split *within* the socialist camp. The People's Republic of China was threatening Soviet leadership of the communist bloc. Khrushchev's troubles with Poland and Hungary would seem minor headaches if the most populous nation on earth successfully defied the USSR.

PROBLEMS IN THE PEACE ZONE

Soviet attempts to penetrate the underdeveloped area from 1957-1962 concentrated on the Middle East, Sub-Saharan Africa, and Latin America.

The Middle East   The Middle East posed a special problem for Soviet foreign policy: Soviet national security was involved because of the proximity of this area to Southern Russia. Caution was therefore required lest Soviet moves call forth even greater American intervention in the Middle East. The United States already had given evidence of its "scheme" to dominate the area. The Eisenhower Doctrine introduced in January 1957 had promised American aid to any Middle Eastern government threatened by "communism." As a result, the Soviets would support local anti-Western regimes to encourage "neutralism," but they would stop short of unconditional aid to local leftists or communists. This might be difficult. The winds of revolution were blowing hot in the Middle East. Governments fell in rapid succession during the 1950's. The chaotic situation seemed ideal for local communist parties, particularly in Syria (1954-1958), and Iraq (1958-1960).

The Soviets had made a heavy investment in military and economic aid to Syria beginning in 1955. The local regime was led by a wealthy landowner, backed by pro-Soviet Army officers and the largest communist party in the Middle East. The United States and Turkey feared Syria soon would become a Soviet satellite.

Eisenhower warned the Syrians on September 7, 1957, that they were close to being dominated by pro-communist elements. American arms were sent to Jordan, Lebanon, and Iraq. In turn, the Soviets charged the United States, Britain, and Turkey with launching a "provocative campaign" against the Syrians. Premier Bulganin threatened Turkey with retaliation if she committed "aggression" against Syria. (The Soviets saw evidence that American soldiers were with Turkish troops along Syria's border.)

The crisis abated when Khrushchev attended a Turkish Embassy reception in Moscow on October 29 as "a gesture toward peace." Perhaps he had decided the United States was not ready to intervene directly in Syria. It would seem more logical that the Soviets never really considered war probable, and merely had been demonstrating their support of Arab independence.

The USSR indicated the specific limits to its support of Syrian leftists a few months later. Syrian nationalists overthrew the pro-Soviet regime and merged their country with Egypt in the United Arab Republic. Moscow stoically accepted the merger. Continued Soviet support of the Syrian pro-communist government probably would have brought greater American intervention and driven the other Middle Eastern states closer to the West. It was less risky to place Soviet bets on Nasser's Egypt, a vacillating and unstable ally in Leninist terms but still strongly neutralist.

To show that there were no hard feelings over the Syrian coup, the Soviets gave Egypt a one hundred million dollar loan in October 1958 to start construction of the mammoth Aswan Dam.[14] They also accepted Nasser's crackdown on Syrian and Egyptian communists, although Khrushchev felt obligated to remind the United Arab Republic in January 1959 that the "struggle" against local communists was a "reactionary affair." Egyptian party members were charged with acting counter to the national interests of the Arab peoples. Khrushchev claimed, however, that there were no more steadfast fighters against colonialism.

Meanwhile, a military coup d'état toppled the pro-Western Iraqi regime on July 14, 1958. The United States suspected that the revolution was communist-led. Worried that the leftist contagion might spread, Washington landed Marines at Beirut, Lebanon and London sent airborne troops to Jordan to support the shaky pro-Western governments of these two countries.[15]

[14] The Soviets were destined to learn how expensive their friendship with Nasser would be, and also about the "quicksand effect" of large-scale aid projects—the need for additional capital to finish the work or risk losing the initial goodwill. Against the recommendation of the Soviet Council of Ministers, Khrushchev unilaterally granted Nasser an additional $227 million loan in May 1964 to finish the Aswan Dam. Marshall L. Goldman, "Communist Foreign Aid: Successes and Shortcomings," *Current History,* August, 1966, p. 84. This precipitous action supposedly was one of the reasons for Khrushchev's ouster in October 1964. *The Washington Post,* October 22, 1964.

[15] Manfred Halperin states that part of the reason for the American landing was the belief that it might be necessary to prepare for intervention against a Soviet-controlled communist-neutralist coalition in Baghdad. See Halperin's article, "The Middle East and North Africa," *Communism and Revolution,* ed. by Black and Thornton, p. 84.

Moscow, however, seemed equally surprised at the coup d'état in Iraq where the local communist party appeared to have no control over the course of the revolution. The USSR also appeared nonplussed over the instant reaction of the West. But the predictable Soviet propaganda soon emerged: Britain and the United States were accused of "gross intervention" in the domestic affairs of the Arab countries. The windows of the American Embassy in Moscow were smashed and the walls smeared with ink. Now came the diplomatic onslaught. Khrushchev called for a summit meeting to terminate the military conflict, and then requested a special session of the UN General Assembly.

In the special session, a Soviet-sponsored resolution was shelved in favor of a more moderate proposal of the Arab states. The crisis soon subsided. But Moscow had profited in several respects. Iraq's new military rulers pulled their country out of the Western-organized Baghdad Pact, and utilized local communists as a prop for the regime. As a result, Soviet economic and military aid began flowing into Iraq. By the spring of 1961, however, the USSR was publicly complaining about the persecution of local communists by the Iraqi government. Yet Soviet aid continued. The USSR wanted to keep its influence, however nebulous, on the Iraqi regime.

Sub-Saharan Africa   Africa south of the Sahara posed different problems for Soviet foreign policy. The Soviets never had been involved in this region long dominated by the West.[16] But as the Western powers began to move out of Black Africa after World War II—or as they were moved out—a huge power vacuum appeared. Opportunities for Soviet penetration quickly arose as leaders of new African states looked for non-Western and non-capitalist economic and military aid.

At first, Soviet action was restricted by the Stalinist legacy of distrust for "national bourgeois" leaders. (Ghana's Nkrumah was so labeled.) In addition, Moscow showed little interest in Africa as an area. All this changed in the later 1950's. Soviet scholars began to look seriously at Africa's potential for revolution. A Soviet Society of Friendship with the Peoples of Africa, and other fraternal organizations, blossomed. In 1959, the University of Friendship of Peoples was founded in Moscow for students from the underdeveloped areas, including Africa.[17] (This university, dubbed "Apartheid U." by African students, soon ran into trouble as Africans objected to excessive indoctrination and racial prejudice.)

[16] Tsarist Russia on the other hand had flirted for many years with attempts to gain influence in East Africa, particularly Ethiopia. See Sergius Jakobson, "Russia and Africa," *Russian Foreign Policy*, ed. by Lederer.

[17] The school later was renamed Lumumba University after the murdered Congolese Premier.

The USSR and Eastern Europe also set aside December 1 of each year as "Quit Africa Day."

Soviet interest at first centered on Guinea. Moscow rushed to the aid of President Sekou Touré when he led his West African country out of the French Community in 1958. Over 1,000 Russian and East European advisors and technicians launched impressive aid projects. The Soviets thought Guinea could provide an African showcase of communist generosity. They may have hoped to found the first Russian dominated bridgehead on the African continent. Touré's ruling party, however, was not ready for the latter role. In 1961, Touré requested that the Soviet ambassador be recalled. He apparently had attempted to force communist representatives on Guinea's government. Anti-Western and leftist governments in Africa were not thereby ready for communism, or not necessarily even steadfast friends of Moscow.

Perhaps a greater damper on Soviet plans for Africa was the outcome of the Congo crisis in the early 1960's. Belgium had granted the almost totally unprepared Congolese their independence in June 1960. Premier Patrice Lumumba immediately requested UN troops to help maintain order—really to help put down the secessionist province of Katanga. When the UN failed to support the latter goal, Lumumba threatened to call in Soviet forces. The Soviets at once offered "volunteers" to demonstrate their support of Congolese "patriots" working for the "complete independence" (meaning the elimination of all Western influence) and unity of their country. Moscow hoped events in the Congo would mobilize opinion in the rest of Africa against the West.

Soviet troops never were sent, and probably never had been seriously offered. But the USSR and Czechoslovakia began airlifting military supplies to Lumumba's government in August. Then came one of the unpredictable turns typical of African politics. Joseph Kasavuba, the Congo President, dismissed his demagogic Premier, and kicked Soviet and Czech embassy staffs out of the country. (Moscow thought Kasavuba "in the hire of American imperialists.") The other independent African states moreover failed to support Lumumba; in general, they backed the UN operation and resented Soviet interference in what Africans considered a basically African affair.

As a result of having his fingers burnt in Guinea and the Congo, Khrushchev adopted a more cautious approach to Africa south of the Sahara. The Soviets realized that African internal politics were too volatile and chaotic to justify full-scale support of any particular leader or clique. The previous optimism about the rapid and automatic drift of new African states into the Peace Zone was gone. Emphasis was now placed on supporting independent African governments with military and economic aid if only to weaken Western influence in Africa. (In

Cameroon, for example, the Soviets promised the reigning "national bourgeois" leaders that they would not support local communists engaged in revolutionary activity.) The immediate concern was to win friends for the Soviet Union, irrespective of the ideological complexion of African governments.[18]

Latin America   The communist movement in Latin America began soon after the Bolshevik Revolution, and communist parties in the Comintern from that area faithfully followed the twists and turns of Soviet foreign policy. Yet the USSR refrained from direct involvement in Latin America. It considered this continent, and especially the Caribbean, to be a stronghold of the United States under the "reactionary cosmopolitan doctrine of Pan-Americanism." The Soviets broke their rule on only one occasion before Cuba—Guatemala in 1954.

Colonel Jacobo Arbenz, the leftist president of Guatemala, had slipped increasingly under the control of the small but tightly organized local communist party. Being good communists, the Guatemalans carefully followed Moscow's general strategic line, and there is some evidence that the Soviets advised the Guatemalan party at various stages in its planned takeover.[19] Moscow was looking for a communist showcase in Latin America, and valued any government disrupting hemispheric unity.

A Swedish boat filled with Czech arms arrived in Guatemala in May 1954. The arms apparently were for a people's militia to oppose the regular army—the last major force frustrating the introduction of a communist regime. Yet the Arbenz regime and its communist supporters collapsed like a house of cards when United States-backed Colonel Carlos Castillo Armas led a 200-man invasion force into Guatemala from Honduras in June 1954. The army had refused to back Arbenz, and the communists found that they lacked mass support for a showdown.

The Soviets must have had their appetites whetted by the near success of their Guatemalan comrades. But Armas' victory proved, according to Moscow, that Latin America was still basically a United States domain. Imagine Soviet surprise, therefore, at the appearance of Castro's Cuba ninety miles off the coast of Florida. Fidel Castro, starting with 82 guerrillas in November 1956, had come to power in Cuba by January 1959. Although Castro did not proclaim his own communist faith until 1961, his closest followers long had been convinced Marxist-Leninists. Within a few months, the local communist party began to play the key role in

[18] For an excellent summary of Soviet policy in Africa up to 1963, see Alexander Dallin, "Political Activity," *Africa and the Communist World* (Stanford, Calif.: Stanford University Press, 1963), ed. by Zbigniew Brzezinski.

[19] For the evidence of Soviet influence on the Guatemalan communists, see Ronald M. Schneider, *Communism in Guatemala, 1944-1954* (New York: Frederick A. Praeger, Inc., 1959), especially Chap. 11.

the regime. The charismatic Castro, however, retained ultimate power.

Washington fumed, but limited itself to economic sanctions. Russia hesitantly stepped in, offering to buy 500,000 tons of sugar at the end of 1959, and five million tons in February 1960. Arms were extended in July 1960.

American-trained Cuban exiles then launched the poorly planned invasion of Cuba—the "Bay of Pigs" fiasco—in April 1961. Moscow must have been even more surprised at the caution and restraint of United States foreign policy. It seemed as if Washington was losing its grip. World communism at last had a foothold in Latin America, in a country no more than a stone's throw from the citadel of imperialism.

But Cuba was the one bright spot on the horizon. On other continents, as we have seen, Khrushchev's grand design for hitting the West through its underdeveloped back door was not doing so well. And the Soviet leader now faced even greater difficulties *within* the communist world.

THE RED GIANTS CLASH

We must now trace briefly the growing dispute between the giants of the communist orbit—Russia, the most powerful socialist state, and China, the most populous. China would challenge Soviet leadership of the Peace Zone, creating profound problems for Soviet foreign policy.

Some conflict between the two states was inevitable as long as each government gave first priority to its national interests. These interests differed and in certain areas clashed, especially along the lengthy Sino-Soviet border. As indicated earlier, this built-in source of disagreement was enflamed by traditional Chinese expansionism and xenophobia.[20] Moreover, Mao Tse-tung and his comrades owed the Soviets little; the Chinese communists had come to power under their own steam—and against Stalin's advice. Peking could afford to be independent from the first.

Normal sources of conflict between any two governments of these nations were compounded because the governments now in power were communist. The Chinese (and earlier Tito) interpreted "proletarian internationalism" to mean that the USSR should give the maximum aid with minimum interference to a fraternal "socialist" regime. Another question concerned the proper strategy and tactics for the world communist movement, particularly whether peaceful coexistence, as the Soviets defined it, would work. Differing Soviet and Chinese approaches to this question reflected differing stages in their economic and social develop-

[20] See p. 269.

ment, the differing character of their revolutions, and disparities in their national power. In particular, the Soviets now possessed and understood nuclear weapons; the Chinese apparently did not.[21] In short, ideological questions broadened and deepened a normal inter-state conflict. The result was bitterness and hatred, especially on the part of the Chinese.

Today Soviets and Chinese are eager to tell their side of the story. Yet for years the existence and depth of the dispute were among the best kept secrets of the twentieth century. Secretary of State Herter, for example, wondered in April 1960 whether the differences between Peking and Moscow were real or significant. We now know that the schism was well-developed in 1959.

The Periods in the Dispute   The growth of the dispute can be divided into five periods.[22] The first stage occurred in the 1956-1957 period. Secret and probably moderate discussions took place between the top leaders of the two parties. The Chinese objected to Khrushchev's denunciation of Stalin at the Twentieth Party Congress in February 1956, to his declared policy of "peaceful coexistence" which Peking thought indicated the desire of the Soviets for a détente with the United States, and to his promotion of peaceful and parliamentary tactics as a means of achieving power for non-ruling communist parties. Khrushchev's courting of bourgeois-nationalist India with Soviet economic aid was particularly galling to the Chinese. Peking reasoned this decreased her share of Soviet aid, and suspected that the Soviets were building up India as a counterforce to China.[23] Irrespective of the issues, the Chinese were upset that such basic policy changes had been decided without consulting Mao Tse-tung. Now that Stalin was dead, Mao considered himself the ranking philosopher-king of the communist orbit.

In October 1957, Khrushchev made one important concession; he

---

[21] In an NBC interview on July 11, 1967, retired Premier Khrushchev quoted Mao Tse-tung as stating in a 1959 meeting in Peking: "Comrade Khrushchev, you have only to provoke the Americans to military action and I will give you as many people as you wish—100 divisions, 200 divisions, 1,000." Khrushchev explained to Mao "that with contemporary techniques his divisions meant nothing because one or two rockets would be enough to turn all the divisions into dust. He [Mao] disagreed, obviously regarding me as a coward."

[22] I use the categorization developed by Robert A. Scalapino in "The Sino-Soviet Conflict in Perspective," *The Annals of the American Academy of Political and Social Science*, CCCLI (1964), 1-14.

[23] The Russians had extended some two billion dollars of "aid" to Peking by April 1956. However, only *one-fifth* of this was loaned on normal credit terms. The bulk had to be paid for with deliveries of Chinese goods (foodstuffs and raw materials) to the USSR or with hard, foreign currency. These strict conditions were in stark contrast to the ten-year low-interest loans Moscow commonly extended to bourgeois-nationalist leaders of the developing countries.

promised to give China a sample atomic bomb and technical data on its manufacture. Nevertheless, the second stage of the dispute began in November of that year when a debate broke out at the Moscow conference of the twelve ruling communist parties. The dispute still was formally secret, but now all other ruling parties were privy to the developing split.

During the second period, the Chinese pressed Khrushchev to adopt a more radical and risky foreign policy. As indicated above, the Chinese did not share the Soviet fear of nuclear war. Moreover, Khrushchev himself claimed Soviet nuclear and missile superiority. The Chinese, probably uninformed of real Soviet military strength, could not understand Soviet timidity. They especially resented Khrushchev's lukewarm support of their attempt to force the Nationalist Chinese from the offshore islands of Quemoy and Matsu in the fall of 1958.[24] Mao, in short, thought that communist states should be stirring things up all over the world. Anything less than vigorous revolutionary struggle only encouraged the imperialists and increased the dangers of war. Since the communist bloc was militarily superior to the West in Mao's thinking, there was no risk of general war. The Soviet and Chinese leaders held fundamentally different views of proper communist strategy for a nuclear age.

Meanwhile, the Soviets were distressed at what they considered a disastrous turn in Chinese domestic policy: the introduction of the "great leap forward"; backyard steel furnaces; and, most of all, the communes—a radical scheme to reorganize China's major resource, her manpower, into huge productive units to speed industrial and agricultural growth. The Soviets were particularly upset when Peking intimated that Mao had solved the problem of building communism in developing countries with the commune scheme, and might even bring China to the communist stage before the USSR. The commune theory constituted a fundamental challenge to Soviet doctrinal leadership of the revolution in the developing areas.

By 1960, Khrushchev apparently had given up hope of reasoning with the Chinese. Pressure would have to be used to bring them to heel. In June 1959, he had withdrawn his earlier promise to help Peking build an atomic capability. This sanction did not work; the Chinese initiated incidents on the Sino-Indian border. And another, more ominous challenge to peaceful coexistence was developing; although details are few, there reportedly was new tension along the Sino-Soviet border with occasional clashes of frontier guards. In June 1960, Khrushchev therefore

[24] See John R. Thomas, "The Limits of Alliance: The Quemoy Crisis of 1958," *Sino-Soviet Military Relations* (New York: Frederick A. Praeger, Inc., 1966), ed. by Raymond L. Garthoff, pp. 114-49.

took a drastic step: all Soviet economic aid to China was cut off; trade sharply reduced; and all Soviet technical experts withdrawn. Khrushchev also bitterly criticized Mao at a closed communist meeting in Bucharest that month; like Stalin, Mao was oblivious to anything but his own interests and spun theories detached from reality.

Mao and the Chinese would not yield in spite of the great economic and military setback created by the suspension of aid. The point of no return had been reached. The third stage of the dispute began in October 1961 at the Twenty-second Party Congress in Moscow. Khrushchev publicly attacked Albania, China's sole European ally, in this case the stand-in for Peking. The non-communist world had been given its first formal glimpse of the great "secret" of the socialist camp. The Chinese replied with attacks on Yugoslavia—the stand-in for the USSR.

Communist parties everywhere were now pressured to stand on the issues and ally with one party or the other. No communist could be neutral because the truths of his earthly religion were at stake. And Moscow paid dearly to get support for its position. The Soviet Presidium granted previously pro-Soviet parties greater autonomy to keep their allegiance. Other socialist states—North Vietnam, North Korea, Indonesia, and Cuba—could afford neutrality in respect to Moscow and Peking. Most parties, ruling and non-ruling, developed pro-Soviet and pro-Chinese wings regardless of formal allegiance.

Rumania was perhaps the most flagrant example of "neutrality" appearing in this period. Sharing a common border with Russia, Rumania balked at Khrushchev's plan to integrate the East European economies through the Council for Mutual Economic Assistance (COMECON).[25] In Moscow's view, it made sense to expand the industrialized states (the USSR, Czechoslovakia, and East Germany) while encouraging the raw material and food producers (Rumania, Bulgaria, and to a certain extent Poland and Hungary) to specialize in their products. For reasons of national interest, Rumania wanted to become fully industrialized. After 1963, Rumania steered an increasingly independent course in foreign economic and political questions while retaining a conservative domestic program.

The fourth stage of the dispute began in late 1962 when "some people" or "some parties" replaced the surrogates in open polemics. Each state was in the midst of an international crisis: the Soviets had shipped missiles to Cuba; the Chinese, against Soviet advice, had attacked India on October 20.

The fifth and final stage of the dispute's growth dates from the public

---

[25] Stalin organized COMECON in January 1948 as his reply to the Marshall Plan. Headquartered in Moscow, the organization made little effort towards centralized planning for the region until Khrushchev's initiative in the early 1960's.

letter of June 14, 1963, from Peking to Moscow.[26] In this lengthy, sarcastic document, the Chinese Central Committee threw down the ideological gauntlet on 25 separate points covering all aspects of communist international and domestic policy. Peking finally denounced Khrushchev and the Soviets by name, and accused them in effect of treason to the cause of Marxism-Leninism. In domestic affairs, the Soviets were "helping to restore capitalism." In international relations among communists, they were charged with "great-power chauvinism, sectarianism, and splittism," and with being the leaders of "revisionism." Peking challenged all communists "to distinguish between truth and falsehood with respect to the differences that have arisen in the international communist movement." What Mao wanted was clear—the overthrow of Khrushchev and his faction. (Khrushchev may have supported a Chinese communist faction which attempted to depose Mao in 1959.)

A Moscow meeting in July 1963 between Soviet and Chinese delegations ended in "suspended" discussions. A further nail was driven in the casket lid of unity when the Soviets concluded successful negotiations with the United States on a partial nuclear test ban treaty that same month. These negotiations, incidentally, also took place in Moscow.

Open polemics had been launched. In March 1964, Peking labeled Khrushchev the "greatest revisionist of all time." He retorted one month later that Mao was a Trotskyite, a racist, and a splitter of the international communist movement. Meanwhile, Khrushchev tried to round up support for an international conference of communist parties. Khrushchev hoped the conference would denounce Mao as the main enemy of international communism and would excommunicate the Chinese party.

The Cuban Missile Crisis We must now return to 1962 for the main thread of Soviet relations with the West. Khrushchev was in trouble that year. His problems were numerous and imposing: he feared that the West had learned the true size of his meager ICBM force; he had not expelled the United States from Europe or won major concessions on Berlin and Germany; the developing countries had not become willing servants of Moscow; China was directly challenging Soviet leadership all over the globe. "Offensive" peaceful coexistence, in short, was not working.

All of Khrushchev's foreign policy problems were grist for the mill

[26] For the full text of this fascinating document see *The Sino-Soviet Rift* by William E. Griffith (Cambridge, Mass.: The M.I.T. Press, 1964), pp. 259-88. For the Soviet "Open Letter" of July 14, 1963, replying to the Chinese charges, see the same source, pp. 289-325.

of his internal opposition. Although many in the West assumed that Khrushchev was solidly in control of Russia, this was not the case. His foreign and domestic policies were openly challenged albeit obliquely, by Presidium colleagues. Molotov, roundly defeated in 1957 along with the "anti-party" group, could even send a letter to Central Committee members criticizing the draft of the new 1961 Party Program.

Khrushchev was under great pressure to show that he could be a bold and imaginative leader. He was especially vulnerable to the charge that he had given up the struggle with the imperialist camp. A quick victory over the United States in international politics might fill the bill. And it would help if the quick victory were inexpensive. Khrushchev did not want to sacrifice his long-range domestic plans to improve agriculture and increase consumer goods. He still hoped to prove that it was possible to have butter *and* guns. (His opponents on the Presidium gave priority to the growth of heavy industry and defense needs.) [27]

Sometime in the summer of 1962, Khrushchev found a promising ploy —the emplacement of ballistic missiles in "socialist" Cuba. Castro described it this way some months later:

> They explained to us that in accepting them we would be reinforcing the socialist camp the world over, and because we had received important aid from the socialist camp we estimated that we could not decline. That is why we accepted them. It was not in order to assure our own defense, but first of all to reinforce socialism on the international scale. Such is the truth even if other explanations are furnished elsewhere.[28]

Castro may have accepted the missiles as the best deterrent he could get from the Russians for the defense of his island against an American attack. Until 1962, Khrushchev had talked about the ability of Soviet-based missiles to defend Cuba, but had carefully refrained from a public commitment to do so. He had stated, for example, on July 10, 1960: "Figuratively speaking, if need be, Soviet artillerymen can support the Cuban people with their rocket fire if aggressive forces in the Pentagon dare to start intervention against Cuba." [29]

Let us now examine Khrushchev's motivations in detail. The Soviet leader apparently thought he had found a way to truly alter the world balance of power. The West may have had doubts about his previous

---

27 For Khrushchev's trouble with the internal opposition during this period see Linden, *Khrushchev and the Soviet Leadership, 1957-1964,* Chaps. 6 and 7.

28 Cited in Horelick and Rush, *Strategic Power and Soviet Foreign Policy,* p. 134. As the authors indicate, this account has "the ring of truth" although at another time Castro said he had asked the Soviets for the missiles.

29 Cited in Elie Abel, *The Missile Crisis* (Philadelphia: J. B. Lippincott Co., 1966), p. 15, an excellent, very readable study of the crisis emphasizing the American decision-making process.

claims of strategic superiority. And Khrushchev based much of his claim that the socialist camp was now supreme on the achievements of Soviet rocketry. But once Soviet missiles appeared 90 miles from the continental United States the question would really be "who is encircling whom"?

The some 64 missiles to be emplaced—approximately 48 medium range (1,000 mile) weapons and at least 16 of intermediate range (2,200 mile) —would almost double the number of Soviet missiles then targeted against the United States. For the only other Soviet missiles which could hit the American continent were the estimated 75 ICBM's located in the USSR.[30] It would have been difficult to have found a cheaper or quicker way to affect the military balance in relation to the United States. On the other hand, one forward missile base in a country led by a man whom the Soviets considered somewhat emotional was not going to permanently solve Soviet defense needs. And the Soviet military probably argued this point. Moreover, they had worried about Khrushchev's continual overemphasis on missiles. The military leaders wanted more arms across the board.

Khrushchev, however, could argue that he "knew" Kennedy and the Americans. The missile ploy would make a difference in *political* questions. And this political advantage was probably more important to Khrushchev than any purely military change in the balance. The Soviet leader may have been right in his analysis. President Kennedy commented several months after the missiles had been removed: ". . . this was an effort to materially change the balance of power . . . not that [the Soviets] were intending to fire [the missiles]. . . . But it would have politically changed the balance of power. It would have appeared to, and appearances contribute to reality." [31]

American officials in general felt they could not permit such a blatant threat to the Western hemisphere. If they did, the Monroe Doctrine and the Rio Treaty would appear farcical. A State Department officer said: "To the Latins, Khrushchev would have looked like a winner." [32] But concern was for more than the Americas. Washington feared all nations allied to the United States by treaty would question the readiness of the United States to defend them. Uppermost in the minds of the President and his advisors was the possibility that Khrushchev would try to use his new missile base to resolve the Berlin question. On October 18,

---

[30] Twenty-four launch pads for medium range missiles and 16 for intermediate range missiles were under construction, but it was assumed that at least the medium range pads could be used twice. See Albert and Roberta Wohlstetter, "Controlling the Risks in Cuba," Adelphi Papers No. 17 (London: The Institute for Strategic Studies, 1965), a thorough and convincing analysis of the strategic issues. Equally good are Horelick and Rush, *Strategic Power and Soviet Foreign Policy*, Chaps. 11 and 12.

[31] *Washington Post*, December 18, 1962.

[32] Abel, *The Missile Crisis*, p. 48.

1962, Soviet Foreign Minister Gromyko reassured President Kennedy at the White House that the USSR would do nothing about Berlin until after the American congressional elections on November 6. But after that, said Gromyko, there would have to be some dialogue over Berlin leading to concrete results—a German peace treaty and the "normalization" of Berlin (the creation of a "free city" and the withdrawal of the Western garrisons).

Why did Khrushchev believe that America would accept a Soviet missile base in Cuba? First, the United States had allowed the Bay of Pigs invasion of Cuba to fail in April 1961. Second, it had done nothing about the notorious Berlin Wall constructed in August of that year. Third, Cuba was well on the way to becoming a Soviet armed camp with thousands of Soviet advisors and the United States was tacitly accepting this fact. President Kennedy warned the Soviets that he would act if Cuba became "an offensive military base of significant capacity for the Soviet Union." But Khrushchev's critical assumption seems to have been that Kennedy would not act even if *offensive* missiles were installed. Based on Kennedy's foreign policy style and undoubtedly on their confrontation at Vienna in June 1961, Khrushchev thought he was dealing with an inexperienced and indecisive young man who could be blackmailed and intimidated. He probably told his unconvinced Presidium colleagues that Kennedy would protest to the Soviet ambassador, and Adlai Stevenson, the American representative to the UN, would raise the issue in the Security Council. But in the end the United States would accept the missile base as a *fait accompli*.[33] Khrushchev could not have been more wrong. No American president—Democrat or Republican—could tolerate such blatant Soviet power ninety miles from the United States.

Meanwhile, an important part of Khrushchev's scheme was to get the missiles in place quickly and, if possible, secretly. He knew that they would soon be discovered by high-flying U-2 photo reconnaissance aircraft; indeed, this was part of his plan to impress United States policy makers. But the *fait accompli* still would work if the time between discovery and operational capability could be minimized.

The missiles were secretly shipped in the holds of Soviet freighters, several among the stream of Soviet ships sailing to Cuba that summer. (American intelligence officers later reflected that two of the freighters had exceptionally wide hatches and rode high in the water—much

---

[33] Kennedy faced criticism at home for his Cuban policy. When he spoke at Yale on October 17—the missile crisis was not yet public—a student carried a placard reading: "More courage, less profile." A common charge of Republicans during the congressional campaign that fall was that the President showed cowardice by doing nothing about the Castro regime.

higher than ships with heavy, bulk cargoes.) To aid security precautions, Khrushchev and his diplomatic corps repeatedly assured Kennedy that Soviet aid to Cuba was purely defensive; missiles emplaced were anti-aircraft weapons. Moscow also disclaimed any need to shift its retaliatory weapons to foreign bases—including Cuba. Soviet rockets were so powerful that launching sites were not needed outside the USSR.

Then the secret broke. On October 14, two United States Air Force U-2 pilots brought back detailed photographs of construction work on offensive missile sites. Intelligence experts could hardly believe their eyes. Less than a month before they had advised the President that a Soviet missile base would never be installed in Cuba: the USSR had reason to believe the American government would react violently; and the Russians had not stationed strategic missiles in Eastern Europe. A base in Cuba was even less probable. The United States, in short, also suffered gross misconceptions about its opponent's behavior.

During the next few days, Kennedy and a handful of close advisors wrestled with the secret and what to do about it. All agreed that the missiles had to be removed. Two tactics were seriously considered: a direct air strike to take out the missile sites—inevitably killing Russians; a "defensive quarantine" to stop Russian ships carrying missiles to Cuba. Kennedy chose the latter, a less provocative and less dangerous tactic. This tactic would give Khrushchev time to reflect, and hopefully decide to withdraw the missiles. If the blockade failed, the United States always could escalate to the air strike.

On Monday evening, October 22, President Kennedy finally revealed Khrushchev's gamble to the world: the missiles were "a deliberately provocative and unjustified change in the status quo which cannot be accepted by this country." Kennedy called upon Chairman Khrushchev "to move the world back from the abyss of destruction—by returning to his government's own words that it had no need to station missiles outside its own territory, and withdrawing these weapons from Cuba. . . ." The President announced that the quarantine would be initiated. Should the offensive military preparations continue, he warned, further American action would be justified; he already had directed the Armed Forces to prepare for any eventuality.[34]

Now it was Khrushchev's turn to sweat, and indications are that he and the Presidium spent the next several days doing so. Moscow's first reaction was a government statement transmitted thirteen hours after Kennedy's speech, charging the President with provocative acts that might lead to thermonuclear war, but giving no hint of the Soviet response. In the UN Security Council, Soviet representative Zorin flatly

---

[34] For Kennedy's speech and other documents on the crisis see The "Cuban Crisis" of 1962 (Boston: Houghton Mifflin Company, 1963), ed. by David L. Larson.

denied that the USSR had installed "offensive armaments" in Cuba. Meanwhile, fresh American photos revealed work was continuing on the missile sites.

On Wednesday afternoon, October 24, Khrushchev called William Knox, a visiting American businessman, to the Kremlin for a surprise audience. Clearly exhausted, Khrushchev admitted to Knox that the Soviet Union had missiles in Cuba. And he wanted the President and the American people to know that Soviet submarines would sink American ships if the United States Navy tried to stop Soviet vessels. That same afternoon, however, a dozen of the 25 Soviet ships on the way to Cuba appeared to be changing course or stopping on the high seas.

On Thursday, word came from diplomatic circles that the Russians were "damn scared" and needed a way out without humiliation. A strange overture came on Friday from Alexander Fomin, a Soviet embassy officer believed to be the head of Soviet intelligence in the United States, through John Scali, diplomatic correspondent for the American Broadcasting Company. Would the United States settle the crisis on these terms: (1) the missiles would be returned to the USSR under UN supervision; (2) Castro would pledge to accept no offensive weapons in the future; (3) the United States would pledge not to invade Cuba? The White House said it saw possibilities in Fomin's terms.

Khrushchev now sent Kennedy a long letter through the American Embassy in Moscow. The letter, not yet published, was stamped with Khrushchev's personal, argumentative style and filled with *non-sequiturs* and imprecision. Yet he was clearly scared and indicated that the Soviets might negotiate; if the President would promise not to invade Cuba "then the necessity for the presence of our military specialists in Cuba would disappear."[35]

On Saturday, October 27, Radio Moscow suddenly broadcast a new letter from Khrushchev to Kennedy raising the price for negotiations: the Russians would remove their missiles from Cuba if the United States would remove its Jupiter missiles from Turkey. Clearly different in style and tone, Washington assumed this letter was a group product drafted by the Presidium.

Refusing to trade America's NATO commitment to Turkey and gambling that Khrushchev was still in control, Kennedy ignored the second letter. He immediately wrote the Soviet leader offering not to invade Cuba if the Soviets would remove their missiles and other "offensive" weapons from the island under UN supervision. To be absolutely certain that Khrushchev understood the United States position, Attorney General Robert Kennedy told Soviet Ambassador Dobrynin that the

---

[35] The letter is paraphrased in Abel, *The Missile Crisis*, pp. 158-62.

United States was ready to begin military action by the first of the week unless the crisis was resolved. Sunday morning, October 28, Radio Moscow broadcast Khrushchev's reply to Washington: the Soviet government had given an order to "dismantle the arms which you described as offensive, and to crate and return them to the Soviet Union" in return for the pledge of the United States not to invade Cuba. The crisis was all but over.

Khrushchev later claimed that Soviet missiles had been deployed in Cuba solely to defend Castro's regime. Moreover, the Soviet aim had been achieved because Kennedy pledged not to invade Cuba once the missiles were withdrawn. Both sides made concessions, stated Khrushchev, but the real winner was "sanity, the cause of peace and security of peoples." In fact, Khrushchev probably withdrew the missiles because he feared a greater loss if he did not. He later admitted that the decision to meet Kennedy's demand was triggered by news that an American attack on Cuba was imminent.

Castro was not convinced that there had been a net gain. He complained bitterly to UN Secretary-General U Thant that the Russians had treated Cuba like a vassal, refusing to allow Cubans to set foot on the Soviet missile sites and then withdrawing the missiles without consulting Cuba. As can be imagined, the Chinese hardly were impressed. Peking accused Khrushchev of committing the two cardinal sins of Leninist strategy: "adventurism" for placing missiles in Cuba if he were overextending himself, and "capitulationism" for then yielding to enemy pressure and withdrawing the weapons. Certain members of the Soviet Presidium and the Soviet armed forces probably shared the Chinese evaluation.

THE HESITANT DÉTENTE

It was easy to read much into Khrushchev's withdrawal of the missiles. Especially in Europe, the crisis was thought to have introduced a new era of stability—a turning point in twentieth-century world politics. The Soviets had tried to change the balance of power, and had learned their lesson.

More realistic analysts reflected that the shoe might have been on the other foot if such a "contest" had taken place over Berlin. The West had seen the ease with which the Soviets could blockade that city, and recognized the difficult, if not impossible, task of defending Berlin with other than nuclear weapons. It also is doubtful that Khrushchev thought of his missile ploy as a final, winner-take-all contest. On the contrary, he thought his ploy would succeed; little gambling was involved.

What about the "retreat"? Did this mean Khrushchev would always give way in the face of Western force? One of the most important ideological dictums is Lenin's exhortation to retreat in the face of superior force. But this did not mean all the way to Moscow in 1962. Soviet vital national interests probably lay far to the West of continental Russia. And the Western powers realized this. The United States did not intervene in Hungary in 1956; the USSR did. In Cuba, on the other hand, American national security appeared compromised by a forward base which obviously was not vital to Soviet security.

President Kennedy nevertheless realized the necessity of giving Khrushchev an out even where Soviet vital interests were not at stake. Speaking at American University the following summer, Kennedy philosophized: "Above all, while defending our own vital interests, nuclear powers must avert those confrontations which bring an adversary to the choice of either a humiliating retreat or a nuclear war."

Khrushchev seemed to accept Kennedy's working formula during his remaining two years in office. There were no more direct confrontations; no new Berlin crises. The USSR moved somewhat hesitantly toward a détente with the United States. It was clearly Khrushchev's only option until he could solve the USSR's basic defense problem—the creation of adequate military power to support Soviet foreign policy objectives. Few still believed Khrushchev's threats to defend "socialist" states around the globe with Soviet rockets.

Yet Khrushchev still did not decide to sacrifice butter for guns, to gain strategic power the hard way. In February 1963, Khrushchev had reluctantly admitted that consumer needs would have to be postponed again so that the "enormous resources" required to keep Soviet military power up with the West could be made available. But two months later he apparently had regained the initiative. The Chairman was talking about the need to give priority to economic development, and telling Harold Wilson, head of the British Labor Party, that the USSR was stopping production of strategic bombers and surface warships. In July 1963, Khrushchev launched another attack on "Stalinism" (the forces which opposed his programs). He argued passionately that socialism had to give the people enough bread, clothing, and leisure time to surpass capitalism or "we shall be idle babblers and not revolutionaries." Then came the "détente" budget of December 13, 1963, reducing Soviet military expenditures by some four per cent.[36] By September 1964, Khrushchev was proposing a revolution in Soviet economic planning. He had been talking about making the consumer king; now he was going to force through the proposition that consumer industries should grow as fast or faster than heavy industry.

[36] For a thorough study of Soviet defense policy during the crucial period after the missile crisis see Thomas W. Wolfe, *Soviet Strategy at the Crossroads* (Cambridge, Mass.: Harvard University Press, 1964).

The most widely hailed indication of the détente with the United States was the partial nuclear test ban treaty signed on August 5, 1963. Negotiations on a treaty of this kind had been going on for some seven years.[37] The sudden desire of Moscow to sign the treaty was prompted in part by the need to give life to the détente. But in the background were strategic reasons. The Soviets still feared that West Germany wanted nuclear weapons, and the treaty would be one more roadblock in her path. Moscow seemed just as worried about China one day possessing a nuclear capability. The treaty could justify the Soviet refusal of nuclear assistance to China and the other socialist countries, and make it politically more difficult for the Chinese to conduct nuclear tests if they developed a capability. Finally, the Soviet military may have been satisfied that a test ban at this juncture would give them a relative advantage in weapons development over the United States, especially in high yield bombs.[38] (In spite of all these advantages, Khrushchev had intimated in April 1963 to Norman Cousins, editor of the Saturday Review, that he was having difficulty selling the treaty to his comrades.)

Other détente measures included the "hot-line" emergency teletype link between Moscow and Washington, an agreement not to orbit nuclear weapons in space (embodied in a UN resolution passed on October 17, 1963), and Khrushchev's unilateral budget cut of December 13, 1963, mentioned earlier. The Chairman hinted that progress in disarmament might come through "mutual example."

Any move toward détente, of course, infuriated the Chinese. The test ban, charged Peking, was a "dirty fake," a "big fraud," and a "sell-out" designed to prevent China and other peace-loving countries from increasing their defense capability—in other words, from acquiring nuclear weapons. More basically, the détente policy "pursued by the Soviet Government is one of allying with the forces of war to oppose the forces of peace, allying with imperialism to oppose socialism, allying with the United States to oppose China, and allying with the reactionaries of all countries to oppose the people of the world." The treaty, claimed the Chinese, was "a concentrated manifestation of capitulationism."[39]

---

[37] The best survey of the arms control negotiations during the Khrushchev years is Khrushchev and the Arms Race (Cambridge, Mass.: The M.I.T. Press, 1966), by Lincoln P. Bloomfield, Walter C. Clemens, Jr. and Franklyn Griffiths.

[38] In the fall of 1961, the Soviets had broken an informal moratorium on testing by the nuclear powers. American experts later reported that the Soviets might have surpassed the United States in "certain categories of weapons" with this test series.

[39] For the Chinese government's July 31, 1963, statement on the treaty see Griffiths, The Sino-Soviet Rift, pp. 326-29. Vernon Aspaturian suggests that the test ban treaty forms the "major watershed" in the evolution of Sino-Soviet-American relations between 1956 and 1967, with both Moscow and Peking admitting that a major realignment of powers had taken place. The USSR and the United States were transformed from "total enemies" into "limited partners-and-adversaries," while China

Moscow could not acknowledge giving up the struggle with imperialism or selling out the socialist camp. The Kremlin therefore claimed it was continuing the struggle for peace and socialism on a different plane by working with those "sober" and "sensible" leaders in the West who now realized the consequences of nuclear war. Such cooperation was vital to frustrate the plans of Western "madmen." This argument, not entirely new in Soviet propaganda, was considerably more sophisticated than the orthodox Marxist approach which does not distinguish among "capitalist warmongers." The "good guys" included President Kennedy, Secretary of State Rusk, Senator Fulbright, and later, President Johnson. Moscow charged that Peking on the other hand was "entering into a bloc" with Goldwater, Teller, de Gaulle, and Adenauer —obviously among the "bad guys."

Perhaps the major foreign policy dilemma Khrushchev faced during his last years in power was having to choose between Washington and Peking. The closer he came to a détente, the more he alienated China. If he had followed Peking's advice on world communist strategy, tension with the United States would have risen. We will never know if Khrushchev could have resolved this dilemma. He was relieved of his duties on October 14, 1964, because of "advanced age" and "deterioration" of his health.

SUMMARY

Khrushchev gambled and lost in the Cuban missile crisis. He needlessly enflamed Soviet relations with China—although the rift probably was inevitable. His erratic, sometimes bumptious style in foreign policy was the despair of his colleagues—and often the delight of the West.

Yet under Khrushchev's regime Soviet power was extended into all the areas of the world, and for a brief time ninety miles from the United States. Although the Soviets retreated in 1962, it was perhaps more significant that they consciously tried to change the world balance of power.

Khrushchev subsequently decided in favor of a hesitant détente with the West. He seemed more intent in his last two years on a great program of internal economic reform. General dissatisfaction with his programs and his style in foreign and domestic politics led to his "retirement." Khrushchev was trying to accomplish too much, too fast, with too little.

---

and the USSR changed from allies to "partial adversaries" and "potential enemies." See his essay, "Foreign Policy Perspectives in the Sixties," Alexander Dallin and Thomas B. Larson, eds., *Soviet Politics since Khrushchev* (Englewood Cliffs, N.J.: Prentice-Hall, Inc., 1968), p. 137.

FURTHER READING

Allen, Robert Loring, *Soviet Economic Warfare*. Washington, D.C.: Public Affairs Press, 1960. Soviet use of economic activity to advance foreign policy.

Berliner, Joseph S., *Soviet Economic Aid: The New Aid and Trade Policy*. New York: Frederick A. Praeger, Inc., 1958. Study by American economist.

Bromke, Adam, ed., *The Communist States at the Crossroads*. New York: Frederick A. Praeger, Inc., 1965. Thirteen specialists trace growing diversity in communist world.

Brzezinski, Zbigniew, ed., *Africa and the Communist World*. Stanford, Calif.: Stanford University Press, 1963. Articles on Soviet policy toward Africa.

Dallin, Alexander *et al.*, *The Soviet Union and Disarmament: An Appraisal of Soviet Attitudes and Intentions*. New York: Frederick A. Praeger, Inc., 1964. Report of a group of Western experts.

Doolin, Dennis J., ed., *Territorial Claims in the Sino-Soviet Conflict: Documents and Analysis*. Stanford, Calif.: Hoover Institution on War, Revolution, and Peace, Stanford University, 1965. Thirty documents from various sources covering period December 1962 to November 1964.

Floyd, David, *Rumania: Russia's Dissident Ally*. New York: Frederick A. Praeger, Inc., 1965. Rumania's split with USSR.

Frankland, Mark, *Khrushchev*. New York: Stein and Day, Publishers, 1967.

Griffith, William E., *Albania and the Sino-Soviet Rift*. Cambridge, Mass.: The M.I.T. Press, 1963. Study of Albania's break with the USSR.

Griffith, William E., *Sino-Soviet Relations, 1964-1965*. Cambridge, Mass.: The M.I.T. Press, 1967. Continuation of *The Sino-Soviet Rift*. Runs from November 1963 to November 1965.

Griffith, William E., *The Sino-Soviet Rift*. Cambridge, Mass.: The M.I.T. Press, 1964. Summary and analysis of developments in Sino-Soviet dispute in 1962-1963, with valuable collection of documents.

Horelick, Arnold L. and Myron Rush, *Strategic Power and Soviet Foreign Policy*. Chicago: University of Chicago Press, 1966. Analysis of Khrushchev's use of Soviet strategic forces in his foreign policy.

Hudson, G. F., Richard Lowenthal, and Roderick MacFarquhar, *The Sino-Soviet Dispute*. New York: Frederick A. Praeger, Inc., 1961. Introductory essays on early stages of the dispute and collection of relative documents from 1957 to 1960.

Jackson, W. A. Douglas, *Russo-Chinese Borderlands*. Princeton, N.J.: D. Van Nostrand Co., Inc., 1962. Geographer's analysis of borderlands and their importance in the Sino-Soviet conflict.

Kennan, George F., *On Dealing with the Communist World*. New York: Harper & Row, Publishers, 1964. Essays on necessity of historical perspective and discrimination when dealing with Russia and Eastern Europe.

Kertesz, Stephen, ed., *East Central Europe and the World: Developments in the Post-Stalin Era*. Notre Dame, Ind.: Notre Dame University Press, 1962. Collection of articles dealing with events from 1956-1962.

Kolkowicz, Roman, *The Soviet Military and the Communist Party*. Princeton, N.J.: Princeton University Press, 1967. Four case studies of army-party relations, concentrating on post-World War II period.

Leonhard, Wolfgang, *The Kremlin Since Stalin*. New York: Frederick A. Praeger, Inc., 1962. Analysis of domestic events and their impact on Soviet foreign policy from 1952 to 1960.

Linden, Carl A., *Khrushchev and the Soviet Leadership, 1957-1964*. Baltimore, Md.: The Johns Hopkins Press, 1966. Analysis of Khrushchev's policies and politics.

Lippmann, Walter, *The Coming Tests with Russia*. Boston: Little, Brown and Company, 1961. American senior journalist's interview with Khrushchev in 1961. See also Lippmann's 1958 interview with Khrushchev, *The Communist World and Ours*.

Lowenthal, Richard, *World Communism*. New York: Oxford University Press, 1964. Collection of articles written since 1955 by Lowenthal on the intellectual decay and political disintegration of world communist movement.

Mehnert, Klaus, *Peking and Moscow*. New York: G. P. Putnam's Sons, 1963. Analysis of Sino-Soviet relations and the evolution of the two societies.

Morison, David, *The U.S.S.R. and Africa: 1945-1963*. London: Oxford University Press, 1964. Summary of Soviet policy toward Africa.

Poppino, Rollie, *International Communism in Latin America: A History of the Movement, 1917-1963*. New York: Free Press of Glencoe, Inc., 1964. Section on Soviet relations with Latin-American communist parties.

Scalapino, Robert A., ed., *The Communist Revolution in Asia*. Englewood Cliffs, N.J.: Prentice-Hall, Inc., 1965. Essays by specialists on communist movements in all major countries of East and South Asia.

Shaffer, Harry G. and Jan S. Prybyla, eds., *From Underdevelopment to Affluence: Western, Soviet, and Chinese Views*. New York: Appleton-Century-Crofts, 1967. Selections by Western specialists and communist authorities on the problems of underdevelopment and proposals for the path to affluence.

Thornton, Thomas P., ed., *The Third World in Soviet Perspective*. Princeton, N.J.: Princeton University Press, 1964.

Zagoria, Donald S., *The Sino-Soviet Conflict, 1956-1961*. Princeton, N.J.: Princeton University Press, 1962. The development of the rift.

11

PRUDENT GLOBALISM

1965-1968

Shortly after midnight, October 15, 1964, TASS reported the results of a Central Committee meeting held October 14:

> The plenary meeting of the CPSU Central Committee granted N. S. Khrushchev's request to be relieved of his duties as the First Secretary of the CPSU Central Committee, member of the Presidium of the CPSU Central Committee and Chairman of the Council of Ministers of the U.S.S.R. in view of his advanced age and deterioration of his health.

Khrushchev's principal responsibilities, noted the Soviet press agency, had been given to two men: Leonid Brezhnev was elected First Secretary of the Party; Alexei Kosygin was appointed Chairman of the Council of Ministers (Premier).

The true story filtered through some days later. Khrushchev, thought by many in the West to be firmly in the saddle, had been fired. The ruling body of the USSR, the eleven-man Party Presidium of the Central Committee, apparently met secretly on Monday and Tuesday, October 12 and 13. The unsuspecting Khrushchev was vacationing at Sochi on the Black Sea. On Tuesday morning, the Presidium reportedly voted ten to zero to remove their absent colleague. (Khrushchev, who still knew nothing of the meeting, would have been number eleven.) The full

Central Committee, some 350 strong, met that night to ratify the Presidium's decision. Mikhail Suslov, the chief party theoretician, took five hours to present the Presidium's main indictment of Khrushchev. The Chairman, with only minutes left of his formal duties, now had been brought to face his accusers. Angry at the way his removal had been rigged, Khrushchev insulted and swore at the Central Committee members.

Details about the indictment surfaced later in a secret forty-page document circulated among Soviet party members, and apparently passed to other communist parties. Suslov had listed 29 specific charges against Khrushchev. Predictably, his handling of the missile crisis was included. (The criticism nevertheless was more for putting missiles in Cuba than for later withdrawing them.) Khrushchev also was charged with personally offending Mao and needlessly worsening the Sino-Soviet dispute.

But there was no single foreign or domestic issue on which dissatisfaction focussed. Khrushchev was charged, for example, with disrupting the Soviet economy, ignoring heavy industry for light industry and consumer goods, creating dissension within the party organization, building five-story apartments rather than larger, more economical units.

Khrushchev's policy decisions, the Presidium implied, reflected his style of leadership:

> The Leninist Party is an enemy of subjectivism and drifting in Communist construction. Hare-brained scheming, immature conclusions and hasty decisions and actions divorced from reality, bragging and phrasemongering, commandism, unwillingness to take into account the achievements of science and practical experience are alien to it. Construction of communism is a live, creative undertaking which does not repeat nor tolerate armchair methods, personal decisions and disregard for the practical experience of the masses.[1]

The Presidium was trying to picture Khrushchev's "erratic" style of leadership as a major reason for his removal. Carl Linden suggests that this may have been more a pretext than a reason. Khrushchev's policy shifts and retreats often came because he met intense internal opposition to his radical programs to change the direction of the Soviet economy, the size and allocation of defense expenditures, and the nature of the party's role in leading the society.[2] Khrushchev in effect had

---

[1] From the *Pravda* editorial of October 17, 1964. Reprinted in *The Current Digest of the Soviet Press*, XVI, No. 40 (October 28, 1964), 3, 6.

[2] Linden, *Khrushchev and the Soviet Leadership, 1957-1964*, Chap. 10. For the opposing view that objections to Khrushchev were not, in principle, to his policies, see Robert Conquest, *Russia After Khrushchev* (New York: Frederick A. Praeger, Inc., 1965), Chap. 10.

stepped on everyone's toes, alienating both conservatives and the more moderate reformers. Even Brezhnev, a Khrushchev protégé now First Secretary, deserted the Chairman in his time of need. The military, who had played a vital role in Khrushchev's rout of the "anti-party" element in 1957, also withheld their support.

Underlying all the specific charges appeared to be the fear of the Presidium that Khrushchev was attempting to consolidate his power. The Chairman may have planned to exchange Presidium members for a personal entourage, as Stalin had tried earlier. One charge had been that he was attempting to replace "collective leadership with the cult of personality"—his personality. Another charge was nepotism. Rumor had it that Khrushchev had tried to elevate Alexei Adzhubei, his son-in-law and editor of *Izvestia,* to the party secretariat. The deposed First Secretary, the Presidium feared, had been scheming to supplant Stalinism with "Khrushchevism."

THE FIRST LINES
OF A FOREIGN POLICY

Khrushchev's successors brought no perceptible difference in the general Soviet line toward the world in their first days in office. The new leaders naturally did not want to rock the boat until the situation stabilized. More probably, they couldn't agree on an alternative program. The coalition which had deposed Khrushchev was united only in its opposition to him. There was an uneasy equilibrium, as after Stalin's death. The same Left and Right tendencies, the modernizing and conservative wings, were present in the Presidium. Finally, any Soviet leader faced international problems largely beyond his control—the destructiveness of nuclear weapons, American economic growth, the existence of China, nationalism, the revolution of rising expectations, and so forth. When one added the constraints of ideological conditioning, it was questionable whether any Soviet leader in the 1960's could find dramatically different alternatives to the policies of Khrushchev. Perhaps the only change could be in style. Given a limited range of maneuver, there nevertheless was much that could be done to improve "offensive" peaceful coexistence. And this is what Brezhnev and Kosygin did over the next several years.

The top leaders at once went out of their way to assure Western ambassadors in Moscow that Khrushchevian peaceful coexistence was here to stay. Moreover, the West could expect improved relations with the Kremlin. *Izvestia,* the government newspaper, called for a treaty banning all types of nuclear testing. In a speech a few weeks later on the anniversary of the October Revolution, Brezhnev stated: "We are coming out for an end to the arms race, for general and complete disarmament, for relieving the peoples from the mounting burden of military expenditures." (Soviet Defense Minister Malinovsky's informal remarks on the same occasion containing a pointed attack on United States Secretary of Defense McNamara were left out of *Pravda*, the party newspaper.)

One major problem the new regime had to face immediately was its approach to the communist world. The crucial issue, of course, was Sino-Soviet relations. Mao Tse-tung had sent "warm greetings" to Brezhnev and Kosygin. Premier Chou En-lai followed with a delegation to the October Revolution celebration in Moscow. Peking underscored Chou's visit with another telegram to Moscow expressing the hope that the two parties would rally on the basis of true communist doctrine. The West was warned: "May imperialism, with the United States at its head, shudder from our monolithic unity."

The unity was illusory. Chou En-lai was intransigent on the main issues. Brezhnev and Kosygin refused to renounce the critical "revisionist" decisions of the party congresses held during Khrushchev's administration. The only Soviet concession was to call off open polemics.[3] The new regime added that a world conference of communist parties was "clearly overdue." (Peking had bitterly denounced this project because Khrushchev had pressed for the meeting to read China out of the communist camp.) A scheduled December meeting of 26 communist parties to plan the conference nevertheless was postponed until the following March, and downgraded to a "consultative" meeting. The postponement, however, was more a concession to the East and West European parties than to the Chinese. These parties still hoped to avoid formalizing the split in the communist camp.

VIETNAM AND THE SINO-SOVIET DISPUTE

The new regime decided on positive action to disprove Chinese charges of "revisionism." Premier Kosygin arrived in Hanoi, North Vietnam, on February 6, 1965, bearing gifts of Soviet anti-aircraft weapons, surface-to-air missiles, and MIG fighters.

Soviet economic aid to North Vietnam during Khrushchev's reign had totaled some 350 million dollars. (China's economic aid during the same

---

[3] The Chinese, if they agreed to a similar relaxation of name calling, soon reopened the wounds. In April 1965, Peking charged that Brezhnev and Kosygin's support of the previous party congress policies indicated that Khrushchev's successors had not in the least changed their "revisionist and great-nation chauvinist nature, irrespective of how many fine words they uttered."

period came to 450 million dollars.) Soviet influence on Hanoi appeared dominant from 1957 through 1960. Chinese influence grew when Hanoi decided to launch the National Liberation Front and infiltrate South Vietnam. The Chinese contrasted their wholehearted support of North Vietnam with Soviet hesitation. There was substance to this comparison. American diplomats who tried to raise the Vietnam issue with Khrushchev during these years found him visibly bored. In any case, Khrushchev apparently decided it was difficult to fight a Chinese campaign to woo a country which obviously seemed in the Chinese orbit. Soviet aid to North Vietnam subsequently decreased in 1963 and 1964. Hanoi appeared to be in the Chinese camp, although the North Vietnamese continually qualified their support of Peking's struggle with the Soviet revisionists.[4]

Kosygin's mission appeared to have two aims: (1) to counter Chinese influence in Hanoi by encouraging pro-Soviet elements in the North Vietnamese communist party and Hanoi to send at least an observer to the "consultative" meeting of communist parties in Moscow scheduled for the following month; and (2) to get part of the credit for the communist victory in South Vietnam which appeared around the corner in late 1964.

A new dimension, however, was given to Kosygin's visit. Forty-nine American fighter aircraft launched the first strike of the concentrated air war on North Vietnam on the very day the Premier was in Hanoi promising "all necessary assistance if aggressors dare to encroach upon the independence and sovereignty" of a brotherly socialist country. The American attack retaliated for the Vietcong raid on the United States base at Pleiku in South Vietnam. But Kosygin may have taken the bombing as a studied, personal insult, designed to demonstrate Soviet impotence. Perhaps he was forced to assume a harsher anti-American stand and give more aid than Russia had intended. For the first time since Korea, a socialist state was under direct attack from the imperialists.

Soviet military assistance jumped dramatically over the next several years. Between 1954 and 1964, an estimated 75 million dollars of Soviet arms had been sent to North Vietnam. Some 225 million dollars of arms were dispatched in 1965 alone; 375 million in 1966, 400 million in 1967, and an even higher figure was planned for 1968.[5] Western sources estimated that the USSR was now supplying North Vietnam with 75 per cent of her arms, including all of the most destructive weapons: surface-to-

[4] For the record of Hanoi's attempt to retain some degree of independence from China during the early 1960's, see John C. Donnell, "North Vietnam: A Qualified Pro-Chinese Position," Communist Revolution in Asia (Englewood Cliffs, N.J.: Prentice-Hall, Inc., 1965), ed. by Robert A. Scalapino, pp. 140-79.

[5] Russia claimed that she had supplied 555 million dollars in arms in 1965. Albert Parry, "Soviet Aid to Vietnam," The Reporter, January 12, 1967, p. 28.

air anti-aircraft missiles (SAM's); the latest anti-aircraft guns; MIG fighters, Russia's largest helicopters, and heavy, mobile rocket launchers. Hanoi sent pilots and technicians to train in Russia, while Moscow had several thousand Soviet advisors on duty in North Vietnam. In March 1965, Brezhnev also offered Soviet "volunteers" to Hanoi, a gesture politely and publicly declined by the North Vietnamese. Hanoi may have feared that the Chinese would ask to come in also. And Moscow may have banked on Hanoi's restraint; the Soviets did not seem eager to escalate the war further with "volunteers."

Moscow had set out to lead the progressive forces of the world in the defense of Vietnam against American imperialism. But Peking wasn't fooled. The Chinese publicly charged that the "modern revisionists" were trying to induce the North Vietnamese to capitulate, while professing support for them. Peking called Soviet aid superficial and implied that the North Vietnamese were being duped by the Kremlin.

Stung by Chinese charges, Moscow claimed that Peking had rejected all appeals from the Soviet and other communist parties to unite against American "aggression" in Vietnam. A confidential letter was dispatched to all fraternal parties in March 1966, detailing Soviet aid and charging that the Chinese were impeding the rail traffic of Soviet arms traveling through China for Vietnam. Peking had demanded the right of inspection of such goods. But the Chinese supposedly were halting the shipments, dismantling the latest equipment so it might be copied, and hijacking some of the best Soviet weapons. This sticky problem reportedly was resolved in the spring of 1967 when the Vietnamese began to assume "physical control" of Soviet arms at the Sino-Russian border.

Meanwhile, Moscow pressed for another "consultative" meeting of communist parties to be followed by a formal world conference. This time the invitation for the preliminary conference was extended to the eighty-one ruling and non-ruling parties. Nineteen parties had attended the March 1965 meeting in Moscow, sixty-six convened at Bucharest in February 1968. Noticeably absent were China, Albania, North Vietnam, and other Asian parties.

Moscow's central purpose was to stage a demonstration of wide support for its policies, in the belief that the Chinese would not attend to complicate matters. At the same time, the Soviets had agreed not to attempt an excommunication of China nor to interfere in the affairs of any fraternal party; otherwise there would have been a very sparse attendance. The Soviets also were watching the "cultural revolution" in China with great interest and concern. They may have hoped that a purged party after Mao could be brought back into the fold.

But the Soviets could not resist attacking the Chinese during the meeting; as a result the Rumanians stalked out. A spokesman for the "neutral" Rumanian delegation said later: "We came here to pave the way for a future conference. We found that there was no exchange of views. . . . A number of fraternal parties were attacked. Therefore, the meeting changed its character." The results of the conference only confirmed what Western observers had suspected: any such attempt to unify communist parties in the later 1960's only accelerated the divisive forces within the world communist movement. "Polycentrism" was here to stay. Yet the Bucharest meeting at Soviet urging scheduled the long sought world conference for November 1968.

VIETNAM AND THE DÉTENTE

The new character of the war in Vietnam inevitably cast a pall on the Soviet-American search for a détente. Soviet diplomats insisted that the USSR was "a party to the conflict," and fully supported Hanoi in her requirement that the bombing be stopped before negotiations could begin. At each stage in the escalation, Moscow warned that the Soviets would increase their aid to North Vietnam. "Frenzied hawks," claimed Moscow, had the upper hand in American policy making. There was the impression in the USSR that the United States had initiated a wide-ranging policy to intervene wherever and whenever a situation ran counter to American interests; Vietnam was only the most dramatic of a list of American attempts to "rollback" history in Africa, the Middle East, and the Dominican Republic.

High American decision makers thought that Moscow wanted out of Vietnam as much as the United States, and that she supported Hanoi only because of her desire to lead world communism and counter Peking. Obviously, the Soviets had these motives. It also was true, as the United States believed, that the Soviets feared a pronounced escalation such as an invasion of North Vietnam. The USSR would have had great difficulty supporting Hanoi in that event. Any massive Soviet involvement would have been the wrong war at the wrong time in the wrong place, given Soviet inferiority in strategic delivery systems and mobile forces, and a recalcitrant China. Indeed, Moscow took great pains to point out that its weapons aid to Hanoi was *defensive*. (The Soviets could not forget the Cuban episode.)

On the other hand, Moscow may have been perfectly content for the conflict to continue at the prevailing intensity. For a relatively cheap investment, Moscow had a ready-made issue to prove that it was not revisionist. Moreover, the Soviets were content to see the United States heavily involved in a peripheral area, split internally, and losing influence with her allies around the world.

There were indications that Moscow was advising Hanoi to go to the peace table. But this may have been because the Soviets sincerely thought that North Vietnam's best chance of winning was through political means. (Many Western commentators agreed.) When negotiations finally began in Paris in the spring of 1968 after a partial bombing pause by the United States, the Soviets stayed in the shadows. They seemed to have little real influence over Hanoi. In any event, they could not press the North Vietnamese because of the Sino-Soviet split. Beyond this, Ho Chi Minh and his colleagues undoubtedly harbored resentment for the Soviet (and Chinese) sell-out of their hopes at Geneva in 1954.

Yet the pressures for the détente still existed. The Brezhnev-Kosygin team demonstrated the flexibility of its foreign policy by agreeing to a draft of a nuclear non-proliferation treaty in January 1968, while pursuing the hard line on Vietnam. As with the partial test ban, the Soviets were bent on frustrating West Germany's entry into the nuclear club. They also could advertise their continuing interest in world peace.

Some observers thought such policies contradictory. But Khrushchev had indicated years earlier that the sacred duty to support national liberation wars was an integral part of peaceful coexistence. Indeed, it could be argued that peaceful coexistence, as the former Chairman had described it, was finally being practiced. Moscow's loudly trumpeted support of North Vietnam had put the USSR squarely in the mainstream of international communism. She could humor the left-wing communist parties by full scale support for revolutionary war, and satisfy the right-wing parties by general support for peaceful coexistence with the West.

Meanwhile, the United States and the Soviet Union made other moves toward solving common problems. In June 1967, President Johnson and Chairman Kosygin held a summit conference at Glassboro, New Jersey—the first meeting between an American president and a Soviet premier since the Kennedy-Khrushchev confrontation in 1961. Little was accomplished except the creation of a more cordial atmosphere and the clarification of positions. But in June 1968, the two powers agreed to bilateral talks on limiting strategic offensive and defensive nuclear weapons systems. Soviet readiness to talk came barely 72 hours after the United States Senate voted to begin work on the Sentinel anti-ballistic missile (ABM) system. Washington's offer to talk, some seventeen months old, had been triggered in turn by news that the Soviets were building an ABM complex. Both nations undoubtedly sought some way out of a very costly, probably fruitless escalation of the arms race. But internal pressures on each government, combined with decades of mutual fear and suspicion, would make substantive agreement difficult.[6]

6 For an excellent analysis of the political and strategic issues involved, see Carl Kaysen, "Keeping the Strategic Balance," *Foreign Affairs*, 46, No. 4 (1968), pp. 665-75.

THE SOVIET UNION
AND THE DEVELOPING WORLD

Khrushchev's successors continued his general strategy toward the developing world, including the Soviet foreign aid program. A few weeks after the transfer of power, Mikoyan, Khrushchev's old comrade on the Presidium, assured Mrs. Gandhi, the Indian Prime Minister, that her military aid agreement was with the Soviet Government—not the deposed Chairman.

But a new emphasis began to appear in the Soviet approach to the developing countries. Brezhnev and Kosygin paid more attention to Russia's underprivileged neighbors—in particular, Turkey, Iran, and Pakistan. Security considerations were naturally important since each state held membership in Western defense organizations. The bait was economic aid to all three, and military aid to Iran—long exclusively supplied with arms by the West.

The Soviets also showed new interest in Asia, picturing the USSR as the friendly big brother of new nations regardless of their internal policies toward indigenous communists or leanings in foreign policy. Thus fresh overtures were made to Malaysia and the Philippines. Neutral, if not pro-Western, Prince Souvanna Phouma of Laos received Soviet support. Moscow did complain about the bloodbath launched against Indonesian communists after their abortive coup in September 1965. Nevertheless, the Soviets granted the new obviously anti-communist Suharto government a moratorium on the 1.2 billion dollar debt owed the USSR.[7]

The friendly big brother posture was enhanced when Chairman Kosygin brought warring India and Pakistan to the conference table at Tashkent in January 1966. Moscow was intent on keeping the Asian subcontinent relatively peaceful to counter Peking. China, in contrast, outraged many Asians by supporting Pakistan in a war Asians did not want. It was clear, however, that the Soviets favored India as the main buttress against China. Moscow apparently refused Pakistan's request for Soviet jets to match the flow of the latest Soviet MIG's to India. By 1968, the USSR had become India's chief source of jet fighters, surface-to-air missiles, heavy artillery, and transport aircraft. In addition, Moscow was selling New Delhi attack submarines and destroyer escorts. In return, the Soviets were said to have requested "technical facilities" at Indian ports for the Soviet navy.

[7] One of Khrushchev's major initiatives in the developing world had been the sale of one billion dollars worth of Soviet arms, and the extension of 650 million dollars in credit to the Sukarno government. Khrushchev wanted to support Sukarno in his efforts to take West Irian from the Dutch, but he also may have looked toward Indonesia to check Chinese expansionism in Southeast Asia. See D. P. Mozingo, "Sino-Indonesian Relations: An Overview, 1955-1965" (Santa Monica, Calif.: RAND, 1965).

There was a distinct tinge of sobriety, however, in the Soviet approach to Africa. The Chinese cultural revolution had led to an almost complete collapse of Peking's considerable efforts on the African continent, and thus to the direct competition for influence between the two communist states. Other plusses on the Soviet scorecard were Soviet MIG's sent to Nigeria in its war with secessionist Biafra, and a new Soviet arms deal with the Sudan. But the Soviets failed to regain their foothold in Ghana after Nkrumah fell. They lost influence in Algeria after Ben Bella was replaced by Colonel Boumediene, in spite of the several thousand Soviet military and civilian advisors still in that country and the 250 million dollars worth of Soviet arms supplied to the Algerian armed forces. Even Sekou Touré's leftist Guinea was moving away from total dependence on communist aid toward economic cooperation with the West.

The obvious instability in Africa led Soviet commentators to reflect on the "internal weaknesses and objective difficulties" of the national liberation movement on the continent. Communism, which the Soviets now realized was a very long term goal for Africa, seemed farther away than ever. With 60,000 party members in an African population of 300 million, a Soviet observer noted that "it is hardly possible to agree with the assertion that in Africa there is a swift spread of the doctrine of scientific socialism."

Moscow made the least headway of all in Latin America, although the Chinese effort on that continent also had collapsed. Successful communist revolutions seemed doubtful with a reported net decline in communist strength in Latin America, little indigenous support, and a prevalence of military regimes. The Soviets therefore traded with existing bourgeois governments. They insisted that such economic cooperation really was designed to help "the peoples" of Latin America.

Castro, who hoped to lead the revolutionary movement in South America, did not appreciate Moscow's line. He noted that "not everything which is red is revolutionary." Moscow retorted by having pro-Soviet Latin-American communists advise that the Cuban experience was not necessarily valid for other countries in the region. Clearly, Cuba was an increasing and costly (more than a million dollars a day) trial for the Kremlin leaders. The last thing Moscow wanted in South America was another "premature" revolution which she might have to support.[8]

The Middle East Crisis   The major Soviet gain in the Third World came in the Middle East after the Israeli victory in the lightning war of June 1967. The origins of this war are still shrouded in

[8] See Herbert S. Dinerstein, "Soviet Policy in Latin America," *American Political Science Review*, LXI (1967), 80-90.

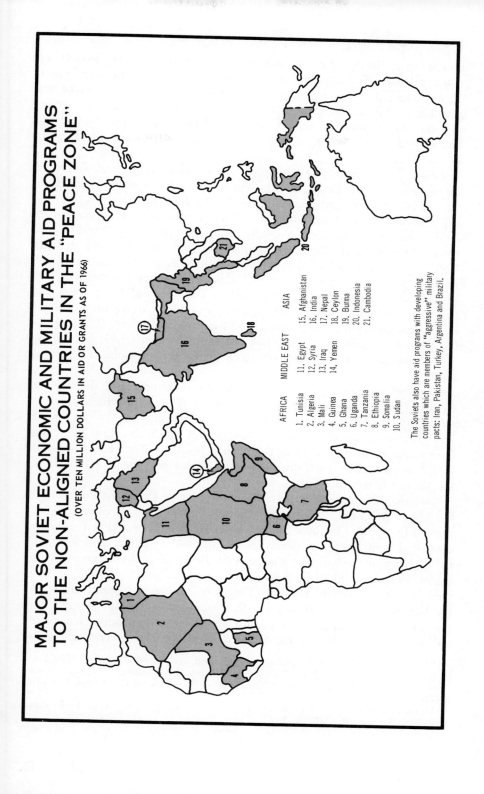

MAJOR SOVIET ECONOMIC AND MILITARY AID PROGRAMS TO THE NON-ALIGNED COUNTRIES IN THE "PEACE ZONE"

(OVER TEN MILLION DOLLARS IN AID OR GRANTS AS OF 1966)

AFRICA
1. Tunisia
2. Algeria
3. Mali
4. Guinea
5. Ghana
6. Uganda
7. Tanzania
8. Ethiopia
9. Somalia
10. Sudan

MIDDLE EAST
11. Egypt
12. Syria
13. Iraq
14. Yemen

ASIA
15. Afghanistan
16. India
17. Nepal
18. Ceylon
19. Burma
20. Indonesia
21. Cambodia

The Soviets also have aid programs with developing countries which are members of "aggressive" military pacts: Iran, Pakistan, Turkey, Argentina and Brazil.

secrecy, specifically the question of whether or not the Soviets encouraged Nasser's increasing pressure on Israel before the war began.[9] In any case, the Soviet Union already had done its part to make war possible in the Middle East. Two billion dollars of Soviet arms, including some of the most advanced examples of Russian military technology, had flowed to the United Arab Republic, Syria, and Iraq in the 12 years before 1967.

Israeli forces destroyed or captured one billion dollars of the Soviet investment—mainly Egyptian arms—in a few days in early June. If the Soviets had encouraged Nasser to the brink, they certainly did not have this outcome in mind and quickly decided against further support of the Arabs during the conflict. Kosygin reportedly used the "hot-line" between Moscow and Washington to assure President Johnson that the USSR would not intervene. Moscow clearly feared escalation if the nuclear powers actively took sides. Algerian Premier Boumediene flew to Moscow shortly after the war had ended. He told the Soviets that national revolutions were suffering successive blows from American neo-colonialism, and supposedly upbraided the Russian leaders: "We feel that the peaceful coexistence motto has become a burden which is crippling your movement." The Soviets retorted: "What is your opinion of atomic war?"

Moscow recovered with remarkable speed—after a hot debate at a Central Committee meeting in June over the manner in which Brezhnev and Kosygin had handled the crisis. Several young "hawks" apparently had proposed more vigorous "Left" support of the Arab cause. They were later demoted or ousted from their party positions. Soviet head of state Podgorny then flew to Cairo in the latter part of June to hand Nasser the Kremlin's new position.

Twenty thousand Egyptians saw Nasser greet President Podgorny in the 110 degree heat at Cairo's International Airport. In private, Podgorny reportedly applied his own kind of heat. He told Nasser that Russia was disgusted with Egyptian cowardice on the field of battle, and was justifiably angry at the way the United Arab Republic had thrown away one billion dollars of military hardware—most of which had not yet been paid for. Russia would resupply Egypt with enough aircraft and tanks for her defense; support beyond that was out of the question.[10] Podgorny's qualified support was almost certainly a compromise hammered out among the factions in the Soviet leadership. The overriding fact, of

[9] For the view that the Soviets were implicated, see Walter Laqueur, "The Hand of Russia," *The Reporter,* June 29, 1967, p. 18. For the opposing view, see Leonard Binder, "The Middle East Crisis: A Trial Balance," *Bulletin of the Atomic Scientists,* XXIII, No. 7 (1967), p. 2.

[10] Anthony Carthew, "Double-Think, Egyptian Style," *The New York Times Magazine,* August 20, 1967, p. 19.

course, was that Moscow's military and diplomatic losses would be compounded unless she gave some support to Egypt.

The resupply actually began before Podgorny's visit. In a textbook operation, hundreds of Soviet transport aircraft ferried the new equipment to Cairo. Later reports indicated that Russia had replaced the major share of the hardware lost in June. Much of the equipment, however, was less sophisticated than earlier shipments. The Russians apparently realized that they had erred by giving their most modern weapons to soldiers who were not quite sure which end of the gun was which. This time the Soviets vastly expanded their corps of military advisors to be sure their investment would be used properly. Before the June war, there had been 500 to 700 Soviet military men in Egypt; now there were over 2,000.[11]

In the interim, the USSR pressed the United Arab Republic to find a "political solution" to the Arab-Israeli problem. The Soviets clearly did not want a repetition of the June calamity. Cairo was not pleased at this qualified support of the Arab position. Nasser thought that the Security Council resolution of November 22, 1967, which the Soviets supported, was neither accurate nor decisive on the withdrawal of Israeli forces. Yet the Soviets were about the only powerful friends Nasser had left, and the only significant outside influence on the mainstream of Arab politics. What little influence the United States may have had in the region was compromised by Arab identification of Washington with the Israeli cause. The dominant Soviet presence nevertheless had its liabilities. With her deep involvement in Egypt, Moscow would find it difficult to stay out if the Arab-Israeli war erupted again.

THE NEW REGIME AND EUROPE

Khrushchev's successors inevitably were concerned about the continuing problem of Germany, and the growing liberalization in Eastern Europe with the predictable loss of Soviet influence in that region. In the long run, Russia's European security needs always took precedence over a "local war" in Vietnam. Brezhnev and Kosygin therefore carried on Khrushchev's program to gain Western acceptance of the *status quo:* Soviet predominance in Eastern Europe, symbolized by Western recognition of the permanent partition of Germany and the Oder-Neisse line as the East German-Polish boundary. The second Soviet goal was to prevent Bonn from gaining nuclear weapons. The

---

[11] Nasser says that he "begged" the Soviets to send additional personnel to retrain his army, but that the Soviet advisors, who had no "command functions," totaled less than 1,000. See William Atwood, "Nasser Talks," *Look,* March 19, 1968.

third goal was to finally end the American military presence in Western Europe, and to weaken—better yet eliminate—NATO.

Some gains were made toward the first goal. West Germany increasingly referred to East Germany as the "DDR" (German Democratic Republic). West German Foreign Minister Willy Brandt announced that the Federal Republic would respect the Oder-Neisse line until a peace treaty was signed—a long-term proposition at best.

Brezhnev and Kosygin continued Khrushchev's bitter attack on the American-sponsored multilateral nuclear force (MLF) in their attempt to bar Germany from gaining nuclear weapons. Washington's plan called for a NATO fleet of some 25 surface vessels each armed with eight Polaris missiles, and manned by mixed crews—including Germans. Kosygin warned that Russia inevitably would give nuclear weapons to *her* allies if the MLF came into being. De Gaulle opposed the MLF for other reasons, threatening to withdraw from NATO if any alliance members participated.

When the steam went out of the MLF proposal in early 1965, Moscow made fresh attempts to lure West Germany closer to the East with increased German-Soviet trade. At the same time, the new Soviet regime gave no indication of resuming Khrushchev's ultimatums on the Berlin question. West Germany then demonstrated its peaceful intentions. The new Kiesinger Government supported a proposal suggested by Khrushchev (1963) and President Johnson (1966) for a balanced reduction of troops in Western Europe. Bonn also decided not to build up the Bundeswehr to the planned 500,000 man level. Meanwhile, Foreign Minister Brandt vowed in March 1968 that West Germany had no interest in obtaining nuclear weapons: "We won't get them, we don't want them, and we don't need them." With Soviet and American agreement on the non-proliferation treaty, the Kremlin could rest more easily.

But Eastern Europe also could rest more easily. Rumania announced in January 1967 that she would enter into full diplomatic relations with the Federal Republic. Until that point, the East European states had considered that the socialist countries would withhold recognition until East Germany was recognized by Bonn.[12] On their part, the Soviets continually beat the drum of West German "revanchism" to hold the East European socialist regimes together through common fear. Moscow apparently was unable to find other tools to enforce conformity—outside of intervention or the threat of intervention on the Hungarian pattern. The attempt launched by Khrushchev to develop common economic ties through COMECON (also called "CEMA") had not been a spectacular success. A rather elaborate planning organization had been

---

[12] The USSR established diplomatic relations with West Germany in 1955, but prohibited the East European states from doing so.

set up along with an "International Bank," a "Common Railway-Wagon Pool," and "Intermetall"—an embryonic version of the European Coal and Steel Community. But East Europeans resisted regional economic planning, which appeared vital for genuine economic integration. The Warsaw Pact had been given more life with combined military planning and joint training exercises. Yet even here success was spotty. The Soviets used the supposed threat from West Germany as cement for the Pact. But the Hungarians, Bulgarians, and Rumanians no longer were especially worried about Bonn.[13]

The Soviet plight in the face of polycentrism was painfully obvious at the Conference of European Communist and Worker's Parties at Karlovy Vary (Karlsbad), Czechoslovakia in April 1967. Rumania categorically refused to attend. Yugoslavia and Albania—the ideological extremities of world communism—also were missing. Since the main purpose of the conference was to "coordinate" the policies of the various European parties, the absence of the recalcitrants preordained its failure. Brezhnev nevertheless told the assembled delegates that the holding of such a conference confirmed the growing trend toward unity within the communist movement and was "the best answer to bourgeois politicians who claim that Communists have split up into their various national groupings."

The chief, formal result of Karlovy Vary was a repetition of the call made at a Bucharest meeting of the Warsaw Pact members in July 1966: an all-European conference to settle European security problems. The objective would be a treaty whereby all European states would renounce the use of force and interference in the internal affairs of other states. In the interim, the socialist countries would work for the withdrawal of "foreign" troops from Europe, the liquidation of "foreign" bases, the establishment of nuclear free zones, and the end of both the Warsaw Pact and NATO when the latter's twenty-year treaty was up for renewal in 1969.[14] It was doubtful if the majority of NATO members were yet ready to eliminate the American presence in Europe. The notable exception was de Gaulle's France, which had dealt a really major blow to NATO by demanding the removal of all alliance forces and their bases from French soil.

The Czech Crisis   The estrangement between the USSR and Eastern Europe was highlighted in the spring of 1968 with the cascading liberalization in Czechoslovakia, long one of the most Stalinist and quiescent of the socialist regimes on Russia's western border. The

[13] See Zbigniew K. Brzezinski, *The Soviet Bloc*, Revised and Enlarged Edition (Cambridge, Mass.: Harvard University Press, 1967), Chaps. 17 and 18.
[14] The Karlovy Vary statement is reprinted in *Survival*, IX, No. 7 (1967), 208-13.

Soviet Union, Poland, and East Germany in particular were uneasy about where the reforms of the new Dubcek regime would end. In July, *Pravda* used the ominous term "counter-revolutionary" to describe the continual pressure for reform from liberal writers, professors, journalists, and students. Deep in the background, Moscow saw "aggressive imperialist forces" at work attempting to undermine the communist world through subversion. Moscow had not yet attacked Dubcek and the Czech party, but the liberal Czech communists had received a clear warning not to let matters get out of hand. The Soviets faced a dilemma if the reforms continued: if Moscow did nothing the liberalization could infect the rest of Eastern Europe and even Russia; if Moscow intervened the Soviets again would demonstrate that communism had to be maintained with force; thus, they would further split the communist movement. Yugoslavia, Rumania, and important non-ruling parties supported Prague.

Recognizing their dillemma, the Soviets increased political and psychological pressures on Czechoslovakia. The USSR and its East European allies (East Germany, Poland, Bulgaria, and Hungary) dispatched letters in early July to the Czech leaders summoning them to a conference at Warsaw. The Czechs rejected the proposal. But the conference was held without them, resulting in the "Warsaw Letter" of July 15. In the letter, the five socialist states termed the growing liberalism in Czechoslovakia "completely unacceptable." The five advised Dubcek and his colleagues to take action against the "anti-socialist and revisionist forces" within their country. These forces, already in control of the press, supposedly sought to end the leading role of the party, install a bourgeois regime, and turn Czechoslovakia against the other socialist countries. The five warned: "We will not permit Imperialism to split the socialist camp from inside or from outside, with or without force. There must be no change in the balance of power." A few days later, Dubcek denied that the Party's leading role was in danger or that the press needed to be curbed.

Meanwhile, Soviet army troops in Czechoslovakia for June Warsaw Pact maneuvers found convenient excuses to delay their withdrawal. A Czech general stated that he could not locate one word in the Warsaw Pact authorizing foreign troops to stay on a member's territory against that country's will. The Czech press, no longer subject to governmental censorship, termed the protracted troop withdrawal a "war of nerves."

The Soviets escalated further, demanding an extraordinary meeting of the full Russian Politburo with the full Czech Presidium—in Moscow, Kiev, or Lvov. Dubcek refused to leave the country, but finally agreed to confer with the Soviets at Cierna, a little Slovakian border town, on July 29. The two ruling bodies argued for three days. Brezhnev repeated the charges made in the Warsaw Letter. The Czechs retorted that they were steadfastly loyal to the socialist commonwealth and to the Warsaw Pact, and refused a Soviet demand for the permanent stationing of Russian troops on Czech soil. Dubcek nevertheless agreed to curb press attacks on the USSR and its allies, and promised that his country would pursue closer political, economic, and military ties with the five. There would be no "independent" Czech foreign policy. (Surprisingly, Dubcek's "Action Program" for internal political and economic reform appeared largely untouched.) On August 3 the other four signatories of the Warsaw Letter met with the Soviet and Czech leaders at Bratislava to rubber stamp the results of Cierna. The Czechs thought they were home free; "normal life" could resume.

The Czechs were wrong. At approximately 11 P.M. on August 20, troops from the USSR, East Germany, Poland, Bulgaria, and Hungary crossed Czechoslovakia's frontier. Pandemonium broke out at a Party Presidium meeting which had been in session since two that afternoon. A shocked Dubcek exclaimed: "This is a tragedy. I did not expect this." He added later: "How is it possible? I have devoted all my life to cooperation with the Soviet Union—and now they have done this to me. This is the tragedy of my own life."

The whole of the country was occupied within hours. Military resistance was futile; the Czech government pleaded with the people not to resort to acts of violence. Yet the ingenious Czechs found other ways of frustrating the invaders: swastikas were painted on Russian tanks; occupying troops found it difficult to find drinking water—taps were mysteriously turned off; road signs disappeared; clandestine television and radio stations sprang up to inform the populace and coordinate the resistance. Most remarkable was the almost unanimous support of the people for their leaders and the Communist Party. The Czechs were unified as never before against the invaders. And this unity apparently made impossible the Russian plan to install a collaborationist government drawn from the conservative opponents of Dubcek's liberalization program. (The Soviet Embassy in Prague seems to have led Moscow to believe that the Czech working people would welcome external "aid" to save their country from a coup by "right-wing revisionists.")

The Soviets, however, needed some kind of government in Czechoslovakia, no matter how distasteful. Warsaw Pact troops could not run the country. The Soviets therefore flew a delegation of Czech government and party leaders headed by President Svoboda to Moscow on August 23. Dubcek and other leading liberals, who had been arrested by the Soviets in the first hours of the invasion, joined the delegation in Moscow after Svoboda refused to negotiate without them.

The next three days were a nightmare for the Czechs; Brezhnev is said to have threatened the dismemberment of their country. Svoboda, Dubcek, and the rest of the delegation were permitted to return home on

August 27 as the legal government. They carried with them, however, strict conditions if they were to continue in power—the so-called Moscow Agreement.

The publicized section of the Agreement promised a phased withdrawal of the over 500,000-man Warsaw Pact force, "as the situation in Czechoslovakia normalizes itself." (A subsequent Czech-Soviet treaty of October 18 legalized the permanent stationing of several Soviet divisions to secure the socialist community against "the increasing revanchist strivings of the West German militarist forces.") The Soviets also seem to have accepted a significant part of Dubcek's program of political and economic reform. On the other hand, there was a cryptic pledge by the Czechs to carry out the decisions of the Cierna and Bratislava conferences, and an ominous commitment to strengthen "socialist" power. They also pledged Czechoslovakia's unfailing support of "the solidarity of the socialist community, the cause of peace and international security." A secret protocol reportedly elaborated on the more important clauses of the Agreement: (1) press censorship would be reintroduced; (2) all "anti-socialist" and "counter-revolutionary" organizations would be dissolved; (3) a number of leading liberals would have to be fired while the Czechs could take no action against the few officials who had collaborated with the invaders; (4) Czech foreign policy would be completely subordinated to the demands of the five occupying powers.

Dubcek and the Presidium faced an extraordinarily difficult task. They would have to convince the Soviets that the Moscow Agreement was being fulfilled. At the same time, the Czech leaders could not appear to collaborate lest they betray the ideals with which they had become identified and lose the support of the people. The liberals were gambling that they somehow could soften the Soviet conditions—censorship was reimposed in a diffused form carried out voluntarily by the news media—but still convince the Soviets that their government was preferable to chaos.

The Soviet-led invasion of Czechoslovakia profoundly shocked many in the West. Détente measures had to be postponed; NATO was rejuvenated. Moscow's ideological leadership of the socialist camp was dealt another major blow. The world conference of communist parties scheduled for November 1968 had to be put off until May 1969. The Soviets were under particularly heavy attack from Yugoslavia and the powerful French and Italian Communist Parties. Most serious, thought many communists and non-communists, was the "Brezhnev Doctrine." First broached in a *Pravda* editorial of September 26, the Doctrine asserted that Moscow and the other communist regimes had the right to intervene in any country in the "socialist commonwealth" to prevent "counter-revolution." Some observers feared a major hardening of Soviet foreign policy on all fronts.

Yet, on balance, the occupation appeared to be a defensive move taken to protect Soviet vital national interests, and the Brezhnev Doctrine an *ex post facto* justification for an unsavory act. The Kremlin reluctantly used force after all other avenues of pressure had been exhausted—and probably with full awareness of the impact the invasion might have on the West and on other communist parties. The military operation itself had been flawless: the result of a carefully conceived contingency plan which undoubtedly had been considered at various times during the summer—and discarded. But at some point around the middle of August, the Politburo—prodded no doubt by the East German and Polish leadership—finally decided that political pressure would not moderate Czech liberalization. Dubcek had received his last warning at Cierna and Bratislava, and the Soviets apparently saw little evidence that he was heeding their advice. Just as worrisome were visits by Yugoslavia's Tito (August 9) and Rumania's Ceausescu (August 15) to Prague; both were public enemies of the Bratislava Agreement and long-time critics of the Warsaw Pact and COMECON. The Soviets also may have been concerned about forthcoming major party congresses in Czechoslovakia. Few of the conservative faction might have remained in power after these meetings, and the Soviets would have to depend on this faction for a collaborationist government.

But what were the Soviet vital interests which were thought to be in jeopardy? The first was certainly strategic. Moscow was very concerned that Czech liberalization—both in domestic and foreign policy—would lead to that country's defection from the Warsaw Pact and probably COMECON. The *Pravda* editorial of September 26 warned that the "anti-socialist elements" in Czechoslovakia in effect had been demanding the "so-called neutrality" of their country, "as a result of which NATO troops would have been able to come up to the Soviet borders, while the community of European socialist states would have been rent. . . . The anti-socialist path, the 'neutrality' towards which the Czechoslovak people were being pushed, would have led their country into the den of the West German revanchists, would have brought it to the loss of its national independence."

The Soviets clearly feared a major change in the European balance of power if the situation in Czechoslovakia were not brought under control—and their forecast may have been correct. Czechoslovakia's defection inevitably would have impacted on the other socialist states. Her natural allies were Yugoslavia and Rumania, leading to the isolation of Hungary —apparently a reluctant partner in the occupation—and eventually, of Bulgaria. The whole central and southern tier of socialist states might have become an anti-Soviet bloc, and that Moscow would not allow. (Dubcek reportedly admitted after the tense confrontation in Moscow that he and his colleagues had underestimated the strategic and military importance the Soviets placed on Czechoslovakia.)

The second factor worrying Moscow was the impact of Czech liberalization on domestic politics in East Germany, Poland, Hungary—and even Russia herself. What was developing in Czechoslovakia was *not* socialism according to the Soviet definition, but a society with freedom of speech, freedom of association, and freedom of the individual—a society where continued rule by the "Party" inevitably would have become more difficult if not impossible. The Soviet Politburo rightly feared the attraction which such a society, claiming to be a unique experiment in "democratic communism," might have for intellectuals and liberals in the rest of Eastern Europe, and ultimately in the USSR.

The Internal Struggle   In 1968 all of the old issues were still being argued in the Politburo: [15] how to allocate priorities among heavy industry, consumer goods production, agriculture, and defense needs; how to keep the populace loyal to the party; how to justify party rule until the millennium; what to do about China; how to effectively influence the policies of other socialist states and communist parties; how to win friends in the Third World of the developing countries; whether to pursue a détente with the West—or a more militant "Left" policy; and whether domestic programs as a whole should receive prority over a more forward, foreign policy—sometimes expressed as the responsibility to support the growth of world communism.

No one leader or faction had yet achieved sufficient power to enforce a consistently Left or Right, radical reform or conservative program. "Collective leadership"—meaning collective compromise—appeared to be standard operating procedure. Brezhnev and Kosygin steered a middle course, leaning a little to the right. This was particularly evident at the Twenty-third Party Congress in March 1966. The party adopted a much more modest and gradual program of economic development—yet it permitted economic reform, including the use of "profit" criteria in business operations, to continue. The citizen-consumer was promised a steadily improving standard of living, but he was reminded that economic progress depended on the "objective laws of socialism."

We have seen the middle-of-the-road foreign policy Khrushchev's successors have pursued except for one vital facet—Soviet defense policy. Compromise, as should now be obvious, was the rule in this instance. There was no crash program—which the Soviet military probably wanted —to outstrip the West in strategic and tactical nuclear and conventional weapons. On the other hand, even the compromise weapons procurement

---

[15] The Party Presidium was given back its old title "Politburo" at the Twenty-third Party Congress in March 1966.

schedule worried the West. The installation of ICBM's was accelerated. Soviet Defense Minister Marshal Grechko declared in February 1968 that the number deployed was now "enormous." As noted earlier, the Brezhnev and Kosygin team also approved the installation of a limited ABM capability. Moreover, there was talk of a Soviet fractional orbital missile system (FOBS).

The United States Department of Defense conceded that the USSR might catch up with the United States by the middle of 1969 in numbers of ICBM's. At the same time, the Department claimed that American forces would continue to have far greater destructive power in their combined land and submarine-based missiles with multiple warheads. (The United States Navy admitted in May 1968 that the USSR was deploying its own missile-carrying nuclear submarines on full-time patrol off the Atlantic and Pacific coasts of America.)

Perhaps the most disturbing development in Soviet defense policy was the apparent intent to construct a powerful, mobile force to bring Soviet armed might to bear anywhere in the world. In the Cuban crisis and the war in Vietnam, the Soviet leaders had only one real military option—the ultimate weapon of the ballistic missile. With these lessons in mind, Khrushchev began the nucleus of the mobile force; Brezhnev and Kosygin accelerated and expanded the procurement program.[16]

In June 1968, a Soviet naval spokesman boasted that the Soviet navy, the second largest in the world, could go anywhere. Russian naval ships had visited ports in India, Somalia, Iraq, Pakistani and Iran; they would call later in 1968 on Algeria, Chile, Japan, Syria, Egypt, Uruguay, and Yugoslavia. Intelligence sources indicated that the Soviets were building two helicopter aircraft carriers, several tank and troop landing ships, were expanding their small naval infantry force, and were giving high priority to long-range supply ships and transport aircraft. It was an open secret that NATO officials were very worried about the more than forty-six modern Soviet warships now cruising the Mediterranean. Three to four had been on station in 1963.[17]

It appeared that the Soviets at long last were replacing Khrushchev's grand deception with genuine weapons. The crucial question for the West was how the Soviet leaders would use their increasing and now flexible military power. Would the Politburo feel more secure, and more ready to compromise with the West in the search for peaceful progress and stability? Would Soviet power breed Soviet militancy? A

[16] See Thomas W. Wolfe, "The Soviet Quest for More Globally Mobile Military Power" (Santa Monica, Calif.: The RAND Corporation, 1967).

[17] Claire Sterling, "The Soviet Fleet in the Mediterranean," *The Reporter*, December 14, 1967. Also see Curt Gasteyger, "Moscow and the Mediterranean," *Foreign Affairs*, XLVI, No. 4 (1968), 676-87.

third alternative, of course, was a more truculent version of the current foreign policy.

SUMMARY

Some of the glamor, excitement—and danger—had gone out of Soviet foreign policy with Khrushchev's retirement. The USSR was now managed, not led.

The Soviet Union, however, was better off with collective leadership. Khrushchev's strategy had been global and adventurist; Brezhnev and Kosygin's strategy was global but prudent.[18] Only time would tell whether collective leadership was destined to continue, and what leader or faction would assume power if it failed.

FURTHER READING

Bromke, Adam and Philip E. Uren, eds., *The Communist States and the West.* New York: Frederick A. Praeger, Inc., 1967. Articles by Western specialists on current international issues between the Western powers and the communist states.

Brzezinski, Zbigniew, *Alternative to Partition.* New York: McGraw-Hill Book Company, Inc., 1965. Comments on the evolution of Eastern Europe.

Conquest, Robert, *Russia After Khrushchev.* New York: Frederick A. Praeger, Inc., 1965. An analysis of Khrushchev's fall from power.

Dallin, Alexander and Thomas B. Larson, eds., *Soviet Politics Since Khrushchev.* Englewood Cliffs, N.J.: Prentice-Hall, Inc., 1968. Articles on foreign and domestic policy, economics, etc.

Goldman, Marshall I., *Soviet Foreign Aid.* New York: Frederick A. Praeger, Inc., 1967. Case studies of Soviet aid programs to both East European and developing nations.

Griffith, William E., ed., *Communism in Europe: Continuity, Change, and the Sino-Soviet Dispute.* 2 vols. Cambridge, Mass.: The M.I.T. Press, 1964, 1966. The interaction between domestic and Sino-Soviet developments within the main European communist states and parties in Western Europe. Two more volumes will cover French and Rumanian communist parties.

Halperin, Morton H., ed., *Sino-Soviet Relations and Arms Control.* Cambridge, Mass.: The M.I.T. Press, 1967. Articles dealing with the impact of arms control issues on the Sino-Soviet dispute.

Herrick, Robert Waring, *Soviet Naval Strategy: Fifty Years of Theory and Practice.* Annapolis, Md.: United States Naval Institute, 1968. Argues that Soviet Navy is still essentially a defensive force.

[18] John K. Jessup, "Tension by Other Means," *Life,* July 26, 1968. Jessup inspired the title for this chapter—"prudent globalism."

Labedz, Leopold, ed., *International Communism after Khrushchev*. Cambridge, Mass.: The M.I.T. Press, 1965. Articles from British journal *Survey* discussing events leading to Khrushchev's fall, the transfer of power, and the potential impact on communist parties around the world.

Zagoria, Donald S., *Vietnam Triangle: Moscow, Peking, Hanoi*. New York: Pegasus (Publishers), 1967. Analysis with documents.

CONCLUSION

Lenin, Bukharin, Trotsky, and Stalin headed a shaky regime controlling a fraction of Tsarist Russia. Their central concern was to exist. The Soviet elite in the 1960's have different concerns. The existence of communism in Russia—or what is called "socialism"—no longer is threatened by external forces. The more sophisticated and reasonable of the Soviet elite must now have some feeling of security. The USSR is the second most powerful country in the world, with the unquestioned ability to wreak devastation on any conceivable enemy. Only "madmen"—Western and Chinese—would dare consider an attack on the socialist motherland.

Contemporary Soviet leaders seem more concerned with increasing Soviet power and influence. This is partly to further Soviet national interests—foremost of which is the defense of the USSR. Few nation-states ever feel completely secure. Partly it reflects the desire of any great power to have its place in the sun. These motivations alone would place the USSR in some degree of conflict with other nation-states.

But, it would seem logical for the hesitant détente to develop into a permanent rapprochement if Soviet foreign policy reflected only the desire to further Soviet national security and to enhance Soviet national prestige.[1] Nothing would promote Soviet security more than increasing

[1] For an interesting program to promote rapprochement see Vincent P. Rock, *A Strategy of Interdependence* (New York: Charles Scribner's Sons, 1964).

Soviet cooperation with the U.S. and its European allies in developing a peaceful and orderly international system. Such policies in turn would promote the stabilization and eventual reduction of the arms race. The Soviets then could channel their defenses toward China, a potential enemy in the communist world, and devote greater resources to the internal development of Soviet society.

Unfortunately, true rapprochement seems a long way off. There is still a very narrow range of interests shared by the Soviets and the Western powers. The most significant goal held in common is the avoidance of nuclear war. Since Cuba, the Soviets also seem reluctant to chance direct confrontations with the West which might escalate into nuclear war. Other common interests are evident in the limited exchanges in cultural affairs, increased trade and commercial ventures—and after seven years of negotiations a Moscow-New York air link.

The Soviets apparently have no overwhelming desire to eliminate perhaps the most basic conflict they have with the West: the fundamental fact that the Soviet leaders hope and work for a different kind of world from the West.[2] The Kremlin's definition of the term "status quo" is change, and change involving "wars of national liberation." The Chinese may label the Soviets cowards, and charge them with conniving with the U. S. to dominate the world. But the fact remains that Khrushchev made the major attempt to change the world balance of power in the 1960's, and his successors have taken practical steps to bring this about while supplying modern weapons to Hanoi and to the Arab states. Around the world, the Politburo continues to support evolutionary and revolutionary changes moving countries towards socialism and into the Peace Zone.

In the process of seeking to build their version of the international system, the Soviets often pursue policies which appear contradictory and confusing, particularly to some party faithful. They support bourgeois-nationalist leaders of developing countries who outlaw local communist parties. They discourage revolutions in Latin America and trade with anti-communist regimes. Often the Soviets aid governments which are formally allied with the West. But such harmony, according to the Soviets, is temporary. The Kremlin is gambling that the complex bag of contradictions called Soviet foreign policy is in tune with the tide of history. The Soviets believe that they and they alone—certainly not the Chinese—can divine the true course of world events.

The Marxist-Leninist ideology, of course, appears to be the chief cause

2 Herbert S. Dinerstein, *Fifty Years of Soviet Foregin Policy* (Baltimore, Md.: The Johns Hopkins Press, 1968), pp. 72-73; Robert Conquest, "The Limits of Détente," *Foreign Affairs*, XLVI, No. 4 (1968); Marshall D. Shulman, " 'Europe' versus 'Détente'?", *Foreign Affairs*, XLV, No. 3 (1967).

of this basic conflict between the West and the USSR. The full impact of ideological conditioning on Soviet decision makers was described in Chap. 3, and will not be examined here. But to sum up: the ideology is the prime source for the Soviet view of the future world, the ever-present cause for Soviet suspicion of Western "realists" and Soviet fear of Western "madmen," and therefore the chief block to the development of significant cooperation between the USSR and the West.

IS THE IDEOLOGICAL IMPACT ERODING?

It would be a pleasure to report that the impact of Marxism-Leninism on Soviet foreign policy is diminishing and will soon die. Unfortunately, such a prognosis seems premature. Nevertheless, we should examine three of the more important arguments that the ideology has lost—or shortly will lose—any significance it may have had in determining Soviet behavior in general, and Soviet foreign policy in particular.[3]

THE LOSS OF REVOLUTIONARY ZEAL

The first argument suggests that the Soviets have lost the ardor of the old revolutionaries. It is certainly true that the Soviet leaders no longer have the zeal of the Old Bolsheviks if by this we mean the desire to communize the world by any means, including revolutionary war, and the vision of impending world revolution. The millennium is pushed further into the future with each year. The "ultimate worldwide triumph of communism" becomes more a conviction based on historical inevitability than a slogan impelling the Soviets to promote revolution. Perhaps even more than before, the revolutionary zeal of Soviet leaders is checked by the need to give first priority to Soviet national interests.

On the other hand, contemporary Soviet Marxist-Leninists may have an even greater feeling of the ultimate triumph of communism. Lenin was ecstatic when the Bolshevik government passed the 72-day existence of the Paris Commune. Today, Soviet leaders are reasonably sure that the USSR will be around for a long while, and they seem to be more confident of eventual victory with the obvious growth of the socialist

[3] For analyses of this complex question see Marshall D. Shulman, *Beyond the Cold War* (New Haven, Conn.: Yale University Press, 1966), esp. Chaps. 4 and 5; Alvin Z. Rubinstein, *The Soviets in International Organizations* (Princeton, N.J.: Princeton University Press, 1964), Chap. 8.

camp.[4] Overly zealous revolutionary activity is unnecessary—indeed is harmful—with final triumph a certainty.

It is difficult, of course, to estimate what impact Soviet problems in leading the camp of socialism may have on Soviet optimism about the ultimate triumph of socialism. The Politburo may wonder even now whether China can be brought back into the fold after Mao's departure. And the permanent loss of China from the socialist camp would leave a gaping hole. (It would be interesting to see how the Soviets would reconcile this eventuality.) The general drift toward polycentrism and diversity of all the socialist states will only accentuate the problem. The Soviets already have difficulties in classifying Yugoslavia. Finally, the Soviets are beginning to recognize that the developing countries are rarely responsible or dependable members of the Peace Zone.

IDEOLOGICAL CHANGE EQUALS IDEOLOGICAL EROSION

The second argument suggests that the changes the Soviets have made in the ideology mean that the ideology has eroded. The first thing to be said here is that change has been required in the ideology since the beginning to make it relevant and vital. As Khrushchev stated a few years ago, Lenin was the greatest revisionist of them all. The real question is about the timing of the change and the nature of the change. Change cannot lag too far behind the situation in the real world. The ideology cannot become too dogmatic. Luckily for all concerned, the Soviet realization of the significance of a modern war fought with nuclear weapons came before, and not after, the Cuban missile crisis. The nature of the change also is extremely important. If the change becomes too far-fetched, there may be great difficulty in maintaining even superficial logic in the ideology. (There has been this danger in the current proposition of a possible peaceful transition from the bourgeois to the socialist stage.) [5]

The need to make the ideology relevant may actually create pressures for a dynamic Soviet foreign policy. The reasoning behind this suggestion is as follows: the Politburo faces a serious challenge in proving to the Soviet people that Marxism-Leninism is a living creed in ques-

---

[4] After careful analysis, one prominent Soviet expert predicts the socialist camp's population will increase by 118.6 per cent in the 20-year period from 1960 to 1980. In the same period, the imperialist camp will grow 10 per cent. S. Strumlin, "The World Twenty Years From Now," *Kommunist*, No. 13 (1961).

[5] Success so far with this method, Cyril Black notes, is limited to the "rather marginal" cases of San Marino and Kerala. Cyril Black, "The Anticipation of Communist Revolutions," *Communism and Revolution*, ed. by Black and Thornton, p. 423.

tions that directly affect their everyday lives; the Marxian dogmas about economics, societal organization, art, literature, and so forth, no longer seem relevant; the entire concept of the party's monopoly on wisdom and therefore its right to rule has been seriously compromised; Khrushchev raised grave doubts about Stalin's infallibility, and Khrushchev's successors characterized him as a bumbling schemer.

One way to renew the confidence of the Soviet people in Marxism-Leninism is to show that ideological prescriptions can win *international* victories. Adam Ulam has written:

> *Somehow* the ideology has to be shown to be important, dynamic, and capable of expansion and conquest. . . . It is this restlessness in the search for a justification of the ideology, a rationale for continued totalitarianism, which opens up incalculable dangers for world peace. Being intelligent men, desirous of learning about the outside world, genuinely interested in improving the lot of their people, the Soviet leaders cannot desire a world conflict. But at the same time, they are driven by an ideological compulsion much more complex than the now obsolete dream of world revolution, to adventurous and aggressive foreign policies.[6]

Perhaps Ulam overstates this particular "compulsion" for Soviet aggressiveness, but we can't ignore the tendency.

THE CHANGING NATURE OF THE LEADERSHIP

A third argument suggests that the current leadership is composed essentially of managers, administrators and technocrats—and not of devoted revolutionaries. This is the "New Class" of Djilas, interested only in protecting and extending its prerogatives, and essentially conservative in nature. Naturally the present leaders have not shared the experiences of the Old Bolsheviks. The contemporary party elite have spent their careers dealing with managerial and technical problems rather than running underground newspapers or planning revolutions. On the other hand, they have undergone a more intensive and thorough indoctrination than did the Old Bolsheviks. It is difficult to conceive how they can escape the ideological conditioning of a lifetime.[7] But perhaps the overriding factor reinforcing the faith of the contemporary elite in Marxism-Leninism is that this is the basic justification for their rule.

The Soviet leaders today probably are more sophisticated about West-

[6] Adam B. Ulam, *The Unfinished Revolution* (New York: Random House, Inc., 1960), p. 278.

[7] For the impact of the conditioning on Premier Kosygin, one of the more "moderate" technocrats, see "A Private Interview with Premier Kosygin," *LIFE*, Vol. LXIV, No. 5 (Feb. 2, 1968), 21.

ern society than their propaganda would indicate. The stereotypes of the "capitalist warmonger" and the "wage-slaves" are being replaced by much more accurate analyses in specialized journals of life outside the USSR. (After his visit to the United States in 1959, Khrushchev himself exclaimed: "I have seen the slaves of capitalism—and they live well!") Unfortunately, such realism does not often extend to Soviet views of Western foreign policy. Here the stereotypes prevail. The U. S. is still the arrogant and aggressive leader of world imperialism, blinded by fear of change and determined to suppress revolution around the world.[8] This image is confirmed in Soviet eyes by the American involvement in Vietnam and American intervention in the Dominican Republic. The old fears, prejudices, and suspicions about Western foreign policy still exist.

In short, the nature of the ideological impact on Soviet foreign policy has changed in kind and degree. Yet those factors tending to erode Marxism-Leninism have been countered by other factors reinforcing the faith.

In the future, the corrosive forces may win out. Soviet leaders may become preoccupied with planning and managing their increasingly complex economy, and attempting to inspire a sophisticated populace indifferent to ideological exhortations.[9] Polycentrism is a galloping force which may absorb much Soviet energy. Soviet sobriety about the possibilities for scientific socialism in the developing nations, buttressed by Soviet realism regarding the actual limits of Russia's influence in these countries, may decrease conflict with the West in the Third World. Soviet fear of imperialism—with the black days of the Cold War only a memory —may become an irrelevant, complicating factor in East-West relations. Marxism-Leninism may finally disappear as a significant component of Soviet foreign policy.

[8] Morton Schwartz, "What Moscow's Washington Watchers See," *New York Times Magazine*, Oct. 8, 1967, p. 50.

[9] On the future of Soviet society, see the debate in *Problems in Communism*, XV, Nos. 1-6 (1966), and XVI, No. 4 (67), particularly the lead article by Zbigniew Brzezinski (XV, No. 1), and the reply by Merle Fainsod (XVI, No. 4). Also see Frederick C. Barghoorn, *Politics in the USSR* (Boston: Little, Brown and Company, 1966), Chap. 10.

SIGNIFICANT DATES
IN SOVIET FOREIGN POLICY

1917   November 7. The Bolsheviks seize power; the "Great October Socialist Revolution."

       December 1917-March 1918. Soviets negotiate with Germans and their allies at Brest-Litovsk.

1918   January. Rumania occupies Bessarabia.

       March 3. Soviet delegation signs Treaty of Brest-Litovsk.

       During Spring and Summer, Allied troops intervene in Russia. The Soviets fight a civil war with "White" opposition.

       November 11. World War I ends.

       November 13. Soviets unilaterally abrogate Treaty of Brest-Litovsk.

1919   January 5-15. Spartacist uprising in Berlin led by German communists.

       March 2-6. First Congress of Communist International (Comintern) held in Moscow.

       March 21. Short-lived Hungarian Soviet Republic established.

       April 7. Bavarian Soviet Republic lasts one month.

1920   January. Allies lift blockade of Russia.

       April 25-October 12. Polish-Soviet War. (Treaty of Riga signed on March 18, 1921, officially ends war.)

       July 19-August 7. Second Congress of the Comintern.

The critical of Comintern [handwritten marginalia]

September 1. Baku Congress of "Peoples of the East" convenes.

November. Soviets defeat remaining "White" forces in Civil War; Allied troops withdrawn except Japanese.

1921 February 28-March 18. Kronstadt revolt. *sailors* [handwritten]

March 15. New Economic Policy (NEP) announced. *stability* [handwritten]

March 16. Anglo-Russian Trade Agreement signed. *forced requisitions stopped — private land* [handwritten]

Soviets sign treaty of "friendship and fraternity" with Turkey.

1921 March 19-31. German communists again fail in revolutionary attempt.

June 22-July 12. Third Congress of Comintern.

1922 April 10-May 19. Genoa Conference.

April 16. Germany and Russia sign Treaty of Rapallo.

October. Japanese leave mainland Siberia.

December 30. Congress of Soviets held in Moscow establishes USSR.

1923 Winter of 1922-23. Lausanne Conference on Turkish Straits.

January 26. Sun Yat-sen and Joffe, a Soviet emissary, agree China not ripe for communism, but Comintern advisors sent to aid Sun.

May 8. Curzon Ultimatum to USSR.

October. Under Russian direction, German communists fail in another revolutionary attempt.

1924 January 21. Lenin dies. Stalin-Zinoviev-Kamenev ally to isolate Trotsky.

February 2. USSR establishes diplomatic relations with Great Britain. Other European countries follow in the "year of recognition."

October 25. "Zinoviev Letter" published by British press.

1925 January 20. Soviets establish diplomatic relations with Japan. Northern Sakhalin Island returned to USSR.

March 12. Sun Yat-sen dies.

October 12. Soviet-German trade treaty signed on eve of Locarno Conference.

1926 March 20. Chiang Kai-shek holds major purge of Chinese communists.

April 24. Soviets sign Treaty of Berlin with Germany.

1927 April. Chiang Kai-shek's forces crush communist uprising in Shanghai. Mao Tse-tung concentrates on organizing the countryside.

May 12. British police raid "Arcos" offices in London; Great Britain breaks off diplomatic relations with USSR.

December. Stalin defeats remaining major opposition to his rule.

1928 August. Soviets not permitted among original signatories of Kellogg-Briand Pact. "Litvinov Protocol" later invites Russia's neighbors to adhere to Pact provisions.

July-September. Sixth Congress of Comintern adopts "Left" tactics.

Fall. Stalin begins collectivization of agriculture. First Five-Year Plan adopted for forced industrialization of Russia.

1929   May-December. Conflict with China over Chinese Eastern Railway. Chinese-Soviet diplomatic relations severed.

October 3. Great Britain restores diplomatic relations with USSR.

1930   July. Litvinov formally replaces Chicherin as Foreign Minister.

1931   September 19. Japan occupies Manchuria; comes into conflict with Soviets over Chinese Eastern Railway.

1932   January-July. Soviets conclude non-aggression pacts with Finland, Latvia, Estonia, and Poland.

November 29. USSR and France conclude non-aggression pact.

December 12. Soviets resume diplomatic relations with China.

1933   January 30. Hitler becomes Chancellor of Germany.

March 27. Japan leaves League of Nations.

May 5. Reichstag extends 1926 Treaty of Berlin.

October 14. Germany leaves League of Nations.

November 16. United States and USSR establish diplomatic relations.

1934   January 26-February 10. Seventeenth Congress of Soviet Communist Party. Stalin sees traces of German imperialism in Nazi foreign policy.

September 18. USSR enters League of Nations.

1935   March 23. Soviets sell Chinese Eastern Railway to Japan.

May 2. Soviets sign treaty of mutual assistance with French in case either attacked by a "European" state.

May 16. Soviets sign similar treaty with Czechs, but this treaty says Soviets will aid Czechs only if France does likewise.

July 25-August 25. Seventh Comintern Congress adopts "Popular Front" tactics.

October 3. Ethiopia invaded by Italy.

1936   March 7. Germany marches into Rhineland.

July. Civil war erupts in Spain.

September. Soviets decide to intervene in Spain with advisors and arms.

November 27. Germany and Japan sign "Anti-Comintern Pact." (Italy joins a year later.)

1937   July 7. Japan invades Chinese mainland.

March 12. German troops take over Austria in the "Anschluss."

1938   July-August. Soviet forces clash with Japanese along Manchurian-Siberian border.

September. Munich Crisis.

1939   March 10-21. Eighteenth Congress of Soviet Communist Party. Stalin warns Russia will not "pull chestnuts out of the fire" for those states opposing Germany and Japan.

May 3. Molotov replaces Litvinov as Foreign Minister.

May-August. Soviets fight major land and air battles with Japanese, who attack Outer Mongolia. Japanese later pull back.

August 23. Nazi-Soviet Treaty of Non-Aggression concluded.

1939   September 1. Germans invade Poland.

September 3. Great Britain and France declare war on Germany.

September 17. Soviet forces occupy Eastern Poland in accordance with secret protocol to Nazi-Soviet Non-Aggression Treaty.

November 30. Soviet troops invade Finland; "Winter War" begins.

December 14. USSR expelled from League of Nations because of invasion of Finland.

1940   March 12. Finns sign peace treaty in Moscow under duress.

April 19. German armies invade Denmark and Norway.

May 10. Germans invade Belgium, Luxemburg, and the Netherlands, and later France.

June 15. Soviet troops occupy first Lithuania, then Estonia and Latvia. "People's Governments" formed; become republics of USSR by August 8, 1940.

June 17. French government requests armistice.

June 27. Rumania cedes Bessarabia and Northern Bukovina to USSR after Soviet ultimatum.

November 12. Molotov journeys to Berlin to carve up the world with Hitler.

1941   April 13. Soviet-Japanese Neutrality Pact concluded.

June 22. German troops invade Russia.

July 12. Great Britain and USSR sign mutual assistance pact.

October-January 1942. Battle of Moscow.

October 30. United States extends USSR one billion dollars of Lend-Lease credit.

December 7. Japanese attack Pearl Harbor.

1942   May 26. Molotov visits Britain; signs 20-year treaty of alliance.

May 29. Molotov visits Washington to request second front.

1943   January 24. Roosevelt proclaims "unconditional surrender" formula at Casablanca Conference.

February 2. Russians win Battle of Stalingrad; the tide turns.

April 25. Soviets break off diplomatic relations with Poland after Katyn Forest massacre revealed by Germans.

May 22. Comintern dissolved.

September 8. Italy surrenders unconditionally.

October 19-30. Moscow Conference of Foreign Ministers of USSR, United States, and Great Britain.

November 22-26. Cairo Conference, at which Roosevelt awards China all territories "stolen" by Japan (the "Cairo Declaration.")

November 28-December 1. Teheran Conference of Roosevelt, Churchill, and Stalin.

1944   June 6. Allies open second front in Europe.

July 26. Moscow gives pro-Soviet Polish Committee of National Liberation control of liberated Poland.

August 1. London-controlled Polish underground army revolts against Germans in Warsaw.

October 9. Churchill visits Moscow; proposes to Stalin "spheres of influence" arrangement for Balkans.

December 3. Greek communists launch civil war.

December 31. Polish Committee of National Liberation proclaims itself the provisional government; recognized by USSR on January 5, 1945.

1945   January 17. Soviet army liberates Warsaw.

February 4-11. Yalta Conference of Roosevelt, Churchill, and Stalin; "Yalta Agreement" on the Far East.

April 12. Roosevelt dies; Truman succeeds.

April 25. San Francisco Conference to found UN opens; Charter signed on June 26.

May 2. Soviets capture Berlin.

1945   May 8. Germany surrenders unconditionally.

July 16. First atomic bomb exploded at Alamogordo.

July 17-August 2. Potsdam Conference of Truman, Stalin, and Churchill (replaced by Attlee).

August 8. Soviets declare war against Japan.

August 14. USSR and China sign Treaty of Friendship and Alliance in Moscow.

August 14. Japan accepts surrender terms; formal surrender on September 2.

September 11-October 2 (London) December 16-26 (Moscow). Council of Foreign Ministers meets to draft peace treaties with defeated countries.

1946   January 19. Iran complains to UN Security Council of Soviet interference in her internal affairs.

February 9. Stalin sees danger to USSR from capitalist West in first speech since end of war.

March 5. Churchill notes existence of "iron curtain" in Fulton, Missouri speech.

1947   February 10. Soviets sign peace treaties with Italy, Rumania, Hungary, Bulgaria, and Finland.

March 12. Truman Doctrine offers economic and military aid to Greece and Turkey to counteract communist moves.

June 5. Marshall Plan offers American economic aid to rebuild Europe.

October 5. Soviets announce founding of Communist Information Bureau (Cominform); European and Asian communist parties adopt "Left" tactics.

1948   February. Communist coup topples Czech government—last democratic regime in Eastern Europe.

June 28. Yugoslavian Communist Party expelled from Cominform.

June 18-August 4. Soviets gradually introduce first Berlin Blockade.

September. Soviets launch "peace" movement.

1949   January 25. Council of Economic Mutual Aid (Comecon or CEMA) founded.

April 4. NATO established.

May 12. Soviets lift Berlin Blockade.

May 23. Federal Republic of West Germany founded.

September 23. United States announces first Soviet atomic bomb test.

October 1. People's Republic of China (PRC) established.

October. German Democratic Republic (East Zone) founded.

1950   January 10. Soviet representative walks out of UN Security Council protesting its refusal to seat PRC representative.

February 14. Soviets and Chinese communists sign 30-year treaty of "friendship, alliance, and mutual assistance."

June 25. North Korea attacks South Korea.

August 1. Soviet representative returns to UN Security Council.

1951   June 23. Soviets suggest Korean ceasefire and armistice.

July 10. Armistice negotiations begin.

September 8. West signs peace treaty with Japan against Soviet objections.

1952   May 26. Allies give West Germany virtually complete sovereignty.

May 27. France, Italy, West Germany, and Benelux nations sign treaty establishing European Defense Community (EDC).

October 5-14. Nineteenth Congress of Soviet Communist Party; Stalin's essay "Economic Problems of Socialism in the USSR" published.

1953   March 5. Stalin dies. Malenkov becomes Premier, and Khrushchev Party Secretary.

June 16. Riots in East Germany after Stalinism eased.

July 27. Korean armistice signed.

August 8. Malenkov announces the USSR has developed hydrogen bomb.

1954   January 12. American Secretary of State Dulles announces "massive retaliation" policy.

January 25-February 18. Council of Foreign Ministers meets in Berlin to discuss Germany and Austria.

April 26-July 21. Geneva Conference on Indochina.

August 30. French Assembly refuses to ratify EDC.

1955   February 2. First major Soviet economic aid project to a non-communist developing country (Indian Bhilai steel mill).

February 8. Malenkov resigns as Premier.

May 6. West Germany joins NATO.

May 14. USSR and East European states sign Warsaw Pact.

May 15. Soviets and Western powers sign Austrian peace treaty.

May 26-June 2. Khrushchev goes to Belgrade to heal the breach.

June 18-23. The Big Four heads of state meet in Geneva.

September 20. Czechoslovakia sells arms to Egypt.

November 17-December 22. Khrushchev and Bulganin tour India, Burma, and Afghanistan.

1956   February 14-25. Twentieth Congress of Soviet Communist Party; Khrushchev condemns Stalin, talks of Peaceful Coexistence and the Peace Zone.

April 17. Cominform disbanded.

June 28. Polish crisis begins with riot in Poznan.

October 19. Khrushchev and company confront Polish leaders in Warsaw.

October 23-November 4. Soviets crush Hungarian Revolution.

October 29-November 6. Suez Crisis; British, French, and Israeli forces attack Egypt.

1957   June 22-29. Khrushchev defeats "anti-Party group" at meeting of Central Committee.

August 26. Moscow reports successful test of ICBM.

October 2. Polish Foreign Minister Rapacki proposes nuclear-free Central Europe to UN.

October 4. Soviets launch Sputnik, world's first artificial satellite.

October. Soviets reportedly promise Communist China a sample atomic bomb.

November 14-16. Twelve ruling communist parties meet in Moscow.

1958   March 19. Khrushchev claims USSR may no longer be encircled by capitalist states.

March 31. Soviets unilaterally suspend testing of nuclear weapons.

May-August. Lebanon Crisis.

August-November. Formosa Straits (Quemoy and Matsu Islands) Crisis.

October. USSR loans Egypt one hundred million dollars for Aswan Dam.

November. Khrushchev launches a new Berlin crisis.

1959   January 27-February 5. Twenty-first Congress of Soviet Communist Party.

May 11-August 5. Unproductive conference of Foreign Ministers at Geneva on Berlin Question.

June. Khrushchev reportedly withdraws promise to aid China in building atomic capability.

September 15-27. Khrushchev's visit to United States.

1960   May 1. Soviets shoot down U-2 plane inside Russia.

May 16. Khrushchev confronts Eisenhower at Paris; summit conference breaks up.

June. Khrushchev withdraws economic aid and technical experts from China.

July. Congo Crisis begins.

1961   April 17. Bay of Pigs invasion by U. S. trained Cuban exiles.

June 3-4. Kennedy meets Khrushchev in Vienna.

August 12. Construction begins on Berlin Wall.

October 17-31. Twenty-second Congress of Soviet Communist Party; new Party program adopted. Khrushchev publicly attacks Albania.

December 9. Soviets sever diplomatic relations with Albania.

1962   October 20. Communist China attacks India.

October 22-24. Cuban missile crisis.

1963   June 14. Public letter from Peking to Moscow.

August 5. Soviet and U. S. representatives sign partial nuclear test ban treaty.

December 13. Soviets introduce "détente" arms budget.

1964   July. Khrushchev schedules meeting of twenty-six communist parties for December 15, 1964, to plan later world conference.

October 14. Khrushchev fired. Brezhnev made Party Secretary, Kosygin Premier. December conference postponed until March 1965.

1965   February 6. Premier Kosygin arrives in Hanoi.

March. Nineteen communist parties attend "consultative" meeting in Moscow.

1966   January 4-10. Kosygin brings warring Pakistan and India together at Tashkent.

March 29-April 8. Twenty-third Congress of Soviet Communist Party.

July. Bucharest conference of Warsaw Pact members calls for all-European meeting to settle European security problems.

1967   April 24-26. Karlovy Vary Conference of European communist parties. Rumania, Yugoslavia, and Albania absent.

1967   June 5-10. Arab-Israeli War. Soviets quickly resupply lost Arab arms.

June 23, 25. President Johnson and Premier Kosygin meet at Glassboro, New Jersey.

1968   January 18. U. S. and Soviet negotiators agree to draft of nuclear non-proliferation treaty.

February 26. Sixty-six communist parties convene in Bucharest for "consultative" conference. China absent. Rumania stalks out.

May 10. American-North Vietnamese negotiations begin in Paris.

June 27. Soviets agree to talk with U. S. on limiting nuclear weapons.

July. Soviets launch serious criticism of Czech liberalization.

August 20. Warsaw Pact Troops invade Czechoslovakia.

OTHER SOURCES FOR
THE STUDY OF
SOVIET FOREIGN POLICY

BIBLIOGRAPHIES

Hammond, Thomas T., ed., *Soviet Foreign Relations and World Communism; A Selected Annotated Bibliography of 7,000 Books in 30 Languages.* Princeton, N.J.: Princeton University Press, 1965. A massive effort by selected scholars. Largely supersedes earlier bibliographies. A basic source for any research on Soviet foreign policy.

Carew-Hunt, R. N., *Books on Communism.* London: Ampersand, Ltd., 1959. A less extensive compilation of books on communism since 1945 with annotations. Updated by Walter Kolarz in 1964.

Horecky, Paul L., ed., *Basic Russian Publications: A Selected and Annotated Bibliography on Russia and the Soviet Union.* Chicago: University of Chicago Press, 1962. The major Russian works on Soviet politics, international relations, economics, law, literature, and history. Basic source for research in Russian language sources.

WESTERN PERIODICALS

Bulletin. Monthly. Published by Institute for the Study of the USSR, Munich.

Current Digest of the Soviet Press. Weekly. Published by the Joint Committee on Slavic Studies, New York. Translations of all major news items and articles from the Soviet press and Soviet periodicals.

East Europe. Monthly. Published by Free Europe Committee, Inc., New York. Articles on current affairs in Eastern Europe.

Problems of Communism. Bimonthly. United States Information Agency. U. S. Government Printing Office, Washington, D.C. Articles and book reviews dealing with all phases of Soviet politics.

Radio Liberty Dispatch. Periodic dissemination. Radio Liberty Committee, New York. Short summaries of current events in the Soviet Union and commentary on world communism.

Research Materials. Periodic dissemination. Published by Radio Free Europe, New York. Analyses of current events in the Soviet Union and Eastern Europe.

Russian Review. Quarterly. Hanover, New Hampshire. Articles and book reviews. Occasional articles on Soviet foreign policy.

Slavic Review. Quarterly. (Formerly *American Slavic and East European Review.*) Major American scholarly review of American Association for the Advancement of Slavic Studies, Inc. Occasional articles on Soviet politics and book reviews.

Survey. Quarterly. Published by Congress for Cultural Freedom, London. A journal of Soviet and East European Studies.

The Yearbook on International Communist Affairs. Annual. Prepared by The Hoover Institution on War, Revolution, and Peace. Stanford, Calif.: Stanford University. First edition dealt with year 1966, ed. by Milorad M. Drachkovitch. Subsequent editions planned. International political activities of the various communist parties and their inter-party relations during given year. See *World Communism; A Handbook, 1918-1965,* also published by the Hoover Institution, Witold S. Sworakowski and Karol Maichel (eds.), for period before 1966.

SOVIET PERIODICALS IN ENGLISH

International Affairs. Monthly. Moscow. Articles by Soviet scholars on Soviet foreign policy and international politics.

New Times. Weekly. Moscow. Necessary for the current Soviet line on foreign policy.

World Marxist Review. Prague. Monthly. English edition of "Problems of Peace and Socialism," the organ of the international communist movement. Emphasizes the Soviet line in international politics.

INDEX

2557